The Circular Supply Chain

Organizations need to stay competitive and transition from a linear make-use-dispose supply chain model to a sustainable one. This book covers techniques and basic principles, historical developments and recent issues facing the adoption of a circular supply chain model.

The Circular Supply Chain: Basic Principles and Techniques presents the key principles and techniques for the effective integration of a circular economy into supply chains. It discusses sustainability, digitization and the application of blockchain to enhance operations within the realm of Industry 4.0. Principles to assist managers in effectively adopting circularity business models for sustainability improvements are provided, along with the historical background, so the reader can have a better understanding for implementation. Case studies and reading comprehension questions are also offered to help with the effective integration of a circular economy into supply chains.

This book is written to assist students, practicing engineers and business professionals that work in the industrial and manufacturing sectors, supply chain management, and with advanced technologies associated with Industry 4.0, sustainability, blockchain and digitalization integration techniques of circular supply chains.

The Circular Supply Chain
Basic Principles and Techniques

Ifeyinwa Juliet Orji and Frank Ojadi

CRC Press is an imprint of the
Taylor & Francis Group, an **informa** business

First edition published 2023
by CRC Press
6000 Broken Sound Parkway NW, Suite 300, Boca Raton, FL 33487-2742

and by CRC Press
4 Park Square, Milton Park, Abingdon, Oxon, OX14 4RN

CRC Press is an imprint of Taylor & Francis Group, LLC

© 2023 Taylor & Francis Group, LLC

Reasonable efforts have been made to publish reliable data and information, but the author and publisher cannot assume responsibility for the validity of all materials or the consequences of their use. The authors and publishers have attempted to trace the copyright holders of all material reproduced in this publication and apologize to copyright holders if permission to publish in this form has not been obtained. If any copyright material has not been acknowledged please write and let us know so we may rectify in any future reprint.

Except as permitted under U.S. Copyright Law, no part of this book may be reprinted, reproduced, transmitted, or utilized in any form by any electronic, mechanical, or other means, now known or hereafter invented, including photocopying, microfilming, and recording, or in any information storage or retrieval system, without written permission from the publishers.

For permission to photocopy or use material electronically from this work, access www.copyright.com or contact the Copyright Clearance Center, Inc. (CCC), 222 Rosewood Drive, Danvers, MA 01923, 978-750-8400. For works that are not available on CCC please contact mpkbookspermissions@tandf.co.uk

Trademark notice: Product or corporate names may be trademarks or registered trademarks and are used only for identification and explanation without intent to infringe.

ISBN: 978-1-032-17155-5 (hbk)
ISBN: 978-1-032-17156-2 (pbk)
ISBN: 978-1-003-25201-6 (ebk)

DOI: 10.1201/9781003252016

Typeset in Times
by KnowledgeWorks Global Ltd.

Contents

Author Biographies xvii

PART 1

Chapter 1 The Circular Supply Chain-Introduction and Historical Development 3
    1.1 Introduction 3
    1.2 Defining Circular Supply Chain 4
    1.3 Circular Supply Chain Management: Meaning and Essence 6
    1.4 Development and Growth of Circular Supply Chains 8
        1.4.1 The Emergence of Circular Economy 8
        1.4.2 The Role of Stakeholders in Circular Supply Chains 10
        1.4.3 Circular Supply Chain Implementation in Industries 11
    1.5 Key Circular Supply Chains Terms and Concepts 13
    1.6 Major Activities and Focus of Circular Supply Chains 16
        1.6.1 Product/Service Design in Circular Supply Chains 16
        1.6.2 Procurement in Circular Supply Chains 17
        1.6.3 Production in Circular Supply Chains 18
        1.6.4 Logistics in Circular Supply Chains 18
        1.6.5 Consumption in Circular Supply Chains 19
        1.6.6 End of Life (EoL) and Waste Management in Circular Supply Chains 19
    1.7 Summary 21
    Discussion and Review Questions 22
    Suggested Materials for Further Reading 22

Chapter 2 The Future of Circular Supply Chain 23
    2.1 Introduction 23
    2.2 Projection Development Along the 4R Framework 23
        2.2.1 Reduce 23
        2.2.2 Reuse 24
        2.2.3 Recycle 24
        2.2.4 Recover 25
    2.3 From Design for Sustainability to Design for Circularity 25
        2.3.1 The Role of Supply Network Collaboration 26

2.3.2 Organizational Change for Circularity in Supply Chains 28
2.3.3 The Importance of Collaboration in the Transition to Circularity in Supply Chains 30
2.3.4 Transition to Circular Economy and Green Employment 31
2.4 Summary 33
Discussion and Review Questions 34
Suggested Materials for Further Reading 34

PART 2

Chapter 3 Sustainability and Circular Supply Chains 37

3.1 Introduction 37
3.2 Sustainable Supply Chain Management 38
3.3 Sustainable Supply Chain Management and the Circular Economy 41
3.4 Organizational Paradigm Shift for Circular Economy 44
    3.4.1 Collaboration as a Facilitator of Circular Economy 45
    3.4.2 Supply Chain Configuration as Facilitator of Circular Economy 48
3.5 Organizational Theories in the Nexus Between Sustainable Supply Chain Management and the Circular Economy 49
    3.5.1 Existing Theories 49
        3.5.1.1 Institutional Theory 49
        3.5.1.2 Stakeholder Theory 50
        3.5.1.3 Natural Resource-Based View 51
    3.5.2 Potential Theories 52
        3.5.2.1 Social Innovation Theory 52
        3.5.2.2 Organizational Learning Theory 53
        3.5.2.3 Social Learning Theory 53
3.6 Summary 54
Discussion and Review Questions 54
Suggested Materials for Further Reading 55

Chapter 4 Reverse Supply Chain Management 57

4.1 Introduction 57
4.2 Definition of Reverse Supply Chain Management 57
4.3 The Reverse Supply Chain 58
    4.3.1 Remanufacturing 61
    4.3.2 Closed-Loop Supply Chain 64
    4.3.3 Measuring Reverse Supply Chain Performance 66

Contents   vii

    4.4   Role of Supply Chain Leadership in Reverse Supply Chains 67
        4.4.1   Transformational Leadership 68
        4.4.2   Transactional Leadership 70
    4.5   Role of Governance Mechanisms in Reverse Supply Chains 71
        4.5.1   Suppliers' Trust and Relational Governance 71
        4.5.2   Legal-Legitimate Power and Contractual Governance 72
    4.6   Summary 73
    Discussion and Review Questions 74
    Suggested Materials for Further Reading 74

PART 3

Chapter 5   Supply Chain Issues in the Circular Economy 77

    5.1   Introduction 77
    5.2   Procurement in the Circular Economy 77
        5.2.1   Demands for Circular Public Procurement 79
            5.2.1.1   Organizational Aspects and Circular Public Procurement 80
            5.2.1.2   Individual Behavioral Aspects and Circular Public Procurement 81
            5.2.1.3   Operational Aspects and Circular Public Procurement 81
        5.2.2   The Role of Intermediaries in Circular Public Procurement 83
    5.3   Product Flow in the Circular Economy 86
    5.4   Closed Loop Supply Chain Planning 88
    5.5   Production Planning in the Circular Economy 93
        5.5.1   Defining Disassembly for Recycling 93
        5.5.2   Mathematical Formulation for Production Planning in Disassembly Systems 94
        5.5.3   From Product to Raw Material Recycling 96
        5.5.4   Mathematical Formulation for Product to Raw Material Recycling Systems 97
    5.6   Summary 99
    Discussion and Review Questions 99

Chapter 6   Sustainable Supply Chain Operations in the Circular Economy 101

    6.1   Introduction 101
    6.2   Green Supply Chain Management in the Circular Economy 101

6.3			Sustainable Consumption and Production in the Circular Economy 104
6.4			Reverse Logistics 106
	6.4.1		The Role of Collaboration in Reverse Logistics 107
		6.4.1.1	Vertical Collaboration and Reverse Logistics 108
		6.4.1.2	Horizontal Collaboration and Reverse Logistics 108
	6.4.2		University-Industry Collaboration and Reverse Logistics 109
6.5			Sustainable Packaging in the Circular Economy 109
	6.5.1		Use of Institutional Theory in Sustainable Packaging Research 112
	6.5.2		Use of Stakeholder Theory in Sustainable Packaging Research 113
	6.5.3		Use of Ecological Modernization Theory in Sustainable Packaging Research 114
6.6			Pricing Circular Products 115
	6.6.1		Consumers' Willingness to Pay for Products with Environmental Attributes 115
	6.6.2		Consumers' Willingness to Pay for "Circular" Products 116
		6.6.2.1	Environmental Information and Consumers' Willingness to Pay for "Circular" Products 117
		6.6.2.2	Environmental Concern 119
	6.6.3		Model Formulation for Pricing and Recycling Investment Decisions 119
		6.6.3.1	Recycling 119
		6.6.3.2	Demand 120
		6.6.3.3	Production Cost 121
		6.6.3.4	Profit 122
		6.6.3.5	Firm's Optimization Problem 122
6.7			Summary 123
			Discussion and Review Questions 124
			Suggested Materials for Further Reading 124

PART 4

Chapter 7 Facilitation of Circular Supply Chains with Digital Technologies 129

    7.1 Introduction 129
    7.2 Digital-Enabled Strategies for Circular Supply Chains 130

Contents ix

        7.2.1   Defining Digital Supply Chain 131
        7.2.2   Industry 4.0 Solutions for Circular
                    Supply Chains 132
   7.3   Industry 4.0 and Sustainable Development in the
       Circular Economy 135
       7.3.1   The Smart Circular Economy 139
       7.3.2   Developing Smart Circular Economy
               Framework 140
               7.3.2.1   Data Transformation Levels 140
               7.3.2.2   Resource Optimization Capabilities 140
               7.3.2.3   Data Flow Processes 141
               7.3.2.4   Maturity Levels 142
   7.4   The Role of Sharing Economy in the Circular Economy 142
       7.4.1   Consumption Work and the Circular Economy 145
               7.4.1.1   The Concept of Consumption Work
                          and Its Relevance to the Circular
                          Economy 145
               7.4.1.2   The Consumption Work of the Sharing
                          Economy 146
       7.4.2   Sharing Economy Platforms and Green
               Consumption Values 148
   7.5   Internet of Things as an Enabler of Circular Economy 151
   7.6   Big data Analytics - An Emerging Paradigm for
       Circularity in Future Supply Chain 155
       7.6.1   Business Intelligence and Data-Driven Insights 157
       7.6.2   Big data Analytics and Data-Driven Insights 158
       7.6.3   Data-Driven Insights and Decision-
               Making Quality 159
   7.7   Summary 160
   Discussion and Review Questions 162
   Suggested Materials for Further Reading 162

Chapter 8   Application of Blockchain Technologies in Circular
                Supply Chains 163
   8.1   Introduction 163
   8.2   The Background and Role of Blockchain Technologies 163
       8.2.1   Traceability 164
       8.2.2   Trust 164
       8.2.3   Transparency 165
   8.3   Blockchain and Circular Economy 166
       8.3.1   Cost 167
       8.3.2   Speed 167
       8.3.3   Risk Control 167
       8.3.4   Sustainability 168
       8.3.5   Flexibility 168

8.4 Blockchain and Circular Supply Chain Management 168
    8.4.1 Key Areas of Blockchain-Enabled Circular Supply Chain Management 168
        8.4.1.1 Supplier Selection and Development 168
        8.4.1.2 Procurement 168
        8.4.1.3 Data Management Resource Deployment 168
        8.4.1.4 Materials Management in the Logistics Process 168
        8.4.1.5 Production and Operations 169
        8.4.1.6 Green Product Management 169
        8.4.1.7 Reverse Logistics 169
        8.4.1.8 Reusing Waste Across Various Circular Supply Chains 169
    8.4.2 Stakeholders in the Blockchain-Enabled Circular Supply Chain Management 169
8.5 Access to Data in the Blockchain Network 171
8.6 Manufacturing Sustainability Challenges and Blockchain-Enabled Solutions in Circular Supply Chains 174
8.7 Summary 178
Discussion and Review Questions 179

PART 5

Chapter 9 Circular Economy and Sustainable Business Performance 183

9.1 Introduction 183
9.2 Circular Business Models 184
    9.2.1 Efficient Material-Technical Loops 184
    9.2.2 Effective Product-Service Loops 185
    9.2.3 Social-Collaborative Loops 186
    9.2.4 Symbiotic Ecosystems 187
9.3 Driving Business Management Sustainability Through Circular Economy 187
    9.3.1 Strategic Planning 188
    9.3.2 Cost Management 189
    9.3.3 Circular Supply Chain Management 190
    9.3.4 Quality Management 191
    9.3.5 Environmental Management 191
    9.3.6 Process Management 192
    9.3.7 Logistics 193
    9.3.8 Service Management 194
    9.3.9 Research and Development (R&D) 194
9.4 Synergizing the Business Areas for Circular Economy Impact 195

Contents xi

    9.5 Environmental Impact of Circular Economy Business Models 197
        9.5.1 Experimentation Toward Circular Business Models 198
        9.5.2 Environmental Impacts of Circular Business Models 199
        9.5.3 Present State of Environmental Impact Assessment 199
    9.6 Firm's Dynamic Capabilities and Circular Economy Development 200
    9.7 Circular Economy Rebound in Circular Business 203
        9.7.1 The Environmental Rebound Effect 203
        9.7.2 Rebound in the Circular Economy 204
        9.7.3 Circular Business Models and Circular Economy Strategies 204
        9.7.4 Mitigation Effects 205
        9.7.5 Rebound and Inequality 206
        9.7.6 Mitigating Rebound in the Transition 206
    9.8 Summary 208
    Discussion and Review Questions 209

PART 6

Chapter 10 Enablers and Associated Risks to Implementing Circular Economy 213

    10.1 Introduction 213
    10.2 The Circular Economy Paradigm and Driving Factors 213
        10.2.1 Win-Win Strategies 214
        10.2.2 The Role of Regulatory Initiatives 214
        10.2.3 Environmental Values as a Key Issue 214
        10.2.4 Supply Risk-Related Drivers 215
    10.3 The Shift Toward Circular Economy 215
        10.3.1 Extending the Life Cycle of Products Through 3R 216
            10.3.1.1 Product-as-a-Service 217
            10.3.1.2 Sustainable Consumption 217
            10.3.1.3 Collection 217
            10.3.1.4 Repair 217
            10.3.1.5 Distribution and Material Movement 217
        10.3.2 Ecological Balance and Protection 218
            10.3.2.1 Energy and Resource Efficiency 218
            10.3.2.2 Clean and Renewable Energy 218
            10.3.2.3 Waste Management 218
            10.3.2.4 Waste to Energy 218

10.3.3 Big Data and Information Flow 219
  10.3.3.1 Cloud Computing 219
  10.3.3.2 Internet of Things (IoT) 219
  10.3.3.3 Data-Driven Analytics and Artificial Intelligence (AI) 219
10.3.4 Government Policies 219
  10.3.4.1 Government Policies Promote Capacity Building 220
  10.3.4.2 Urban Planning 220
  10.3.4.3 Legislation and Regulation 220
10.3.5 Consumer Behavior 220
  10.3.5.1 Education 220
  10.3.5.2 Persuasive Communication 220
  10.3.5.3 Cultural Factors 221
10.4 TOE Classified Enablers of Circular Supply Chain 221
  10.4.1 Technological Enablers 222
  10.4.2 Organizational Enablers 222
  10.4.3 Environmental Enablers 223
10.5 Risks Associated with Circular Supply Chains 223
  10.5.1 Government and Regulatory Issues 227
  10.5.2 Economic and Financial Issues 228
  10.5.3 Technological Issues 228
  10.5.4 Societal Issues 229
  10.5.5 Organizational and Managerial Issues 230
  10.5.6 Infrastructural, Supply Chain and Market Issues 230
10.6 Summary 231
Discussion and Review Questions 232

Chapter 11 Behavioral Perspectives to Implementing Circular Economy 233

11.1 Introduction 233
11.2 The Role of Purchasers in the Circular Economy 233
11.3 Organizational Citizenship Behavior for the Environment and Circular Purchasing 236
11.4 Eco-Labeling as a Behavior Change Tool 237
  11.4.1 Drivers to Adopting Product Labeling Schemes 238
    11.4.1.1 Knowledge and Awareness 238
    11.4.1.2 Trust 239
    11.4.1.3 Consumer Preferences and Perceptions 239
    11.4.1.4 Business Influences 239
  11.4.2 Impacts and Outcomes of Labeling Schemes 241
    11.4.2.1 Behavioral Impacts and Outcomes 241
    11.4.2.2 Environmental Impacts and Outcomes 241

Contents xiii

		11.4.2.3 Business Impacts and Outcomes 241
	11.4.3	Interventions to Support the Adoption of Labeling Schemes 242
11.5	Eco-Label and Circular Economy 242
11.6	Summary 245

Discussion and Review Questions 246
Suggested Materials for Further Reading 246

PART 7

Chapter 12 Deployment Considerations for Implementing Reverse Logistics 249

    12.1 Introduction 249
    12.2 The Stages in the Reverse Logistics Process 251
        12.2.1 Financial and Economic Consideration 254
        12.2.2 Return Loop Consideration 254
        12.2.3 Social Consideration 255
        12.2.4 Environmental Consideration 256
        12.2.5 Infrastructure and Technology Consideration 257
        12.2.6 Management and Organizational Consideration 259
        12.2.7 Consumer Awareness and Incentives 260
    12.3 Current Trends and Future Developments of Circular Supply Chains in the Retail Industry 261
    12.4 The Overall Impact of Circularity on Contemporary Logistics 263
    12.5 Summary 264

Discussion and Review Questions 265
Suggested Materials for Further Reading 265

Case 1 The Use of Reusable Plastic Containers in Tomato Logistics System: A Case Study in Nigeria 273

    C1.1 Introduction 273
    C1.2 Tomato Production in Nigeria 273
        C1.2.1 Unit of Measure in the Trade 274
        C1.2.2 The Nigerian Tomato Supply Chain 275
        C1.2.3 Current Practice 275
            C1.2.3.1 Farmers 276
            C1.2.3.2 Middlemen at the Northern Markets 276
            C1.2.3.3 Dealers at the Northern Markets 276
            C1.2.3.4 Dealers at the Southern Markets 276
            C1.2.3.5 Dealers' Agents at the Southern Markets 276

		C1.2.3.6	Transporters and Their Agents at Both Sets of Markets................................ 276
		C1.2.3.7	Raffia Basket Suppliers 277
		C1.2.3.8	Retailers at the Southern Outlet Markets... 278
		C1.2.3.9	Supermarkets.. 278
		C1.2.3.10	Suppliers of Inputs and Services to Farmers 278
		C1.2.3.11	Consumers... 278
	C1.3	Reusable Plastic Crate (RPC).. 278	
		C1.3.1 RPC Management Systems 279	
			C1.3.1.1 Ownership Issues.................................. 282
			C1.3.1.2 Pool Size 282
			C1.3.1.3 Return Rate... 283
		C1.3.2 Cycle Time 284	
		C1.3.3 Maintenance of Crates 285	
		C1.3.4 Service life of Crates and Trip Rate 285	
		C1.3.5 Cost of Packaging.. 285	
	C1.4	Distribution of the Benefits of Using RPCS 286	
		C1.4.1 Backhaul Distances... 287	
		C1.4.2 Environmental Considerations 287	
	C1.5	The Way Forward 288	
		C1.5.1 Suggested Operational Model 288	

Case 2 Implementing Circular Economy in the Automotive Industry: A Case Study in Nigeria 291

	C2.1	Introduction 291
	C2.2	The Case Study of the Presidential Task Force on Clearance of Abandoned/Accident/Scrap Vehicles from Police Stations, Highways and Public Places in Nigeria.. 294
		C2.2.1 Work Design.. 296
		C2.2.2 Funding of the PTF Activities................................ 296
	C2.3	Metal Scrap Industry 296
		C2.3.1 The Global Perspective 296
		C2.3.2 Types of Scrap Metals 297
		C2.3.3 Users of Scrap Metals/Utilization Capacity............ 297
		C2.3.4 State of Metal Scraps in Nigeria 297
		C2.3.5 Sources of Scrap Metals.. 298
	C2.4	The Test Run Phase 298
		C2.4.1 Findings from the Test Run..................................... 299
		C2.4.2 Limited Expansion Stage 299
		C2.4.3 Reversal into Lull Period... 300
	C2.5	Critical Element of Success 301
		C2.5.1 Administrative Set-Up... 301

		C2.5.2	Roles Specifications	301
		C2.5.3	Bureaucratic Interference	302
		C2.5.4	External Forces Influence	302
		C2.5.5	Hostile Attitude of Metal Scraps Keepers	302
	C2.6	Prospects		303
		C2.6.1	Environmental Sanity	303
		C2.6.2	Growth of Recycling Plants	303
		C2.6.3	Inputs to Existing Industries	304
		C2.6.4	Funds Generation	304
		C2.6.5	Costing the PTF Performances	304
		C2.6.6	Going Forward	304
Suggested Materials for Further Reading				305
Index				307

Author Biographies

Ifeyinwa Juliet Orji, Ph.D., is an Assistant Professor in the Business School of Soochow University, PR China. Her research interests include green manufacturing, sustainable supply chain management, and operations management. She has previous research experience in the MIT Global Supply Chain and Logistics Excellence (SCALE) Network. Ifeyinwa has published in journals such as Omega: The International Journal of Management Science, Computers and Industrial Engineering, International Journal of Production Economics, International Journal of Production Research, Journal of Business Research, Transportation Research Part A: Policy and Practice among others. She serves as a reviewer and associate editor for many reputable journals and has received several awards for excellence in research.

Frank Ojadi, Ph.D., is an Associate Professor at the Lagos Business School, Nigeria. Dr. Ojadi's teaching and research interests are in operations management – design and implementation of logistics and supply chain management optimization. His research works have been published in Supply Chain Management: An International Journal, International Journal of Production Research, and International Journal of Logistics: Research and Applications. His case studies and technical notes include Sensational Foods Ltd, Talent Drycleaners (among the 15 top-selling cases for 2009, 2010 and 2011 in the category of production and operations management by the European Case Clearing House), Clearing of Imports at the Lagos Seaport, Economic Regulation of Industries and Industrial Sectors, Reforming the Nigeria Police Force, Nigerian Maritime Security, Maritime Administration in Nigeria. He is a member of the editorial board of Journal of Transport and Supply Chain Management, South Africa.

Part 1

1 The Circular Supply Chain
Introduction and Historical Development

1.1 INTRODUCTION

The global economy was 9.1% and 8.6% circular in 2019 and 2020, respectively, highlighting a massive and expanding circularity gap. The worsening circularity gap demonstrates the persistence of the linear economy's take-make-dispose production and consumption tradition, which promotes high rates of resources extractions, unending material wastages and low levels of end-of-use processing and cycling. As the world continues to consume 100 billion tonnes (Gt) of materials annually, the future outlook is grim because the global economy is breaching several milestones. The manufacturing sector is one of the notorious villains in the widening circularity gap. As a resource-intensive space, the manufacturing sector has the largest ecological footprint. The processes and products of the manufacturing techniques deplete a significant amount of virgin materials, consume excessive energy, emit prohibitive quantities of greenhouse gases and generate significant quantities of solid landfill wastes. The manufacturing sector's wasteful nature and circularity gap are even more pronounced in emerging economies like China, with tremendous manufacturing activities where manufacturing wastes account for a huge percentage of landfill wastes. Typically, business-as-usual in the manufacturing industry encompasses the linear economy model of materials production and consumption. Therefore, the main reason for the manufacturing sector's massive circularity gaps is the dominance of manufacturing techniques that operates based on the take-make-waste tradition of the linear economy.

Hence, a circular approach to manufacturing is considered a strategic path to reduce the sector's circularity gap. The manufacturing sector is considered a significant sector with a high potential to implement circular economy strategies due to the discrete nature of manufacturing processes and the growing adoption of eco-friendly products and technologies. Likewise, manufacturing companies are required to implement a circular economy to protect natural resources, reduce material wastage and solid wastes and also minimize the environmental footprint of manufactured products. The circular economy reverses and reinvents the take-make-dispose tradition of the linear economy to closed loop material production and manufacturing model, enabling the reuse and recycling of wastes and resources. Circular manufacturing facilitates the reuse and recycling of manufactured products and maintains components and resources at their highest intrinsic values for a more extended period. It enables components to be kept in a continuous loop of use, reuse, repair and recycle, thereby reducing manufacturing waste and negative externalities such as carbon dioxide emissions. In the circular economy, economic growth is decoupled from resource consumption and the notion of waste is eliminated by maintaining products, components and materials at their highest utilities and values.

Recently, the concept of a circular economy has gained widespread attention in academic institutions and significant traction within policy and business perspectives. Major companies such as IKEA, Philips and H&M have adopted ambitious circular economy agendas to strengthen their commitment to sustainable development. On a European Union level, the Circular Economy Action Plan proposed by the European Commission aims to further the realization of the circular economy and many European member states have adopted a variety of implementation strategies. The circular economy is still subject to conceptual and terminological un-clarity and debate, which are unlikely to aid its implementation. The circular economy has been referred to as a "catch-all" philosophy, which consists of a multitude of different definitions and is interpreted in different ways by different actors. Nevertheless, there is a consensus on the potential of the circular economy to necessitate a systemic view on resources and their lifecycles and a fundamental systemic change rather than "a bit of twisting of the status quo". Furthermore, recent plans presented in light of the COVID-19 pandemic consider investing in the circular economy as a way to create 700,000 new jobs by 2030 and strengthen supply chains. Despite these pro-active measures, thus far the realization of a circular economy in practice has been rather limited and still appears to be in its early stages.

We begin our study by:

- Defining circular supply chains.
- Discussing briefly what circular supply chain management entails.
- Presenting the historical development of circular supply chains.

1.2 DEFINING CIRCULAR SUPPLY CHAIN

Basically, supply chains are the backbone of economies and society, and largely interact with nature, with such interactions being very complex and triggered by mutual interrelations and feedbacks between supply chains, nature and the economy. They consist of physical facilities scattered geographically that assist in the movement of raw materials from the initial suppliers to the manufacturers and finished products from the manufacturers to the end users. Supply chains are strategic for actualizing sustainability objectives and increasing overall organizational performance and competitiveness. Companies' resolve to be sustainable encourages their supply chains to act on health and environmental issues since no single company can solve such issues on its own. Addressing these issues requires systemic change across the whole supply chain. Nowadays, supply chains are becoming circular because they form a closed loop connecting the supply chain from its beginning to the end. Today, with the growing awareness and global concerns on environmental sustainability, circular supply chains are formed. A schematic of a circular supply chain is presented in Figure 1.1. In circular supply chains, not only closed loop

The Circular Supply Chain

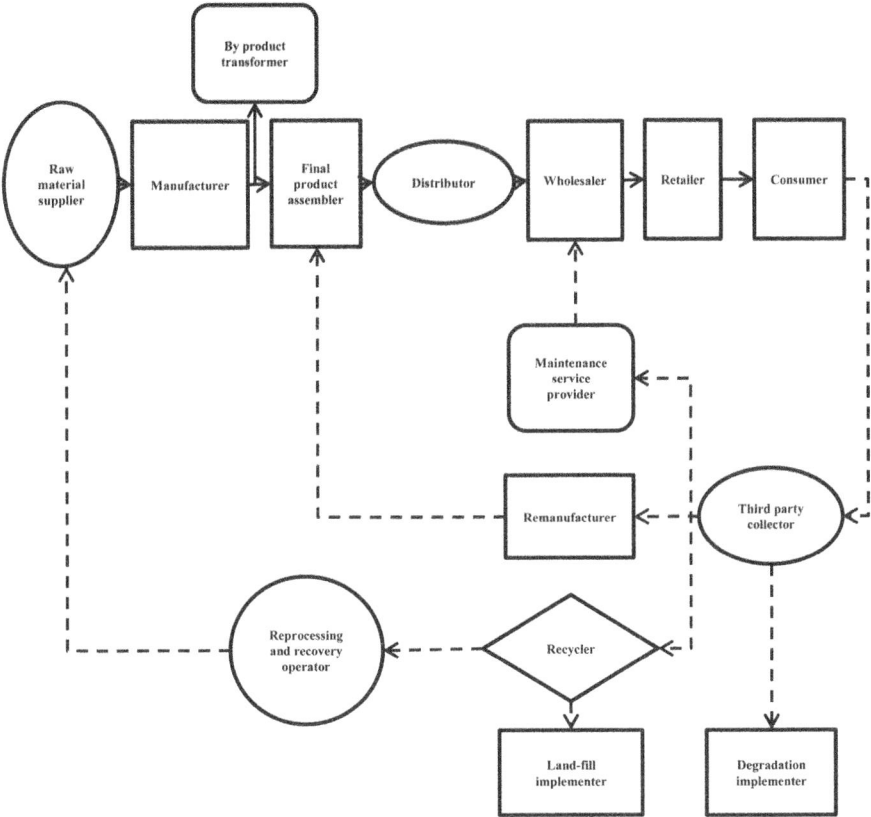

FIGURE 1.1 Circular supply chain.

supply chain processes and triple-bottom-line-based sustainability are encouraged, but proposals on zero wastes and regenerative supply chains are well advocated.

Generally, a circular supply chain comprises partners such as upstream raw material suppliers, product manufacturers, distributors, wholesalers, retailers, third-party collectors for scraps and wastes, remanufacturers, recyclers and so on (see Figure 1.1). The circular supply chain focuses on highlighting the risks of resource paucity and ecological degradation from an industrial perspective. Circular supply chain comprises the returns and recycling through managing waste materials and changing such into products, which can be re-marketed, thereby returning back into the economy. The circular supply chain can help in minimizing the demand for new natural resources supporting the reuse of existing materials, functioning in a closed loop to optimize the product life cycle and reduce scraps and unfavorable ecological impacts in the supply chain practice by means of reprocessing. In fact, in other to find opportunities for wealth creation for companies, there is a huge need to improve resource management and ensure it follows environmentally safe practices. As such, the concept of circular economy was developed in response to this need. The circular economy is restorative and excretes waste with design by more suitable materials, products and systems design enabled via innovative business models. The end cycle of products could result in awareness. Consequently, technologies' production that is essential for waste handling and estimation of economic and environmental benefits related to the circular economy could be a vital output in this regard.

Furthermore, the circular supply chain innovation enables the opportunity for value recuperation from product streams that were traditionally treated as waste. For instance, polyethylene terephthalate (PET) bottles can be reused after recycling, which brings value to the construction industry by including light concrete to the bottles to produce a material for insulated walls for the house. In yet another instance, manufacturers can reuse textile supplies by transforming them into insulation, thereby creating value for the construction industry.

1.3 CIRCULAR SUPPLY CHAIN MANAGEMENT: MEANING AND ESSENCE

In recent years, given the increasing scarcity of resources, the concept of circular economy (CE) has become popular and consistently advocated by academic scholars, policy makers, and industry managers/practitioners. The circular economy has been defined as an economy that is restorative and regenerative by design. Such an economy aims for a zero-waste mission through circulating scarce resources by means of biological (natural decomposition) and technical (reuse, remanufacturing, refurbishing and recycling) cycles. Additionally, the circular economy paradigm evolved as an approach that aims at sustaining the circularity of resources and energy in a closed loop chain. In fact, the circular economy is defined as an economic system that minimizes resources consumption and eliminates waste while simultaneously emphasizing on the continuity of economic development. Indeed, the concept of circular economy has been developed over the past decade to help deal with the global problems of environmental degradation and resource depletion/scarcity resulting from industrial activities. Moreover, the integration of circular economy-related concepts in available literature on supply chain management is dated back to related literature streams like industrial ecology, sustainable supply chain management, reverse logistics and closed loop supply chain management. These literature streams have emphasized on how organizations can effectively interchange resources and wastes, incorporate environmental and social issues into firms and also recover after-use products for capturing additional economic benefits. The transition to a circular economy requires a transformation in supply chain management, which has given birth to a new concept, circular supply chain management.

In this context, circular supply chain management is the integration of circular thinking into the management of the supply chain and its surrounding industrial and natural ecosystems with the goal of achieving zero waste. It is defined *as the configuration and coordination of the organizational functions marketing, sales, R&D, production, logistics, IT, finance and customer service within and across business units and organizations to close, slow, intensify, narrow and dematerialize material and energy loops to minimize resource input into and waste and emission leakage out of the system, improve its operative effectiveness and efficiency and generate competitive advantages.* Contrary to the traditional concepts like closed loop supply chain management and sustainable supply chain management, the concept of circular supply chain management offers greater potential and clearer processes for progressing supply chain circularity. For instance, circular supply chain management enables value recovery across different supply chains partnering firms in the same industry and/other industries, while closed supply chain management can rarely reuse/recycle all materials within the original supply chains. The introduction of circular economy principles in supply chain management confronts firms with new considerations in product design, procurement, manufacturing, logistics, sales, product use and information management. For instance, a firm's product design may now be reviewed in terms of product lifetime (extension), product/component reuse guidelines and other circular redesign strategies.

Likewise, a firm's material procurement in a circular economy necessitates that firms monitor the properties and inventories of components which in turn requires the organized collection and exchange of data across the supply chain network. Basically, wastes are available from manufacturing practice as substitutes of inputs, which may involve assessing: (a) processing techniques needed (waste treatment or waste processing, (b) the mismatch in both quality and quantity of manufactured wastes since these are manufactured upon demand, (c) the economic viability of the synergy and (d) the contractual clauses. In the logistics context, this may necessitate changes and additions in distribution networks (e.g. pipelines to facilitate heat exchange, recycling networks or reverse logistics in case of extended producer responsibility [EPR])). Sometimes, the integration of circular economy principles may affect sales and require a business model transformation and may also affect consumers' consumption patterns. Supply chain actors or governmental agencies that are responsible for minimizing impacts due to product use may coordinate awareness campaigns and sustainability education to influence consumer behavior. Finally, a firm's information management is affected. For instance, by the need to manage the new logistics or by the need to keep track of the environmental impacts of product components, where there is often a duality between the benefit of information sharing and protecting a firm's competitive advantage. These circular developments in supply chains are often the result of convergence activities of firms, i.e., identifying new opportunities in which the unique value proposition is delivered through a collaboration of multiple stakeholders, typically from different sectors (e.g., integration of products or shared knowledge creation).

Furthermore, circular supply chain management is the integration of circular thinking into the management of the supply chain and its surrounding industrial and natural ecosystems. It systematically restores technical materials and regenerates biological materials toward a zero-waste vision through system-wide innovation in business models and supply chain functions. These functions are from product/service design to end of life (EoL) and waste management, comprising all stakeholders in a product/service lifecycle including parts/product manufacturers, service providers, consumers and users. Circular supply chain management significantly facilitates sustainable supply chain management and green supply chain management by a regenerative dimension. It progresses sustainability thinking by a systematic application of circular economy's circular thinking in all supply chain stages and functions. As with the circular economy philosophy, circular supply chain management is applicable to manufactured products as well as service products. In circular supply chain management, organizations cooperate with others internally and externally to maximize the utility of goods/materials. It presents a promising vision to direct supply chain managers to achieve a breakthrough performance in resource efficiency and, consequently, profitability.

Additionally, circular supply chain management reduces the negative social, environmental and economic impacts. The goal of circular supply chain management is to strengthen circular supply chains, which contrast with traditional (linear) supply chain and closed loop supply chain. A linear supply chain extracts resources from the geosphere and the biosphere and disposes off EoL products, packaging materials and wastes from multiple supply chain stages, with unwanted items often deposited in landfills. A closed loop supply chain results in environmental performance improvements by bringing back goods and packaging materials to the producer to recover value. For instance, closed loop remanufacturing of photocopiers can conserve 20%–70% of materials, labor and energy and also minimize waste by 35%–50% as compared to conventional manufacturing. Nevertheless, the extent to which value is recovered in a closed loop supply chain is often limited due to efforts that are restricted within the original supply chain (producer's supply chain). Additionally, such efforts do not necessarily include secondary supply chains or comprise new auxiliary channel members.

1.4 DEVELOPMENT AND GROWTH OF CIRCULAR SUPPLY CHAINS

In this section, we present insights on the emergence of circular economy, the role of stakeholders in the circular supply chains and the implementation of circular supply chains in industrial sectors as precursors to the study of the development and growth of circular supply chains.

1.4.1 THE EMERGENCE OF CIRCULAR ECONOMY

The concept of the circular economy was first mentioned by the economist Kenneth Boulding in 1966. Then, environmental economists Pearce and Turner further discussed the circular economy in their book *Economics of Natural Resources and the Environment*. The circular economy emerged as an umbrella concept to achieve sustainability and encompasses a wide range of strategies for slowing, narrowing and closing materials and energy flows to handle the structural waste. Many politicians and experts have also defined a variety of concepts of the circular economy. The implementation of the circular economy dates back to 1996 in Germany with the promulgation of the "Closed Substance Cycle and Waste Management Act". Next, in 2000, the Japanese government issued a law to promote the circular economy. This law sought to transform society with high society. The successful implementation of the circular economy in these two countries inspired the Chinese government to create its circular economy mode. In 2008, the Chinese government passed the "Circular Economy Promotion Law" and defined the concept of the circular economy as a broad term referring to reduction, reuse and recycling in all stages of the value chain.

In 2013, the "Circular Economy Development Strategy and Recent Action Plan" was issued by the State Council of China. In the same year, the National Development and Reform Commission (NDRC) of China announced the first group of 40 pilot cities in China for the circular economy. Because of the increasing attention on the circular economy, since 2000, a large amount of literature has been published from various perspectives such as supply chain, sustainable buildings, new product design, renewable energy, smart cities and industrial parks and EoL vehicles. Additionally, there is literature evidence on a circular supply chain that focuses on the emerging policy of circular economy within the China context. Other studies address rapid economic development and eco-industrial initiatives that are related with environmental degradation in China, which are comparable with strategies implemented in the Western and Eastern parts of Asia. Within the Indian context, circular economy business models present some lessons on reduce, recycle and reuse.

In business models, the shift to a circular economy requires critical modifications in supply chain operations that relate to product/service design, manufacture, use, waste management and reprocessing. As such, many circular economy practices at the firm's micro-level that are related to supply chain operations have been implemented by some firms. For instance, some academic researchers in their study indicated a multidisciplinary clique of researchers in economics, engineering, management, operational research and other fields is examining the selection of circular economy practices and analyzing their influences on manufacturing operations. Likewise, other research scholars in their study categorized how circular economy practices are relevant for implementing the sustainable development goals (SDGs). In yet another study, some research scholars focused on the subject of circular economy practices between Chinese manufacturers differing in environmental-oriented supply chain collaboration and the performance implications. Also, some academic researchers studied the circular economy practices in the leather industry. Additionally, some research scholars reviewed incorporating a circular economy with distinct supply chain functions such as product/service design, procurement, production, logistics, consumption, EoL and waste management.

Furthermore, the circular economy transition is regarded as a model to redirect the path of economic development and revert societal and environmental effects to earlier stages in which planetary boundaries were not exceeded. In addition, the circular economy narrative proposes a future in which the concept of waste is phased out, aiming at a model of economy that overcomes the actual effects of human activities that exceed the resilience of ecosystems on a global scale. The concept of circular economy has gained increasing attention in academics, policy making and business practice; it advocates deep transformation of the economic system challenging how modern industrial societies design and produce goods. From this perspective, circular supply chains represent a basic building foundation for the transition toward a circular economy. The circular supply chain integrates a circular economy theory in the firms' supply chain and presents novel opportunities for sustainability improvement of supply chain processes. Likewise, the integration of industrial ecology in the supply chain can assist with the adoption of circular supply chain practices to achieve sustainable development. In fact, the adoption of a well-designed reverse logistics network can influence the operational activities and performance of circular supply chains. Thus, organizations are constantly making efforts to integrate the circularity concept in their supply chains, and as such, the practical and advanced IT system for tracking EoL products in organizations improves the product rate of return.

1.4.2 THE ROLE OF STAKEHOLDERS IN CIRCULAR SUPPLY CHAINS

The involvement of all the relevant stakeholders such as suppliers, customers, supply chain members and company's employees plays a significant role in the adoption of circular supply chains. Consequently, the interests of customers in buying circular products will be protected by developing appropriate standards, the formulation of assurance policies and the inspection of certifications for recycled/remanufactured products. The circular supply chain decouples an organization's socioeconomical and environmental growth by extracting resources and environmental losses. It implies returning waste to the production cycle to manufacture new products instead of wasting materials with embedded resources. Hence, companies that take the decision to redesign their supply chains based on circular economy aspects can eventually actualize improvements in economic, environmental and social performance. Circular initiatives in the supply chain context emphasize on the interactions between supply chain management and the circular economy. Indeed, the circular supply chain concept integrates the circular economy philosophy into an organization's supply chain and, as such, considered an alternative solution to the traditional linear supply chain model. In traditional supply chains, natural resources are usually converted into products and delivered to the end customers for use. After the end-of-use phase, products are usually dumped into landfills, generating an enormous amount of waste and ecological deterioration issues.

Meanwhile, the circular supply chains focus on regenerative and restorative aspects of the circular economy. It also employs 6Rs principles such as reuse, recycling, repair, remanufacturing, reduction and refurbish to create a closed loop system that minimizes resource inputs, waste, pollution and carbon emissions across the supply chain. The 6Rs principles of the circular economy facilitate the socioeconomic and environmental performance of manufacturing organizations. Many countries in the Europe continent have well-established policies, laws and regulations that encourage organizations toward adopting circular supply chain strategies in their manufacturing units, showing their maturity in the circularity issues. Hence, the concept of the sustainability of the circular supply chains has attracted significant global companies such as Google, Renault and Unilever due to its economic and ecological benefits, although it is still in its initial stages in several developing countries. Likewise, circular supply chains have become a popular research domain over the years due to cases in which it has been successfully applied. For instance, some academic scholars in their study analyzed healthcare industry circular supply chain collaboration in Vietnam and investigated thought and determining impacts on the link in a circular supply chain and circularity business model. Some research scholars in their research carried out a study on the principal dimensions that are involved in the development of circular supply chains. Most studies have discussed a procedure to integrate the circular economy and the supply chain to form a reverse supply chain that considers design, operations and EoL operations for product management. This

The Circular Supply Chain

procedure can improve effectiveness over its entire lifecycle through value recovery (such as reuse, repair, remanufacture or recycle) of after-use products either by the original producer or by a third party.

1.4.3 Circular Supply Chain Implementation in Industries

However, in many industrial sectors, the implementation of circular supply chain has increased at the micro-level. For instance, some academic researchers in their study offered "material supply chain sustainability" initiatives through green engineering and circular economy principles focused on the electronics industry. Then, other academic researchers in their study acknowledged that textile companies faced challenges in producing circular goods. In yet another study, some academic authors performed a thorough analysis of parameters connected with e-waste and metal flows in the Australian metal value chain. The metal losses associated with e-waste are reported to be US$60–70 million per year. Some academic researchers presented discussions on circular economy implementation in biochemical and agricultural industries and the critical gaps. Other researchers in their study analyzed the risks of using circular economy initiatives in producing supply chains. Another research scholar analyzed the food supply chain wastes and plastics in other to create viable organic "waste-to-resource" opportunities. Ultimately, the integration of circular economy and supply chain management can facilitate environmental sustainability as evidenced in past published studies coupled with economic performance improvements.

Furthermore, we present some of the incentives for implementing the circular economy concept in supply chains. First and foremost, an incentive to implement the circular economy concept in business practices is to explore the retained value of waste or underutilized resources. In essence, the circular economy business model presents business with opportunities for a new vision that wastes can be exploited as resources. As such, the fast-paced advancement of the circular economy infrastructure at the regional, industry and supply chain levels stimulates organizations to recover value from wastes. Additionally, another incentive for implementing the circular economy concept is to reduce supply chain vulnerability. In this context, the depletion of available natural resources tends to constitute a wave of concerns about the supply of raw materials in the long run. Basically, supply chains are increasingly complex and geographically dispersed in the pursuit of low costs and efficiency and such developments increase supply chain risks during operational disruptions and market uncertainties. A circular economy creates restorative and regenerative cycles of resources in a circular flow and such a model helps firms with an effective method to establish secure supply chains against mishaps like supply shortage, price fluctuation and resource depletion. In fact, organizations are utilizing the circular economy as an operations strategy to minimize supply chain vulnerability, although the basic goal is in environmental performance improvements. A third incentive indicates that implementing the circularity concept in supply chains can aid in addressing environmental concern and regulation changes. This shows that although the environmental gains of circular economy are widely recognized, most companies are not inspired to hastily commence implementation due to environmental performance or regulatory compliance. In fact, companies are mostly pragmatic in their circular economy pathway, commencing an implementation at the point that retained value of waste or underutilized resources can be explored. This pragmatic approach adopted by companies is understandable since most businesses exist to make profits.

Nevertheless, this decision to make profits may hinder their long-term progress in the circular economy journey during conflict between environmental and economic performance. Yet another incentive is in social sustainability improvements as a result of implementing a circular economy. For instance, companies usually utilize the circularity method to increase recycling and remanufacturing activities and thereby create more local jobs and the firms utilize these jobs to increase labor intensity. In addition, firms utilize circular information systems to encourage fragmented local farmers to increase individual propensity. As such, the social sustainability implications of a circular economy present additional insight on the role of circular economy in sustainable development. Also, there are reports on the economic and operational advantages of implementing a circular economy in supply chains of various companies. In most cases, companies experienced economic improvements, mainly due to reduced materials and energy utilization, maximum resource use and reduced disposal costs. Some firms developed new revenue sources by resale and selling wastes and by-products. Interestingly, business experience increased cost savings through reusing than through a recycling process. For instance, in the electronics and electrical equipment sector, refurbished products resulted six times more added value than recycled products. In the context of printing paper, reutilizing paper through erasing the information rather than by traditional recycling would provide cost savings without any upfront investment. This shows that through the use of careful design for reverse engineering and technological support, "slowing resources loops" can be most cost-efficient than "closing resources loops" in business practices.

The circular resource use at firm and supply chain levels (e.g., a sharing economy) allows companies to conduct business without substantially investing in production equipment. Thus, it minimizes the capital constraints and market entry obstacles, which are especially important to small- and medium-sized enterprises. Another benefit of implementing circular economy practices in companies is to facilitate improved supply chain relationships. For example, the development of the circular economy model presents new avenues for supply chain collaborations. Reverse logistics expects supply chain partners to collaborate to restructure material flows, design for disassembly and ensure information sharing for supply chain circularity. Indeed, manufacturers utilized the "product-service system" (PSS), where companies change their tenets from physical product delivery to providing integrated product-service offerings in the form of renting or leasing. Supply chain partners are more likely to develop strategic collaborations through long-term and customized maintenance and disposal services in product-service systems. The utilization of regenerative energy and restorative materials enhances the continuity in resource supply and thus facilitates trust between purchasing firms and their suppliers. The circular economy model hugely extends the supply chain operations to a broader scope than those in a linear supply chain system, thereby presenting opportunities to solidify supply chain relationships. The circularity of material resources also minimizes the purchasing costs and enables shared advantages of circular economy in supply chains. The increasing utilization of recycled products hugely saves manufacturing costs and minimizes purchasing costs. Therefore, the optimized purchasing costs tend to enhance supply chain collaborations/relationships. Furthermore, implementing circular economy practices in supply chains can encourage developing supply chain resilience. A circular economy helps to develop a more self-sustaining manufacturing system, which protects the flow of resources from price fluctuation, seasonality and disruptions in supply. Additionally, the rapidly changing market and external disruptive events (e.g., COVID-19 pandemic) cause a huge threat to supply chain stability. Thus, innovative uses of circular economy can be a means to supply chain resilience improvements coupled with traditional mechanisms (e.g., operational slack).

1.5 KEY CIRCULAR SUPPLY CHAINS TERMS AND CONCEPTS

The rising global population has led to increased demand for raw materials, water and energy and thus, the access to natural resources is constantly creating more stress. In this context, the circular economy is required to be implemented to achieve resource efficiency. Circular economy and business models should be developed using relevant inputs from waste production, energy and carbon footprints. In addition, the nexus between the circular economy and sustainability should be further strengthened and implemented in circular supply chains. This kind of supply chain contradicts linear supply chains, which exist with the aim to reevaluate all waste for recycling, reusing, refurbishing, etc., for achieving zero waste. In the circular supply chain, waste and by-products from the production stage are likely to occur, while in the consumption stage, reuse waste is likely to occur based on consumer's skill and competence. In recent times, products related to wastes are used as by-products in resource recovery like bioenergy, electric energy or cleaning water by utilizing innovative technologies. Through the application of appropriate and innovative technologies, different types of processing wastes can be recovered to manufacture different types of products. Likewise, the collaborations between suppliers and customers in the supply chain network may assist in extending the product life span and usage through integrating value as 9R. The importance of the 9R strategies for the circular supply chain and circular economy are presented in Table 1.1 with illustrations of the recoveries made in all the processes. In Table 1.2, the 9R strategies are presented in detail with some examples as well.

In the circular supply chains, the optimal use of all resources, products remanufacturing, reusing and recycling are highly critical for value recovery from manufacturing operations and from waste. Additionally, the circular supply chain transforms waste into products that are defined as value-added products or waste to value products. Moreover, the sustainable use of products is dependent on upstream and downstream information sharing and integrating processes in a circular supply chain can minimize waste and losses. The sharing of information and knowledge while collaborating with supply chain partners may likely increase the value from recycling and reusing waste.

Furthermore, the circular supply chain and sustainability measures provide economic, social and environmental benefits to the stakeholders and customers. A circular economy and sustainability play critical roles in the manufacturing industry

TABLE 1.1
Definitions of the 9R Concepts and Strategies in the Circular Supply Chain

Strategies	Definition/Explanation
Refuse (R0)	This entails rejecting the product or using it with the same function but in a different product and, as such, extends the usage of an existing product. It is considered to be highly significant in circular supply chains. Some examples include final products and returns.
Rethink (R1)	This refers to utilizing products more intensively or sharing products with other partners including renting, sharing and leasing. Rethink is characterized in the circular economy since the circularity concept requires the rethink operation to a large extent.
Reduce (R2)	This refers to reducing usage of natural resources, raw materials, energy, inputs and waste and is essential in circular supply chains to reduce resource consumption and pollution.
Reuse (R3)	This can be defined as the further use of products that are still in good and the same physical conditions as their original form and exhibit similar functions. Examples include pellets, packages, etc.
Repair (R4)	This is defined as fix, restore and maintenance of broken or faulty products so that it can be used again with its original function and operations. Repair can assist in correcting product defects (decay or damages) in a product thereby restoring it to increase its durability, serviceability or usable conditions. In other words, repair is associated with the maintenance of equipment or machines
Refurbish (R5)	This entails updating, modernizing or restoring an old product/item, and it is associated with part replacement or light manufacturing. Certain product parts are often changed and presented to the market again with specified safety, quality or working standards e.g. pallets, equipment, etc.
Remanufacture (R6)	In this process, some of the parts of the old products are utilized in a new product and, as such, can be defined as second-life production. Here, parts of the old products are utilized in a new product with the same operational function. In remanufacturing, used products are reused without losing their original functionality. E.g. automobiles
Repurpose (R7)	In repurpose process, certain parts of the product or the whole product are utilized for an entirely different purpose or with a different function in a different product. In the repurpose process, products are utilized in different functions and in this case, products are processed to have an entirely new functionality and a different identity. E.g. pallet-furniture, box-vase
Recycle (R8)	The recycle involves a chemical transformation from raw materials to a finished state. The raw materials are converted to be used for many products and this process plays a significant role in the circular economy by reducing waste and landfill
Recover (R9)	This process refers to certain products that cannot be recycled and remain as waste and evaluated as a source of energy. It involves the collection of products at the end of their life span disassembling, sorting and cleaning such products so that it can become part of a new system

TABLE 1.2
Examples of the 9R Strategies in the Circular Supply Chain

Supplier	Processor/ Manufacturer	Distributor/ Wholesaler	Retail	Consumer
Reuse (pallets, packaging)	Reuse (packaging, pallets)	Refuse (final product, transport methods, returns)	Refuse (final product)	Refuse (final product)
Recycle (energy, etc.)	Recycle (energy, packaging materials, plastics, used oils)	Recycle (packaging materials, cardboard, plastics)	Recycle (plastics, packaging materials, cardboard)	Recycle (glass, paper, plastics, unused products) Recycle (glass, paper, plastics, unused products)
Remanufacture (raw materials)	Repair (machines, components, equipment, production line)	Repair (equipment, machines)	Repair (equipment, machines)	Rethink (plastic, glass bottles, unused products)
Refurbish (pallets, equipment)	Refurbish (machines, equipment)	Refurbish (equipment, machines)	Refurbish (equipment, return product package, machines)	Reuse (by-product, cardboard, glass, plastics, final product, container)
Reduce (water consumption, energy, pollution, raw material)	Rethink (renting, sharing, leasing)	Reduce (pollution, energy, damage and spoilage)	Reduce (damage and spoilage, pollution, energy, water, inaccurate forecasting)	Reduce (pollution, cost)
Repurpose (water, by-products)	Reduce (energy, raw material, energy, water consumption)			Repurpose (boxes, pallets, by-products, final products)
	Recover (raw materials, water)			Refurbish (final product)
	Remanufacture (packaging, plastics)			
	Repurpose (by-products, water)			
	Refuse (raw material, final product)			

when dealing with higher demand for products and higher costs with higher energy consumption. The sustainable supply chain is based on "doing more and better with less". In a circular economy, resources and waste must be minimized and resources preserved by extending the product life cycle by either reuse or some other strategies to provide further value. Nevertheless, in many industries, many by-products cannot be properly processed within a manufacturing plant and this condition hence offers opportunity for cooperation with other firms and development of an eco-industrial network. In addition, circular economy-based sustainability is associated with product waste minimization and improved 9R concepts/strategies performance; better utilization is made of resources with maximum value at different stages.

Moreover, upcycling is a relatively new sustainable mode of production that "prolongs the life of old objects by creatively reusing and reshaping them into new products". Upcycling shares the product reuse benefit with other sustainable practices including recycling, namely the conversion of waste into reusable materials. However, despite both sustainable practices involving the repurposing of old products, in contrast to recycling, upcycling does not imply the downgrading of raw materials. In recycling, the process of downgrading requires energy and water usage. Moreover, not all of the material in the original product will be reclaimed and a portion of raw material still does become waste. In upcycling, there is no degradation of the material and the lifespan of the material is extended. More importantly, it requires creativity and originality to reform the existing product into something useful and nice again.

1.6 MAJOR ACTIVITIES AND FOCUS OF CIRCULAR SUPPLY CHAINS

The shift to circular supply chains necessitates considerable changes in business models, supply chain configurations and practices related to product/service design, production, consumption, waste management, reuse and recycling. Some firms have adopted various micro-level circular economy practices since there are implications for logistics flows at all supply chain stages. Such circular economy practices include green design, green procurement, cleaner production and EoL management based on Reduction, Reuse and Recycle (3R principles).

1.6.1 Product/Service Design in Circular Supply Chains

Product/service design has significant roles in facilitating materials and energy recirculation in circular supply chains. It is the starting point of applying circular thinking in supply chain functions. Circumventing measures lie in sustainable EoL product and waste management, resource circularity, modularity and design standardization and supply chain collaboration. Drawing upon the concepts of circular economy and sustainability, the product/service design functions require to be basically transformed as the product/service design hugely influences the whole value chain of products and services. Sustainable packaging design and product labeling have also been regarded as significant aspects of the circular design strategy. Designers must respond to various social, environmental and economic requirements and must adopt holistic methods to solve problems. Such designers must transform their design thinking and interpretation of related operations that result in transition to circular economy by developing products and services that meet the circular business model criteria. Moreover, the significance of chemistry to offer the basis of innovative products (e.g. designed to be reused or the feedstock renewed through natural processes) is critical to creating a world without waste. There is research evidence on design functions that provide various design strategies and circular business models based on the notion of product life extension and closed loop systems. For instance, some academic researchers in their work presented a clear distinction between circular product design and green design. Also, Moreno et al. (2016) proposed a conceptual model and mapped the identified circular design strategies against circular model archetypes. In addition, some research scholars identified design guidelines that are needed for a better circular product and suggested the urgent need to integrate lifetime extension and guidelines for product reuse in the strategies for circular product design.

Likewise, there has been an increased adoption of design for dismantling (DFD) in many industries due partly by recent technological developments that provide costs savings and extended product responsibility regulations. The DFD provides values to products not only at the EoL stage but also during the usage, lifetime and maintenance stages. Some academic researchers evaluated the use of the DFD approach by minimizing the number of incompatible polymers in vehicle dashboards. The DFD method led to easy polymers separation and recycling with mechanical methods and also eliminated chemical separation methods. Also, some research scholars developed a robust method to compute the disassembly time modeled using the Maynard operation sequence technique (MOST). The robust method is titled the "ease of Disassembly Metric" (eDiM). Important implications for design for a better circular economy were also presented in the computer industry and in the key domain of managing critical materials supply. Furthermore, since circular supply chains require a complete rethinking of the design approach for products, processes/operations and supply chains, design for circularity is regarded as a cornerstone of circular supply chain management. Thus, research opportunities in this domain include supply chain design for EoL, circular economy driven process innovations, design for recycling, design for remanufacturing and new product design methods.

1.6.2 Procurement in Circular Supply Chains

The procurement activity in circular supply chains will necessitate re-defining associated price, time, quality and value for money principles. The circular economy needs raw materials to be technically restorative or biologically regenerative so that there are no negative environmental impacts. Although the topic of green procurement has been actively researched in extant literature, there is a dearth of studies on procurement management in circular supply chains. Drawing upon the circular supply chain concept, a framework was developed for public procurement, which comprises technical and non-technical product/service specifications that offer guidelines for minimizing raw material utilization and increasing resource efficiency through recovery and lower waste generation. In a similar vein, some academic researchers in their study provided insights on green industrial acquisitions and emphasized on resource efficiency improvements. Their study presented possibilities for the complete reuse of used products materials while considering the environmental advantages and disadvantages of diverse options for industrial product acquisitions. Moreover, procurement is a strategic function of many organizations that plays a significant role in firm's sustainability performance improvement. However, the research on integrating the concept of circularity in procurement is much less than in other operations in the supply chain. Since the circular supply chain expects products with stronger features (such as reliability, reusability, durability, easy resources recovery and minimal wastages), much research is required to incorporate circular thinking into procurement management. This will aid in reducing environmental impacts of products/services through their life cycle.

1.6.3 Production in Circular Supply Chains

Manufacturing organizations are constantly making efforts to adopt sustainable manufacturing strategies and circular economy in their supply chains to mitigate negative environmental impacts. Indeed, this stems from the need for these organizations to increase competitive edge since reduction of resource consumption in the production operations has become important in today's sustainability era. Within this context, green manufacturing has become a widely accepted model for sustainable development. This model incorporates concepts such as resource and energy conservation, environmental protection and waste reduction along the production economy. Some research scholars in their study suggest that green production adoption improves brand image, regulatory compliance and investor's interest while also offering long-term cost savings. Yet still, firms struggle with implementing green manufacturing due to perceive high cost of investment. Improving the efficiency of materials with regard to minimized industrial waste generation and resources consumption has resulted in the development of many strategies in the manufacturing sector. Within the circular supply chain context, green manufacturing and cleaner production have been employed for material efficiency improvements. Cleaner production is considered to be broader than green manufacturing since it also covers service operations. In fact, it is defined as a production need that is not only concerned about fulfilling human needs by sustaining the environment against negative impact. It also aspires to prevent the use of harmful and non-renewable inputs, increase economic efficiency and reduce damage to humans and environment. As such, cleaner production is highly significant in achieving a circular economy. Nevertheless, cleaner production has not been fully implemented in many industrial sectors, and more so, very few studies have explicitly integrated the circular economy philosophy into cleaner production. In sum, cleaner production operations are regarded as a critical enabler of circular supply chain practices at a micro-level, which has implications for other supply chain functions such as circular product design, consumption and EoL and waste management.

1.6.4 Logistics in Circular Supply Chains

Consumers and government regulations alike have pressured organizations to redesign their logistics networks to become more environmentally friendly while being cost efficient. Green logistics is considered manufacturing and distributing goods in a sustainable manner, taking account of social and environmental criteria. This also involves measuring the environmental impacts of different distribution strategies, minimizing energy requirements in logistics-related operations, minimizing wastages and residual wastages treatment. Although traditional logistics concerns forward distribution (i.e., the transport, warehousing and inventory management from suppliers to customers), reverse logistics also plays a vital role toward sustainable development. Circular supply chain management is expected to have numerous implications for logistics management. Likewise, many efforts to integrate the circularity concept into reverse logistics have been observed. For instance, some academic researchers in their study proposed a conceptual model of a closed loop recovery system that integrates national postal service networks into reverse logistics to aid in optimizing circular economy operations. Also, some research scholars illustrated the critical roles of secondary markets in mining product value and also assist in promoting product reuse with regard to reverse logistics, circular economy and sustainability. Additionally, an attempt has been made to ember circular economy values in consumer retail reverse logistics and also develop a model to compute reverse logistics emissions and explore the influential criteria for reverse logistics carbon footprints.

1.6.5 Consumption in Circular Supply Chains

The philosophy of a circular supply chain has stimulated a transition toward a more sustainable consumption model in which valuable resources are reused, and less waste is created. Moreover, the shift to circular supply chains requires changes in consumer behaviors, and this may require an awareness campaign and sustainability education. In essence, the product design operation must be altered in order to reach optimal values. For instance, a Dutch company has now commenced designing and producing a mobile phone that is totally repairable and this is expected to dramatically alter consumer's attitudes. Consumption in the context of circular solutions is fast becoming a research domain that has garnered increased attention from scholars with interests particularly in studying the drivers, barriers and dynamics. However, in spite of early studies on sustainable consumption, there is still a dearth of studies on the consumer perspective on circular products. Consequently, research studies are required to investigate how circular products can be made to become more appealing to customers. For instance, marketing strategies based on demonstrating product reliability, innovative offerings, warranty and quality control mechanisms assurance may be developed to shape positive consumer attitudes toward circular products. Indeed, it is highly important to explore strategies and incentives for changing consumer behaviors to support the cause of circularity since many consumers are unwilling to return used products. In sum, there is a huge need to design appropriate policies and firm-level measures to encourage awareness on circular consumption and highlight consumer attitudes toward circularity practices.

1.6.6 End of Life (EoL) and Waste Management in Circular Supply Chains

In circular supply chain management, EoL and waste management are considered to be essential for recovering the remaining value within a product to its maximum utility. The recirculation of used materials and components has critical environmental and economic performance implications. Nevertheless, there is a minimal insight of the potentials of EoL management for a circular economy in many industrial sectors. There exist various EoL resource recovery methods, namely repurposing, remanufacturing, refurbishing and recycling. *Refurbishing* is a process to restore used products to a functional and satisfactory condition without dismantling the products completely. Refurbishing can be employed to regain value from used products and minimize waste. An efficient refurbishing method enables easy maintenance, recovery and product modification after the EoL cycle. Nevertheless, there is a huge requirement to develop guidelines and standards from refurbishing since the lack of such can result in variations in production, quality issues and poor recognition of products. *Repurposing* is regarded as the identification of new utilization for a product that can no longer be utilized in its original form. There is also a concept known as *re-contextualizing*, which entails the utilization of an obsolete product or its components without any remedial actions in a different context than its originally designed use. Within a circular economy context, it has been observed that 9% of the EoL notebooks could be repurposed as thin computers without incurring any cost based on a recent feasibility study of 246 notebook computers. *Remanufacturing* is preferred to other EoL processes because the remanufactured products are higher in quality, have a longer extended life and more environmentally friendly since it recovers the residual value of used products bringing them to a new-like condition.

Nevertheless, there is ambiguity surrounding the true meaning of other related circular economy activities, namely repair, reconditioning, refurbishment and uncertainty in managing intellectual property issues in many industrial sectors hinder organizations from adopting a remanufacturing strategy. On the other hand, throughout the world, there is still a lack of consumer acceptance of remanufactured products, which prevents supply chains from unlocking the full potential of remanufacturing. Additionally, the diversity of product types, design features and material compositions pose serious policy and practical challenges. Likewise, various research scholars have recommended different strategies and methods to manage and optimize remanufacturing operations in a circular economy context. For instance, some academic researchers presented adaptive remanufacturing to recommend the utilization of an EoL product core to create a similar but non-identical product, hence, enabling more viable lifecycles when in comparison to traditional remanufacturing. Also, there have been developed simulations for prediction of the remanufacturing system performance operating under uncertainty. Several examples of the circular economy-enabled recycling practices exist in various industrial sectors. An integral aspect of the circular economy model is the steel industry. Due to the recyclable nature of the steel raw material, steel scrap is a key resource that can be utilized in steelmaking and also recovered from products. Some barriers classified as economic, policy and technology-related hinder metal recycling and reuse. On the other hand, better regulations and effective use of taxation, establishment of extended producer responsibilities systems and encouraging R&D in metals are some of the possible remedies to the barriers. Indeed, recycling systems for post-consumer plastic packaging have huge potential to positively contribute toward circularity.

Moreover, providing insight on the links between economic activities and waste generation is highly important to assist in achieving circular economy goals.

Incorporating a circular economy into EoL materials management, which is concerned with collecting waste for material recovery, can be hindered by certain challenges. Nevertheless, it is highly important that in supporting other EoL operations, for instance, reuse, the collection systems need to be improved to prevent physical damages to the EoL products during the collection process. Such a system that enhances resources circularity by strengthening the link between resource recovery and waste treatment is described as a circular integrated waste management system. This is highly significant in the case of waste electrical and electronic products since they are often vulnerable to damage.

Furthermore, many countries have adopted product take-back schemes using the concept of EPR, where producers are physically or financially conferred with the responsibility to collect EoL electronics and their recovery in order to remove hazardous materials from landfills. Optimizing EPR schemes can assist in promoting the collection and recycling of both critical and hazardous materials by closing materials loops and also incentivizing green design. The expansion of circular economy necessitates producers to systematically take-back products for resource recovery through EoL management. Hence, EoL and waste management environments must strive to address: (a) liability due to toxic substances utilized in manufacturing, (b) liability due to materials mismanagement during the lifecycle and (c) liability due to products malfunctioning. Furthermore, future research efforts should focus on investigating the feasibility and effectiveness of an EPR legislation. This will be intended to hold producers accountable for their products even longer after a sale to end customers. PSS is an alternative method that serves as a "functional service" model in which the producers retain the ownership of physical products and act as service providers focusing on the service needs of end customers. The PSS can be designed to assist in facilitating EoL management by manufacturing companies and can substantially minimize the requirement of production operations in a shared economy, thereby resulting in lower environmental consequences.

1.7 SUMMARY

Supply chains consist of physical facilities scattered geographically that assist in the movement of raw materials from the initial suppliers to the manufacturers and finished products from the manufacturers to the end users.

A circular supply chain comprises the returns and recycling through managing waste materials and changing such into products, which can be re-marketed, thereby returning back into the economy. It can help in minimizing the demand for new natural resources supporting the reuse of existing materials, functioning in a closed loop to optimize the product life cycle and reducing scraps and unfavorable ecological impacts in the supply chain practice by means of reprocessing.

Likewise, the circular economy is restorative and excretes waste with design by more suitable materials, products and systems design enabled via innovative business models. The end cycle of products could result in awareness. Consequently, technologies' production that is essential for waste handling and estimation of economic and environmental benefits related to the circular economy could be a vital output in this regard.

The historical development of circular supply chain provides interesting background information on the continuing evolution of this strategic domain. The discussion and review questions included in this chapter and subsequent chapters provide insights into the basics of the circular supply chain concept.

DISCUSSION AND REVIEW QUESTIONS

1. Briefly describe circular supply chain.
2. Identify the key circular supply chain concepts.
3. Describe the 'Refuse' and 'Refurbish' as key strategies in circular supply chain.
4. Define circular supply chain management.
5. Briefly discuss each of these terms related to the main activities of circular supply chain:
    a. End of Life (EoL) and waste management
    b. Procurement
    c. Green design
6. Who are stakeholders and what is their role in the development and growth of circular supply chain?

SUGGESTED MATERIALS FOR FURTHER READING

Asta, R. (2017). Artisanal network turns corporate waste into quality goods, Ellen MacArthur Foundation Case Studies, https://www.ellenmacarthurfoundation.org/case-studies/waste-recovery-netwrok-turning-corporate-waste-into-handmade-goods.

e-Choupal (2017). Improving income levels of Indian farmers through better access to information, Ellen MacArthur Foundation Case Studies, https://www.ellenmacarthurfoundation.org/case-studies/improving-income-levels-of-indian-farmers-through-better-access-to-information.

Ellen MacArthur Foundation (2015). Towards a circular economy: Business rationale for an accelerated transition, https://www.ellenmacarthufoundation.org/assets/downloads/publications/TCE_Ellen-MacArthur-Foundation_26-Nov-2015.pdf.

Fuller, R. B. (1969). *Operating manual for spaceship earth*. Southern Illinois University Press.

Moreno, M., De lo Rios C., Rowe Z., Charnley F. (2016). A conceptual framework for circular design, Sustainability, 8(9): 937.

Moula, M. E., Sorvari, J., & Oinas, P. (2017). Constructing a green circular society, https://helda.helsinki.fi/bitstream/handle/10138/231630/ebook2017(pdf).pdf?:sequence=1. (Accessed 15 March 2018).

Papanek, V. J. (1972). *Design for the real world by Victor Papanek*. Academy Chicago Publishers.

Popa, V. N., & Popa, L. I. (2016). Green acquisitions and life cycle management of industrial products. In: *The Circular Economy, IOP Conference Series: Materials Science and Engineering.* IOP Publishing, 012112.

The circularity gap report 2020, Global (2020). Global circularity gap report – circularity gap reporting initiative, circularity-gap.world. (Accessed 2nd May 2022).

2 The Future of Circular Supply Chain

2.1 INTRODUCTION

In this chapter, you will learn about the different projections on the concepts of circular supply chain classified as the 4R framework. You will also learn the strategies that are important in the transition to circularity in supply chains and circular economy.

2.2 PROJECTION DEVELOPMENT ALONG THE 4R FRAMEWORK

The circular economy has traditionally been discussed as a means to achieve environmental sustainability by decoupling economic growth from the arbitrary consumption of resources. The circular economy represents a paradigm change toward a more sustainable economic system where resource input, waste, emission and energy leakage are minimized by closing, narrowing or slowing energy and material loops. Supply chains are the basic unit of activity enabling circular flows whereby circular supply chain management is the integration of circular thinking into the management of the supply chain and its surrounding industrial and natural ecosystems. The circular economy's future development remains uncertain and has received only limited attention in literature. For instance, scholars have explored different scenarios and corresponding enablers of circular economy's potential development. Others discussed the circular economy's future implementation scope based on its current adoption in various sectors or developed circular economy roadmaps for specific industries.

Practices to operationalize circular supply chains are commonly conceptualized in "R" frameworks. Different "R" frameworks have been used in academia and practice, such as 3R, 4R, 6R or even 9R. They all include a value retention hierarchy, where the "R"s' order reflects the priority in terms of circular economy conceptualizations discussed by scholars. The 4Rs also incorporate the "Rs" of the more nuanced frameworks as sub-dimensions. Hence, we detailed the various "R" practices along the 4R framework, discussed their potential to reduce supply chain dependencies and introduced some future-oriented projections.

2.2.1 REDUCE

The 4R framework's hierarchy starts with "Reduce". From a product perspective, "Reduce" aims at waste prevention by simply using less (packaging) material per manufactured unit. Furthermore, products can be redesigned for longer lifetimes, decreased product exchange rates, and reduced resource consumption. From a consumer perspective, "Reduce" practices aim to intensify resource utilization by designing product-service systems (i.e., sharing or leasing models whereby the producer retains product ownership at the end of life [EOL]).

"Reduce" practices such as dematerialization approaches (product and packaging) can limit the need to procure raw materials, thereby decreasing dependencies from material suppliers. Prolonging product lifetimes reduces the rate of product exchange and thus reliance on material and component suppliers. Sharing or leasing models limit the number of products requited to satisfy overall customer needs, further decreasing dependencies on suppliers. Moreover, such models can diversify the customer base by attracting new, environmentally conscious segments or consumers that cannot afford one-tome purchases.

2.2.2 Reuse

The second priority in the 4R framework concerns "checking, cleaning, or repairing recovery operations, by which products [...] can be reused", whereby the products retain most of their resource value. This includes directly reusing a product "as-is" as second-hand for the originally intended purpose. In case a product does not fulfill its full functionality any longer, repair activities aim to restore a product to working order. Another "Reuse" practice is to upgrade or downgrade a product (i.e., refurbish), thereby exchanging components to alter its quality and bring it "up to the state-of-art". Finally, repurposing practices refer to using discarded products or components for a different use case. Direct reuse and repair operations can slow down production loops by keeping product lifetime high, thereby reducing the need for production materials. Upgrades or downgrades through refurbishment can increase a product's utilization time, reduce exchange rates and decrease reliance on material and component suppliers. Reparability and upgradability can increase customer dependence, as there is potential for additional monetization and consumer lock-in. Second-hand operations can address previously un-served segments and diversify the customer base. Lastly, repurposing practices target entirely new markets and decrease dependence on existing customers.

2.2.3 Recycle

Recycling is a key strategy in the transition to a circular economy that maximizes the value and utility of materials from products reaching their inevitable EOL. "Recycling" begins with resource streams after product usage and aims to keep components and materials in circular loops as long as possible. Thereby, the structure of the original product is lost. "Recycle" practices can be differentiated between recycling of materials and remanufacturing. The latter refers to completely disassembling a product and using some or all of its components to produce a new product with the same functionality. For material recycling, components of discarded products are further broken down, classified into distinct material categories and reused to produce new parts. Recycled materials have a broad application field and are also termed "secondary material". Particularly in the light of material shortages, secondary materials can be a promising lever to decrease dependence on virgin raw material providers. Likewise, it has been observed that integrating recycled materials can increase a company's bargaining power toward raw material suppliers. Also, some research scholars found that leveraging remanufactured components can decrease the reliance on component suppliers by reducing the required volume per supplier. Moreover, on the sale side, recycled materials and remanufacturing can attract additional customer segments.

2.2.4 Recover

The last "R" practice in the 4R framework refers to capturing energy embodied in waste, for instance, through incineration. This practice has the lowest priority among the circular economy approaches, though it is still considered preferential compares to processing waste into landfills. Some academic researchers showed that energy recovery could satisfy a considerable share of an industrial system's energy need, diversify energy supply and decrease dependence on utilities. They specifically argued for the "Recover"- practice's potential to reduce import dependence from international oil and gas providers.

2.3 FROM DESIGN FOR SUSTAINABILITY TO DESIGN FOR CIRCULARITY

Sustainability in the field of design is a popular research stream. Since the middle of the twentieth century, seminal design thinkers such as Buckminster Fuller and Viktor Papanek have raised awareness of sustainability aspects in the design professions. The scope of design has expanded entailing a "shift from insular to systemic design innovation". Design approaches have progressively expanded their focus from initially addressing sustainability in isolation (a single actor striving to, e.g., improve recyclability and product efficiency) to systemic approaches such as product-service systems for sustainability which involve a large degree of complexity and require a variety of actors. The expanding scope of design represents a larger shift in the role of designers, moving from object-centric thinking to a more system-based design approach, which challenges designers to perform strategic roles to an increasing extent. For example, activities such as establishing future visions and facilitating strategic dialogs between actors and co-design processes have been attributed to the enhanced roles of the design professions. Accordingly, the role of the designer has become progressively more entangled with the roles of other actors.

Within the context of the circular economy, it is apparent that various design for sustainability (DFS) approaches (e.g., cradle-to-cradle, bio-mimicry, eco-design) are instrumental for design practice. Some DFS approaches have been criticized for their failure to consider social dimensions, and the same critique has been made of the circular economy. On a conceptual level, the circular economy has been criticized for assuming a solely "technological fix" approach and neglecting relevant social factors such as challenging consumption behavior and sufficiently oriented lifestyles. Nevertheless, within design research, considerable efforts are being made to address the social implications and human-centered factors of a circular economy. An important distinction has to be made between sustainable development from the perspective of the current linear economy and of the circular economy. Sustainable development from a linear perspective may emphasize waste reduction, recycling and the reduction of pollution. The circular economy, conversely, does not strive to optimize what is already there but rather to rethink the system starting from the notion of a "closed loop" of resources that avoids the generation of waste. This assumption of an ideal state can be considered utopian, but in the context of design, it focuses attention on the following question: "how can designers generate truly sustainable or circular innovations if the current methods only lead them to optimize what is already there?"

The circular economy, thus, presents specific challenges for designers, such as for example, thinking in terms of multiple lifecycles, anticipating the reality of an alternative economy, adopting a deeper understanding of materials, the concurrent development of the product design and business model and assuming a systemic view on resources and their lifecycles. The shift to a circular economy challenges designers, especially with regard to the cultural barriers that hinder the adoption of circular practices to take on the roles of solution providers rather than object creators and to develop trans-disciplinary skills and understanding. Furthermore, there is the need for systems thinking in design practice and education in the context of design for a circular economy.

2.3.1 The Role of Supply Network Collaboration

Some research scholars have pointed to supply chain design and collaboration as key enablers in the transition to a circular economy. Likewise, various alternatives have been put forth to address the need to strengthen existing relationships among actors and develop new ones in the realm of EOL product recycling. These alternatives include circular supply chain, closed-loop supply chain, green supply chain, sustainable supply chain and reverse supply chain, all of which emphasize how collaboration improves the financial and environmental performance of supply chains. Furthermore, the "supply network" is regarded as a more accurate depiction of a system design than the supply chain. On the one hand, using the metaphor of a network is not that important when discussing how original equipment manufacturers could take back their own products for remanufacturing and remarketing in closed-loop supply chains that resemble chains. On the other hand, using the network metaphor is very relevant when discussing product and material recovery and waste minimization by actors other than the original equipment manufacturer in open-loop and circular supply chains. These supply networks involve a plethora of actors engaged in a complex web of relationships.

Moreover, supply chains are typically viewed as linear systems of sequential, dyadic exchange relationships containing information, material and monetary flows. Nevertheless, this view of supply chain relationships as linear and dyadic has been described as an "oversimplification" which, for instance, is evident in multi-tier supply chain management literature. Modern supply chains are complex network structures rather than dyads.

Ultimately, the literature on supply networks originates from two distinct lines of research: descriptive research within the field of industrial marketing and purchasing and prescriptive research from the fields of strategic management, operations management and logistics. Both these lines of research acknowledge the growing complexity of supply structures and the increasing interconnections among members of those structures. Similar to the transaction cost approach, the network perspective argues that stable long-term relationships between industrial actors emerge due to the complexity and heterogeneity of exchange. These relationships among actors develop through involvement in exchange and adaptation processes, and over time they both become increasingly important to the actors and increase interdependence between the actors.

Additionally, managing a supply chain involves coordinating flows within and between supply chain members who collaborate to maximize profits. Supply network collaboration is, however, not only important for economic performance but also for environmental performance. For instance, it has been concluded by some academic researchers that "the existing literature has given tremendous importance on the collaboration with supply chain partners to improve environmental and economic performance". When studying this important phenomenon, researchers commonly depict relationships as reflecting three types of collaboration. *Vertical collaboration* refers to a relationship between a buyer and a supplier. *Horizontal collaboration* refers to a relationship between two suppliers or between two buyers. *Lateral collaboration*, which includes both vertical and horizontal collaboration, refers to a relationship involving either two buyers and a supplier or a buyer and two suppliers. All three types of collaboration are important in a circular economy, where actors need to organize holistically, as compared to organizing in silos to achieve efficiency in a linear economy. This directs attention to supply network designs that enable supply network collaboration.

However, in recent years, as the circular economy model has emerged, supply network design has become crucial as a key aspect in the transition to a circular economy. The literature on supply chain management, however, has largely focused on material and product flows rather than the regenerative principles of a circular economy. The aim of closing the loop in a circular economy aligns particularly well with the concept of closed-loop supply chains, which has received considerable attention recently. The closed-loop supply chain concept generally concentrates on industry needs to configure supply chains to achieve product recovery and comply with regulations on extended producer responsibility. Research on the topic is largely concerned with how original equipment manufacturers can take back their own products for remanufacturing and remarketing. Within the context of climate change mitigation in general and the circular economy in particular, supply networks have additional role of not only recovering products but also recovering materials and minimizing waste. Complicating matters even further, in a circular economy, residual waste from one process or supply network should become a resource for another process or supply network. The open-loop supply chain concept fills this gap by emphasizing product and material recovery and waste minimization through the involvement of actors other than the original equipment manufacturer. Although the closed-and open-loop supply chain concepts individually allow detailed study of specific product recovery options in a circular economy, it is required to combine them in order to respond to demands for holistic organization in a circular economy. The circular supply chain concept addresses this need since it refers to narrowing, slowing and closing material and energy loops by working toward environmental, economic and social sustainability with actors within and across supply chains.

In other words, actors in a circular supply chain need to find other actors whose processes can feed into their own or which their own processes can feed into; this implies a need to strengthen existing collaborations and supply chain design and develop new ones.

Moreover, contrary to recovery options higher up in the waste hierarchy, recycling is typically not performed in closed-loop systems. With some rare exceptions, such as PET bottle recycling, recycling is handled through open and much more complex systems. While closed-loop supply chains have received a lot of attention in the past two decades, recycling systems are often simplified into reverse supply chains with characteristics very similar to those of forward supply chains but with a stochastic supply. The advent of circular economy research, however, has brought back attention to the EOL product domain as a complex issue involving a plethora of actors who collaborate outside typical supply chain boundaries. Indeed, there is scholarly evidence that pinpoint the need for collaboration to span several industrial sectors in the transition toward a circular economy including the food industry, the plastics industry, the furniture industry, the electronics industry, the construction industry, the textile industry, the steel industry and the municipal waste management. Typically, the motivation for supply network collaboration in the context of EOL products is to improve financial performance (to reduce logistics costs), environmental performance (to reduce resource use) or improve social performance (to increase the level of commitment between supply chain partners through shared visions). Some academic researchers have identified certain drivers for collaboration in supply networks, such as access to external knowledge, information sharing, government support and organizational support. Barriers to collaboration in supply networks include a corporate cultural mismatch between internal and external organizational cultures (e.g., old habits and ways of thinking), a lack of alignment among supply network members and power imbalances.

2.3.2 Organizational Change for Circularity in Supply Chains

In circular supply chains, it is advocated that waste should be removed by closing material flows in the supply chain. This needs a systemic approach for supply chain partners to incorporate their operations with other partners since actions of one partner can influence other partners. Since the concept of circular economy is relatively novel, the academic literature is still limited but growing fast. There is an expectation to clarify circular supply chain as highlighted in prior published studies. The issues that arise during the implementation of circular economy practices depend on the ambiguity in understanding circular economy. This ambiguity tends to introduce different interpretations that effectively provide challenges and opportunities to the implementation of circular economy. These challenges are magnified when the implementation of circular is focused on the lower levels, i.e., the supply chains. Supply chains are an increasingly significant domain in the circular economy literature that needs more research on implementing circular economy strategies, including the material closed loops and the new business models. Nevertheless, the debate is still unclear on the organizational changes that supply chains are likely to implement in order to ensure a smooth transition toward circular economy. Hence, a question remains to be tackled, which is "What are the required organizational changes toward circular economy in the supply chain?"

The organizational changes within supply chains have mostly concentrated on integrating sustainability goals, i.e., sustainable/green supply chain management with some of its concepts seemingly useful for circular economy advancement. These concepts are particularly transaction cost economics, agency, complexity and information. Moreover, there is research evidence that circular economy can be promoted through enacting changes in policies, laws, risk reduction measures and strict governance. The literature on circular economy has presented relevant catalogs of possible required changes in the supply chains. Available published literature have highlighted lack of technology, poor governmental policies and lack of practical knowledge and awareness as the main challenges to implementing circular economy.

Additionally, changes are also needed from individual companies in the supply chain. Nevertheless, the literature on circular economy seems to lack a holistic and systematic insight of the barriers that companies face during supply chain redesign. By then, the literature revealed the multidisciplinary character of the required changes to implementing circular economy like brand image, eco-efficient technologies and financial risks. Moreover, the requirements for transitioning to circular economy create a new organizational form in inter-firm collaborations and these forms stimulate the rise of new institutions enhancing sustainability. They suggest two pathways: the product-as-service arrangements (PAS-a) and status quo arrangements (SQ-a). PAS-a implies changes with a wider range, particularly with respect to ownership of partners in the supply chain (Schraven et al., 2019). This highlighted that next to responsibility, the significance of the required changes to circular economy should be better understood.

Currently, the circular economy literature has produced minimal data on responsibility. Firstly, some sources recognize the government agencies as impactful partners in the circular economy since they can assist in sharing large amounts of infrastructure and resources and can also apply oversight to the industry to control disruptive effects that may arise from implemented changes. Additionally, governance structure can assist to align supply chains to system changes. Secondly, responsibility may emanate from circular economy business models of partners which drive circular supply chains. On the one hand this might be because businesses consider competitive advantages amidst the changes that stem from external pressures. On the other hand, the needed changes for implementing circular economy in supply chains translate to radical implications for business models of partners and expose businesses to more challenges that might altogether impede change. The significance of changes may differ to supply chain partners, and this may be a result of a mix of classed off barriers, making changes complex to implement. Also, it might be because supply chain changes are situational and need to be clarified on a case-by-case basis. We then arrive at another important question which is "What are the possible clarifications for the responsibility and importance of circular economy changes?" In the economic context, the implementation of circular supply chains may be considered challenging and the bottom-up initiatives at the level of the supply chain might require to be incentivized through some form of top-down governmental support. This pinpoints the responsibility of government agencies to develop reasons for proper responsible change agents within the supply chain.

2.3.3 THE IMPORTANCE OF COLLABORATION IN THE TRANSITION TO CIRCULARITY IN SUPPLY CHAINS

There is a growing emphasis by companies on exploring better efficiency of resources and processes at different stages of production and consumption to encourage the circular economy principles in their supply chains. Circular supply chain sustainability can also assist in facilitating safe and high-quality products and minimizing waste which are directly related to business collaboration and integration of circular economy strategies. Hence, integration means that parties need to collaborate and communicate transparently to achieve their goals. Supply chain collaboration and integration with extended responsibilities/obligations to partners are critical for the successful implementation of circular economy. Generally, supply chain collaboration is classified as internal or external collaboration, which can be extended to become horizontal and vertical integration. Specifically, a collaboration between companies or companies and their stakeholders/partners is known as external collaboration, while the integration of a company's different functions is also known as internal collaboration. In a similar vein, vertical collaboration occurs between companies and their suppliers or their customers, while horizontal collaboration occurs between companies and their competitors.

Information and knowledge sharing with internal and external partners is highly critical for supply chains. Moreover, internal and external collaboration can be achieved with the aid of information systems, data sharing and process integration. Transparency cab be enhanced from system integration and collaboration and it is an effective tool for internal and external collaboration. Likewise, information visibility is essential for supply chain sustainability improvement and the management of production or process-related risks and ensuring sustainable collaboration. Traceability can provide tracking of all operations that begin from origin to the life span of the product, also, traceability is associated with information provision. Furthermore, information sharing is important for the coordination of a supply chain since such is required to exist between supply chain partners for the effective integration of the circular economy concept into supply chain management. Throughout the supply chain network, there is a need to define the aims and an equal information distribution to all partners is considered critical. Managers are required to communicate with external stakeholders to share the environmental performance of their organizations. Nevertheless, it is not considered a simple process to implement due to a lack of knowledge about the flow of materials, processes and products in the supply chain. Various supply chain members/partners, often suppliers, may decide to hold back information about their environmental performance and its probable effect on the customer and this is a term called information asymmetry.

Moreover, in the supply chain, traceability is associated with the product origin and its genetic situation, origin of inputs, product physical location, process visibility and accessibility of reference standards associated with the product. The efficient utilization of resources and production methods in a clear way that is according to standards coupled with transparency and traceability at every production stage is very significant for circular economy traceability. On the other hand, operations are not made visible, issues may arise that are associated with production safety, resource utilization and standards compliance, and there may be too much information that is hidden at every stage of the supply chain. Nevertheless, some firms may be unwilling to share real information about their product such as the origin, quality and safety issues. This might stem from the need to mislead customers about the environmental benefits of the product and environmental practices of a firm. The purpose is to increase the eco-friendly image of the company rather than dwell on any negative environmental impact.

2.3.4 Transition to Circular Economy and Green Employment

There is an intense debate about the potential of green growth to create or destroy employment. In fact, there are two ways to assess the direct impact on employment; one on changes in employment focusing on the green industries and the other involves counting the jobs created by companies that adopt green technologies and the effects on employment taking into account the specific circular and innovative strategies at the firm-level. Circular economy strategies can be classified as *eco-process* and *eco-product innovations*. Eco-process innovations could lead to the reduction of the use of energy, materials and water, replacing non-renewable resources by renewable energy, recycling of waste, water or materials, while the product redesign to extend its lifetime is related to product eco-innovation in order to introduce an environmental-friendly product in the market. Considering this classification, the effects of each environmental innovation strategy on employment differ. On the one hand, product eco-innovations have a positive effect through increased demand for new products of the firm, but it also can cause a negative effect through the substitution of non-green products. On the other hand, the adoption of eco-process technologies has a positive effect on employment if their introduction implies to hire new employees (but only if the innovation is not labor saving).

Another possible classification distinguishes between end-of-pipe and cleaner technologies. The former could have a positive effect because it may require additional employees with higher skills. The latter can have a positive effect through the hire of new and more specialized qualified employees, but also a negative effect because these technologies may lead to labor savings due to the employee substitution effect when incorporating more recent technologies (cleaner technologies). This negative effect on employment can occur when the firm redesigns the production process to try to increase labor productivity and human resources are substituted by capital.

Moreover, circular business models that purpose to slow or close resources loops are linked to the principle of Reduce in the 4R framework. Nevertheless, circular economy implementation at micro-level includes eco-design and design for the environment to improve the circularity within the company's production processes. Although Reduction (more efficient use of scarce resources), Reuse (ensuring repair and secondary use of products) and Recycle (recycling materials and waste) are considered as preliminary steps toward circular economy, these strategies have different degrees of novelty. Indeed, within this approach based on the 4R framework, we assume that the adoption of the diverse circular economy practices incorporates different levels of new knowledge, i.e., the newer knowledge required to adopt such a strategy, the higher number of green jobs the firm will have.

Regarding the circular economy principle of *Reduction*, firms aim to minimize the inputs of raw materials, energy and water, increasing the level of "eco-efficiency" in their production processes. The reduction of inputs enables to improve business performance through cost-saving (eco-efficiency) at micro-level while also contributing to increasing environmental and social benefits at macro-level (resource-efficiency). This objective is easier to implement by introducing incremental technologies or more-efficient appliances and machinery. The adoption of eco-process innovations has been shown related to embodies technology in machinery and equipment and incremental eco-innovations. Moreover, the effects on employment of more incremental technologies (end-of-pipe solutions or eco-process innovations) have been found negative or not significant in the previous empirical literature. For instance, some academic researchers pointed out that this objective "can be achieved by using fewer resources per unit of value produced and by replacing more harmful substances in favor of less harmful ones per unit of value produced". Environmental benefits are achieved by the reduction of resources used, but their complexity and formalization do not require pre-innovation conditions either by the hiring of technical specialists.

Likewise, the *Reuse* principle is related to "any operation by which products or components that are not waste are used again for the same purpose for which they were conceived". In the context of a circular economy, the reuse allows to close the material and energy cycle (close resource loops), maximize waste use and minimize the use of virgin materials. Based on life cycle assessment (LCA), reuse enables to increase the resource efficiency and decreases the environmental harms. The reuse implies to achieve the technical maximum reusability of materials and secondary use of products after their original use. These purposes probably involve the adoption of radical process innovations. It has been argued in extant literature that reuse and remanufacturing activities are labor intensive as in linear models of production. Since the adoption of radical process requires the concentration of technical specialists, firms seek to achieve new knowledge and greater technological leadership through the hiring of employees with greening skills and capabilities.

Additionally, *Recycling* is a basic principle of circular economy because it enables to reduce substantially the environmental impact compared to disposal of waste in landfills. The internal management of recycling by the firm is considered a cleaner technology, while if this process is organized and supported by third companies, is an end-of-pipe technology. In this regard, recycling is identified with the reuse action because it involves higher resource efficiency through the optimization of resources' use within the firm while facilitating or selling waste to third companies does not imply any radical change in the production processes. Moreover, the configuration of recycling as an organized commercial activity through Solid Waste Management Systems, mainly in the developed countries, makes easier the recycling by an increasing number of firms. In a similar vein, it has been found that the impact on green employment is concentrated in recycling processing countries but not in the solid waste collection sector and scrap materials companies.

Furthermore, to gather the maximum benefits of the circular approach, it is necessary to move beyond incremental changes. It involves identifying new ways of delivering value to users while designing out waste. The transition toward a circular economy requires the development of new products (eco-product innovations). Nevertheless, the design for disassembly, reuse, recycling or durable products implies the adoption of radical product innovations or upstream innovations. In this context, it can be argued that design strategies enable to slow resource loops through designing long-life products (higher attachment, trust, reliability and durability) and design for product-life extension (ease of maintenance, repair, upgradability, adaptability, standardization, compatibility and dis and reassembly) and to close loops through design taking into account technological and biological cycles. These strategies require specialized and qualified workers in green technologies to implement these changes. Thus, the empirical evidence shows that eco-product innovations generate a positive direct effect on employment. Indeed, some academic researchers show that there is a positive link between eco-innovation of products and services and the creation of new green jobs.

2.4 SUMMARY

Supply chains are the basic unit of activity enabling circular flows whereby circular supply chain management is the integration of circular thinking into the management of the supply chain and its surrounding industrial and natural ecosystems. The circular economy's future development remains uncertain and has received only limited attention in literature.

Practices to operationalize circular supply chains are commonly conceptualized in "R" frameworks. Different "R" frameworks have been used in academia and practice, such as 3R, 4R, 6R or even 9R. They all include a value retention hierarchy, where the "R"s' order reflects the priority in terms of circular economy conceptualizations discussed by scholars.

The 4R framework's hierarchy starts with "Reduce". "Reduce" practices such as dematerialization approaches (product and packaging) can limit the need to procure raw materials, thereby decreasing dependencies on material suppliers.

Within the context of the circular economy, it is apparent that various DFS approaches (e.g., cradle-to-cradle, bio-mimicry, eco-design) are instrumental for design practice.

Supply chain design and collaboration are regarded as key enablers in the transition to a circular economy.

The organizational changes within supply chains have mostly concentrated on integrating sustainability goals, i.e., sustainable/green supply chain management with some of its concepts seemingly useful for circular economy advancement. These concepts are particularly transaction cost economics, agency, complexity and information.

Supply chain collaboration and integration with extended responsibilities/obligations to partners are critical for the successful implementation of circular economy.

DISCUSSION AND REVIEW QUESTIONS

1. Can you identify some future-oriented projections of the circular supply chains conceptualized in the "R" framework?
2. List the key ways in which organizational changes can aid in the transition to circular economy.
3. Explain how collaboration can be a key enabler of implementing circular economy.
4. Circular economy can impact green employment
   a. What are the ways to assess the direct impact of circular economy on employment?
   b. How are circular economy strategies classified?
   c. Do they impact of the various classified strategies differ? How?

SUGGESTED MATERIALS FOR FURTHER READING

Schraven, D., Bukvic, U., Di Maio, F., & Hertogh, M. (2019). Circular transition: Changes and responsibilities in the Dutch stony material supply chain. Resources, Conservation and Recycling, *150*, 104359.

Part 2

3 Sustainability and Circular Supply Chains

3.1 INTRODUCTION

With increasing concerns over climate change, firms are constantly being pressured by a range of different stakeholders to consider sustainable development goals in their decision. With regards to their supply chain activities, many firms are now reporting their sustainability performances. Being triggered by demanding regulation and market pressure, companies are increasingly developing new inclusive approaches to manage sustainable performance with their partners, that is, suppliers and customers. The quest for sustainability has started to change the competitive landscape forcing organizations and supply chains to rethink their processes, technologies, products and business models. Supply chains are the main source of carbon in the environment that lead to global warming and climate change. Additionally, the rapid emergence of new technologies is significantly decreasing the product lifecycle, resulting to an increased waste. These notions have caused an increasing environmental preoccupation. Coupled with the consequent legislation and the potential economic benefits, these have changed the focus of supply chain management toward their environmental impacts on production and earth resources' preservation. As such, the domain of sustainable supply chain has acquired a huge significance from researchers as well as industry practitioners and managers. A sustainable and green production system involves balancing global and local efforts to satisfy customer requirements without disturbing nature. Hence, a sustainable supply chain needs management policies for profit maximization, resources consumption reduction and environmental pollution minimization.

On the other hand, the circular economy has many perspectives and, in some instances, has been presented as reliable means for assessing firms' sustainability performance. Academic scholars, in their studies on circular economy, opine that it is an essentially contested concept, as such, there is currently no known definitional consensus on circular economy. This might be attributable to the complex and diverse agendas that exist in its conceptualization, operationalization and development. Generally, the circular economy is utilized to provide an antipode to the perspective that the economy is a "materially open" or "linear" system – where natural resources are converted into production and consumption without considering waste along the product life cycle. The literature streams on circular economy have often concentrated on defining linear economy problems rather than managing the processes of circular economy. These processes are usually investigated under different principles depending on whether they occur at the regional or industry level (e.g., industrial symbiosis or metabolism), supply chain level (e.g., reverse logistics or closed loop supply chains), or at the organizational level (e.g., the material circularity index). Moreover, macro global levels of circular economy have also been proposed. The utilization of system-type descriptors comprising biological metaphors or more technical phrases like "circular", "closed loop" and "circularity" is regarded as the distinguishing circular economy aspect. Academic scholars that evaluate the state-of-art in the circular economy research are more particular on its general non-theoretical stance and investigate the rate of complementarity across potentially relevant theories.

This chapter discusses the organizational paradigm shift to a circular economy with insights into sustainable supply chain management coupled with the nexus between sustainable supply chain management and the circular economy. Furthermore, the organizational theories that exist at the nexus between sustainable supply chain management and circular economy are presented in this chapter.

3.2 SUSTAINABLE SUPPLY CHAIN MANAGEMENT

Past published studies calls for a radical rethinking to design and implement strategies not only at the company level but also at the extended supply chain level. This culminates in UN sustainability goals adopted by the UN in 2015, detailing the 2030 Agenda for Sustainable Development, a blueprint for global welfare for current and future generations. In fact, some UN sustainability development goals (SDGs) are linked to supply chain issues. For instance, UN SDGs encourage companies to sign up to and implement credible and robust ethical sourcing frameworks and also ensure sustainable consumption and production patterns through responsible consumption. In response, some leading companies like Hewlett-Packard, IBM and Walmart have begun to integrate sustainability into their supply chain business models for making it a reality. As early as 2005, the CEO of Walmart, Lee Scott made a commitment to sustainable development in their global supply chains, thereby motivating more than 200 suppliers to reduce the negative environmental impacts of their products. Even in sectors such as automotive, major OEMs such as Jaguar Land Rover have placed sustainability at the core of their business and supply chain strategies with their REIMAGINE initiative (REFS). According to Jaguar Land Rover, the REFS strategy entails two brands and distinct personalities both connected by elements of quality and sustainability that underpin Jaguar Land Rover's future of modern luxury by design.[1] This means that Jaguar Land Rover will lead on clean energy and continue to advance its role in the circular economy; together with their partners, they will design a new quality benchmark in environmental, societal and community impact for a luxury business.[2] Likewise, major consultancies have taken take an interest in highlighting sustainability plans. For instance, McKinsey provided insights on how the trading of credits can help companies and the world to meet ambitious goals for reducing greenhouse-gas emissions among other sustainability initiatives.[3]

Against this backdrop, sustainable supply chain management has become popular among research scholars. Prior published articles in extant literature indicate how organizations are faced with pressures to be more sustainable from stakeholders.

---

[1] https://www.jaguarlandrover.com/reimagine
[2] https://media.jaguarlandrover.com/news/2021/06/sustainability-drive-jaguar-land-rover-strategy-new-executive-appointment-and
[3] https://www.mckinsey.com/business-functions/sustainability/our-insights

These pressures encountered by organizations motivate the adoption of sustainable supply chain management practices. Sustainable supply chain management is defined as *strategic, transparent integration and achievement of an organization's social, environmental and economic goals in the systemic coordination of key inter-organizational business processes for improving the long-term economic performance of the individual company and its supply chains.*

There exists quite a number of conceptual differences between sustainable supply chain management and traditional supply chain management as evidenced in extant literature. In the context of system boundaries, the sustainable supply chain management has political, informational, legal, cultural and technological boundaries, while the traditional supply chain management has the organizational, proximal (spatial) and economic boundaries. With regards to relevant flows, the sustainable supply chain management adds water and energy flows, while the traditional supply chain management has material, service, financial, information and waste flows. In the context of relevant stakeholders, the sustainable supply chain management has stakeholders like governments and non-governmental organizations (NGOs), while traditional supply chain management has managers, customers and stockholders. With respect to impacts of decision, the sustainable supply chain management has the interrelated social and environmental impacts and trade-offs, while the traditional supply chain management has "pure economic" performance metrics. In the context of supply chain tiers, a wider range of issues exist, and hence, multiple supply chain tiers are explicitly considered in sustainable supply chain management, while in the traditional supply chain management, the supply chain staff at one firm or the buyer-supplier relationship is considered. With regards to the degree of cooperation, while cooperation is important in traditional supply chain management, there is a greater need for cooperation in sustainable supply chain management. Finally, the time scale of problems is about 1–5 years in traditional supply chain management, but then it is about 1–20+ years (generations) in sustainable supply chain management.

Nevertheless, academic scholars are of the opinion that the conceptual differences between supply chain management and sustainable supply chain management are not fully addressed. For instance, numerous studies fail to consider all the relevant stakeholders, responsibility for multiple tiers of the supply chain, longer product lifecycle time scales or rigorous treatment of trade-offs between the triple bottom line (TBL) dimensions of sustainable supply chain management situations. This suggests that academic research scholars in the domain of sustainable supply chain management are more concerned that the domain is more conceptually familiar with supply chain management than with the real-life practice of sustainable supply chain management. In addition, research on sustainable supply chain management is in dire need of theoretical developments that can adequately inform practice and utilize quite a few range of possible research paradigms to conduct such studies. In essence, there is a lack of focus on the new perspectives in theory and application of a narrow and traditional methodological focus for most studies, thus leading to confusion on the phenomenon of sustainable supply chain management. Consequently, significant aspects of the study of sustainable supply chain management may be systematically missed through a reductionist perspective instead of building a comprehensive accumulation of learning.

Indeed, organizations are unduly pressured to implement supply chain sustainability from the TBL perspective to increase competitive and collaborative advantage. The effective actualization of sustainability in companies hugely emanates to a large extent on their supply chain coming up with a set of sustainability prerequisites that relate to the TBL perspective. In fact, sustainability within a supply chain context from a TBL perspective refers to the management of materials, information and capital flow, as well as collaboration and cooperation among the supply chain partners while implementing all sustainable developmental goals imitative from the TBL of economic, social and environmental dimensions. Many researchers have addressed supply chains from the TBL perspective. The concept of TBL originally served as an accounting framework that included environmental and social dimensions within the conventional finance-centric business performance model. The TBL evaluates economic, environmental and social performance simultaneously. To achieve unique long-term sustainability performance, the three sustainability pillars – economic, environmental and social dimensions, should be incorporated. Notably, some of the measures of economic sustainability include cost minimization, flexibility, improved quality and increased operational efficiency. These economic sustainability measures can aid in improving existing processes, material flows reduce damaged goods and waiting time for the overall competitiveness of sustainable supply chains. Likewise, the notable measures of environmental sustainability include pollution control, green design and resource optimization. For instance, through implementing sustainable supply chains, there is bound to be improved product lifecycle management, which helps in waste reduction, better recycling and resource consumption and reduced greenhouse gas emissions. In a similar vein, notable measures of social sustainability include visibility and information disclosure, workers' health and safety, rights of stakeholders. Table 3.1 shows some of the TBL performance measures for sustainable supply chain management.

TABLE 3.1
TBL Performance Metrics of Sustainable Supply Chains

Economic Metrics	Environmental Metrics	Social Metrics
• Price/cost	• Environmental competence	• Work safety procedures
• Financial capacity	• Green product design	• Compliance with regulations
• Quality	• Regular environmental audits	• Information disclosure
• Production methods/ technological capability	• Presence of training facilities	• Social responsibility
• Flexibility	• Environmental management system	• Employee welfare
• Order procedures	• Efficient energy consumption	• External stakeholders
• Delivery time/reliability	• Efficient water consumption	• Community influence/projects
• Productivity	• Waste minimization	• Employee welfare package
• Economic value added		• Employee training
• Investment in sustainable processes		• Customer acceptance

3.3 SUSTAINABLE SUPPLY CHAIN MANAGEMENT AND THE CIRCULAR ECONOMY

In time past, the research domains of sustainable supply chain management and circular economy were regarded as separate fields without distinct interrelationships and correlations. This trend has changed in recent times with the popularity of scholarly articles that integrate circular economy principles into sustainable supply chain management. Thus, researchers are beginning to expect that a clear understanding of the synergies that exist between the concept of circular economy and supply chain management can aid in actualizing supply chain sustainability objectives. Sustainable supply chain management has developed for decades as a solution for multi-level social and environmental improvement, while a circular economy also has many perspectives and generally has been introduced for investigating sustainability at multiple levels. Likewise, research scholars opine that sustainable supply chain management can result in an incremental shift toward "weak sustainability" since it solely concentrates on resource efficiency. Contrarily, the circular economy emphasizes a radical shift to "strong sustainability" through reducing the rate (reuse, repair and remanufacture) and closing (recovery and recycling) resource loops with the purpose of preserving raw materials and product components at their maximum value and utility. This radical shift propagated by the circular economy is bound to face hurdles with regard to the management of inter-organizational and inter-industrial sector material and energy flows. Moreover, the sustainable supply chain management emphasis on cleaner production and resource efficiency in the supply chains is identified as "narrowing down the resources loop" in the circular economy literature due to minimizing the resource usage related with the product and the manufacturing process.

Additionally, the circular economy literature terms the cleaner production and resource efficiency as "weak sustainability" due to the implicit assumption that resources are abundantly available, hence, the weak sustainability focuses on minimizing resources utilization by streamlining the material flow in the system. On the other hand, strong sustainability calls for fundamental changes to the manner goods and services are manufactured and consumed to preserve the finite set of resources at mankind disposal. Hence, the circular economy tenets of "slowing and closing resources loops" cause a transition from weak sustainability to strong sustainability by prioritizing resources' reuse and recovery. Slowing resources loop is facilitated by product designs that allow repair and remanufacturing, hence, slowing down the resources' flow. Nevertheless, the ultimate purpose of actualizing a restorative and regenerative circular economy system is enhanced by resources' recycling that closes the material and energy loops. The overlap between sustainable supply chain management and circular economy takes place in the recycling activities toward the downstream supply chain operations. Closed loop supply chains have extended the traditional reverse logistics concept to comprise remanufacturing, reusing, repairing, refurbishing and recycling (5Rs) to restore product value within the same supply chain. The open loop supply chains extend the closed loop for the 5Rs to manufacturing systems outside the supply chain. A cooperative and collaborative effort to recycle and recover resources in the industrial ecosystem is also a central principle of the circular economy philosophy, and it is referred to as industrial symbiosis in the literature on circular economy. An effective industrial symbiosis entails the exchange of materials, water and energy streams between industrial partners to reduce the collective resource utilization and environmental impact.

Furthermore, depending on how resources are looped back for reuse, circularity archetypes can be categorized as closed loop circularity and open loop circularity. Closed-loop circularity involves returning products at the end of life to their origin/original supply chains for recovery of value. On the other hand, in an open loop circularity archetype, various companies across different supply chains work together to maximize resource circularity. For instance, HP works together with its supplier, Flex on reverse logistics and remanufacturing of discarded electronic equipment while both firms feed local supply chains the remaining of materials that cannot be returned back into HP products. Furthermore, circularity archetypes can also be classified by the nature of involved processes: a restorative cycle is necessary for technical materials (e.g., plastics and metal), while a regenerative cycle is essential for biological materials (e.g., food waste). Most companies use the restorative cycle during implementing the circularity concept. This is because most products in the market utilize technical materials, which require reuse, repair, refurbishment, remanufacturing and/or recycling to actualize resource circularity. In the case of regenerating biological materials, businesses usually concentrate basically on composting in the agri-food and packaging industries. Additionally, technology and logistics service providers play a critical role in analyzing resources regeneration.

Ultimately, the growing interest in having a clearer understanding of the overlap between sustainable supply chain management and circular economy could potentially aid in revealing positive synergies. The environmental dimension of sustainable supply chain management aims to reduce the negative consequences that arise from the environment during supply chain processes. Likewise, the circular economy paradigm extends the boundaries of the environmental dimension of sustainability by espousing a more holistic goal of a production system that is not just restorative by regenerative by design. The restorative and regenerative design involves the reduction of resource usage, waste, emission and energy through streamlining, slow-pedaling and closing of material and energy loops. The sustainable supply chain management has adopted some of the circular economy initiatives such as reverse logistics and the "Reduce, Recycle and Reuse", but then the basic difference between the both concepts lies in the mission/intent. The circular economy is an idealist philosophy that targets a "regenerative" manufacturing system that continually sustains the resources circulation and energy within a closed system, therefore, minimizing the need for new raw materials and inputs into the manufacturing system. Although it is practically impossible to obtain a perfect circularity, yet still, the circular economy principles show a more effective method in balancing the interrelationship of environmental protection and economic growth. In a similar vein, some sustainable supply chain management practices partially implement the circular economy restorative principle and in a more reactive manner. For instance, the "Reduce, Recycle and Reuse" goal is to recover the material with a focus on reducing the supply chain's environmental footprint, while the restorative principle of a circular economy manufacturing system also aims to repair past damage by encouraging the utilization of more environmentally friendly materials.

Nevertheless, in spite of some of the overlaps, circular economy is still considered different from sustainable supply chain management and a shift from linear to circular supply chains necessitates a radical transition from the existing business models and practices. For instance, a prior published study conceptualized sustainable supply chain management as an incremental and circular economy as a radical technological innovation that is aimed at achieving sustainability. The radical innovation conceptualization brings the emphasis on the people and the ability to commence the technical processes to enhance circularity adoption in supply chains. Furthermore, the overlaps between sustainable supply chain management and circular economy are mapped on a "sustainability paradigm-level of change" framework shown in Figure 3.1.

The sustainability paradigm signifies a spectrum between weak sustainability and strong sustainability. The weak sustainability indicates environmental management paradigms that emphasize the reduction of the environmental footprint, while the strong sustainability requires more structural changes in the manner society and firms create value. There is also a notion of sustainability orientation to relate the shift from weak sustainability to strong sustainability to the mindset and attitude of the organizational partners. Sustainability orientation is defined as the deeply rooted values, beliefs and behavioral cultures that form a company's sustainability operations and show that it influences a company's performance.

Moreover, the emerging concepts of closed loop supply chains and open loop supply chains bring sustainable supply chain management closer to circular economy, but then, it does not capture the philosophical goals of circular economy's

Context	Sustainable supply chain management	Circular economy
Sustainability paradigms	Weak sustainability	Strong sustainability
Levels of change- organizational and societal	Incremental	Radical
Principles	<ul><li>Cleaner production and resource efficiency</li><li>Closed loop supply chains</li><li>Open loop supply chains</li></ul>	<ul><li>Industrial symbiosis and shared consumption patterns</li><li>Circular business models</li><li>Open loop supply chains</li></ul>

Increased sustainability orientation →

FIGURE 3.1 The overlap between sustainable supply chain management and circular economy.

manufacturing system. So that it becomes both restorative and regenerative as a more proactive manner to balance economic development and ecological sustainability. A restorative circular economy system facilitates recuperation to the original state, while a regenerative circular economy system targets recuperation to a new and usually a higher state of value. Subsequently, closed loop supply chains and open loop supply chains target value recovery in supply chains, while circular economy manufacturing system aims at opportunities for more value creation from the recovered material. The open loop supply chains and industrial symbioses have created pathways for the utilization of supply chain wastes to be utilized by other industrial sectors to recover value. Nevertheless, the circular economy literature argues for a radical shift in the way organizations and societies manufacture and consume goods and services. The restructuring of current value creation architecture through business model innovation is recognized a means to find opportunities that would facilitate a regenerative circular economy system. For instance, an Australian firm implemented a close loop supply chain by coming with an innovative idea of using old printer cartridges, soft plastics waste and recycled glass to manufacture a road surface that lasted 65% longer than the traditional asphalt. Prior published studies in extant literature refers to circular business models (CBMs) as initiatives that identify value creation opportunities to slow, narrow and close resource loops.

The ongoing viability and large-scale use of CBMs such as the use of recycled materials for high-quality asphalt manufacturing are largely hinged upon the reconfiguration of printer plastic and glass products supply chains to provide their industrial wastes to the construction supply chain as input materials. This extends the traditional supply chain perspective to a broader "supply chain network" or "industrial ecosystems" where supply chains work together and reconfigure the supply chain systems to share low entropy wastes for potential utilization as an input to the manufacturing processes of other supply chains. This resulted in the popularity of the concept of circular supply chains in the extant literature which has been defined as the configuration and coordination of the supply chains to close, narrow, slow, intensify and dematerialize resource loops. As shown in Figure 3.1, the overlap between sustainable supply chain management and the circular economy is the circular supply chain domain which strengthens the ongoing viability and large-scale adoption of CBMs. We further develop this literature stream to opine that circular supply chains are influenced by establishing (a) collaboration within the supply chain network and reconfiguration of the supply chains for industrial symbioses and (b) a persuasive organizational narrative that encapsulates a stronger orientation toward sustainability.

3.4 ORGANIZATIONAL PARADIGM SHIFT FOR CIRCULAR ECONOMY

The near consensus in the emerging literature on circular economy and sustainable supply chain management indicates that a transition to circular supply chains is a strategic change initiative that requires a paradigm shift. An organizational paradigm shift necessitates an emphasis on people and the ability of an organization to affect the collective behavior of all organizational actors toward the new

Sustainability and Circular Supply Chains

organizational objective. The stream of the theory of sense-making can be utilized to conceptualize organizational narrative as a prevailing discourse that is due to the shared understanding of the management and employees that relates to the transition to circular supply chains. Hence, the absence of a persuasive organizational narrative that is grounded on normative principles adversely influences both the implementation of collaboration and supply chain configuration and the expected circular economy goal of environmental performance improvements. Some academic researchers in their study identified the recursive relationship between organizational change and a persuasive organizational narrative by deciphering the links between organizational social interactions. Likewise, the literature on sustainability orientation has currently established the nexus between sustainability awareness and environmental performance.

The literature on circular economy has also begun to observe the significance of social constructions to enable the transitions to circular supply chains. For instance, some academic researchers in their study identified the staff mindset and commitment as the most critical enabler for the adoption of circular economy practices in small and medium enterprises. In a similar vein, some research scholars identified that the organizational actors' cognitions sustainability awareness and a deeper insight on circular economy's economic benefits contribute to the transition to circular supply chains. These results signify a recursive relationship between the organizational narrative and the transition to circular supply chains. In essence, a compelling circular economy organizational narrative would influence the supply chain environmental performance directly, and it would influence the process facilitators (collaboration and supply chain configuration). Additionally, some academic researchers in their study inferred that current practices of circular economy would assist to understand its present level of implementing circular economy. Yet other research scholars in their study categorized corporate management's sustainability advocacy as an element of institutional pressure that influences the implementation of circular economy practices. In sum, a recursive relationship of circular economy organizational narrative with both the supply chain environmental performance and the process facilitators (collaboration and supply chain configuration).

3.4.1 Collaboration as a Facilitator of Circular Economy

Research scholars investigate collaboration among companies along the supply chain and particularly employ the governance view to discuss the role of collaboration in actualizing supply chain sustainability. Other scholars analyze the governance mechanisms which describe initiatives, processes and practices to manage relationships with internal functions and external partners that focal companies can employ to manage their supply chain sustainability. Consequently, the collaboration factor remains critical since it is one avenue for firms to form strategic alliances, share information and/or reduce costs to improve performance and thus realize increased competitiveness. For instance, a prior published study presented supply chain collaboration as comprising cooperation, mutual understanding and joint efforts affects the market and sustainability performance of an organization. The collaboration construct within the domain of sustainable supply chain management mainly involves the relationships between the upstream and downstream actors, supplier selection and environmental collaboration with customers.

Nevertheless, the open loop supply chains and circular economy's industrial symbioses collaborative emphasis entails a broader supply chain network perspective where supply chains from many industries share their low entropy wastes and by-products to be utilized as an input material. Industrial symbiosis is a central area of circular economy literature that depends on cooperative organizational behaviors to enable the emergence of an industrial ecosystem that simultaneously reduces the resource utilization of virgin input materials and the output of waste products and emissions. For example, a past published study presented the notion of "industrial chains" to emphasize the significance of collaboration between many supply chains in a larger supply chain network that usually covers over many industries. This suggests that a transition to circular supply chains is facilitated when the traditional upstream and downstream collaborative interactions are widened to involve organizations beyond the immediate industrial boundaries of a supply chain. Indeed, for many industries, the transition toward a circular economy is rather challenging because firms need to collaborate with actors within and beyond immediate industry boundaries. Businesses are more likely to establish vertical collaboration than horizontal collaboration during implementing circular economy initiatives.

Vertical collaboration is hinged on developing circular resource flows in buyer-supplier relationships within focal companies' supply chains and mostly beyond supply chain dyads. Focal firms usually cooperate with both downstream and upstream companies to optimize circular resource flows. On the other hand, horizontal collaboration primarily operates in the form of secondary marketplaces. Purchasing firms gain more procurement/buying channels and cost savings in place of underutilized resources. Likewise, the circular economy literature identifies challenges beyond vertical approaches and emphasizes the need for horizontal collaboration and further actors within and outside the industry. Within this context, horizontal collaboration is regarded as more essential than vertical collaboration to facilitate functional circular supply chain management through the closing (recycling, recovery) of resource loops. The key strategic pre-conditions for the energizing horizontal collaboration for circular supply chains include developing a circular economy enabling environment, innovating a CBM and forming of strategic alliances with specialized partners within and outside the industry. Through horizontal collaboration, firms can effectively and systematically integrate the circularity concept into supply chain management, thereby orchestrating circular economy-oriented supply chains for utmost sustainability goals. The sustainable supply chain management literature concentrates on managing vertical collaboration with upstream suppliers or downstream customers.

There is research evidence that collaborative approaches and shared governance approaches in a vertical dimension indicate functional instruments to successfully manage sustainability issues. However, while vertical collaboration is widely studied in extant literature on sustainable supply chain management, there is still a dearth of studies on horizontal collaboration with external forces like the NGOs, competitors, etc. This is in spite of the emergence of the topic of supply chain governance on third-party collaboration in sustainable supply chain management literature. In fact, various published studies on the synergy between circular economy and supply chain sustainability still emphasize on vertical and third-party relations, which do not entirely provide insights on the circularity principles. Although research that emphasizes the governance perspective on sustainable supply chain management has shown that governance mechanisms for vertical collaboration can aid in actualizing sustainability in supply chains, the circular economy concept requires close collaborative relationships with multiple partners within and outside the industry and sector. This tends to emanate into new challenges to supply chain management in aspiring to vertically connect with suppliers and customers while also making efforts to horizontally connect with competitors and other actors like NGOs, government bodies, universities, etc.

Therefore, new governance mechanisms are pre-requisites for a circular economy to enable formal and informal rules that are changing to form the basis of inter-organizational collaboration schemes, which tends to demand the analysis of incentive structures. This is because the main problem that firms that engage in circular economy practices, face, is to arrange collaborative and business relationships under the constraint of an institutional system that is aligned with the linear economy principles. It is argued that circular economy principles should be of high importance for various supply chain stakeholders (local authorities, entrepreneurs, construction industries, financial institutions) in order to reduce the negative impacts on environment, while simultaneously using natural resources more sustainably. Indeed, circular supply chain management is closely related to sustainable supply chain management initiatives that concentrate on the minimization or the delay of unintended negative impacts on the environment due to cradle-to-grave material flow. This recent pattern of life cycle thinking indicates that waste could be utilized as an alternative resource offering new business opportunities while simultaneously encouraging environmental protection.

Basically, there are opportunities in multiple stages of a supply chain to collect and share the wastes and by-products in the wider supply chain network. For instance, the paper supply chain has a number of transformation processes such as wood logging, pulping, paper production and paper cutting. The paper supply chain is a part of a wider forest industry supply chain network with dyadic supplier-buyer relationships between pulp mills and fuel supply chain's heating plants for bark chips. This signifies that the purpose to identify and establish industrial symbioses needs to be distributed across the supply chain stages. Consequently, this was termed a significant operational aspect of industrial symbiosis in supply chains and suggested the implementation of local waste and by-product collection and delivery systems. Some academic researchers in their study identified the centralized responsibility for pursuing industrial symbioses the main challenge to circular supply chains and recommended that all supply chain tiers must work together to take responsibility for analyzing and implementing opportunities to share resources in the broader supply chain network.

The few studies on the challenges and drivers of implementing circular supply chains classify improved technologies and information sharing across the value chain as a manifestation of successful industrial symbioses. The identification of industrial symbioses opportunities requires new process discoveries and input-output mapping of multiple stages of a supply chain within the industrial ecosystem. This data intensive operation is enhanced by augmented information sharing and coordination within the broader supply chain network. For instance, some research scholars in their study identified information exchange within global configurations as the main enabler of supply chain collaboration. The final step to establishing industrial symbioses partnerships is also heavily dependent on technological development. The use of low entropy wastes and by-products in place of virgin resources usually requires new and innovative transformation processes that entail substantial research and development efforts. The adoption of emerging technologies like the Internet of Things and big data analytics also assists in monitoring, tracking and automating the reverse flow of products. Collaborative relationships within the value chain to develop the knowledge base and expertise on both the identification and adoption of the opportunities for industrial symbioses is the main facilitator for the shift to circular supply chains. Ultimately, the collaboration within the supply chain network positively affects supply chain environmental performance.

3.4.2 Supply Chain Configuration as Facilitator of Circular Economy

The collaboration within the supply chain network is geared at identifying opportunities for industrial symbioses, but in most cases, the existing supply chain configurations need to be redesigned to implement industrial wastes and by-products sharing. Hence, as expected, the emerging literature on circular supply chains has concentrated in reverse flow management in supply chains. The introduction of reverse logistics enables closed loop supply chains to use recycling, repairing, refurbishing, remanufacturing and reusing for resource conservation with the same supply chain. Nevertheless, the open loop supply chain entails cross sector waste management and the use of by-products which necessitates systemic variation in the supply chain network to enable sustained resources recovery and delivery. Some research scholars investigated supply chain redesign for circular economy and inferred that there is uncertainty about the quantity, mix, timing and location of resources pick-ups and deliveries restricted the ability of reverse flows to reach an economic scale. Some academic researchers recommended that the supply chains with similar supply and distribution structures are more likely to reduce the returns flow uncertainty, hence, facilitating circular supply chains. In a prior published study, the academic authors utilized the notion of "supply chain complexity for circular economy" to characterize the geospatial compatibilities within the supply chain. Their study recommended stakeholders' joint decision-making to position the recycling facilities for compatible supply and distribution channels within the supply chain.

A significant aspect of supply chain design enabling a shift to circular supply chains is the inherent flexibility of the existing supply chain structures to introduce and broaden the reverse product flow to the extended supply chain network. The global supply chains of large organizations with dispersed geographic locations find the reverse logistics as particularly difficult but then, the open loop supply chains open up the possibility of sharing the low entropy wastes and by-products within the industrial ecosystem that may be physically close. Nevertheless, this is largely reliant on the ability of an organization to shatter the "linear lock-in" according to

Sustainability and Circular Supply Chains

an academic research scholar who's study posited that circular supply chains are more likely to be developed from new start-ups that are still establishing their supply chains. For established global supply chains, emerging methods such as redistributed manufacturing provide pathways to break the "linear lock-in" by product manufacturing at multiple scales and locations, hence, minimizing the spatial complexities for the reverse product flow. Additionally, some academic researchers in their study analyzed the impact of redistributed manufacturing on the supply chain structures of many industries and observed blurring of industrial boundaries beyond the boundaries of traditional supply chains. Consequently, supply chain configuration is considered a process facilitator by designing/redesigning and restructuring supply chains to physically connect with partners in the industrial ecosystems for resource sharing, which then reduces the supply chain environmental footprint. Therefore, supply chain configuration positively influences supply chain environmental performance.

3.5 ORGANIZATIONAL THEORIES IN THE NEXUS BETWEEN SUSTAINABLE SUPPLY CHAIN MANAGEMENT AND THE CIRCULAR ECONOMY

Despite the recent trends toward theorizing, available published studies in extant literature on the nexus between sustainable supply chain management and the circular economy still remain non-theoretical. Indeed, most studies in the area focus on prescriptive, descriptive and technological solutions rather than present insights on theory development and advancement. The most applied organizational theories at the interface between sustainable supply chain management and circular economy studies include institutional theory, resource-based view (RBV) and stakeholder theory. The natural RBV is an extension of the traditional RBV that concentrates on more sustainability-oriented resources. It describes how a firm's competitive advantage changes over time with regard to the impact of environmental concerns in organizational relationships. The institutional theory provides a description of the roles that institutions (social norms and rules) play in strategic organizational decision-making. Stakeholder theory provides a description on how and why managers respond to pressures from stakeholders like government agencies, industry, consumers and NGOs.

3.5.1 Existing Theories

We present a detailed explanation on each of the above-mentioned organizational theories applied to the nexus between sustainable supply chain management and circular economy.

3.5.1.1 Institutional Theory

The institutional theory is applied in organizational studies to consider how societal pressures influence organizational processes. The main premise of the institutional theory is that "organizations and the individuals who exist in organizations are suspended in a web of values, norms, beliefs, rules and assumptions that partially originate from them". Generally, institution includes societal factors and cultural elements with important economic consequences. The institutional theory emphasizes the long-term social processes of transferring cultural elements between individuals and social collectives. The sources of institutional forces are complex and nuanced and of three types as follows: (1) coercive forces – arise from the power of centralized government, large corporations and foundations; (2) mimetic forces – arise from the need to copy or mime, others' strategies due to the uncertainty of competition and (3) normative forces – as result of social expectations through the process of professionalization to create a pool of almost interchangeable individuals. Subsequently, the institutional theory is applied to consider how isomorphic forces contribute to the adoption of sustainable supply chain management operations. A further research direction could entail providing insight on the influence of internal forces, ways government agencies might identify and target core firms to promote the sustainable supply chain management adoption and the reason for the much heterogeneity in sustainable supply chain management practices. The research on sustainable supply chain management has seen critical linkages with institutional theory, while the circular economy is only beginning to be linked with an institutional theory perspective. In part, the major reason for this lack of institutional theory perspective in circular economy research is due to the levels of analysis and the non-theoretical nature of the research. It is expected that the linkage with institutional theory in circular economy research continues to become popular as broader societal issues like equity and inclusiveness begin to make headway. The nexus between sustainable supply chain management and circular economy provides the important potential to diffuse institutional theory across these domains, where investigations on sustainable supply chain management using institutional theory explanatory theory can be transferred to sustainable supply chain management supported circular economy activities, business models and strategies.

3.5.1.2 Stakeholder Theory

In stakeholder theory, managers are viewed as operating firms in an endogenous dynamic social system whose feedback are sought in their firm's environment to manage the consequences of the externalities that result from the firm's operations. The two main components of stakeholder theory are salience and identification. The identification entails a normative typology that describes the reason for firms' managers paying attention to a certain type of individual or group. Generally, the stakeholder may either possess legitimacy or not. Legitimacy can be made by any stakeholder that is negatively impacted by externalities. Nevertheless, legitimacy typically de-emphasizes the rules for decision-making employed by managers to decide how and when a latent stakeholder's legitimate claims should receive attention, even though it determines who should receive the utmost attention. On the other hand, salience defines the essence of legitimate claims. As such, stakeholders with legitimate claims become actual stakeholders, not the potential ones, when they gain either urgency or power. Urgency occurs when the stakeholder's claim on the utmost attention of the manager is regarded as critical or sensitive. Moreover, salience is related to the pressure concept, which is a core aspect of institutional theory and often related with stakeholder theory. In a similar vein, when stakeholders do not possess power, then their legitimate and urgent claim has a salience attribute. Thus,

Sustainability and Circular Supply Chains   51

by integrating power and urgency to the normative assessment, stakeholder theory provides a clear explanation on the reasons for which managers focus attention on stakeholders' requirements. Accordingly, within the context of the utilization of theory in sustainable supply chain management and circular economy, stakeholder theory is typically utilized to consider the extent of active procedures for stakeholder inclusion in decisions, especially the relevant stakeholders and how such stakeholders' requirements are attended to as against internal firms' requirements. A further research direction could contribute to the stakeholder theory by providing insights on how national boundaries and various kinds of pressures and stakeholders are linked with sustainability strategies across supply chain and circular economy members. Currently, the appropriation of stakeholder theory is still in a nascent stage in the circular economy research, while in research domain on sustainable supply chain management, it can be said to be fully realized/appropriated. Nevertheless, the stakeholder theory can further aid the investigation of the nexus between sustainable supply chain management and the circular economy. For instance, although the circular economy does not always involve integrating environmental and social sustainability dimensions, stakeholders may decide to broaden the horizon beyond technological and policy concerns to integrate "strong sustainability" advancements.

3.5.1.3 Natural Resource-Based View

The natural RBV is an extension of the traditional RBV, which states that firms' competitive advantage is mostly derived from the policies they utilize to manage internal resources and capabilities. However, RBV considers societal welfare while natural RBV considers competitive advantage that emanates from explicitly considering the resources in the natural environment and the relevant stakeholders in the firm environment. According to the natural RBV, stakeholder and institutional perspectives are considered as linked to the external aspect of the strategies. Within the context of the nexus between sustainable supply chain management and circular economy, natural RBV posits the ideal organizational strategies as follows:

First, product stewardship considers environmental performance across the entire product life cycle, from the design stage to the disposal stage. This strategy entails important variations to the manner in which supply chains are configured with the long-term objective of "closing-the-loop in the operations". Second, clean technology describes varying a firm's relationship to the physical environment through variations in technology rather than "incremental improvements to today's products and processes". Third, base of pyramid provides a description of altering a firm's relationship to social inequality, particularly in low-income countries, by identifying procedures to supply the unmet demands of the poor and involves the development of novel capabilities. Extant studies of natural RBV in sustainable supply chain management and circular economy research have proved some of the hypotheses about the capabilities that strengthen success under different strategies. There is also research evidence that success in pollution prevention is related to the management of material flows and that process improvement and project management capabilities increase the impact of pollution prevention strategies on financial performance. Additionally, there is research evidence shows that managers invested in pollution control but underinvested in cost-effective pollution prevention. Furthermore, in the context of the reviews on the application of theory in sustainable supply chain management, natural RBV is typically utilized to consider how inter-organizational and intra-organizational resources (identified using RBV) influence the adoption of sustainable supply chain management by suppliers. In the future, research direction can be geared toward providing insights on how inter-organizational learning takes place and by identifying procedures for the quantitative analysis of the resources and capabilities.

3.5.2 Potential Theories

Likewise, we present potential theoretical perspectives to expand the nexus between sustainable supply chain management and the circular economy. With the increasing popularity on the scholarly and practical interests in sustainable supply chain management and the circular economy, there is a need to broaden the current conceptual understanding and theoretical boundaries. This will include promising theories in social science that can be essential in providing theoretical perspectives on the nexus between sustainable supply chain management and the circular economy. Consequently, these under-utilized theories can be applied to show the significance of information feedback across multiple levels of analysis and what such a framework entails for wider issues. The theories are summarized as social innovation, organizational learning and social learning using the systems thinking perspective with an emphasis on organizational, social and environmental strategic planning. These theories provide a description of the individual and organizational networks that tends to improve the society through social and environmental institutions.

3.5.2.1 Social Innovation Theory

The social innovation is a practical and significant phenomenon in modern society. It comprises innovators that adopt organizational innovations with the goal of resolving pressing social and environmental issues, and thus, innovation plays a critical role in the development of a modern society. Despite its significance, social innovation is still an essentially contested concept with specific and direct theoretical constraints still elusive. It signifies novel theoretical and practical phenomena with foundations across the social science discipline. In essence, socially innovative actions within the social innovation context should be framed as part of the process of changing the dominance of existing institutions where social innovation actors are regarded as the main protagonists but not necessarily exclusive drivers. A significant application of social innovation theoretical lenses would entail incorporating with the organizational learning theory in the sustainable supply chain management and circular economy research stream. For instance, research can analyze how social innovation actors develop and adopt innovations coupled with other significant organizational issues like leadership, interactions between individuals' motivations and organizational and network structure, which have been so far neglected. Hence, social innovation is viewed as a potentially emancipatory theoretical lens since it assists in considering the actions of the wider scope of sustainable supply chain management and circular economy actors within the above noted social innovation context. Consequently, this will enable exploring situations in which sustainable supply

Sustainability and Circular Supply Chains

chain management and circular economy interact with existing or new social norms, beliefs and views, which can be related to the next broad-based potential interpretative theory of social learning.

3.5.2.2 Organizational Learning Theory

The organizational learning theory comprises interactions that exist between individuals and collectives. This position constitutes challenging conceptual and methodological issues for its wider application. Individual learning takes place only when the learner changes their decisions or goals due to the response to information stimulus and feedback from the environment, which pinpoint to the learner about an original decision that needs adjustment. Two types of information-feedback cycles exist in the organizational learning theory, which consists of action cycles and learning cycles; in action cycles, automatic decisions are used and actions are adjusted based on goals and perceived outcomes of decisions, while in learning cycles, goals or decisions are altered in the face of perceived problems. The learning cycle has three feedback loops, namely: (1) a *double-loop learning* loop which signifies adjustments in goals and decisions, (2) a *cultivating alternatives* loop in which an individual entertains several competing diagnoses of a problem in their mind, which are then tested in a group process of acting and interpreting until sense is made of the problem by the individual with a correct and timely solution and (3) and *interpretation* loop in which the openness to new information by an individual is shaped by the plausibility of their current diagnosis which in turn affects their ability to perceive errors in that diagnosis. Currently, organizational learning theory is fully realized in research on sustainable supply chain management and circular economy. A further research direction could improve organizational learning by standardizing the constructs across theories in a single conceptual model. This would enable researchers in the sustainable supply chain management and circular economy domain to utilize this theory in an easy manner. Additionally, how social and environmental pressures like regulatory pressures and stakeholder feedback affect organizational and individual decision-making within organizational units and operational systems can be studied.

3.5.2.3 Social Learning Theory

The social learning theory can also be considered an essentially contested concept with possibilities to broaden the understanding and perspective of the nexus between sustainable supply chain management and the circular economy. It proposes cultural change processes especially changes in norms, due to changing conditions that occur in the natural environment. These processes proposed by the social learning theory are often guided by an open-ended, consensus-driven process that is informed by long-term thinking and the requirement that macro-societal systems can be designed so that it can be capable of adjusting to changing conditions more quickly. The social learning theory is hinged on the processes of social cooperation and proposes mechanisms that cultures would utilize to learn from failures or from potentially disruptive events like health pandemics. Consequently, social learning theory presents affordances that address problems in narrow views of evidence-based policy. These perspectives result in command-and-control policy making rather than learning policy systems. Social learning theory proposes the redesign of relationships across institutions and of policy cycles as part of a more holistic perspective of evidence for evidence-based policy. The social learning theory views learning processes as involving simultaneous cycles of action and learning, just like the organizational learning theory and similar challenges to those encountered in group-based organizational learning processes. Furthermore, social learning theory views society as having a structure that consists of feedback loops with its behavior being driven in large part by unintended consequences of past actions – systems thinking perspective. In sum, the social learning theory has the most potential as an interpretive theoretical view for considering the inter-organizational processes that result in significant policy changes over time in the nexus between sustainable supply chain management and the circular economy. Due to the rise in the adoption of digital infrastructure by businesses, novel opportunities are presented for redesigning material flow and information feedback systems across supply chains. Thus, social learning can potentially assist managers to have insight on the resulting distributed and institutional processes.

3.6 SUMMARY

Manufacturing companies around the globe face rising costs in treating, preventing and controlling environmental issues. For instance, manufacturing companies in the United States spend tens of billions of dollars annually to solve environmental problems. The Carbon Disclosure Project reports that managers in these companies are laden with the burden to perceive more physical risk from climate change and higher pollution abatement costs, but less opportunity for reputation building with customers with respect to environmental issues. In the supply chain downstream, companies are encouraged to improve sustainability performance albeit not under backlash for failure to do so.

Sustainable supply chain management has developed for decades as a solution for multi-level social and environmental improvement, while a circular economy also has many perspectives and generally has been introduced for investigating sustainability at multiple levels.

At the nexus between sustainable supply chain management and the circular economy, many opportunities exist for research to broaden the conceptual boundaries. For instance, in sustainable supply chain management, by considering more tiers, stakeholders, impacts and time scales and thereby further showing the nature and complexity of today's business environment and in circular economy, considering institutional and social issues.

DISCUSSION AND REVIEW QUESTIONS

1. What is sustainable supply chain management?
2. What are the conceptual differences between sustainable supply chain management and supply chain management?
3. Mention the overlaps between circular economy and sustainable supply chain management.

4. Collaboration and supply chain configuration are the process facilitators of circular economy. Why?
5. List some existing theories at the nexus between circular economy and sustainable supply chain management.
6. Are there potential theories that can be employed to study the overlaps between sustainable supply chain management and circular economy? Outline the potential theories.

SUGGESTED MATERIALS FOR FURTHER READING

Adams, R., Kewell, B., & Parry, G. (2018). "Blockchain for good? Digital ledger technology and sustainable development goals", in Leal Filho, W., Marans, R., & Callewaert, J. (Eds.), World Sustainability Series, *Handbook of Sustainability and Social Science Research* (pp. 127–140). Springer. https://doi.org/10.1007/978-3-319-67122-2_7.

Gonzalez-Ricoy, I., & Gosseries, A. (2016). *Institutions for future generations.* Oxford: Oxford University Press.

Brazil, H. P., & Sinctronics (2017). Creating a reverse logistics ecosystem, *Ellen MacArthur Case Studies,* https://www.ellenmacarthufoundation.org/case-studies/creating-a-reverse-logistics-ecosystem.

Penrose, E. T. (2009). *The theory of growth of the firm.* Oxford University Press, United Kingdom.

UN (2016). #Envision2030: 17 goals to transform the world for persons with disabilities, Accessed Aug 01, 2021, #Envision2030: 17 goals to transform the world for persons with disabilities | United Nations Enable.

UN (2019). The sustainable development goals report, United Nations Publication issued by Department of Economics Soc. Aff.

4 Reverse Supply Chain Management

4.1 INTRODUCTION

This chapter gives an overview of reverse supply chain management. Important aspects of reverse supply chain management comprising of reverse supply chains, remanufacturing and metrics for reverse supply chain performance. Additionally, the role of supply chain leadership coupled with the role of governance mechanisms in the reverse supply chain are discussed.

4.2 DEFINITION OF REVERSE SUPPLY CHAIN MANAGEMENT

In the last decades, green and sustainable supply chain management practices have been developed, trying to minimize negative consequences of production and consumption processes on the environment. In parallel to this, the circular economy discourse has been propagated in the industrial ecology literature and practice. Circular economy is defined as an economic paradigm where resources are utilized as long as possible, with maximum value extracted from them while in use; the paradigm has its conceptual root in industrial ecology, emphasizing the benefits of recycling waste materials and by-products. The principles of circular economy thereby extend the boundary of green supply chain management by devising methodologies to continuously sustain resources circulation within a quasi-closed system. It pushes the frontiers of environmental sustainability by focusing on the idea of transforming products in such a way that there are workable relationships between ecological systems and economic growth. Consequently, it reduces the need for virgin resource materials for economic activity and this economic paradigm is opposed to the current linear take-make-dispose resource model that generates enormous waste. At the micro-level, the implementation of circular economy practices would push for the design of circular or reverse supply chains, enabling products at the end of their life cycle to reenter the supply chain as a production input through recycling, reuse or remanufacturing.

Hence, reverse supply chain management is defined as a series of activities that are required in order to retrieve a used product from a customer and either dispose of it or reuse it. The topic of reverse supply chain management has gained considerable attention in industry and academia due to mounting regulatory pressure, growing environmental concerns and increasing benefits (i.e., material conservation, reduced energy consumption and waste and lower prices). Generally, companies that have been most successful with their reverse supply chains are those that are able to closely coordinate their reverse with their forward supply chains, creating a closed-loop system, therefore maximizing value creation over the entire product life cycle. Nevertheless, it is also observed that reverse supply chains can also be open-loop where raw materials are recovered by parties other than the original manufacturers and utilized in the production of different products. The idealistic paradigm of the circular economy might also result in a series of challenges. For instance, it is argued that in the European context, which is mainly dominated by free-market and neo-liberal ideologies, companies are already capturing most of the economically attractive opportunities to recycle, reuse and remanufacture. This leads them to claim that reaching higher levels of circularity may entail an economic cost that Europe cannot cope with, especially as companies are already struggling with high resource prices. Thus, policy interventions are also needed alongside innovative business models that are currently adopted by companies.

Indeed, rapid technological development, shorter product life cycles, and globalization have increased supply chain resources, leading to depletion of the already limited resource and waste generation. Moreover, the waste quantity has kept increasing at an alarming rate, which has yet to be properly managed. These are happenings for products with significant residual values, such as e-waste, end of life (EOL) vehicle, etc. The average rate of recycling e-waste in the European Union is about 38% and in China, there has been a reported significant gap between the value of collected e-wastes and the subsidy funding provided by the government. The dependency on the subsidy and underperforming waste management signifies how the current reverse supply chain system is infeasible in the long term. Developing reverse supply chain system that can be economically and environmentally sustainable has become the stakeholders' interests. By doing so, integrating product reuse, reconditioning and recycling in the reverse supply chain has become necessary to allow companies to minimize resource consumption, waste and cost. Additionally, the growth of environmentally aware/conscious customers and the interest in remanufactured products have offered business opportunities for reverse supply chains, while adhering to strict environmental protection laws. These environmental protection laws include the EU directives on waste electrical and electronic equipment (WEEE) (Directive 2021/19/EU), Council Directives 75/442/EEC Article 1 on waste. Therefore, the reverse supply chain system is compelled to be: (1) able to efficiently perform various complex operations and (2) responsive and adaptive in coping with demand uncertainties.

4.3 THE REVERSE SUPPLY CHAIN

There are two major trends in the research on reverse flow of supply chain development which include waste management and reverse supply chain. Reverse supply chain is defined to focus more on value creation, while waste management concerns the treatment and removal of waste. It is also defined as the series of activities required to retrieve a product from a customer in order to dispose of it or recover its remaining value. Furthermore, reverse supply chains involve moving products from customers back to sellers or manufacturers and disassembling them in an ecological manner. It consists of a series of activities required to collect used products from consumers and reprocess them to either recover their leftover market values or dispose them. Strict environmental regulations and diminishing raw material resources have intensified the importance of reverse supply chains for industry. In addition to being environment friendly, effective management of reverse supply chain operations leads to higher profitability by reducing transportation, inventory and warehousing costs. Moreover, reverse supply chain operations have a strong impact on the operations of forward supply chain such as the occupancy of the storage spaces and transportation capacity.

The reverse supply chain idea fully reflects the vision of environmental protection and the efficient utilization and reuse of resources. It is a process by which a manufacturer systematically accepts previously shipped products or parts from the point of consumption for possible reuse, remanufacturing, recycling or disposal. The reverse supply chain processes have been defined as follows: reuse is the process of directly reusing the product with cosmetic repairs apart from cleaning and checking; recycling is the process of recovering raw materials where the shape of the material changes; cannibalization is the process of reusing good parts and components that are recovered from used products; repair or reconditioning is accomplished by restoring out of specification products to working conditions but not to as good as new condition; remanufacturing and refurbishing is the process of transforming or restoring the condition of the used parts to its original condition as good as new. Consequently, the reverse supply chain can be organized into five sequential key steps, namely product acquisition or collection of returned product, reverse logistics, inspection and disposition, reconditioning or remanufacturing and selling and distribution. In this context, reverse logistics comprises of the product returns from customers, through collectors and recyclers to suppliers or manufacturers. This practice has huge economical valuations in all industries and assists supply chain players to minimize the environmental impacts – mitigating energy use and minimizing the amount of greenhouse gas emissions to the air – and to enhance resource use, attaining global sustainability. Hence, a large number of companies are utilizing reverse logistics to collect and recycle used products. In fact, four major classifications of return items have been defined: recycling of wasted products, reusable products, repair services and remanufacturing.

The benefit of reverse supply chains is that by reusing, remanufacturing and recycling used products and components, it is possible to reduce landfill waste drastically. Indeed, the use of reverse supply chains is one of the approaches to minimizing the environmental impact of e-waste in order to increase the amount of product materials recovered from the waste stream. Nevertheless, the concerns in achieving circular economy have intensified efforts to improve resource use efficiency through the use of a variety of waste management techniques which includes recycling and reuse. Particularly, the annual amount of waste within the EU territory is around 4 million tons which included WEEE. The WEEE is regarded as the most hazardous but equally profitable waste since it contains valuable materials and/or parts. High amount of waste electrical and electronics is mainly as a result of the linear economic pattern adopting "take-make-dispose" paradigm whereby the waste is disposed and disregarded for being further processes. To solve this problem, the circular economy presents another approach that is considered useful. As depicted in Figure 4.1, consequent upon the reverse part of its cycle, the waste can be taken back and further processed as the alternative supply source of production process in the circular economy.

The purpose of the reverse supply chain is to recapture or create value, as well as to perform proper disposal through various product recovery approaches that fit these circular economy objectives. Product recovery is a process that aims at reusing the collected, used products from the user with the purpose of minimizing the amount of waste that is sent to landfills. One type of product recovery is remanufacturing, which offers a situation in which old products can be utilized as new, by means of carrying out some necessary operations such as disassembly, refurbishing

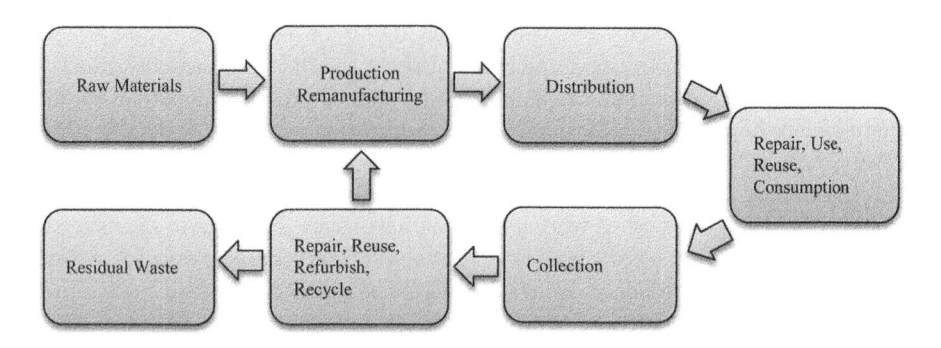

FIGURE 4.1 The reverse supply chain cycle in the circular economy.

and replacement activities. In this context, the product recovery management model has provided as a system to recover economic value of the used products as reasonably as possible to reduce the quantity of waste to the barest minimum. The inclusion of waste prevention and reuse is the favorable alternative to recycling, as reuse can extend product's lifetime, especially for short life-cycle products. Additionally, the purpose of waste management starts to shift from developing environmentally safe disposal to creating economically attractive options of economic value extraction. This is evident in how some recent studies on waste management have begun to emphasize on optimizing the waste management operations subjected to fulfilling demand or maximizing revenue. These studies consider value creation for the user over the efficient waste treatment found in other existing studies on waste management. The increasing alignment in interests and practices of both reverse supply chain and waste management to becoming the means for sustainable value creation has urged the development of an integrated reverse supply chain system. This kind of system can necessarily accommodate various reverse flow operations of the supply chain while being feasible and self-sustaining in the long term.

Furthermore, in reverse supply chains, returned/used products are transported to inspection and disposition locations, where disposition actions are determined including remanufacturing, reuse and recycling. The new and never used products are restocked to the forward distribution channels, while other products are sold for remanufacturing and recycling. Then, the remanufactured products are sold in secondary markets for additional revenue. In certain cases, companies are mandated to recycle used products due to hazardous materials (e.g., in the case of refrigerators in the United States). In this context, reverse supply chains need to be not only well managed but also tightly integrated. Figure 4.2 shows a three-stage, capacitated reverse supply chain which consists of contracted collectors, capacitated manufacturers and demand points geographically dispersed in secondary markets. The contracted collectors supply returned/used products to the manufacturer and the manufacturer remanufactures good-as-new products, and delivers to demand points. Each demand point specifies order quantity and delivery deadline and the manufacturer is imposed penalties if it cannot deliver finished products to demand points on or before requested deadlines.

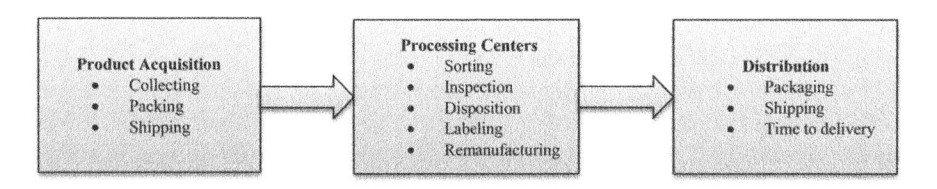

FIGURE 4.2 Reverse supply chains with remanufacturing.

4.3.1 REMANUFACTURING

The traditional business practices of landfilling products after their useful life are not considered sustainable anymore due to two reasons. Firstly, such practices increase the depletion of natural resources and thereby increase the cost of extracting more raw materials to fulfill consumers' demand. Secondly, such practices destroy the natural ecosystem through soil, water and air contamination. Hence, worldwide business legislations are beginning to force firms to identify ways of minimizing resource consumption and waste generation. For example, the extended producer responsibility (EPR) can extend the responsibilities of manufacturers to the post-consumer stage of the lifecycle of the products. Likewise, the EPR mandated recycling, minimum recycled content standards, energy efficiency standards, disposal bans and restrictions. Advance recycling fee (ARF), advance disposal fee (ADF), virgin material taxes/subsidies and deposit/refund schemes are some of the relevant laws which push manufacturers toward industrial sustainability and reducing solid waste generation. There is an existing solution to both of the above-mentioned problems in the form of recovery-and-reuse policy that reduce both natural resource consumption and solid waste generation. The recovery-and-reuse policy is based on 6Rs that reduce, reuse, recycle, redesign, remanufacture and refurbish. Remanufacturing involves the recovery of used products so as to convert such products into useful products and is regarded as a profitable approach of minimizing natural resource depletion and waste generation.

The intention of remanufacturing is to revive residual business value from used products through either component replacement or reprocessing and gives them a new life. Traditionally, remanufacturing is considered an economical option when compared to manufacturing products because it makes possible to get a product to meet the market demands for a lower price value than a brand-new product. Nevertheless, in recent times, it is gaining more importance and relevance due to its environmental benefits when compared with the economic ones. Presently, remanufacturing is considered a highly sustainable practice due to its higher absolute environmental impact in most industrial sectors that depend on non-renewable resources. Due to its economic advantages, remanufacturing provides a new approach for sustaining an edge in a hyper-competitive market environment. Hence, based on a commercial viewpoint, 100% may seem more desirable due to low remanufacturing costs. Nevertheless, in the broader outlook, with considerations for other operational costs like management, recovery and logistics, the results may vary significantly. Hence, the concept of hybrid manufacturing-remanufacturing systems was developed through which partial demand is satisfied with remanufacturing while the remainder is fulfilled from traditional manufacturing process.

Furthermore, remanufacturing is enabled by the collection and reprocessing of used products that result in additional reverse logistics and management activities in the supply chain. Because transport packaging is one of the largest contributors to manufacturing waste, increasing transportation can raise the generation of solid wastes from supply chain management. Hence, this simultaneously impacts on the overall sustainability and economics of remanufacturing. In this context, many industries have contemplated utilizing reusable transport packaging rather than disposable packaging. RTIs, also known as returnable transport items, are reusable secondary transport packages like crates, pallets, rail-cars and containers critical to the sustainability of logistics operations. Prior published studies in extant literature highlight that the reuse of transportation packaging minimizes both energy consumption and solid waste generation from transportation and cuts down CO_2 discharge by up to 16%. However, the utilization of returnable transport items requires adequate coordination with supply chain activities to achieve the expected benefits to the full extent. This might be attributable to the mismanagement of RTIs being able to create additional complexities for high volume and high-value packaging materials and increase the costs of management and transportation of the system. The severity of these issues is further exacerbated in closed-loop supply chain due to the complex recovery system. Therefore, it is important to regulate the management of RTIs for a smooth circulation of materials in the multi-echelon supply chain environment.

However, all these economic and environmental benefits that accrue from remanufacturing, closing the loop and reuse have some financial implications. They all increase the complexity and uncertainty of the activities that can arise from reverse logistics operations. These operations can generate undesired in-process costs in the remanufacturing system if not well managed. Moreover, the randomness of the rate of return and the remanufacturing cost makes it problematic for manufacturing companies to smooth manage the process. Generally, stochastic failure and rate of repair increase the complexity, costs and production time for manufacturing process. As such, this adds to the inherent complexity of closed-loop supply chains with the additional costs imposed by recovery operations. In sum, remanufacturing is the most desirable option for EOL product management than a scrap or spares recovery since it minimizes the environmental impacts, results in lower loss of value and can create new market opportunities. Remanufactured products are often offered as an alternative option to the original products to the customers that are attracted by the brands but do not desire to pay the price of a new/original product. For instance, there are a number of industries such as automobiles and electronics in which the price of remanufactured/reconditioned product is lower than original products in order to capture the demand. Indeed, remanufacturing is usually considered as a recovery process in which a returned (recovered) item is converted through several operations like disassembly, cleaning, testing, part replacement/repair, and reassembly to a "like new" one which is equivalent to the original manufactured product. Examples of such remanufactured products include mostly high-value industrial products such as aircraft or automobile engines, aviation equipment, railroad locomotives equipment, medical equipment, machine tools, copiers, electrical and electronic equipment, toner cartridges, cellular telephones, single-use cameras, etc. On the other hand, recycling is the process of recovery of reusable materials, components and products for reuse in the forward production channel from the raw material stage to the final product stage.

Product remanufacturing has been going on for quite some time and, an average profit margin of 20% was reported for the remanufacturing firms which directly employ 350,000 workers in the United States. Product recovery management encompasses the management of all used and discarded products, components and materials that fall under the responsibility of a remanufacturing company. The goal of all product recovery management is to recover as much of the economic and ecological value as reasonably possible, thereby minimizing the ultimate quantities of waste. Since remanufacturing requires different competencies than manufacturing, it becomes unclear whether to implement remanufacturing activities or to implement manufacturing activities for new products. Remanufacturing focuses on value-added recovery rather than just material recovery, i.e., recycling. In remanufacturing, used products can range in condition from slightly used products with only minor cosmetic blemishes to significantly damaged and needing extensive rework. The critical operating decision for remanufacturing is to establish a proper sorting policy given variable conditions of returns just to have an understanding of which product is to be reused or which one is to be repaired and which one is to be recycled ultimately. It has been a practice for quite some time on the part of manufacturers to pay lowest acquisition prices for the collection of old used products of worst quality class from customers and highest price for best quality class. Clearly, remanufacturing cost is assumed to increase as product condition worsens.

Nevertheless, it would not be practical for any manager to fix price for each product being collected according to its condition. In order to overcome this challenge, organizations generally assign a fixed number of quality grades of the returns and assign acquisition prices according to the quality grades for the entire range of collected products. Each price is assigned to a group of products having similar nature of defects and where remanufacturing/repairing cost in a reverse supply chain center would lie within a narrow band. For instance, for a three-stage closed-loop supply chain, grade one may signify products with virtually no parts replacement but needs a touch-up or tweaking or testing to bring it to shape. The highest price could be paid for such a range of products for collection from the customers since the remanufacturing cost will be least. In a similar vein, grade two signifies products with major repair with parts replacement without complete product dismantling. The second highest price could be paid for such range of products. The worst grade of quality means products with worst condition where some parts after dismantling may be scrapped but manufacturers would be more interested in salvaging costly raw material by recycling the same internally or externally to convert them into ingots like aluminum alloys and zinc. The raw materials ingots could be then utilized again for manufacturing the components in the first stage in forward supply chain. Lowest acquisition prices could be paid for such products since the recycling cost would be the highest among all the costs of reverse supply chain entities.

4.3.2 CLOSED-LOOP SUPPLY CHAIN

Due to resource shortage and environmental degradation, manufacturing companies are facing the challenge of coordinated production and environmental development. These manufacturing enterprises are required to make the integrated optimization for the forward logistics of new products and reverse logistics of waste products. Several companies in many countries have begun to recognize the strategic value of incorporating environmental principles into business policies and have developed innovative product recovery programs to recover and reuse their EOL products. Forward supply chain ensures an efficient and effective of new products/parts and delivery of the same to the customers. Similarly, a reverse supply chain comprises of activities involving acquisition, collection, delivery, reprocessing of the used parts/products to recover leftover market value or dispose it. The integration of forward and reverse supply chains is termed as closed-loop supply chain. It is also defined as the design, control and operation of a system to maximize value and dynamic value recovery throughout the life of the returns of different types and quantities. The closed-loop supply chain focuses on the integration of material flows, information flows and financial flows throughout both forward and reverse chains. This kind of supply chain helps companies in recognizing potential benefits and overcoming the challenges associated with their strategies and operations. The closed-loop supply chain, especially the reverse logistics system with the third-party reverse logistics provider, is very significant for materials recycling, resource saving and environmental protection activities.

The concept of closed-loop supply chain refers to the integration of forward and reverse supply chains. It is a supply chain that integrates the reverse flow and sells the remanufactured products in the same market as new ones. In recent times, the management of these supply chains has garnered a lot of attention in both the academic and industrial sectors since it is one of the main drivers of sustainability and circular economy. The management of closed-loop supply chain refers to the design, control and operation of a system for value maximization over the product lifecycle with dynamic value recovery from different types and volumes of returns over time. The market for multiple lifecycle products continues to grow, the current estimates signify that remanufactured product sales exceed $100 billion per year in the United States and it is also a large volume in other countries. Remanufacturing companies, such as HP, Dell, Apple, Xerox, Caterpillar, Kodak, Gazelle and ReCellular hire more than 500,000 people in more than 70,000 companies saving approximately 14 million tons per year in material. In all, closed-loop supply chain management is one of the most relevant problems for the operations management community and a proper design of the reverse channel is important for environmental and financial benefits improvements.

Moreover, the disassembly process is a part of the reverse flow in closed-loop supply chain and is a critical step in facilitating circular economy. The disassembly process consists of a set of activities aimed at extracting the subassemblies, raw materials and/or other forms from EOL products. The implementation of the disassembly process can assist in facilitating supply chain sustainability, since it also practically offers employment opportunities and decrease the amount of WEEE. It helps in creating a market of EOL products while augmenting the image of the company involved.

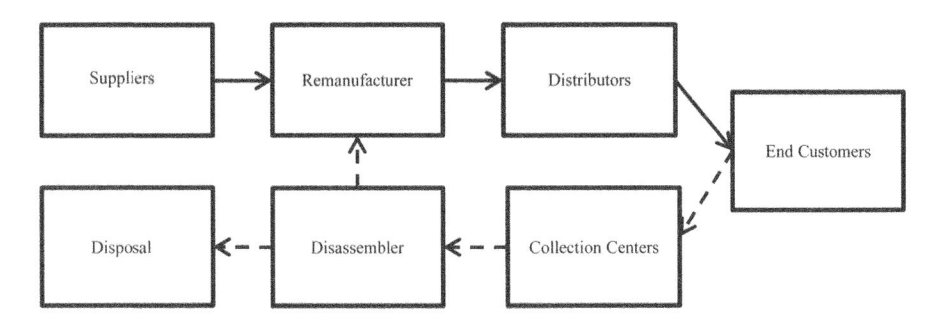

FIGURE 4.3 Closed-loop supply chain.

In compliance, the forward supply chain that is the popular form utilized in linear economy must be redesigned into closed-loop supply chain by integrating the reverse flow corresponding to WEEE. Nevertheless, the disassembly process is regarded as an expensive process because of its complexity as labor intensive and time-consuming process. Additionally, collecting EOL products can be considered as an indispensable operation that precedes the disassembly process. The collection process is considered as a transportation activity that has the potential to increase the supply chain's total cost. When compared to the assembly process that has been widely studied in extant literature, the supply side of disassembly process is less structured and more unstable. As such, it requires to be managed in order to avoid inefficiency that leads to high cost. Considering this process as a part of closed-loop supply chain presented in Figure 4.3, dealing with the supply side of EOL products as a collection process may be required. Indeed, the circular economy requires a closed-loop supply chain by integrating the disassembly and its corresponding operations to form the reverse flow. When compared with the forward flow, its differences comprise of geographical location, financial and inventory aspects. It deals with many dispersed collection centers as supply sources to collect EOL products and transport them to producer or recovery facilities such as disassembly facility or disposal area. Its lack of proven and effective inventory management coupled with unclear financial implication results in inconsistency.

As part of sustainable supply chain, the closed-loop supply chain is designed to manage the recycling and recovery process of EOL products. It generally involves a manufacturer taking care of the reverse logistics process in which the goods are returned directly by the original manufacturer or through indirect channels. All the returned goods are resold in primary or secondary market after necessary disposition. Essentially, a closed-loop supply chain extends the normal forward supply chain by including reverse supply chain channels for remanufacturing, product return, resale and recycling/recovery. Initially, growing attention on closed-loop supply chain issues originated with public awareness. Then, government legislation forced producers to manage their EOL products. The importance of the environmental performance of products and processes for sustainable manufacturing and service operations is increasingly being recognized. As part of closed-loop supply chains, reverse supply chains concentrate on taking back products from customers and recovering added value by reusing the entire product, and/or some of its modules, components and parts. In recent times, product and material recovery has received attention throughout the world, with its three main motivators including economic value to be recovered, governmental legislations and environmental concerns. Collection centers are one of the most significant actors in the product recovery systems and they play a critical role in sustainable development. They deal with activities such as acquisition of EOL products from end users, reverse logistics, product disposition and dispatching of the products to the remanufacturing/repair facilities or disposal sites.

Furthermore, closed-loop supply chains include three main types of returns: commercial returns, end-of-use returns and EOL returns. Commercial returns refer to the returns made with customers' consent in several days after the purchase. This type of returns is handled by small-scale processes such as repairs. End-of-use returns are made when products are replaced with better alternatives due to dissatisfaction of consumers even while existing products are still working properly. This type of returns requires more treatment such as remanufacturing to be able to rejoin the forward flow. EOL returns take place when products are no longer functional. This kind of returns can typically be handled by a single recovery option, recycling, after which they can be utilized as raw materials. Despite these well-defined categories, returns are non-homogenous in practice, and there is uncertainty in their timing, quantity and quality. These issues arise due to several reasons including the limited information of resources and collectors about the products' selling date and life cycle and the compatibility of the waste recycling system with the daily habits of customers. From the business perspective, the presence of uncertainty makes it more challenging to plan the recovery and remanufacturing activities and this may have an impact on profitability. For instance, in the case of an e-waste recovery system, profitability is affected by uncertainty in product, collection and market such as variations in returned products' age and return mix. Hence, it is critical for decision-makers to account for uncertainty in product/material recovery systems.

4.3.3 Measuring Reverse Supply Chain Performance

Due to stakeholders' pressures, firms' focus on economic performance needs to be accompanied by care for social and environmental performance. Similarly, alternative economic models are shaping the development of new forms of supply chains; this is the case of the circular economy paradigm, which is embracing the notion of restorative industrial systems. Consequently, reverse supply chains can be considered as one of the significant approaches to implementing circular economy practices at the inter-organizational level. Generally, reverse supply chain designs a set of operations to recover EOL and after-use products and intermediate by-products by the original equipment manufacturers (OEMs), suppliers or any third parties. These operations can be related to an open-loop process, where the materials or products are retrieved and reused by parties other than the original manufacturers, or a closed-loop process. In the closed-loop process, retrieved products are returned back to the original manufacturers for refurbishment, recycling and reuse. The transformation of traditional linear supply chains into reverse supply chains aims at ensuring that waste can be minimized while reducing the excessive utilization of virgin materials for environmental protection.

TABLE 4.1
Some Reverse Supply Chain Performance Metrics

Performance Measures	Items to Be Measured
Flexibility	i. Ability to manufacture products with high reusable and recyclable materials
	ii. Ability to integrate traditional practices with reverse supply chain practices (i.e., dismantling parts and recycle)
	iii. Ability to provide new infrastructure for new products research and development
Quality	i. Ability to remanufacture and refurbish returned products
	ii. Availability of recyclable/reusable materials in products
	iii. Availability of material recovery plan and warranty returns
Cost	i. Cost of remanufacturing, replenishment and reproduction of returned products
	ii. Cost of processing recyclable products
	iii. Cost of storing returned products
	iv. Cost of retrieving returned products
Time	i. Lead-time of product recycling and reuse
	ii. Lead-time for unsold products to be remanufactured/refurbished
	iii. Lead-time for warranty returned products to be refurbished/remanufactured

Several performance measures have been created in order to keep track of reverse supply chain performance and these can be categorized as cost, time, quality and flexibility. Table 4.1 shows some of the initial measures for measuring reverse supply chain performance. Likewise, in order to ensure that environmental performance is maximized across supply chains, the adherence of suppliers to sustainability standards must be monitored as well. Nevertheless, the reverse supply chain implementation has a number of risk management implications. For instance, the availability of stable and predictable product streams to be recovered, where the environmental benefits lie in reducing the risk of the non-availability of related resources. Additionally, the relationships among various stakeholders at multiple tiers of reverse supply chains are often less stable and more problematic to establish than in forward supply chains, since product returns are based on their life cycle and on the marginal value-of-time. As such, close coordination and alliances are required to fully realize the reverse supply chains potential. From this perspective, purchasing/buying firms can play a significant role as facilitators of these activities through mechanisms for governance and leadership approaches.

4.4 ROLE OF SUPPLY CHAIN LEADERSHIP IN REVERSE SUPPLY CHAINS

For a long period of time, leadership has represented a prolific research stream in the fields of management and organizational behavior. In recent times, the leadership research stream has been extended to the inter-organizational setting and notably, the concept of supply chain leadership has been emerging. The development of this research stream can be observed from the initial discussions on channel leadership (based on manufacturer-retailer relationships), supply chain governance (comprising elements of both contractual and relational governance) and institutional forces that are based on the concept of isomorphism. In particular, supply chain leadership is defined as a relational concept that involves the supply chain leader and one or more supply chain follower organizations that interrelate in a dynamic, co-influencing process. The supply chain leader is characterized as the organization that demonstrates higher levels of the four elements of leadership in relation to other member organizations. Such member organizations include the organization capable of greater influence, readily identifiable by its behaviors, developer of the vision and that established a relationship with other supply chain organizations). In a similar vein, supply chain leadership can be defined as the ability of the buying firm to influence a supplier to achieve a common goal within the supplier's organization. In addition, the leadership style of a buying firm has the potential for improving a firm's capital which comprises suppliers' commitment and supply chain relationships. Notably, supply chain leadership has deduced an antecedent of supply chain performance improvement by focusing on the buying firms' ability for articulating vision for the future, communicating the vision and motivating supply chain members. It has been identified that supply chain leadership is the antecedent of supply chain performance improvement including relationship commitment, supply chain efficiency, organizational learning and supply chain agility. Additionally, strong leadership and commitment are necessary in order for improving the competitiveness of buying firms that are also influenced by the extent of suppliers' dependency on them. In order for a particular buying firm to take care of the specific needs of different suppliers and efficiently facilitate the sustainability operations of the whole supply chain network, such suppliers should depend on a multi-faceted and adaptive style of leadership. A visible leadership indicated by the buying firm can help multiple stakeholders in implementing plans on environmental sustainability. In essence, a buying firm is responsible in enforcing sustainability initiatives and exhibiting the required leadership behaviors (such as control, audit, motivation and reward) in order to ensure that the suppliers adhere to its sustainability plan. Till date, there is an observation of a similar dynamics in relation to the implementation of sustainability initiatives by third-party logistics providers, pinpointing the expectation for the focal firm leadership and coordination. Generally, within the context of supply chain management, a distinction is usually made between *transformational* and *transactional* styles of leadership.

4.4.1 Transformational Leadership

Transformational leadership is characterized by four main dimensions, namely inspirational motivation, individualized consideration, idealized influence and intellectual stimulation, as shown in Table 4.2. A leader usually is acting as a role model when adopting a transformational style, thereby motivating followers toward better performance and generating awareness about missions and visions of the group. Based on this concept, transformation leadership within the supply chain context refers to the potential ability of a buying firm to motivate and stimulate its supply chain members' actions and behaviors. By exhibiting transformational leadership,

TABLE 4.2
Dimensions of Transformational Supply Chain Leadership

Dimensions	Description
Individualized consideration	Buying firms also emphasize on followers' individual needs, particularly for achievement and growth. Followers' individual requirements can be achieved in several ways including the leader acting as a coach or mentor. Individualized consideration is significant in promoting new learning opportunities for the suppliers
Idealized influence	A buying firm acts and behaves in ways that its followers will view them as a role model. A buying firm is needed to lead by example, which results in being admired and respected
Inspirational motivation	Buying firms should be able to motivate and inspire their supply chain members by providing meaning and suggestion. By demonstrating inspirational concepts in the leader's style of management, a buying firm will be able to generate enthusiasm, team spirit and optimism among their suppliers
Intellectual stimulation	Buying firms should be able to stimulate followers' intellectual capacity to be more innovative and creative. There are a few ways of stimulating supply chain members' (such as upstream suppliers) intellectual capacity including questioning assumptions, reframing and redefining problems or issues, and providing new ways of approaching old practices

supply chain leaders can facilitate information sharing and communication, which is considered critical for supply chain collaboration. Moreover, it has been highlighted that a buying firm practicing transformational leadership can encourage organizational learning. It is also claimed there is a positive relationship between transformational leadership approaches exhibited by the buying firm and their operational performance. Transformational leadership of the buying firm can expand organizational innovativeness and result in a higher financial performance of the organization. Additionally, transformational leadership by the buying firm can enable itself to manage organizational change, articulate vision and develop suppliers' commitment.

In the fast-food retail industry, closed-loop practices could only be implemented in the presence of a collaborative relationship between buying firms and their logistics service providers. The planning and implementation phases of recycling should involve both parties in order to ensure that waste collection and transfer activities are more organized and at the same time, improve the sense of responsibility of logistics service providers. Moreover, the successful implementation of closed-loop supply chain strategies is dependent on the ability of the buying firm to coordinate upstream and downstream supply chain members comprising of suppliers, retailers and distributors. Due to the dynamic nature of the supply chain environment, a buying firm should be able to engage with supply chain members in all tiers and orientations (downstream or upstream) to make sure that the requirements of reverse supply chain initiatives are well addressed. A buying firm is expected to establish shared goals with supply chain members, in such a way that the reverse supply chain strategies implementation will be of benefit to all of them. A buying firm should inspire supply chain members to work together to ensure the new orientation toward a reverse supply chain can be implemented. The ability to coach and mentor the suppliers toward reverse supply chain initiatives foster suppliers' willingness to work together with the buying firms' reverse supply chains strategies. In addition, acting as the mentor, role model or mentor, buying firms will allow suppliers to learn about reverse supply chains initiatives which are currently being implemented. Hence, this will directly influence suppliers' ability to learn, replicate and imitate buying firms' reverse supply chain strategies, which will result in such suppliers improving their own reverse supply chain activities. In sum, the central idea of transformational leadership is the ability of buying firms to inspire suppliers, so that they will simultaneously transcend their normal performance and develop suppliers' self-interest to excel and commit to buying firms' plan.

4.4.2 Transactional Leadership

Transactional leadership is characterized by two dimensions, namely *management-by-exception* and *contingent reward*. *Management-by-exception* entails that a buying firm tends to monitor deviances in members' assignment and take corrective action if necessary through management-by-exception practices. On the other hand, through using the *contingent reward*, a buying firm will assign suppliers and agree on goals and objectives with potential rewards or actual rewards in exchange for attaining the assigned levels. *Contingent reward* has been observed as a reasonably effective construct in motivating followers to achieve higher levels of performance and development that can contribute to organizational growth and competencies. Transactional leaders clarify followers' roles and expectations, then providing rewards for those who meet the requirements. Based on this idea, transactional leadership in the context of supply chain management is conceptualized as the behavior of buying firms in clarifying suppliers' requirements and roles: monitoring, rewarding and auditing suppliers. It has been deduced that buying firms that are committed toward contract compliance (such as quality monitoring and defect inspection) are practicing transactional leadership. Moreover, by exhibiting a transactional leadership style, a buying firm can initiate rewarding behaviors that trigger information sharing between two parties. While through a transformational leadership, a buying firm inspires the supplier to do more than contracted, transactional leaders strive to ensure that suppliers do exactly as expected.

The suppliers' adoption of reverse supply chain practices can also be maximized by using transactional supply chain leadership. A buying firm will be able to monitor and keep track of suppliers' performance by comparing it to a certain set of pre-determined rules and requirements using a transactional approach. Similarly, rewards can be offered to supply chain members in order to promote compliance; buying firm is also able to utilize punishment schemes. In addition, the immediate feedback on improvement and potential corrective actions can be shared with the suppliers through enforcing close tracking of reverse supply chain initiatives. Suppliers tend to adhere to rules and regulations so that they are able to reduce the risk of potential losses or complications such as business termination. Clearly, the main motivation for monitoring, rewarding and punishing suppliers is to ensure their products or components are aligned to quality requirements of the buying firm; this technique indirectly affects and improves suppliers' reverse supply chain performance. Being inactive in monitoring the adoption of reverse supply chain initiatives by suppliers entails that there is less suppliers' communication, feedback and monitoring. This therefore, indicates a lack of collaborative operations between buying firms and suppliers in realizing environmental sustainability in supply chains.

4.5 ROLE OF GOVERNANCE MECHANISMS IN REVERSE SUPPLY CHAINS

From the supply chain perspective, governance can be interpreted as the set of interaction principles between buying firms and suppliers. These interaction principles stimulate the approaches and tasks that ought to be performed by the buying firms and suppliers in order to achieve mutually agreed goals and objectives. Governance can be defined as a multidimensional phenomenon, encompassing the initiation, termination and on-going relationship maintenance between a set of parties. Going further, any kind of governance should be able to place emphasis on organizing, monitoring and enforcing rules between parties. Governance mechanism refers to the safeguards stipulated by forms to govern inter-organizational exchange, reduce exposure to opportunism and protect transaction-specific investments. Predominantly, these mechanisms were created to minimize opportunistic behaviors of exchange parties majorly through contractual governance and legal-legitimate power. Nevertheless, the progression of governance theory suggested that the influence of governance mechanisms is also critical in reducing conflict and strengthening cooperation between supply chain partners. Additionally, it can help to foster information and knowledge sharing, improve supply chain agility, flexibility, financial and non-financial performance and cultivate environmental sustainability as well. Generally, contractual governance refers to the definition of supply chain members' responsibilities through formal agreement, while relational governance is focused on relationships' regulation among supply chain members through informal rules such as trust, flexibility, fairness and solidarity.

4.5.1 SUPPLIERS' TRUST AND RELATIONAL GOVERNANCE

Trust is regarded as the most significant mechanism for relational governance when compared to others since it is deemed to play a critical role in improving supply chain performance. Indeed, trust has been extensively considered as a central factor in enhancing inter-firm relationships, particularly between buying firms and suppliers. Similar to contracts, trust has been considered as one of the best mechanisms for organizational control. From the supply chain perspective, trust can be defined as one's belief that one's supply chain partner will act in a consistent way and carry out his/her agreed responsibility. Suppliers' trust toward buying firms can culminate into many benefits in supply chain operations such as encouraging suppliers' investment, involvement, collaboration, information sharing, sustainability performances and suppliers' performance improvements. Investing in facilitating suppliers' trust often leads to economic benefits and reduces transaction costs. Nevertheless, suppliers' opportunistic behaviors can be reduced as trust results in minimizing perceived risks and uncertainty in supply relationships. Suppliers' trust toward buying firms is extremely prevalent when the buying firms' dependency on suppliers is high. But then, when this dependency on suppliers is high but buying firms fail to foster suppliers' trust on them, then there is a high possibility that suppliers can develop opportunistic behaviors. The ability of a buying firm to enhance suppliers' trust will foster suppliers' initiatives toward reverse supply chain practices as they will feel confident and secure to work together in actualizing such objectives. Similarly, suppliers are willing to share information and knowledge, collaborate and even involve themselves in designing reverse supply chain initiatives and operations that can be utilized throughout supply networks.

Nevertheless, buying firms should realize that they are laden with the responsibility to enhance suppliers' trust. Through a transformational style of leadership, a buying firm tends to work collaboratively with suppliers, thereby providing any needed assistance, support and motivation. In these circumstances, suppliers will assume that the buying firm is committed to their success. However, the concept of transformational supply chain leadership can strengthen buying firms to mentor and train suppliers, and to assist them to express their ideas, thereby improving their strengths. By being actively involved in the discussion with suppliers, providing the needed feedback and suggestions, coupling with providing rewards when due, the value of buyer-supplier relationships can be optimized. In a similar vein, a great amount of information will be distributed across the supply network, assistance and support will be provided by the buying firms to the suppliers and consequently, suppliers will be confident in the relationship. This results in a higher extent of trust between suppliers and the buying firms. However, transactional supply chain leadership can assist suppliers to understand buying firms in a better manner. The practice of monitoring and auditing suppliers results in the buying firm to have a close communication and thereby fostering collaboration. Through having close contact and communication, uncertainty about buying firm behaviors can be minimized and this tends to increase the suppliers' trust. Additionally, the existence of clear and fair reward mechanisms has a positive influence on the trust toward buying firm.

4.5.2 Legal-Legitimate Power and Contractual Governance

Interactions usually occur between two or more parties that have interests and objectives that differ in supply chain relationships. Likewise, opportunism, disagreement and conflict may be ignited as each supply chain partner strives toward their own benefits and goals and thereby signaling the expectation for contractual governance. Contractual governance has been found to be a pivotal tool for enhancing and monitoring supply chain performance and relationships. It depends on the use of formal contracts, legal contracts, explicit contracts or legal safeguards to manage the relationship between buying firms and suppliers. A formal or legal agreement that is regarded as an instrument of control is the official written document specifying supply chain partner's expectations and obligations. One of the main aims of having contracts is to exert control or influence over the supply chain partners with the assistance, enforcement or involvement of another party including the legal system. This signifies the readiness of the buying firm to exert legal-legitimate power toward its suppliers. *Ex ante* details are usually outlined in the contracts to enhance the monitoring process of supply chain members. Moreover, the contract is designed to plan for unforeseen circumstances and to ensure agreement on issues like quantity, price, quality and products specifications. A contract might comprise of a number of clauses, obligations expectations and non-compliance expectations. Through the use of power and contract, buying firms are able to promote suppliers' adherence. Reverse supply chain initiatives can be put in place in the contracts thereby allowing buying firms to reduce suppliers' non-conformance behaviors. Going further, through using a contract to exert power, the buying firms will be able to improve supplier performance since suppliers will aim to avoid conflicts with the buying firms that might degenerate to legal disputes. Nevertheless, suppliers will endeavor to avoid contracts' breaching since it can result in financial (such as payment or order delay) and non-financial (such as future business loss) losses.

The transformational leadership is dependent on the leaders' ability to inspire followers in such a way that they will transcend the requirements or normal performance, and likewise, develop followers' self-interest to excel and commit with leaders' plan. On the other hand, the nature of transactional leaders is to identify performance expectations and ensure that followers (suppliers) adhere to requirements. The main motivation for leading the suppliers (followers) is to make sure that the buying firms' plan is carried out as planned. Hence, both styles of leadership will essentially contribute to a greater exercise of power, which will also result in better supplier performance in adopting reverse supply chains.

4.6 SUMMARY

Reverse supply chain management is defined as a series of activities that are required in order to retrieve a used product from a customer and either dispose of it or reuse it.

The reverse supply chain idea fully reflects the vision of environmental protection and the efficient utilization and reuse of resources. It is a process by which a manufacturer systematically accepts previously shipped products or parts from the point of consumption for possible reuse, remanufacturing, recycling or disposal.

Supply chain leadership can be defined as the ability of the buying firm to influence a supplier to achieve a common goal within the supplier's organization. Notably, supply chain leadership has deduced an antecedent of supply chain performance improvement by focusing on the buying firms' ability for articulating vision for the future, communicating the vision and motivating supply chain members.

As part of a sustainable supply chain, the closed-loop supply chain involves a manufacturer taking care of the reverse logistics process in which the goods are returned directly by the original manufacturer or through indirect channels.

Within the context of supply chain management, a distinction is usually made between *transformational* and *transactional* styles of leadership. *Transformational leadership* is characterized by four main dimensions, namely inspirational motivation, individualized consideration, idealized influence and intellectual stimulation.

Transactional leadership is characterized by two dimensions, namely *management-by-exception* and *contingent reward*.

From the supply chain perspective, governance can be interpreted as the set of interaction principles between buying firms and suppliers. Governance can be defined as a multidimensional phenomenon, encompassing the initiation, termination and on-going relationship maintenance between a set of parties.

Contractual governance refers to the definition of supply chain members' responsibilities through formal agreement, while relational governance is focused on relationships' regulation among supply chain members through informal rules such as trust, flexibility, fairness and solidarity. Trust is regarded as the most significant mechanism for relational governance when compared to others since it is deemed to play a critical role in improving supply chain performance.

DISCUSSION AND REVIEW QUESTIONS

1. Define reverse supply chain management.
2. What is closed-loop supply chain?
3. Give a detailed illustration of the importance of remanufacturing the circular economy.
4. Discuss the role of reverse supply chain in the circular economy.
5. Mention some of the metrics and specific items for measuring reverse supply chain performance.
6. Explain the role of governance mechanisms in reverse supply chains.
7. Outline and explain the different dimensions of transformational supply chain leadership.

SUGGESTED MATERIALS FOR FURTHER READING

Grant, D. B., Trautrims, A., & Wong, C. Y. (2017). *Sustainable logistics supply chain management: Principles and practices for sustainable operations and management*, 2ed, Kogan Page, New York.

Pienaar, W., & Vogt, J. (2012). *Business logistics management: A value chain perspective*, 4ed. Oxford University Press.

Part 3

5 Supply Chain Issues in the Circular Economy

5.1 INTRODUCTION

In this chapter, important issues related to the supply chain in the circular economy are discussed. Consequently, detailed discussion is presented on procurement in the circular economy including aspects of circular public procurement and the role of intermediaries in circular public procurement. Additionally, an overview of product flow in circular supply chains coupled with planning of closed loop supply chain and production operations in the circular is illustrated.

5.2 PROCUREMENT IN THE CIRCULAR ECONOMY

Procurement in a circular economy implies seeking to purchase work, goods or services that close the energy and material loops within the supply chain and minimize or eliminate waste. The first step in environmental protection and implementing circular economy is collaborating with green suppliers and buying eco-friendly raw materials. Consequently, circular suppliers that focus on reducing waste in their network and benefit from both forward and reverse flows are regarded as the most significant factor in environmental protection. Circular purchasing and sustainable purchasing, both increase the level of complexity of purchasing. Yet, sustainable purchasing is related to creating value for society, economy and the environment, which could include minimizing material use. In contrast, circular purchasing is more related to closing the material loop and minimizing waste, by, for instance, reducing, recycling and reusing materials. Hence, circular purchasing is more narrowly defined than sustainable purchasing. In fact, the supplier selection problem in the circular supply chain network is a process that is of huge importance that it can have an enormous impact on minimizing environmental degradation and the supply chain costs. In other words, the purchasing of eco-friendly and reusable raw materials can result in the reduced waste and utilization of raw materials depending on proper circular supplier selection. Hence, the circular supplier selection encompasses both economic, social responsibility and environmental aspects with specific consideration for labor rights and promoting safe and secure work environments for employees. As such, circular supplier selection contributes a substantial challenge to achieving SDG 8 (i.e., decent work and economic growth).

Furthermore, the circular supplier selection is considered as the process of selecting suppliers in a closed loop supply chain. As the first level of the network, suppliers have a noteworthy impact on the efficiency of the whole network. Around 70% of the products' overall cost is associated with the cost of purchasing raw materials from suppliers. Hence, selecting the suppliers and implementing common and circularity criteria simultaneously assists in increasing network efficiency and reducing costs.

In a similar vein, the main environmental damage is from suppliers and manufacturers. Consequently, selecting the right supplier can minimize both environmental damage and costs and result in circularity of used materials. The circular economy imposes suppliers to provide raw materials that are technically restorative, recoverable and regenerative and would not have negative effects on the environment.

Moreover, the real-world complexity that is associated with selecting suppliers creates the need for simplified but thoughtful, sustainable supplier selection. The complexity increases even more when adding environmental aspects and it is therefore not surprising that environmentally sustainable supply chains have attracted growing popularity in literature and practice. Most environmentally sustainable supply chains presented in extant literature propose to screen suppliers in the forward supply chains based on their organizational performance, e.g., complying with ISO standards or green product design. An overview of the most frequently utilized environmentally sustainable supply chain aspects available in published studies is presented in Table 5.1.

Additionally, purchasing in the circular economy requires more than just waste management. A broader system perspective is needed that encompasses the entire life cycle of products and processes and the interaction of this system with the environment and the economy. The circular economy is concerned with the creation of self-sustaining production systems. Purchasing professionals are the gatekeepers to the supply chain; their activities are aimed at controlling and tracking incoming materials and products. Purchasers are able to connect the goals of their organization to the goals of the suppliers and internal and external end users. In collaboration with suppliers, they have a role in decreasing supplier risks and in increasing product innovation. They provide the connection between suppliers and internal business functions such as production and R&D. Their important role and strategic position within the organization means that they can contribute to the bottom-up transition toward circularity. For instance, purchasing professionals and supply chain managers can collaborate with suppliers to gain access to required materials

TABLE 5.1
Environmentally Sustainable Supply Chain Aspects

Organizational Aspects	Related Attributes
Process design	Internal recycling at the supplier; waste water; solid waste; energy consumption; use of recycled materials; air pollutants; emission and release of harmful substances.
Product design	Product design for material reuse, recycle and recovery; green packaging; excess package reduction, toxic and hazardous components.
Miscellaneous	Management commitment; staff training on environmental issues; environmental performance of the suppliers' suppliers; social responsibility
Environmental management systems	ISO 14001; end-of-pipe control; green process planning; continuous monitoring; regulatory compliance; up-to-date air, water and pollution permits.

and end users in order to ensure that the products or services can be reused or recycled and that value is created. The pricing, time and value for product principles that purchasers use in their daily work are constantly evolving due to the transition toward a circular economy.

Notably, green public procurement is a process whereby public authorities seek to procure goods, services and works with a reduced environmental impact throughout their life cycle when compared to goods, services and works with the same primary function that would otherwise be procured. On the other hand, sustainable public procurement is a process whereby organizations meet their needs for goods, services, works and utilities in a way that achieves value for money on a whole life basis in terms of generating benefits not only for the organization but also for the society and the economy, while minimizing damage to the environment. Likewise, the circular public procurement is the process by which public authorities purchase works, goods or services that seek to contribute to closed energy and material loops within supply chains, while minimizing and in the best case avoiding negative environmental impacts and waste creation across their life cycle. The three types of procurement have similarities that raise the level of complexity in public procurement, compared to tendering and procuring scenarios based on purchase at the lowest upfront price.

5.2.1 Demands for Circular Public Procurement

In light of current consumption, resource and climate changes, the European Commission published in 2015 the Circular Economy Action Plan, and later did the European Parliament encourage the combination of the knowledge of green public procurement with circular economy principles. The public procurement and purchase of products, services and works amount to approximately EUR 1800 billion, equivalent to 14% of the European gross domestic product. Further, does it describe how circular public procurement can influence markets and by that creates greener and more sustainable products and services through the use of procurement techniques. Compared to a business-as-usual mode, circular public procurement practices are considered approachable to facilitate environmental, social and ethical production and consumption. Yet, the adaptation and transformation toward a circular economy are in a nascent stage, which is also the case for public tendering and procurement. Moreover, circular economy theories have evolved since the 1970s and recently received huge attention from a diverse range of stakeholders. Circular economy minimizes incineration and landfill; is regenerative and restorative by design; operates by default on renewable energy; maintains resources at their highest value at all times. It inherently has a higher complexity than linear transactional value chains; and thus embeds a potential to decouple growth in the extraction of virgin resource from monetary growth. Accordingly, the circular economy addresses the United Nations Sustainable Development Goals, specifically goals 6–9 and 11–17, indicating that a circular economy helps to meet the needs of the present without compromising the needs of the future. Green and sustainable public procurement has likewise gained status as addressing social challenges through public procurement activities. Circular public procurement is a new field in both academia and practice and the elements of green and sustainable public procurement can facilitate and develop circular public procurement processes. Various aspects, namely organizational aspects, individual behavioral aspects and operational aspects, play significant roles during developing circular public procurement processes.

5.2.1.1 Organizational Aspects and Circular Public Procurement

Awareness and knowledge through education, training and clear political goals are considered crucial factors to enhance circular public procurement and to support effectiveness in the tender process. Hence, organizational structures must have the potential to deliver information. The issue of awareness and knowledge can be related to the size of the firm. The size of procuring organizations does not necessarily affect efforts toward effective use of circular public procurement. Nevertheless, this is the case of internal resource allocation that actually supports increasing organizational capabilities toward understanding circular public procurement opportunities. The inclusion of circular public procurement principles is often as a result of random, cautious and unsystematic patterns of experimentation. To achieve an effective use of circular public procurement implies focusing on developing cultural, managerial and operational structures, and being able to support systematic and focused processes. The integration of circular public procurement objectives in organizational strategies is clearly imperative in the effort to prevent a lack of organizational capabilities, proper responsibility and functional roles from acting as barriers for large and small public organizations. Transformational senior managers should incorporate organizational circular public procurement planning, strategies, cross-department commitment and goal setting, which should further be supported by political, administrative, cultural and funding measures to enhance effective implementation of circular public procurement processes.

Public procurers are often resistant to pay a price premium to include circular public procurement due to budget constraints. The integration of policy goals in tenders leading to inclusion of required criteria in tenders pushes, however, contractors to adopt strategic circular public procurement policies to mitigate the operational staff's risk perception. This is why policy makers should consciously emphasize circular public procurement values in operations and communications, using EU and national soft regulation as an indirect support. In contrast, direct support comes from political commitment, environmental knowledge, the organizational structure and the focal interpretation of regulatory framework. National differences in the application and interpretation of legislation and regulations between mandatory and voluntary utilization do also occur. Additionally, the private sector imitates the public sector regarding the use of specific certifications. If the objective of public institutions is to change markets toward more circularity, then demanding innovative new solutions have the largest impact. The quality of contracts is the result of contingent processes of negotiation, making market dialogue and sharing experiences through interdisciplinary iterative processes to be highly efficient in terms of supporting greater circularity in public purchasing. Finally, effective circular public procurement contracts are based on the enhancement of technical, legal and economic capabilities in the procurement department or staff.

5.2.1.2 Individual Behavioral Aspects and Circular Public Procurement

The individual behavioral aspects describe the challenges related to agency, cross-departmental management, beliefs, awareness and individual guidance that can also be influenced by human agency embedded in enduring socioeconomic structures. Transforming the public purchase process from a linear approach focused on the lowest price as the only decision variable toward relying on the best relation between quality and price from a long-term perspective, requires a change in the intertwined behavioral practices and socioeconomic structures. Likewise, change agents play a pivotal role in developing individual engagement through knowledge dissemination and fostering collaboration. The exchange of information and the strategic transfer of knowledge are thus important aspects in transforming the behavioral practices of individuals. Enlightened public buyers, often motivated by trust, which they can make a difference and the actions they take are essential in an effort to adopt circular public procurement. An effective commitment to change characterized by an inherent belief in the benefits of circular public procurement, acts as a mediator for ecological sustainability, procedural justice and a circular public procurement-oriented vision of change. In order to develop an effective commitment to change, it requires the crucial step of establishing structures for individual learning and training concerning circular public procurement opportunities.

The information on circular attributes in general and on circular public procurement specifically, provides additional authority, capacity and motivational energy and only a small amount of guidance can result in big impacts on transformational and individual development. Awareness and knowledge of circular public procurement principles, therefore, have a profound effect on individual behavior and practices and are even considered more important to the implementation and dissemination of circular public procurement than additional financial resources. Furthermore, the knowledge about the long-term impacts of not pursuing circular public procurement can shift the public purchasing approach from a shortsighted focus on the point of purchase cost, toward public procuring with a long-term life cycle costing perspective. One important factor to keep in mind in the transformation is, that knowledge silos represent a weak link in the dissemination of circular public procurement development, but can be mitigated by best practice training, workshops and monitoring. Understanding the power of relational norms and mandatory transformational development targets is essential too. To support the development of individual circular public procurement practices, public institutions must seek to create a work environment, where individuals understand and can appreciate the value of transforming public purchasing from a linear to a circular model.

5.2.1.3 Operational Aspects and Circular Public Procurement

Within the operational context, the circular public procurement is a purchasing system based on pre-requirements, calls for tender, selection, awarding and contracting. Nevertheless, these attributes also play a role in linear public purchasing. The difference lies in taking a circular public procurement approach to five basic consecutive steps, which involve developing internal policies, setting purchasing criteria, creating internal procedures for assurance practices, establishing supplier relations management and building internal circular public procurement capacity.

Likewise, process and decision outcomes are evaluated using life cycle assessment, eco-labels and other strategic circular economic tools in general as the first operational area. However, lack of training, linear economic prioritization and a failure to take measurements able to shed light on possible outcomes, will hamper effective processes. Some mathematical tools proposed for prioritizing operational aspects/tasks include the analytic hierarchy process, the Hurdle analysis and so on. In this context, involving the purchase of computers and a set of qualitative recommendations can provide the procurer with guidelines to navigate among various possibilities available in the process.

The second operational area involves the use of life cycle assessment to enable criteria setting and as an evaluation tool to help procurers to understand the amount of emissions produced and embedded and this is associated with a specific purchase. Integrating carbon emission calculations as evaluation criteria in tenders acts as market communication and stimulates eco-innovation among suppliers. For instance, it is clear that the environmental impact of road construction is due to the combustion of fossil fuels in the transport of materials. The third operational area relates to the use of standards, standardization and legal aspects, which can drive market development in a preferred direction. Unfortunately, evidence shows that circular public procurement principles are either not considered in tender processes or given any special attention in tenders and contracts because past practices are favored to avoid legal conflicts. Public procurers are therefore encouraged to use a defined, operational innovation space to reduce risk when innovating complex circular public procurement processes or eco-labels if products are off-the-shelf solutions. Furthermore, ignorance toward including relevant circular public procurement criteria, decrease with the use of a mandatory market analysis and the justification of choices in the event of non-compliance with possibly useful circular public procurement criteria. Award criteria must be linked to the contract's subject matter and value for money is defined as a combination of quality, quantity, risk, timeliness and cost from a life cycle perspective. The inclusion of all the parameters of value for money enhances the most economically advantageous tenders defined as the best relation between price and quality from a long-term perspective.

The fourth and final area of operational tools relates to supplier selection issues and describes the four specific strategies named ignore, incorporate, insist and integrate. Supplier management meets both internal and external obstacles and proactive strategic positioning through supplier selection requires skills. Environmental criteria are an example of this kind of decision tool; nevertheless, the empirical evidence indicated that environmental criteria have minimal influence on supplier selection. In a similar vein, the norms of strategic importance in effective long-term structures relate to the importance of individuals' understanding of how to allow relational norms to flourish. Purchasing managers, therefore, need key suppliers with shared values and expectations to enhance the quality of long-term relationships. In a specific tender process, where the subject matter is of an extra complex nature, a competitive dialogue procedure allows the creation of relationships with possible suppliers. This is an aspect that can mitigate perceived risk among procurement professionals and enhance innovation in relation to the preferred solution.

5.2.2 THE ROLE OF INTERMEDIARIES IN CIRCULAR PUBLIC PROCUREMENT

The progression of sustainable development through a more circular economy requires improving resource efficiency by prolonging the value of products or services within supply chain markets. Connecting production and consumption to add value to waste materials can drive these improvements by reducing the amount of raw materials needed. Products or services that are part of a circular economy are attractive to buyers as they provide new revenue streams while reducing costs. However, the circular economy model has not been proven in many sectors, and the need for agreement between players before products are on the market creates uncertainty regarding effective consultation processes. Coupled with the high potential of the model, its early stage in private markets creates opportunities for demand-side intervention to increase the uptake of products and services that are part of circular supply chains. Public procurement activities can drive sustainable development by creating demand-side pressure in markets. The demand created via all types of public procurement is sizeable, amounting to up to 19% of GDP across Europe. Leveraging public demand for a more circular economy depends on contracting authority's ability to integrate information that has been captured during various activities undertaken or participated in during the procurement planning process in the pre-procurement phase. However, public agencies are often limited in their internal knowledge, which hinders the environmental benefits of procurement through inadequate technical specifications and award criteria.

The consultation of external groups, including potential suppliers, other government agencies and experts is one means by which to supplement internal knowledge and improve procurement outcomes. With regards to innovation procurement, this has been viewed as a type of "user-producer interaction" or "interactive learning". These interactions transfer information across institutional boundaries to further learning, which in turn is associated with higher project performance. Despite this, such consultation is not common across Europe. When it does occur, interactions are often through negotiated procedures rather than more open discussions of sustainability, such a long-term consideration of raw materials or material wastes. For public procurements of products that are part of circular supply chains, the effectiveness of pre-procurement consultation becomes an integral success factor in the ensuing procurement and its market impacts.

Intermediation can facilitate such consultation processes in public procurement. Intermediation can establish or enable the link between actors with complementary skill sets or interests, focusing on the roles of multiple intermediaries in supporting the generation and diffusion of innovation through public procurement. As the individual or institution carrying out intermediation activities, an intermediary provides support for interconnected functions required to further a project. Intermediaries can serve sustainability transitions through taking a systemic role in acting multilaterally within networks, moving beyond the role of information broker between buyer and supplier. Intermediaries are also referred to as change agents, which are known as internal or external individual or team responsible for initiating, sponsoring, directing, managing or implementing a specific change initiative, project of complete change program. Intermediation has also been discussed in more detailed terms of interaction, such as facilitating the process of coordination, cooperation and collaboration. *Cooperation* is defined as mutual engagement and alignment of the "multi-actor network". Through cooperation, participants learn from each other and share experiences. *Collaboration* is a "recursive process where people or organizations work together in an intersection of common goals by sharing knowledge, learning and building consensus. *Coordination* is a quality indicator of collaboration for "shared understanding" of goals, activities and contributions.

The ways in which intermediaries help to further projects depend in part on their roles and characteristics. The three types of intermediation include demand articulation, actor and linkage formation and innovation process management. The three types of intermediation are differentiated based on their roles such as:

1. *Hard* intermediaries, articulating technical possibilities;
2. *Soft* intermediaries, articulating business and innovation strategies and
3. *Systemic* intermediaries, articulating demand and strategy development.

While all three of the latter include activities of articulation, alignment and learning, *systemic* intermediaries have additional roles of "identifying, mobilizing and involving relevant actors; Organizing discourse, alignment, and consensus; and management of complex, long-term innovative projects.

Moreover, there are four roles of intermediaries in public procurement particularly:

1. Performers of the project or purchase,
2. Brokers linking externally to markets and internally within organizations,
3. Content experts with technology, market, and diagnostic expertise and
4. Trainers building buyer capacity for future projects.

Their roles are further shaped by the market effect of the procurement, distinguished by those which trigger or respond to an innovation. Transferring knowledge is a key function of intermediaries, as they develop and disseminate particular information collected to actors. In this sense, the concept of intermediaries as *brokers* has been well-established. Brokers act within "multi-party, learning-action networks" to transform information on technology and markets. Social network theory supports that these brokers benefit from negotiation, creating relationships to fill structural holes which create knowledge gaps between individuals, organizations and sectors. A key function of "intermediary actors" is seen as knowledge aggregation through the codification of tacit knowledge. In this sense, intermediaries can include standardization institutes, industry associations stimulating technical knowledge production, and firms who are involved across multiple "local practices". Intermediaries can also create conditions enabling the *creation* of knowledge gained through experience. Intermediation facilitates "learning and cooperation in the innovation process" to achieve "alignment and learning of the multi-actor network". Learning-action networks for sustainable purchasing are based on relationships that "lay over and compliment formal organizational structures linking individuals together by the flow of knowledge, information and ideas". Ultimately, based on public procurement, we suggest that government agencies can use the process of intermediation – through the use of intermediaries – to work a given system or network, facilitating the creation and codification of knowledge as part of demand articulation.

Likewise, interactions in public procurement have been examined mainly with respect to public procurement partnerships rather than broader consultation prior to procurement. Basically, trust "facilitates action" in the same way as authority (for governments) and prices (for markets). It builds social capital and can improve connectivity between public, private and non-profit actors. Partnerships with suppliers and the trust those are based on are "paramount" to including social and environmental factors in the purchasing process. Under the New Public Management paradigm, government works more closely with businesses, social enterprises and NGOs and cooperation with these actors can generate knowledge to be incorporated in public procurement. Considering relationships in these more complex environments, the information provision role of intermediaries is seen as being driven by the creation of "awareness and transparency" by intermediates, supporting the creation of "market enabling communication and trust between the parties". In this way, social capital is a key component of intermediation, as it can improve linkages between government, market and non-profit actors.

A central challenge to public procurement is balancing procurement goals with the competition. Market players can provide information used to better design a tender call, which must preserve fair competition while promoting other goals such as a more circular economy. Public procurement has undergone a shift from simple market consultation toward "relationship contracting", which includes "collaboration, networks, strategic alliances and partnerships". Collaboration in pre-procurement initiatives to inform demand can serve as a modern form of competition to bring in market information to procurement processes. The knowledge benefits of stakeholder engagement may make them an even more effective tool in public procurement than conventional competition aspects. Indeed, both competition and collaboration can be required. The transition to a more circular economy includes both of these aspects as actors collect and disseminate information along the supply chain and seek to "influence the performance of supply chain members". Collaboration enables more horizontal rather than hierarchical structures, facilitating "knowledge competence and teamwork". Aspects of collaboration that may affect participation and hinder projects must be considered in intermediation. For example, collaboration may not affect cost reduction or operational performance, and firms may also capitalize upon collaborative initiatives to preserve or enhance their organization's interests or as a platform to promote them through legitimacy instilled. The propensity for organizations to be engaged to further their own agendas should be considered especially when industry collaborates with government – an important consideration when examined in the context of public procurement. Supplier opportunism occurs and by creating environments that reward desired behaviors to motivate supplier performance. As partnership goals in public procurement can be separated from project goals and potential for learning, innovations and collaboration from project success, intermediation prior to procurement can be disentangled from the procurement itself to be examined as an important mechanism with the potential to influence business models.

5.3 PRODUCT FLOW IN THE CIRCULAR ECONOMY

Generally, circular supply chains include forward supply chains and reverse activities and these reverse activities of circular supply chains include a collection of waste/EoL products (discarded products), reverse logistics, quality assessment and remanufacturing, recycling and other forms of recovery or disposal. Basically, there are two types of circular supply chains, namely closed loop systems and open loop systems. Closed loop systems aim to return products to their point of origin and examples include Xerox's copy machines and Kodak's cameras. Open loop systems aim to employ other parties rather than the original producers to recover the value of the discarded products. Examples include recycling firms and the exchanges taking place within industrial symbiosis networks where waste and by-products of one firm serve as feedstock for another firm. Circular and forward supply chains have different product flows. Forward supply chains extract virgin materials to respond to customer demand. When customer demand increases, virgin material extraction increases. Therefore, forward supply chains have demand-driven product flows and are unconstrained in supply as long as virgin materials are available. In contrast, circular supply chains fulfill customer demand by extracting the remaining value of discarded products and looping them back into the economy. As such, the supply of discarded products is constrained by the consumption of the primary product it derived from. In a similar vein, within the forward supply chains, customers may dictate the demand for discarded products, as such resulting in demand-driven product flows. It is only when discarded products leave the circular loop and enter landfills and waste incineration without energy recovery that the product flows become supply driven.

First, the constrained supply of discarded products may lead to inter-market trade and transport operations. When a firm increases its intake of discarded products, the other waste handling activities that operate on the same market may fall short of discarded products. In response, the short-falling waste handling activity may source discarded products from a market located in a different geographical area. The subsequent increase in demand experienced on the other market may, in turn, create a shortage for the waste handling activities operating on this market. This ricochet effect continues until the demand in all involved markets is satisfied; this happened when the chain of trade reached an end market. An end-market satisfies the newly expressed demand while meeting its own domestic demand for discarded products. End-markets either have an abundant supply of discarded products (which might otherwise be absorbed by supply-driven activities such as landfills or incinerators without energy recovery) or replace the missing discarded products with virgin material. The transport that occurs because of the above-described situation can be divided into direct and indirect transport. Direct transport refers to the transport between the buyer and the first-tier supplier, while indirect transport refers to the transport following the trade operations between different geographical markets. Basically, transport that occurs beyond the first tier in supply network has an environmental impact. In fact, indirect transport can play a significant role when selecting a supplier in the forward supply chain with transportation sometimes canceling out the benefits of preferred food production methods. Additionally, transport emissions depend on the selected supplier and the transport occurring in the supplier's upstream supply chain. Changing the first-tier supplier may reduce the environmental impact of transport just like selecting supplier for discarded products may trigger a chain of trade and as such, circular supply chains should also consider the environmental burden of both direct and indirect transport.

Second, the affected end market determines the affected waste handling activity. The identification of the affected waste handling activity that runs short of supply is sensitive to the long-term expanding or decreasing nature of the end market. The increase in demand on an expanding market (i.e., the increasing availability of discarded products) arguably affects the marginally most-preferred waste handling activity – i.e., the waste handling activity which processes more discarded products over time. The opposite logic also holds true: a decrease in demand on a declining market affects the least preferred waste handling activity. The affected waste handling activity influences the environmental performance of circular supply chains as processing a discarded product in one way avoids its processing by another waste handling activity. In general, the waste hierarchy favors waste handling activities that take advantage of the usability and residual value of discarded products. The waste processing results in a lower environmental burden when *disposal < energy recovery < recycling < reuse < reduction < prevention*. To quantify the environmental performance of both the open loop and closed loop circular supply chains, firms should consider which waste handling activity runs short of supply when they express a demand for a given discarded material.

Moreover, the usability of discarded products which refers to the extent to which discarded products fulfill the function of the substituted virgin materials may affect the environmental performance of circular supply chains in several ways. First, discarded products may have a lower quality than their virgin counterparts. For example, municipal solid wastes may have a lower heating value than fossil fuels and recovered fibers may have a lower flexural strength than virgin fibers. A lower usability may increase the number of discarded products needed to substitute a given virgin counterpart. This may result in increased transport and diverting more material from other waste handling activities. Second, discarded products may require additional processing such as disassembling, cleaning, melting and quality checks. These additional processing activities may have an impact on the environment. Third, in industries with capacity constraints, such as process and capital-intensive industries – the production output may decrease when the use of discarded products hampers production efficiency. To a constant output, other firms (with varying environmental performances) may have to produce and transport missing products. The impact of the constrained supply and demand-driven circular supply chains, as well as the impact of the usability of the discarded products as explained, are not usually reflected in environmentally sustainable supply chains. Nevertheless, the environmentally sustainable supply chain framework can assist companies to progress toward sustainable societies by offering cleaner products and by substituting virgin resources with discarded products.

The ability to plan for the collection of returned products, the component/product recovery process, the proportion of products to be manufactured at different quality levels (QLs) and product design for recovery remains a significant challenge to supply chain managers. In reverse logistics, returned products can include the following: after use (end of life (EoL) or before EoL); returned under warranty; defective; obsolete products returned by the retailer (obsolescence due to emergence of new model or new technology) and products returned by consumers under exchange programs. The collection of EoL, returned or defective items should be driven by reasonable profit if third-party logistics is to be involved. Most of the returned products do not have any value in terms of functionality, but they do offer materials that can be reprocessed. For short life cycle products like copiers, computers and cell phones, several components can be recovered to obtain functional values if the condition of the product permits. Conditions, however, are often unknown – and the same can be said for the mix of returned items. It is also crucial to address the fact that consumers do not typically have any motivation to return products. As such, logical planning should set collection options that provide consumers with the motivation to return products without any extra hassle like finding a collection center. Based on these two vital collection-related factors, successful development would involve retailers and selling outlets in the collection of returnables through appropriate promotional steps that would include reasonable incentives for motivating consumers. The consumer should know from the moment of purchase that the product may be returned at any outlet or retail centers with a call to company representatives or carrying the product to the retail centers. Using retail outlets in this way will provide a collaborative network of collection centers when more than one company chooses to use the same retail outlets.

To be successful, a reverse logistics system must have product recovery and collection of returnable equally effective. The recovery process can be handled by the original manufacturer of the product or 3P logistics, but since it is very difficult to pre-determine the quantity and quality of returned products, it may not be feasible for a manufacturer to open a recovery facility for their returned or reverse-channeled products. Economic factors suggest that the most suitable recovery option would be a 3P recovery service provider (RSP) or a network of RSPs. It may be noted at this point that product recovery in a reverse logistics situation is both complex and time consuming. Recovery processes for different product types would involve different levels of expertise. Modularity in reverse logistics is a way to avoid the futility of returned built-to-order type products and sometimes to cope with the take-back law. Modular product design is an established approach for accelerating product development and creating a range of variation in product design.

To obtain reverse logistics-related business advantages or even comply with the regulatory requirements, supply chains should that reverse logistics is a complex business process, and the recovered products would always be in a competing situation with new products. A reverse logistics-based supply chain may categorize products at three QLs: QL1 could be products that use all new components/modules; QL2 could be products that use a mixture of new and recovered components/modules and QL3 could be products that use only recovered components/modules. This business provision would allow supply chains to use an "if-what" analysis to decide the proportion of each QL produced as a way to optimize profit.

5.4 CLOSED LOOP SUPPLY CHAIN PLANNING

This section addresses the planning problems presented by a closed loop supply chain that involves a set of products P of different designs D, manufactured in a set of plants L using a set of modules M and marketed through a set of retailers C. The modules are built by the plants to suit different designs, using K components supplied by a set of V suppliers. The supply chain collects the returned – EoL, defective (DF), broken or unused (BU) – products from the customer through retailers C using a contractual agreement. The returnables from customers are converted into equivalent products P (same denotation as original product) for easy accounting by the retailers C are sent to the assigned RSPs R for the recovery of modules, then recovered modules SQ_{rm} are sent to the plants.

The RSPs are paid based on an agreement regarding the recovery services. Each returned product obtained through the retailer is dismantled and modules are recovered by the RSPs under this agreement. The supply chain uses a modular product design both for production and the recovery process. The supply chain produces and markets each of its products at three QLs: $q = 1$, $q = 2$ and $q = 3$ as a way of making the recovered products business-worthy.

- $q = 1$ means QL products are manufactured using new modules,
- $q = 2$ level products use a predefined mixture of new and recovered modules and
- $q = 3$ level products use only recovered modules for their production.

The objective of the model is to maximize supply chain profit by using optimum modular design for production and recovery, optimizing returnables obtained through retailers, initiating recovery by the RSPs and production of the products at three QLs, deciding the optimal mixture of products at different QLs and optimizing transportation to distribution centers and distribution of the products to the retailers. Figure 5.1 provides a schematic framework for the reverse logistics-based supply chain.

The MIP model, which considers modular product design and integrates a reverse logistics process for the collection of returned products, their recovery process and production of products at different QLs – all with the objective of maximizing overall supply chain profit. This model assumes that the cost of products increases as the number of modules increases. For each product and each design, a

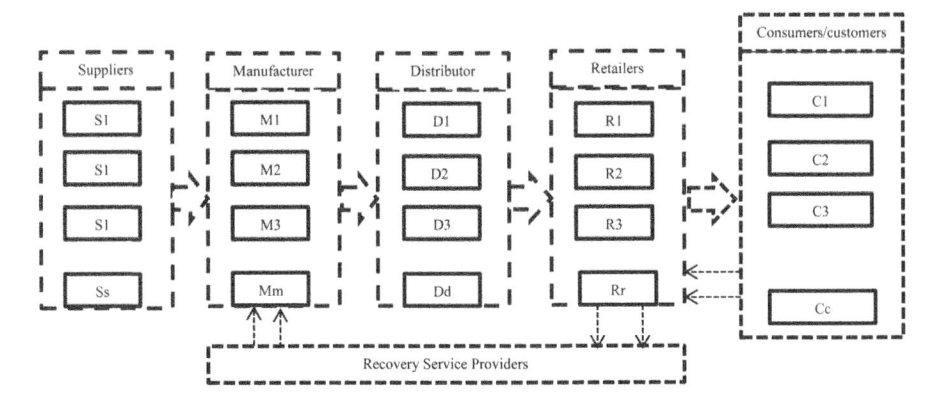

FIGURE 5.1 Reverse logistics-based supply chain schematic framework.

standard number of modules are used, and there is a standard cost associated with each modular design.

Objective Function: maximize Profit (5.1)

$$\text{Profit} = \text{Revenue (REV)} - \text{Total Cost (TC)} \tag{5.1a}$$

$$REV = \sum_{t \in T} \sum_{q \in Q} \sum_{c \in C} V_{tqc} \sum_{j \in J} L_{tqjc} \tag{5.1b}$$

$TC =$ Retailer's payment for the collection of returnables (RP)
  + Transportation from retail outlets to recovery service providers factory (TRR)
  + Payment to recovery service providers for recovery of modules (PRM)
  + Purchasing cost of new component (PNC) (5.1c)
  + Production cost (PC)
  + Transportation cost of products to distribution centers and
  + Distribution cost from distribution center to retailer (TCD)

$$RP = \sum_{t \in T} \sum_{c \in C} CC_{tc} \sum_{r \in R} B_{tcr} + \sum_{c \in C} FC_c e_c \tag{5.1d}$$

$$TRR = \sum_{t \in T} \sum_{c \in C} \sum_{r \in R} B_{tcr} TC_{tcr} \tag{5.1e}$$

$$PRM = \sum_{r \in R} \sum_{m \in M} RV_{mr} SQ_{mr} + \sum_{r \in R} FR_r \cdot n_r \tag{5.1f}$$

$$PNC = \sum_{v \in V} \sum_{k \in K} SQ_{mr} NK_{vk} \sum_{v \in V} FV_v \cdot u_v \tag{5.1g}$$

$$PC = \sum_{t \in T} \sum_{q \in Q} \sum_{i=I} MC_{tqi} \sum_{d \in D} x_{tdqi} + \sum_{t \in T} \sum_{i \in I} FP_{ti} m_{ti} + \sum_{m \in M} \sum_{i \in I} NQ_{mi} NC_{mi} + \sum_{m \in M} \sum_{i \in I} FM_i o_i \tag{5.1h}$$

$$TCD = \sum_{t \in T} \sum_{i \in I} \sum_{j \in J} TR_{tij} \sum_{q \in Q} y_{tqij} = \sum_{t \in T} \sum_{j \in J} \sum_{c \in C} WC_{tjc} \sum_{q \in Q} L_{tqjc} + \sum_{j \in J} FD_j w_j \tag{5.1i}$$

Constraints:

$$\sum_{d \in d} Z_{td} = 1 \quad \forall p \tag{5.2}$$

$$\sum_{i \in I} x_{tdqi} \leq BM z_{td} \quad \forall t, d, q \tag{5.3}$$

$$\sum_{d \in D} x_{tdqi} \leq m_{tt} CM_{tqi} \quad \forall t, q, i \tag{5.4}$$

$$\sum_{t \in T} \sum_{d \notin D} \delta_{tdm} \sum_{i \in I} \sum_{q \in Q} x_{tdqi} = G_m \qquad \forall m \qquad (5.5)$$

$$\sum_{r \in R} B_{tcr} = \sum_{q \in Q} D_{tqc} \sum_{s \in S} R_{tc}^s PS_{tc}^s \qquad \forall t,c \qquad (5.6)$$

$$\sum_{r \in R} B_{tcr} \leq e_c MQ_{tc} \qquad \forall t,c \qquad (5.7)$$

$$\sum_{p \in P} \sum_{c \in C} B_{tcr} \sum_{d \in D} \delta_{tdm} = SQ_{rm} \qquad \forall tr,m \qquad (5.8)$$

$$SQ_{rm} \leq n_r CR_{mr} \qquad \forall tr,m \qquad (5.9)$$

$$G_m - \sum_{r \in R} SQ_{mr} = \sum_{i \in I} NQ_{mi} \qquad \forall m \qquad (5.10)$$

$$NQ_{mi} \leq o_i CO_{mi} \qquad \forall m,i \qquad (5.11)$$

$$\sum_{p \in P} \sum_{d \in D} \delta_{tdm} \sum_{q \in Q} x_{tdqi} = NQ1_{mi} \qquad \forall m,i,q=1 \qquad (5.12)$$

$$\sum_{p \in P} \sum_{d \in D} \delta_{tdm} \sum_{i \in I} \sum_{q \in Q} x_{tdqi} = \sum_{r \in R} SQ1_{mr} \qquad \forall m,q=3 \qquad (5.13)$$

$$\sum_{p \in P} \sum_{d \in D} \delta_{tdm} \sum_{i \in I} x_{tdqi} = MX_m \qquad \forall m,q=2 \qquad (5.14)$$

$$PM1 \sum_{i \in I} (NQ_{mi} - NQ1_{mi}) + PM2 \sum_{r \in R} (SQ_{mr} - SQ1_{mr}) = MX_m \qquad \forall m \qquad (5.14a)$$

$$\sum_{m \in M} \left(\sum_{i \in I} NQ_{mi} \right) CN_{mk} = \sum_{v \in V} NS_{vk} \qquad \forall k \qquad (5.15)$$

$$NS_{vk} \leq u_v CS_{vk} \qquad \forall v,k \qquad (5.16)$$

$$\sum_{d \in D} x_{tdqi} = \sum_{j \in J} y_{tqij} \qquad \forall t,q,i \qquad (5.17)$$

$$\sum_{i \in I} y_{tqij} \leq w_j CD_{tqj} \qquad \forall t,q,j \qquad (5.18)$$

$$\sum_{i \in I} y_{tqij} = \sum_{c \in C} L_{tqjc} \qquad \forall t,q,j \qquad (5.19)$$

$$\sum_{p \in P} \sum_{q \in Q} L_{tqjc} \leq BN\beta_{jc} \quad \forall j,c \tag{5.20}$$

$$\beta_{jc} \leq w_j \quad \forall j,c \tag{5.21}$$

$$\sum_{j \in J} L_{tqjc} = e_c D_{tqc} \quad \forall t,q,c \tag{5.22}$$

$$u_v; w_j; e_c; z_{pd}; m_{pi} n_r; o_i; \beta_{jc} \in \{0,1\},$$
$$\forall p \in P, i \in I; j \in J, c \in C, d \in D, v \in V, r \in R, m \in M, k \in K \tag{5.23}$$

The objective function in Eq. (5.1) maximizes profit. Profit is computed in Eq. (5.1a) by subtracting total cost (*TC*) from revenue (*REV*). *REV* in Eq. (5.1b) is earned by supplying products to customers at a customer expected price. The components of *TC* are defined in Eq. (5.1c). The retailer's payment (*RP*) in Eq. (5.1d) is computed considering the amount collected and sent to retailer, the per unit cost of collecting and the fixed contractual cost for the collection arrangement. Per unit collection costs include promotional steps for convincing the customer to return; collection of returnables; storing and carrying the returnable inventory until transported to RSPs by the supply chain. Eq. (5.1e) considers the per unit transportation cost for sending collected returnables from retail outlets to RSPs. Eq. (5.1f) computes the cost of recovered modules based on total quantity recovered and per unit recovery cost. Cost of new components (*PNC*) in Eq. (5.1g) is computed based on the quantity received from the suppliers at the quoted prices and the fixed cost for ordering the suppliers. Eq. (5.1h) computes the total production cost (*PC*) of the products based on the quantity of products produced and fixed cost for setting the plant for such production. It also includes the cost of making new modules and the setup costs for module production, the transportation and distribution cost (*TCD*) in Eq. (5.1i) computes the cost of transporting products from plants to distribution centers; sending products from distribution centers to retailers and the fixed cost of opening distribution centers.

According to constraint (5.2), a product can have only one design, once the design for a product at a QL is decided, constraint (5.3) ensures production of the product based on its design and QL. Constraint (5.4) limits production quantity and quality for a product based on plant capacity. Eq. (5.5) determines the modules required for production. Products collected by each retailer are estimated in Eq. (5.6) using a scenario-based analysis. According to constraint (5.7), retailers will collect returnables within the maximum limit fixed in the contractual agreement with the supply chain. Constraint (5.8) determines the modules recovered by the RSPs from the returnables. Constraint (9) limits recovery by the RSPs within their capacities. Eq. (5.10) determines the quantity of new modules that are to be manufactured. Constraint (11) limits production of new modules according to the capacity of the plant. Eq. (5.12) determines the new modules to be used for producing products at $q = 1$ level (new). Eq. (5.13) determines recovered modules for producing products at $q = 3$ level (second hand). Constraint (5.14) determines the total quantity of modules needed for $q = 2$ level products (that uses mixture of new and old modules), and constraint (5.14a) determines the new and recovered modules to be used based on the predefined proportion by the $q = 2$ products estimated in the constraint (5.4). Constraint (5.15) determined the components required for the new modules to be procured from the suppliers. Eq. (16) limits the components supplied by the supplier based on their capacities. Eq. (5.17) balances the production quantity with the quantity transported to the distribution centers. Constraint (5.18) limits the transported quantity to the distribution centers within their capacity. Constraint (5.19) balances the inputs to the distribution centers from the plants and the output from the distribution centers to the customers. Constraint (5.20) distributes products to the retailers from the assigned distribution centers. Constraint (5.21) ensures that open distribution centers are assigned to retailers. Constraint (5.22) ensures the satisfaction of customer requirements by the products distributed to the customers. Constraint (5.23) imposes integrality.

5.5 PRODUCTION PLANNING IN THE CIRCULAR ECONOMY

The interference between the reverse and forward flows affects the production planning process, which includes: (i) the planning of the recovery and raw material procurement and (ii) the planning of the production activities required to transform input materials into finished products to satisfy customer demands, covering both remanufactured and new products. The reverse flows affect the decision levels of production systems in different proportions as follows:

- **The operation production problems** refer to short-term decisions, such as line balancing or scheduling. Once the mid-term needs are determined, these decision-making problems can, in most cases, assimilate the reverse production streams without additional constraints or costs in objective functions.
- **The mid-term production planning problems** seek to assist managers/firms at tactical level in deciding how much and when: to produce and order new goods, disassemble and remanufacture. Apart from the option of preparing waste for reuse, three other loops support the circulation of production flows in industrial systems without entering the environment via the recovery of products, materials and production residues. All of these circular economy-oriented flows change the structure of the traditional linear production path by adding an additional layer of complexity to the mid-term production planning.
- **Strategic planning problems** operate at the supply chain level by integrating procurement, distribution and recovery decisions. Although the strategic circular economy decisions are of crucial importance and investment, their posing and making are less frequent and take place upstream in the supply chain network.

5.5.1 Defining Disassembly for Recycling

The first crucial step in most processing operations of EoL/use products is disassembly. Allowing a selective retrieving of desired parts or components, it truly belongs to the area of environmentally conscious manufacturing and product recovery. Disassembly appears in different recycling options (from product to raw material recycling), which results in planning problems with particular specifications. From an engineering point of view, disassembly can be defined as a systematic and selective process of separating an item into components, subassemblies or other groupings. Within the realm of operations management, quantitative disassembly problems can be classified into four generic types of problems:

- **Disassembly-to-order** (also known as *disassembly leveling*) determines the lot size of a mix of different types of EoL/use products to be disassembled for satisfying the demand of parts or components. Two optimization criteria are either minimizing the number of products to be disassembled or the sum of costs related to the disassembly process. EoL/use products can have parts in common. The parts commonality means that products or subassemblies share their parts or components.
- **Disassembly lot-sizing** (also called *disassembly scheduling*) for a given disassembly structure, schedule the quantity of disassembling EoL/use products and their components in each period of a planning horizon in order to meet the demand of their parts or components. The considered optimization criterion seeks commonly to minimize the sum of a combination of costs: setup, penalty, overload, lost sales and inventory holding. Additionally, disassembling scheduling includes timing of disassembling, unlike disassembly-to-order.
- **Disassembly line balancing** assigns disassembly tasks to qualified workstations while respecting the precedence relations. The objective usually aims at minimizing the number of workstations, the idle time of workstations, the cycle time, etc., or a combination of these parameters.

5.5.2 Mathematical Formulation for Production Planning in Disassembly Systems

Two classes of problems revolve around production planning in disassembly systems, namely disassembly-to-order and disassembly lot-sizing. The class of disassembly scheduling problems can allow:

Distinct structure and number of product types: Both cases of single and multiple product types have been addressed by various research scholars in extant literature. It should be noted that it is not so much the number of product types but rather their structure that increases the problem complexity. Two product structures can be distinguished:
  i. *assembly type*, where each child item has at most one parent, i.e., a given product type does not allow parts commonality and
  ii. *general type*.
With or without parts commonality: Owing to interdependencies among different parts or components of EoL/use products, disassembly lot-sizing problem with parts commonality becomes more complex.

Multi-level demand: Relatively minimal research addresses problems which integrate both disassembly-to-order and scheduling decisions. These two interrelated problems are separately treated in the literature.

Partial or complete disassembly: No information about parent-child matching between items is required in complete disassembly setting, the root-leaf relationship being sufficient. Against the complete disassembly planning, partial disassembly setting involves mainly two questions:
  i. To what depth the products have to be disassembled in each period of time horizon? And
  ii. In the case with parts commonality, which disassembly sequence has to be performed?

Capacitated or un-capacitated: Similar to production planning problems in assembly systems, the resource capacity constraint is an important consideration due to its industrial soundness.

Consider a given disassembly Bill of Materials (d-BOM) with an assembly structure. All items are numbered level by level: 1, 2,...,μ, $\mu+1$,...N, where 1 represents the root index and μ is the index of the first leaf item. All indices greater or equal to μ correspond to leaf parts. The disassembly of one unit of parent i results in α_{ij} units of part j. Denote in parentheses (i) the parent of a part i.

For this basic d-BOM, a generic version of the disassembly lot-sizing problem is formalized, which aims to determine the disassembly quantity and timing X_{it} of all parents $i(\forall i < \mu)$ in order to meet the demand of leaf parts $d_j(\forall j \geq \mu)$ over a planning time horizon 1,2,....P. Let the objective function be cost-based and include two costs unrelated to disassembly timing. A fixed setup cost g_i is required if any disassembly operation of part $i < \mu$ is performed in period p. This condition is verified via the indicators $Y_{it}, \forall t \in [[1,P]], \forall i \in [[1,\mu-1]]$.

In order to satisfy the demand of leaf items, partial disassembly is allowed during the planning horizon. An inventory holding cost is h_i is thus incurred when I_{it} parts of type i are stored from period p to period $p+1$ to meet future demands $\forall p \in [[1,P]], \forall i \in [[2,N]]$. The available quantity of the root item is supposed to be unlimited. A generic version of the disassembly lot-sizing problem is given below:

$$\text{Minimize} \sum_{p=1}^{P}\left[\sum_{i=1}^{\mu-1} g_i Y_{ip} + \sum_{i=2}^{N} g_i I_{ip}\right] \quad (5.24)$$

Subject to:

$$I_{i,p-1} + \alpha_{(i),i} X_{(i),p} = I_{it} + d_{it} \qquad \forall p \in [[1,P]], \forall i \in [[\mu,N]] \quad (5.25)$$

$$I_{i,p-1} + \alpha_{(i),i} X_{(i),p} = I_{it} + X_{it} \qquad \forall p \in [[1,P]], \forall i \in [[2,\mu-1]] \quad (5.26)$$

$$I_{i,0} = 0 \qquad \forall i \in [[2,N]] \quad (5.27)$$

$$X_{ip} \leq M Y_{ip} \qquad \forall p \in [[1,P]], \forall i \in [[1,\mu-1]] \quad (5.28)$$

$$I_{ip} \geq 0 \qquad \forall p \in [[1,P]], \forall i \in [[2,N]] \qquad (5.29)$$

$$X_{ip} \geq 0 \text{ and integer} \qquad \forall p \in [[1,P]], \forall i[[1,\mu-1]] \qquad (5.30)$$

$$Y_{ip} \in \{0,1\} \qquad \forall p \in [[1,P]], \forall i \in [[1,\mu-1]] \qquad (5.31)$$

The set of equalities (5.25) and (5.26) expresses the flow conservation constraints. As constraints (5.27) specify, the initial inventory level of each part is null. Constraints (5.28) involve a setup cost in each period if any disassembly operation is realized in that period. The definition domains of all variables are stated in constraints (5.29)–(5.30). Note that besides the cost-based objective function (5.24), another optimization criterion considered in the literature seeks to minimize the number of products to be disassembled, i.e., $\Sigma_{i=1}^{P} X_{1i}$. Even if rare, of importance to mention is the explicit consideration in the mathematical models of circular economy issues other than those related to the disassembly process per se. For example, the legislative and environmental requirements imposed by the Directive 2002/96/EC appear in the constraints of a mathematical model proposed for a case study encountered in a manufacturing enterprise of electric heating appliances.

5.5.3 From Product to Raw Material Recycling

In this section, we discuss the production planning systems including the following recycling operations:

i. the conversion of worn-out goods into new or good as new ones, and
ii. the flow back of material obtained during disassembly into production as valuable material.

These recovery operations fall within the concept of *remanufacturing*. Various terms can be enumerated that are often confused with remanufacturing, such as restoring, reconditioning, repurposing and refurbishment. No clear-cut definitions and distinctions between these recovery options exist in available published studies. One thing is certain, remanufacturing becomes a standard term for an industrial recovery process of returned products, which requires several processing operations including often the disassembly operation.

Manufacturing and remanufacturing are two alternative and competing production ways that share the same industrial environment and often lead to the same serviceable products. Accordingly, production planning systems for remanufacturing raise new questions for production and inventory management, the well-posedness of which heavily depends on the systems settings. In the production planning literature, the classic lot-sizing problem has been extended with a remanufacturing option under different settings with or without final disposal options, as illustrated in Figure 5.2. The arrows in Figure 5.2 depict the direction of material flows. A significant part of available published studies operates on production systems, where manufactured and remanufactured products are identical and assimilated as *serviceable products*.

Supply Chain Issues in the Circular Economy

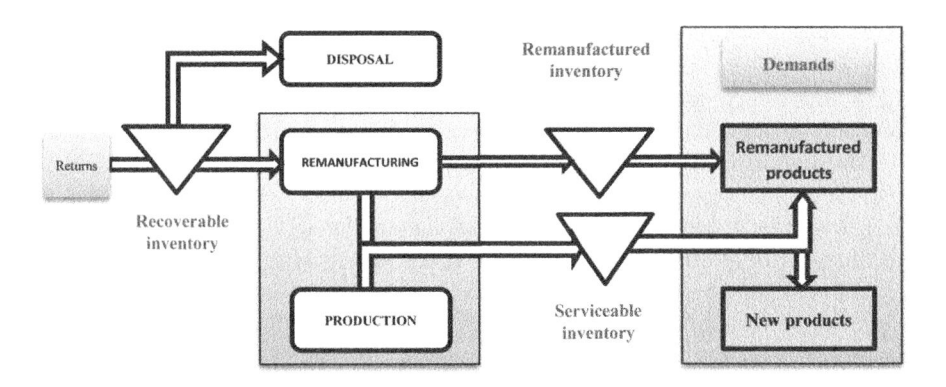

FIGURE 5.2 Production systems including remanufacturing.

Another part distinguished the newly produced from remanufactured products in customer demand.

5.5.4 Mathematical Formulation for Product to Raw Material Recycling Systems

In seeking to better define industrial contexts, various academic scholars have investigated different variants of the lot-sizing problem with manufacturing options (LSR). Apart from the classical capacitated and un-capacitated cases of the lot-sizing problem, it is important to review the main remanufacturing-oriented characteristics of this problem which tends to define a nomenclature within the scientific community:

Joint or separated setups: Both configurations have been studied in the literature, namely when:

- Manufacturing and remanufacturing are performed in two separate processes, each having its own setup cost. This problem is commonly called *lot-sizing with remanufacturing and separate setups*.
- Manufacturing and remanufacturing share the same production routes and have one joint setup cost. Defined on this assumption, the problem is known as *lot-sizing with remanufacturing and joint setups*.

Stationary or time-dependent parameters: Special cases of lot-sizing problems with manufacturing options (LSR) with stationary parameters have not been neglected and a number of useful analytical results have been derived for them.

Inventory management: The integration of product returns and remanufacturing-related goods into the production environment affects the traditional inventory management. In this respect, decisions related to the recoverable (of product return), serviceable (of identical manufactured and remanufactured products) and remanufactured inventories are inherent to lot-sizing problems with manufacturing options (LSR) problems for a suitable coordination between the regular policies of procurement and remanufacturing.

With or without products substitution: In contrast to the classical lot-sizing problem, one of the main specificities of lot-sizing problems with manufacturing options (LSR) lies on the demand that can be fulfilled from a single stream of serviceable products or be fitted into two categories of newly produced and remanufactured ones.

The general form of the lot-sizing problem with remanufacturing, time-dependent parameters and separated setups can be formally defined. Let the planning horizon be spread over P periods. Denote by d_p the demand for serviceable products and r_p the quantity of returns $\forall p \in [[1,P]]$. The related industrial process involves the following costs: unit production costs for manufacturing (remanufacturing) $t_p(\hat{t}_p)$, setup costs for manufacturing (remanufacturing) $h_p(\hat{h}_p)$, unit holding costs for serviceable products e_p and returns e_p, $\forall p \in [[1,P]]$.

Let $X_p(\hat{X}_p)$ be the quantity of manufactured (remanufactured) products and Y_p be ($\hat{Y}_p$) the binary indicator for manufacturing (remanufacturing) in period $p \in [[1,P]]$. Variables I_p and $\hat{I}_p$ are used to express the inventory levels of serviceable products and returns, respectively. The lot-sizing problem with manufacturing options (LSR) problem with time-depended parameters and separated setups can be formulated as follows:

$$\text{Minimize} \sum_{p=1}^{P} \left(t_p X_p + \hat{t}_p \hat{X}_p + h_p Y_p + \hat{h}_p \hat{Y}_p + e_p I_p + \hat{e}_p \hat{I}_p \right) \quad (5.32)$$

Subject to:

$$\hat{I}_{p-1} + r_p = \hat{I}_p + \hat{X}_p \qquad \forall p \in [[1,P]] \quad (5.33)$$

$$I_{p-1} + \hat{X}_p + X_p = I_p + d_p \qquad \forall p \in [[1,P]] \quad (5.34)$$

$$I_0 = \hat{I}_0 = 0 \quad (5.35)$$

$$\hat{X}_p \leq \sum_{i=p}^{P} d_i \hat{Y}_p \qquad \forall p \in [[1,P]] \quad (5.36)$$

$$X_p \leq \sum_{i=p}^{P} d_i Y_p \qquad \forall p \in [[1,P]] \quad (5.37)$$

$$\hat{X}_p, X_p, \hat{I}_p, I_p \geq 0 \qquad \forall p \in [[1,P]] \quad (5.38)$$

$$\hat{Y}_p, Y_p \in \{0,1\} \qquad \forall p \in [[1,P]] \quad (5.39)$$

The objective function (5.32) minimizes the sum of production, setup and holding costs associated with manufacturing and remanufacturing processes. The sets of equalities (5.33) and (5.34) express the flow conservation constraints. Both serviceable and returns inventories are initialized via constraints (5.35). Constraints (5.36) and (5.37) track the manufacturing and remanufacturing setups. Binary and non-negative requirements are imposed in constraints (5.38) and (5.39).

5.6 SUMMARY

The first step in environmental protection and implementing circular economy is collaborating with green suppliers and buying eco-friendly raw materials. Consequently, circular suppliers that focus on reducing waste in their network and benefit from both forward and reverse flows are regarded as the most significant factor in environmental protection.

Green public procurement is a process whereby public authorities seek to procure goods, services and works with a reduced environmental impact throughout their life cycle when compared to goods, services and works with the same primary function that would otherwise be procured.

Sustainable public procurement is a process whereby organizations meet their needs for goods, services, works and utilities in a way that achieves value for money on a whole life basis in terms of generating benefits not only for the organization but also for the society and the economy while minimizing damage to the environment.

Circular public procurement is the process by which public authorities purchase works, goods or services that seek to contribute to closed energy and material loops within supply chains while minimizing and in the best case avoiding negative environmental impacts and waste creation across their life cycle.

Closed loop systems aim to return products to their point of origin and examples include Xerox's copy machines and Kodak's cameras. Open loop systems aim to employ other parties rather than the original producers to recover the value of the discarded products.

To be successful, a reverse logistics system must have product recovery and collection of returnable equally effective. The recovery process can be handled by the original manufacturer of the product or 3P logistics, but since it is very difficult to pre-determine the quantity and quality of returned products, it may not be feasible for a manufacturer to open a recovery facility for their returned or reverse-channeled products.

The first crucial step in most processing operations of EoL/use products is disassembly. From an engineering point of view, disassembly can be defined as a systematic and selective process of separating an item into components, subassemblies or other groupings.

DISCUSSION AND REVIEW QUESTIONS

1. What is procurement and why is it important in the circular economy?
2. Differentiate between circular purchasing and sustainable purchasing in the circular economy.
3. Outline the role of intermediaries in public procurement.
4. Explain the two main types of circular supply chains.
5. Discuss the product flow in the circular supply chain.
6. Define disassembly from an engineering point of view.
7. Within the realm of operations management, mention the four generic types of quantitative disassembly problems.

6 Sustainable Supply Chain Operations in the Circular Economy

6.1 INTRODUCTION

In the circular economy, products, components and materials are utilized at the maximum level and reach zero-waste idealism. Consequently, biological products can be safely returned to the biosphere, while other products can be remanufactured, recycled and refurbished to attain maximum waste. Furthermore, in the circular economy, there are restorative and regenerative cycles so that both biological and technical ingredients can be safely disposed of to gain the maximum utility. Also, unique to the circular economy philosophy, no waste has arisen. A circular economy is a new economic concept which is first adopted by China, in contrast to the linear economy. Within the circular economy, the linear sequence of "take-make-consume", which is the classical flow of traditional business models is converted by the new sequence of "take-make-consume-dispose". The purpose of circular economy is to maintain the maximum level of utility and value of the products and materials via methods like design, maintenance, reuse, remanufacturing, repair and recycling and also decreasing waste. Due to the ongoing fierce competition in the market environment, companies are constantly laden with the burden to integrate circular economy in their supply chain strategies.

6.2 GREEN SUPPLY CHAIN MANAGEMENT IN THE CIRCULAR ECONOMY

The rate of consumption of natural resources has risen with the world population growth. Recently, more than 8.5 million tons of toxic materials and more than 30,000 million tons of CO_2 emissions are released annually (http://www.worldometers.info). These statistics are considered alarming and just two estimating factors for environmental degradation coupled with other factors like aridity, water pollution, deforestation, species extinction, etc. All these factors are equally important and should be given critical consideration. The critical question is, what approaches can be implemented to minimize these destructive processes? In response, the implementation of green supply chain is regarded as one of the most effective approaches to controlling and reducing these damages, even though the efficient use of natural resources also contributes to achieving SDG12 (Responsible Consumption and Production).

Likewise, the purpose of the circular economy is for waste and pollution decrease, minimal resource consumption, sustainability improvements, collaboration and efficient management of resources (i.e., materials, labor, natural resources and information). The circular economy is characterized with environmental requirements based on the 3R principle, namely, Reuse, Reduce and Recycle for resource use and environmental protection. Additionally, circular economy can assist in gaining environmental, economic and social sustainability improvements. Indeed, the circular economy aspires to reduce material consumption and carbon emissions and thereby supporting cleaner production, green design and waste management. The transformation from a linear economy to a circular economy necessitates organizations to redesign their supply chains. Within this context, the circular economy is effective to ensure the transition from the traditional supply chain to the green supply chain and results in additional pressure on the company. The structure of green supply chain in the circular economy is shown in Figure 6.1.

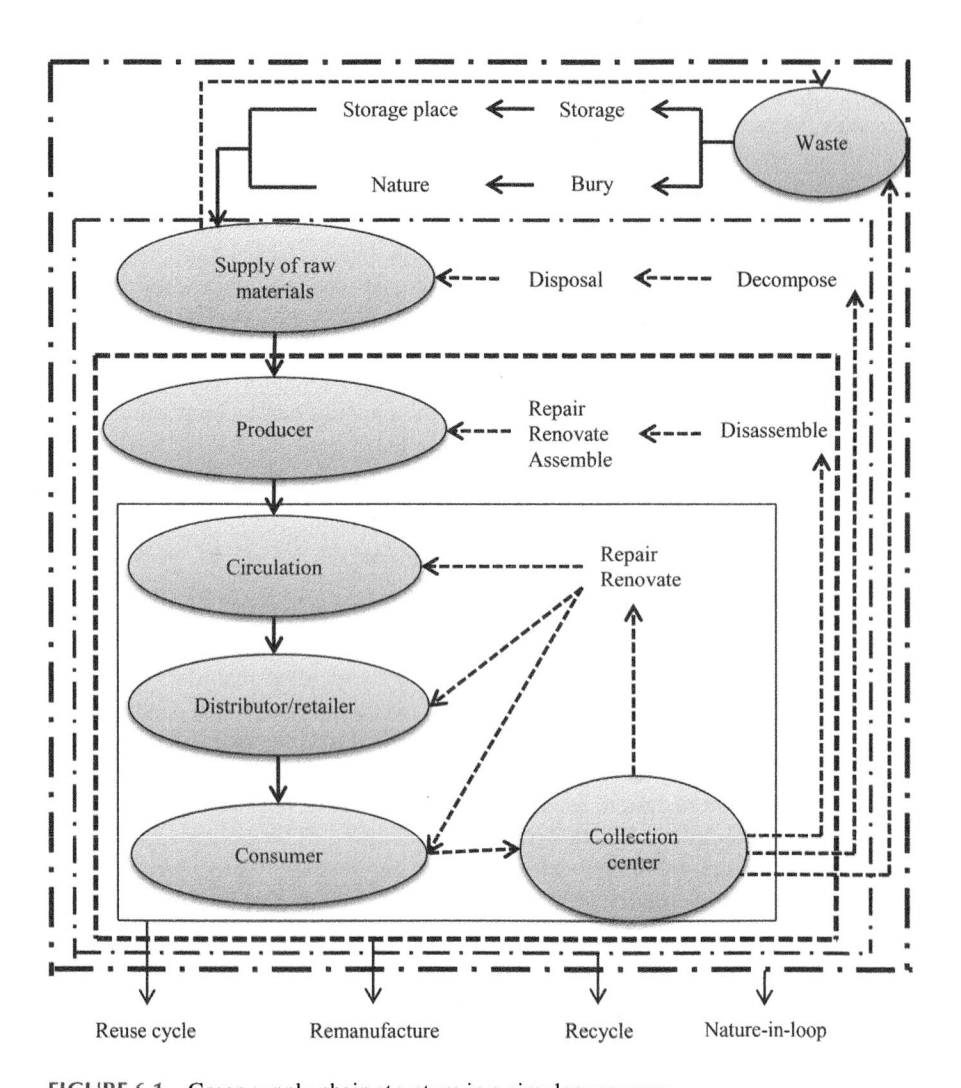

FIGURE 6.1 Green supply chain structure in a circular economy.

The circular economy focuses on protecting the environment and conserving resources and hence, significantly supporting green supply chain management implementation. Therefore, within the circular economy, green supply chain management should integrate the 3R principles of reuse, reduction and recycling in each supply chain cycle to achieve the goals of economic and environmental performance improvements. The integration of green supply chain management in the circular economy is necessary to attain an optimal balance of social, economic, operation and environmental performance improvements for an organization. Green purchasing is regarded as the first step in implementing green supply chain management. Green supply chain management has a broader definition since it aims to minimize the life cycle impacts of products and integrate eco-design. Also, green supply chain management can facilitate efficient resource utilization and allocation, decreasing the utilization and production of environmentally harmful materials and the concepts of reuse and recycling products. Implementing green supply chain management is considered a semi-closed loop that encompasses eco-design, green material, green logistics, green production and green consumption. When compared with the traditional supply chain, green supply chain management is characterized by greenness in product design, selection and purchase of raw materials, production, distribution of final products and after sale services. Generally, the supply chain can be extended in terms of green procurement/purchasing, closed-loop supply chain and reverse logistics supply chain. The extended supply chain is described as all the elements of the traditional supply chain including facilities, suppliers, distribution and customers coupled with feed forward flow of information and materials and integrated green operations. Such integrated green operations include product recycling and packaging, reuse and remanufacturing operations. In addition, green supply chain management involves the purchase of less harmful materials and minimized material utilization with greater utilization of renewable and recyclable materials as circular economy implementation.

Furthermore, green supply chain management emphasizes the procurement/purchase as an internal environmental management function that includes the concepts of reuse, recycle and source savings. It involves green operations such as material procurement, production, packaging, logistics, marketing and reverse logistics. These operations refer to the forward supply chain operations such as manufacturing, procurement, material sourcing and selection, warehousing and inventory management, distribution, shipping and transportation. This process entails collaboration between an organization and its vendors and customers. The different elements of supply chain management consist of suppliers, manufacturers, distributors, retailers, consumers, recyclers and government agencies. These supply chain partners are involved in integrated planning, organizing, directing, controlling and coordinating material, information, capital and knowledge in green supply chain management. Green supply chain management encompasses a wide range of inter-relationships between organizations designed to reduce the impact of the materials flow and to obtain environmental information on materials. The environmental cooperation and alignment in the supply chain need direct involvement with its vendors and customers to arrive at environmentally sustainable solutions. Green supply chain management provides a range of benefits for companies, such as reducing manufacturing, logistics and overall business costs, maximizing profits, reducing environmental impact, increasing customer satisfaction, improving brand image, revenue and market shares. Other benefits include market expansion, competitors differentiation, enhancing corporate social responsibility, improving profits and increasing product recovery solutions. In addition, there are benefits associated with green supply chain management such as improving employee satisfaction, employee acquisition, engagement and retention, acquiring new customers, developing new products and increasing ecological efficiency. Ultimately, the main operations in green supply chain within the circular economy include green design, green purchasing (e.g., certified suppliers and purchase of eco-friendly materials), green/sustainable packaging and transportation, product reuse, and remanufacturing or recycling. Thus, there are different applications of supply chain operations that integrate with the circular economy such as product and service design, procurement, production and logistics.

6.3 SUSTAINABLE CONSUMPTION AND PRODUCTION IN THE CIRCULAR ECONOMY

Circular economy activities are increasingly significant in developing and developed economies as the Sustainable Development Goals have been implemented by United Nations Member States (e.g., SDG 9 emphasizes inclusiveness and sustainability through economic growth and sustainable industrial practices). Circular economy facilitates sustainable consumption and energizes public and private investment, which eventually results in economic growth. At the moment, research studies and industrial practices in circular economy signify that the practice of recycling and realizing material cost savings in manufacturing sectors can facilitate economic activities through eco-product development, remanufacturing and refurbishment. In real life situation, the new investment injections to a circular economy system must emanate from resource regeneration and must optimize resource and environmental sustainability within the closed-loop system in the supply chains. The closed-loop system refers to the multiplier effect in the supply chains, which tends to increase investment and consumption. Over the last decade, significant attention has been devoted to closed-loop supply chain systems and evidence suggests that such can aid in the transition toward a circular economy at the supply chain level.

Clearly, the multi-loop supply chain system activities widen the economic benefits. Yet still, studies on circular economy rarely relate the activities to economic benefits since many studies focus on resource input optimization through minimization of waste, emissions, energy leakage and resource input, and maximization of product service output through multi-loop closing, eco-design, remanufacturing, refurbishing and recycling. Beyond material costs saving through recycling and reuse, untapped opportunities exist for economic growth through a circular economy. Circular economy entails that each time there is an injection of new demand into the circular investment or consumption flow, there is likely going to be a multiplier effect as a result of this injection, due to which there is more investment and more value creation. This multiplier effect can be linked to causing an increase in the multi-loop supply chain systems, thereby arising from any new circular economy

Sustainable Supply Chain Operations in the Circular Economy

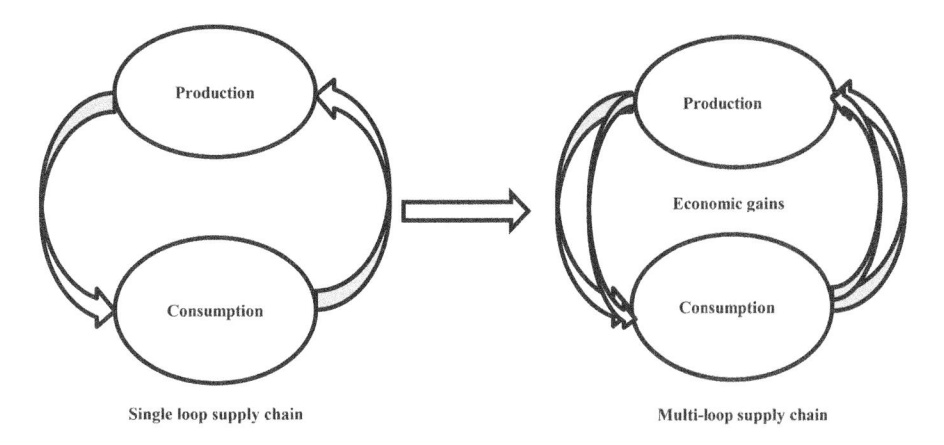

FIGURE 6.2 Single loop supply chain to multi-loop supply chain system.

investment and consumption spending based on innovative business models and activities of circular economy.

Hence, to actualize and maximize the multiplier effects from the circular economy, the traditional, closed-loop supply chain system can be reconsidered as a multi-loop supply chain system, as shown in Figure 6.2. According to Figure 6.2, in the multi-loop supply chain system, reused and recycled materials from a previous life cycle are rejuvenated with new values and functionality. The life cycle assessment tool in the multi-loop supply chain systems tends to monitor/control the diffusion effect of the circular economy. Various studies only emphasize the circular economy diffusion effect on the operations and neglect the multi-loop supply chain system operations and this results in increased economic gains. Additionally, the multi-loop supply chain system operations have more innovative business models to facilitate the multiplier effect for maximizing economic gains.

Moreover, multi-loop supply chains exhibit certain limitations on resource/material, technology limitation and consumption pattern perspectives. In the context of resources or materials, multi-loop supply chain systems need to collaborate and coordinate together for maximizing the reuse and recycle potentials and to capture added values by incorporating all supply chain operations. Such industrial symbiosis draws firms closer in innovative cooperation that enhances the goal of the closed-loop system, which involves multiple supply chains by using the available resources for re-manufacturability or recyclability to actualize by-product or wastes' new life cycles. Likewise, technology limitation is a key challenge for products or wastes' new life cycles that could reform the materials or resources into an up-cycled new product and result in the re-design of a product service system. For example, the sharing service for umbrella, launched in Japan, is a re-designed product-service system that gives the same utility or function of an umbrella when it is not otherwise utilized, hence, maximizing its value over its physical life span. Additionally, all products or product-service systems at multi-period closed-loop supply chain can be re-designed and become raw materials or resources of the subsequent new product life cycle, hence increasing values of the resources or materials. Sustainable consumption is a growing awareness that enhances variations in environmental costs and stimulates further sustainable production and consumption patterns.

6.4 REVERSE LOGISTICS

The circular economy is presently an important issue in the manufacturing sector, and its interest has grown in recent years among industries and academic scholars alike. The emerging markets that are economically considered as developed are constantly promoting the implementation of circular economy in their companies. For instance, it has been proposed in a prior published study that transforming the linear model of the value chain (i.e., take-make-dispose) process to the circular supply chain is carried out by integrating reuse, remanufacturing, and recycling processes. Nevertheless, to effectively manage the circular economy-oriented value chains, the organization needs to enhance the management of the recovery and remarketing operations that are supported by the "Reverse Logistics" program. In the past decade, there has been a renewed interest in reverse logistics with the first contribution to the topic beginning in the 1960s and 1970s. It has observed that in implementing an environmentally conscious program, companies typically reflect three phases: reactive, proactive and value seeking. Newly introduced environmental standard regulations usually force organizations to a reactive response to them. These organizations may examine environmental issues from time to time, but they do not actively pursue competitive advantage through environmental practices. Quite unlike reactive companies, proactive companies often implement reverse logistics programs such as recycling and reuse and even attempt to develop a competitive advantage by designing effective environmental programs. Such companies tend to manufacture products that generally satisfy customers' environmental concerns. On the other hand, value seeking companies incorporate environmental programs into their business strategy. Most companies in this phase have advanced environmental programs with extremely efficient reverse logistics systems.

Additionally, the reverse logistics concept seeks to evaluate the end of life of products and components. It is the driving force that sustains the circular flow of materials, as it promotes products' return to the supply chain for value extraction. The circular economy and reverse logistics concepts have a similar orientation, for example, both concepts are concerned about environmental and economic improvements. Nevertheless, the circular economy concept is more broadened than the reverse logistics concept since it not only concentrates on the reverse aspects but also on the forward aspects of the supply chain, which involves the newer materials. Reverse logistics is an integral part of the circular supply chain network and could have a significant economic impact since it generates about 2.15 billion euros in revenue through effective e-waste recycling. Hence, the ReSOLVE conceptual framework is characterized by the circular economy-based business model and development strategies. The ReSOLVE conceptual framework comprises of six strategies namely (i) Regenerate, (ii) Share, (iii) Optimize, (iv) Loop, (v) Virtualize and (vi) Exchange.

Furthermore, there is growing interest in the concept of circular economy over the years due to the need to reduce the use of natural resources by continually sustaining materials, resources and energy circulation in closed loop systems, which tends to

Sustainable Supply Chain Operations in the Circular Economy

result in the minimization in need for raw material inputs for manufacturing. The recent efforts of society to encourage the dimensions of sustainability, namely economic, environmental and social dimensions, have led to the beginning of the current transition. Likewise, the management of end of life products is critical to addressing the principles of circular economy. Several methods have been recommended to determine how introducing end of life products into a closed-loop production system could result in benefits to manufacturers. The most cost-effective practice is the products reuse, followed by refurbishing, recycling and remanufacturing. Products disposal is the least beneficial of all the options since no value is recovered when materials/products are landfilled. While remanufacturing and reuse operations prevail in closed-loop supply chains, recycling operations operate in open-loop systems where end of life products are delivered to different organizations from those that are developed originally.

Within this context, reverse logistics has become one of the significant competencies of the modern supply chain, where products not only flow from producers to customers (downstream) but also from customers to producers (upstream). Unlike traditional linear logistics from producer to customer, reverse logistics refers to the reverse flow that-combined with linear logistics – determines a closed-loop supply chain. Indeed, reverse logistics is regarded as a major issue for enterprises due to the necessity of managing every single stage in which products are handled and distributed toward producers, with multiple recovery options, which has led to a considerable number of uncertainties for companies. Reverse logistics is considered a key component of the circular economy since the circular economy would not be possible without the reverse flow-enabled by reverse logistics of end of life products and components essential for their recycling or regeneration.

6.4.1 The Role of Collaboration in Reverse Logistics

Intuitively, introducing reverse logistics requires a significant process, product and distribution channel redesigns that imply complex interactions between the firm and the other participants in the supply chain and value chain. Additionally, regulations increasingly induce firms to take responsibility for the packaging and products that reach their end of life to achieve environmental benefits. Nevertheless, implementing reverse logistics can help firms to achieve not only environmental goals but also economic goals. Indeed, reverse logistics can result in economic benefits. Such benefits include savings from the reuse of low-cost inputs at a fraction of the manufacturing costs from raw materials, the recovery of the value still integrated in the used product, the reduced transportation and disposal costs and the revenue generated by the sale of salvaged materials. Likewise, firms that aspire to innovate their logistics by re-designing their processes need to collaborate with both supply chain partners and non-industry partners. Collaboration may imply sharing decisions in planning and inventory management; information on market demand, in-transit items, inventory levels and other operational aspects and visibility on the entire remanufacturing process. Circular economy relies on collaboration between accountable stakeholders and this is enabled by close supply chain collaboration with partners within and beyond their immediate industrial boundaries, including suppliers, product designers and regulators. The importance of collaboration is also to increase transparency and create joint value internally within organizations. As such, logistics imposes inter-organizational collaboration since a firm cannot fully implement reverse logistics on its own.

Different types of collaboration (vertical and horizontal) relate with the reverse logistics as presented below.

6.4.1.1 Vertical Collaboration and Reverse Logistics

The collaboration between a firm and its customers and suppliers, jointly referred to as "vertical collaboration" and, in most cases, focuses on dyadic customer-supplier collaborations is considered very popular. From an institutional theory perspective, the pressure exerted by customers and suppliers, i.e., the market pressure has a coercive effect on firms that can bring them to introduce environmental innovations in general and to implement reverse logistics in particular. Furthermore, since regulations may induce competing firms to an excess of isomorphism and the corresponding loss of competitive advantage, vertical collaboration may contrast this phenomenon, offering opportunities to develop capabilities and differentiate themselves from the competitors in the way they approach reverse logistics. Additionally, customers and suppliers can be significant sources of critical resources based on the view of resource dependence theory. The collaboration with customers and suppliers benefits the firm by reducing transaction costs and increasing resource and knowledge sharing. Indeed, collaboration with new customers and suppliers can reduce the uncertainty in the operating environment, help to fill the demand for returned products and create value in closed-loop supply chains.

Furthermore, customers and suppliers may have established routines that can maximize the frequency and intensity of their socio-technical interactions, nurturing their absorptive capacity and, in turn, the effectiveness of their collaborations. Collaboration with customers in reverse logistics is considered imperative. On the one hand, customer groups encourage firms to reduce waste disposal and reuse parts from an environmental and social perspective. On the other hand, when customers do not feel prompted to comply with reverse logistics activities, the firm can experience significant losses. Indeed, since closed-loop supply chains are likely to suffer from uncertainty regarding the rate and quality of the returns, collaboration with customers can be a critical success factor. Likewise, collaboration with suppliers is the bottom line to reducing purchasing costs and addressing technical challenges. Collaboration with suppliers is a key facilitator in managing reverse logistics. For instance, the collaborative re-design of the packaging in a reverse logistic perspective can bring mutual benefits to both manufacturer and supplier. Suppliers can participate in re-designing the packaging to reduce material and recover products or parts, which customers can buy as service parts.

6.4.1.2 Horizontal Collaboration and Reverse Logistics

Horizontal collaboration, which usually involves two or more firms at the same level in the supply chain, may result in a joint venture through a reverse logistics alliance center. A firm constantly compares its strategies and practices with those of its best competitors treating them as benchmarks based on the institutional theory

Sustainable Supply Chain Operations in the Circular Economy

perspective. The resulting mimetic process takes an essential role in motivating a firm toward reverse logistics. Interestingly, firms not only imitate their most successful peers, but they also imitate those organizations with which they have social ties. As such, horizontal collaboration could lead to isomorphic responses for product recovery, which may increase economies of scale. Horizontal collaboration can also inhibit power imbalances among competitors since collaboratively shared information with a competitor can enhance recycling. Moreover, some wastes are not commercially viable in small volumes and teaming up among competitors when interacting with suppliers can open new opportunities. In a similar vein, recycling facilities that collaborated with one another rather than compete obtained better results than non-collaborating ones. Particularly, when the competitors share parts of the supply chain (e.g., wholesalers, logistic partners or distributors), then active collaboration among them can set standards and accelerate the implementation of reverse logistics in the industry. Additionally, competitors have the advantage of a common knowledge base and understanding of relevant technologies deriving from their positions in the same or similar markets enhancing collaborative innovation.

6.4.2 University-Industry Collaboration and Reverse Logistics

Universities and research institutions can shape decision-makers' professional perspectives in organizations by presenting economic and social benefits of reverse logistics in both professional (such as international conferences and publications) and educational settings (such as masters and doctoral programs). The corresponding normative processes that act as motivators can also trigger collaborations among firms and research institutions to implement the change. Indeed, the specialized scholars on the topic often own knowledge that can help firms identify the innovations they need to enable reverse logistics innovations. There have been multiple cases where firms collaborated with universities and research centers to acquire the knowledge needed to draw value from waste. The university-industry collaboration enhances learning. Likewise, the collaboration between universities and firms active in complementary fields is particularly successful. In fact, there is a huge need for interdisciplinary and trans-disciplinary collaboration among different disciplines including those pertaining to natural sciences, engineering sciences and management sciences.

6.5 SUSTAINABLE PACKAGING IN THE CIRCULAR ECONOMY

The packaging industry plays a significant role in the world economy, with a market value that has rapidly risen over the last few years and is projected to reach $1 trillion in 2020 from $839 billion in 2015. Despite the critical role that packaging play in the supply chain and in the economy, there is currently an absence of evident execution of Extended Producer Responsibility (EPR) policies with respect to packaging. Companies continually depend on packaging options that are considered to be environmentally degrading such as single-use plastics and multi-layered packaging coupled with the unsustainable disposal of packaging by end users which creates ecological strains. Additionally, with recent technological advancements and the emergence of global supply chains, the product is manufactured, assembled, packaged and finally sold in different global regions. This tends to increase the packaging requirements for handling raw materials, product components and parts and the final delivery to end users, which results in increasing the packaging waste created at each stage. Hence, such unsustainable packaging practices have become a threat to sustainable development goals and the ultimate progression of circular economy. In many countries around the globe, packaging accounts for 15–20% of total municipal waste. In particular, plastics packaging accounts for 50% plastics wastes globally, with Asian countries like China, Indonesia, Philippines, Vietnam and Thailand depositing more plastic waste into the ocean than the rest of the world. Ingestion of plastic kills around one million seabirds and 100,000 marine mammals every year, while plastic incineration releases toxic gases into the atmosphere that cause a host of human respiratory and kidney problems. Furthermore, data collected from FedEx, UPS and USPS show that 165 billion packages are shipped in the United States per year, which utilize up cardboard packaging made from approximately 1 billion trees.

Given the impact of packaging on several ecosystems, there is potential to explore its significance within the circular economy, which is essentially restorative and regenerative by design and purposes to extract much value from materials, products and components over a long period of time. In this context, the linear take-make-use-dispose packaging approach is becoming obsolete while more sustainable approaches or minimizing packaging utilization and packaging waste management through separation, collection, recovery and recycling are taking center stage. Likewise, the "New Plastics Economy Global Commitment" movement, started by the United Nations and Ellen MacArthur Foundation' has been signed by 250 organizations including major food and beverage companies, governments and packaging manufacturers and targets to remove and plastic waste and pollution at its source. More than 60 countries have also introduced bans and levies to curb the single-use plastic packaging waste (UNEP, 2018). Multi-national companies like Nestle and Danone are aiming to commercialize 100% bio-based recyclable bottles for still water. At the consumer end, there is an increasing transition to greener choices like bio-degradable and compostable packaging and an increasing demand for sustainable packaging for products. Consequently, the changing consumer behavior and the zero-packaging stores such as Nada in Vancouver and Original Unverpackt in Berlin have become popular with the aim of eradicating the need for grocery packaging encouraging consumers to bring their own containers.

Hence, the rising popularity on the negative impacts of packaging on the environment and society is attracting interest from various stakeholders in the supply chains. Sustainable innovation in industrial packaging along a supply chain necessitates collaboration among the supply chain partners coupled with the internal and external variations in companies within a supply chain in order to be actualized. Nevertheless, as packaging impacts supply chain costs such as transportation, warehousing, order processing and information carrying and lot sizing costs, operations and supply chain management research has basically considered packaging from an economic viewpoint to enable cost efficiency in supply chains. Indeed, the packaging industry significantly impacts on the costs and environmental efficiency of the overall supply chain beginning from packaging material procurement and packaging design and development phases to logistics and end of life handling phases. Nevertheless, with increasing pressure for supply chains to implement sustainable development, it becomes highly essential to have an in-depth understanding of the significance of packaging in developing a circular economy. Furthermore, a conceptual framework is presented herein for sustainable packaging the circular economy, which highlights the support of organizational theories along with circular economy elements, as shown in Figure 6.3. Through the use of the circular economy framework for sustainable packaging presented in Figure 6.3, a fully integrated supply chain can be realized in the circular economy. This will be able to highlight the synergy between the product, packaging, supply chain processes and their environmental implications in the design stage in a way to minimize re-handling and product return and reuse. As such, its associated packaging is strengthened at minimum environmental and societal hazards. The significance of the government in developing policies

Circular Economy Design
- Sustainable material selection
- Standardized product parts
- Design for ease of end of life sorting

New Business Models
- Supply chain integration
- Greener technologies
- Zero packaging business models

Renewable Energy and Resources

Emissions from logistics and processing

Eco-friendly design and manufacturing

Storage and distribution with minimized re-handling

Energy Recovery

Reverse flow of product

Consumption

Reverse flow of packaging for reuse/repurpose/remanufacture

Reduced Emissions and Zero Waste

Enablers and Favorable System Conditions
- Role of government agencies
- Access to incentives
- Supply chain collaboration

Reverse Cycles
- Risk management
- Logistics efficiency
- Return, reuse, recover, remanufacture, sorting, collection

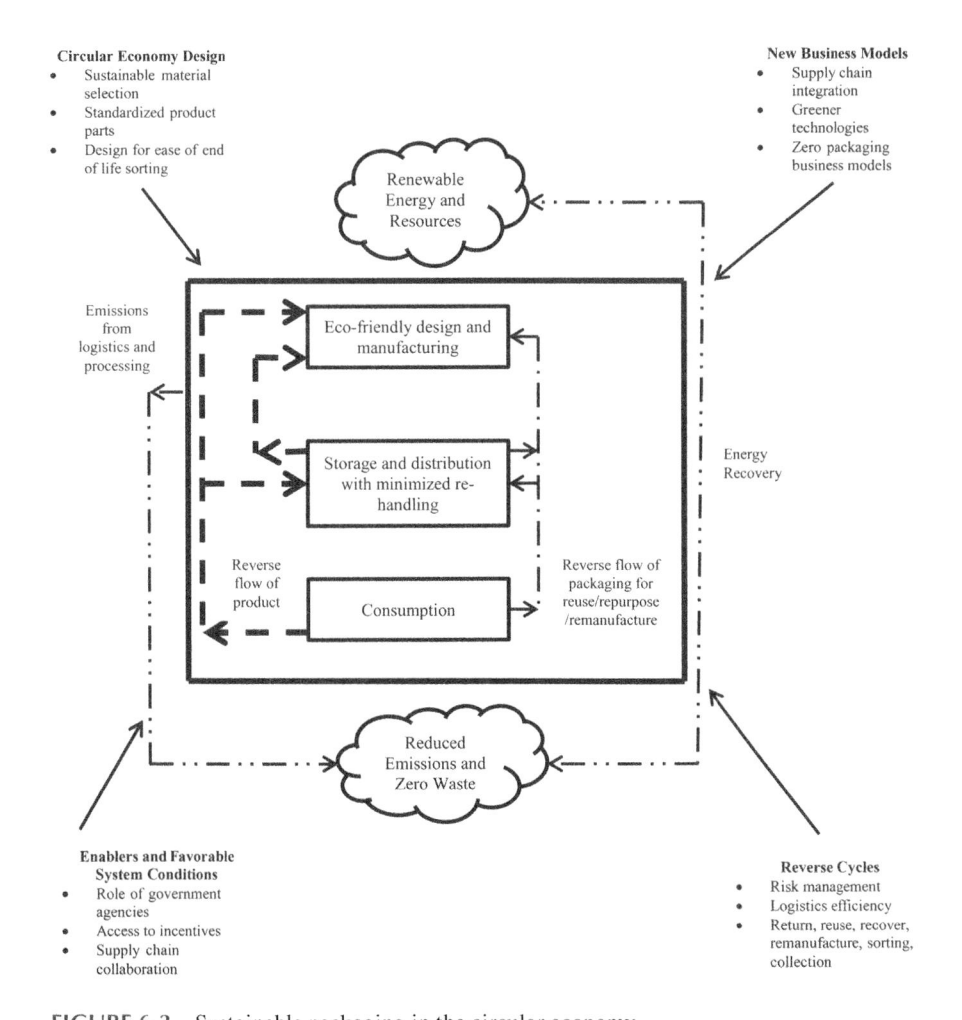

FIGURE 6.3 Sustainable packaging in the circular economy.

and implementing regulations and community awareness on packaging handling is, therefore, considered a critical enabler that can aid this is a self-sufficient and regenerative process.

Prior research studies in the domain of sustainable packaging fall within themes like adoption of sustainable packaging practices and the comparison and selection of eco-friendly packaging systems/alternatives. Such themes comprise the same principles that exist in the **circular economy design**. Moreover, there is an emerging holistic understanding of the potential driving factors, challenges/barriers and opportunities that exists in pursuit for a more sustainable packaging design, development and selection of eco-friendly packaging design solutions and packaging standardization. To the end goal of creating both environmental and economic benefits that will aid in the shift toward a circular economy. Likewise, many studies have addressed different **new business models** that range from the more traditional focus on integrating reduce/reuse/recycle strategies to redesigning supply chain nodes with zero-packaging flexibilities. Probably, with respect to a circular economy, the most researched area in sustainable packaging is that of **reverse cycles**. This is evidenced in focus on downstream recovery and logistics network structures and the "Reuse/Recycle/Remanufacture and/or Return of Packaging" theme that supports the recovery of packaging for continued usage within the supply chain presenting its positive influence on nature and the cash flows of the organizations. Furthermore, the circular economy element of **enablers and favorable systems** include government policies, collaboration between players, incentives to players in the supply chain to adopt circular economy strategies. Research studies that are categorized under "Adoption of sustainable packaging practices" and "Packaging waste management" have also advocated for the use of collaborative approaches among supply chain partners or incentive structures to promote adoption of sustainable strategies. This will enable reducing packaging waste generated and also enable/promote sustainable efficiency in the supply chain.

We then present some of the current and future research directions in the sustainable packaging domain with respect to three organizational theories, namely institutional theory, ecological modernization theory and stakeholder theory.

6.5.1 Use of Institutional Theory in Sustainable Packaging Research

Studies in the domain of sustainable packaging have provided insights on the coercive and normative drivers that are related to the institutional theory. Coercive drivers comprise of government regulations and legislations like EU directives on packaging and packaging wastes. Likewise, a prior published study investigated the normative drivers by consumers on organizations as presented by a survey. Nevertheless, there are still some significant questions that need to be analyzed using the institutional theory through future research directions, even though there are currently available published studies in the sustainable packaging domain. Government agencies have an option of implementing policies that nudge or boost organizations and the population to adopt a particular practice. In addition, there is practical insight on the role of government in advanced/developed economies through various directives and regulations on packaging waste. Hence, there is a huge need to provide insights on the questions that pertain to whether the government should choose a command-and-control approach to policy making or direct the organizations through encouragement to adopt sustainable packaging strategies, especially in developing countries. Furthermore, the kinds of incentives that are required by different supply chain partners to conform to a particular packaging strategy need to be studied. Moreover, in the era of globalization, how enterprises imitate strategies such as product and packaging stewardship from various countries operating under the same as well as different supply chains needs to be studied. Also, the kinds of mechanisms that accelerate the diffusion of such packaging strategies need to be studied. Additionally, with regard to normative drivers, how the differences in ethical and cultural values in different regions affect customer and market pressures to be sustainable for a company that serves different customer segments globally need to be investigated.

6.5.2 Use of Stakeholder Theory in Sustainable Packaging Research

Product packaging in the supply chain has resulted in quite a lot of negative externalities on the environment, and thus, a significant part of the literature on sustainable packaging has concentrated on the topic. Likewise, there have been attempts to study the societal aspects of packaging by different authors. Also, some past published research in extant literature evaluated packaging approaches through the role of stakeholder such as downstream retailers and upstream suppliers. Questions that pertain to the role of internal and external stakeholders take center stage during the transition from a take-make-dispose approach to a circular economy approach. As earlier mentioned, future research efforts in the sustainable packaging research domain need to emphasize on integrating the supply chain partners through collaboration and cooperation to achieve required sustainability goals. Hence, whether collaboration between different supply chain stakeholders such as suppliers, logistics players, recyclers and customers can enhance packaging design and minimize the need for packaging materials needs to be studied. Also, the kinds of incentive schemes that can be used to affect the stakeholders with non-conformance attitudes need to be addressed.

Additionally, whether facilities' sharing between competing supply chains such as warehouses, forward and reverse logistics facilities, sorting and recycling facilities of packaging leads to improved economic and environmental performance needs to be studied. If in affirmative, then what type of contracts and relationships need to be implemented between such organizations to aid the sharing process. Also, the integration of product and packaging decisions is considered to be required for an optimum packaging system and has been highlighted in available published studies. Therefore, the kinds of mechanisms and management strategies that are required within and outside an organization to encourage internal and external stakeholders to collaborate together rather than working independently need to be addressed. Besides the future research directions that are outlined from a review of available published studies, further evaluation of the research output on sustainable packaging research can lead to other research avenues. For instance, it should be investigated whether standardization of packaging within and across different supply chains can result in better organizational performance in terms of sustainability. Additionally, future research needs to study the acceptance of service-based packaging models (e.g., renting, leasing, etc.) rather than ownership of the packaging among customers in different countries. Furthermore, the kinds of training and education programs that are required to develop the mindset and skills of employees to think from a circular economy perspective while designing/procuring packaging need to be studied.

6.5.3 Use of Ecological Modernization Theory in Sustainable Packaging Research

The ecological modernization theory signifies that the only approach to solving environmental problems with continued industrialism is through the adoption of clean technologies, organizational change and development and implementation of critical innovations that are strengthened by appropriate regulations. Within the sustainable packaging contextual research, there have been issues that pertain to organizational change for sustainability. Also, there have been issues related to reduced end of life waste creation along supply chain strategic and operational improvements in the sustainable packaging literature. In a similar vein, comparison of packaging choices that save costs as well as reduce the negative environmental impacts, use of technology and so have been studied in extant literature. The environmental and social expectations for the packaging industrial sector are rapidly evolving and becoming popular since it is a fast expanding business sector as a result of varying product markets and dynamics of consumers. There are various kinds of packaging that have succeeded in disrupting the industry such as flexible packaging, smart packaging. The analysis of the sustainable packaging literature indicates that there is a huge need to be more focused on studying all the three dimensions of sustainability as well as the three layers of packaging (primary, secondary and tertiary layers) simultaneously. Hence, research questions to provide insight into the kind of packaging that should be adopted by all firms within a supply chain and which would not only reduce environmental impacts and economic costs but also raise the standard of living of the society should be addressed. Also, it should be studied to know how environmental policies which encourage better investment in public infrastructure for end of life packaging treatments can be enacted. Additionally, how the redesigning of the primary and/or secondary layer of packaging reduces the requirement for a tertiary layer of packaging should be studied.

Furthermore, ecological modernization theory and circular economy factors raise issues for future research such as: analyzing how organizations respond to technological disruptions such as biomimicry, big data analytics, blockchain, etc., in packaging. Also, the feasibility of applying digital technologies such as the internet of things for managing packaging returns in developing nations and their underdeveloped counterparts should be studied. Additionally, how packaging innovations can be tailored to fit the industrial sectors like chemical, pharmaceutical, e-commerce and automotive that are generally regarded as environmentally intensive coupled with their appropriate industry-specific packaging rules to minimize waste from these industrial sectors. Furthermore, it should be studied the type of industrial sectors that can collaborate harmoniously for implementing industrial symbiosis with regard to packaging materials and wastes. The advancement of the circular economy is geared toward nudging future research and practitioner efforts in packaging practices along the supply chain network.

6.6 PRICING CIRCULAR PRODUCTS

Circular products are typically defined as having one or two important features. Either they are produced with recycled materials (and thus help close the production loop), or they have an extended life cycle because they are more durable or can be resold as second-hand.

6.6.1 CONSUMERS' WILLINGNESS TO PAY FOR PRODUCTS WITH ENVIRONMENTAL ATTRIBUTES

The recent adoption of the circular economy paradigm by the EU Commission highlights consumers' critical role in advancing circular economy objectives and expanding markets for circular products. Willingness to pay (WTP) is defined as the maximum price a buyer accepts to pay for a given number of goods or services and is a direct measure of consumers' real valuation of the product for his utility. It differs from a products' actual price because WTP does not account for the amount of money required by the seller to conclude the transaction. Consumers' WTP may change with variations in product features or qualities. If consumers value these additional features or qualities, they tend to believe that product utility is greater and so they are willing to pay more. In some instances, additional features or qualities may relate to a product's environmental attributes tends to improve consumers' perceived value of the product. The relation was confirmed for different types of products such as packaging, Energy Star air-conditioner and eco-labeled food, remanufactured domestic apps and eco-friendly t-shirts. Improved perceived value is derived from several factors. In some instances, it relates to consumer expectations that the product impacts higher intrinsic value based on how the product was produced because of fair labor practices or sustainable production processes and these practices are consistent with consumers' personal beliefs and values.

In other instances, consumers' perceived value from products with fewer environmental impacts may derive from stronger expectations for quality and improved health. In other cases, research scholars have found that consumers are willing to pay more for products just because they offer fewer environmental impacts. This relation was confirmed for different types of products such as cars and highly efficient white goods and green food. Furthermore, it has been found that WTP premium price positively influence the intention to buy green packaged products of Indian young consumers. The rationale behind it is that since Indian consumers are price sensitive and are not willing to pay for more product attributes, it is relevant to know whether consumers are agreeing to pay a premium price for eco-friendly packaging. Nevertheless, the expectation is that these relationships will differ for "circular" products, where environmental attributes might be insufficient at increasing WTP because the perceived quality attributes are diminished.

6.6.2 Consumers' Willingness to Pay for "Circular" Products

Circular products are created in a way that optimizes resource efficiency. Resource efficiency is optimized by minimizing the environmental impact of the product lifecycle. This is achieved by revising the traditional product design process, which is defined as a linear mode – consisting of production, consumer use and disposal. Circular products modify these design processes in two ways. The first involves using disposed products as inputs in manufacturing processes toward the creation of a new product. This "closed loop" design model divers waste that otherwise would end up in landfill. Examples of circular products include the production of goods that are made from recycled materials, such as compost and animal feed that is created from organic waste or garments made from fiber scraps or recycled plastic bottles.

The second type of circular product involves design processes that extend a product's life cycle. Here, products are developed in ways that enhance their durability or incorporate features that make them more easily reused, remanufactured or refurbished. By extending the product life cycle, good maintain their original purpose but in use for a longer period of time before they are ultimately land-filled. Examples include reused or second-hand products. Other examples include remanufactured and refurbished products that are upcycled at the end of their life cycle by upgrading and/or partially modifying them prior to re-entering the market. Regardless of their form, circular products – like other products that have positive environmental attributes – may improve consumers' perceived value of the product. This is because circular products may provide higher intrinsic value by diverting waste from landfills and these practices are congruent with some consumers' personal beliefs and values.

However, some consumers may assign a negative quality value to circular products, despite their environmental attributes. In such an instance, consumers are willing to pay *less* for circular products than new products that are made from virgin materials. Generally, the recycled and reused/second-hand products represent the most significant quota of circular products in the market, and consumers are thus more familiar with them. Consumers' negative quality value that is derived from circular products relates to the fact that recycled inputs are produced from post-consumer waste that is introduced into a manufacturing process. Generally, this waste requires reprocessing before it can be utilized in another product. For instance, some circular clothing is made from plastic bottles, which are reprocessed to create plastic fibers. Because of their reprocessing, these fibers may be perceived as being weaker or contaminated by their original productive use.

Similarly, related to goods that are reused or second-hand, the products maintain their original form and use, although they may be improved slightly before they are resold. For example, related to clothing, consumers may perceive that second-hand clothing may have a shorter product life because the fibers are more stressed than would be the case for a new product. Additionally, consumers may perceive that second-hand clothing may have been contaminated during their prior use and thus have lower quality expectations for these garments.

Contamination perceptions can derive from a real or imagined change in an object's state. Related to clothing, real changes include stains or imperfections found on a used garment or impurities or imperfections detected in a recycled one (e.g., color irregularities, textile look and touch-feel, etc.). Imagined changes derive from consumers' metal associations. Negative mental associations include greater perceived risks for personal health. They also relate to consumers' perceptions of reduced hygiene and feelings of disgust for something that could have been contaminated by pathogens because the circular product has been used by somebody else and/or for other uses. Disgust tends to increase as the object becomes more intimate (e.g., closer to bodily intake) because of the higher direct exposure to the potential pathogens.

In other instances, consumers' contamination perception may devalue a circular product because the product has been touched or used by another person. This feeling is likely to be stronger for garments because consumers perceive that they still harbor the essence of their previous owner. This feeling is probably stronger for second-hand garments; however, it can also attain clothes made from recycled material when the recycled materials clearly derive from a second-hand garment. Moreover, used garments retain their original form and involve few (if any) modifications prior to re-entering the market. Consumers of used circular products, therefore, are likely to experience dissonance that diminishes their perceived quality value. Dissonance is the state of mind that holds opposing and even irreconcilable ideas at the same time. Dissonance is due to consumers' negative perceptions about wearing second-hand clothes and relates to fear of contamination and personal space invasion. In this case, the positive environmental value of the circular product cannot outweigh the negative perceived risk of purchasing product that may be of inferior quality. This diminished value is expected to be greater than for used products because they retain their original form and so consumers can more readily identify them as being used.

By contrast, for remanufactured circular products, invasion of personal space may be lessened. The reproduction process, i.e., the industrial process involved in recycling and the material that result in the recycled product, may help consumers create cognitive distance between the recycled product and the fact that it is made from used inputs. If so, it should be expected that there will be a higher devalue for second-hand garments than for garments made from recycled material.

In fact, two factors are considered highly significant to the willingness of consumers to pay for "Circular" products. The factors are presented below:

6.6.2.1 Environmental Information and Consumers' Willingness to Pay for "Circular" Products

Absent or vague environmental information can limit consumers' decision-making process and reduce their purchases of products with environmental attributes. Environmental conscious consumers cannot select the most environmentally friendly product alternative if they are not provided with any information about products' environmental attributes. By contrast, environmental information can influence consumers to purchase products with environmental attributes and fewer negative impacts. This is because providing consumers with environmental information positively increases their awareness and enhances their perceptions about the effectiveness of their purchasing decision. In particular, the provision of information increases consumers' perceived behavioral control (PBC) and perceived consumer effectiveness (PCE). PCE is a measure of the subject's judgment in the ability of individual consumers to affect environmental resource problems. PCE reflects a consumer's beliefs in being able to attain outcomes in a particular sphere of activity. When applied to green purchasing it measures consumer's perception of being able to obtain a positive environmental impact through the purchase. In the case of large-scale environmental issues, such as climate change, the large number of people involved in the problem negatively affects single consumer's PCE. The provision of clear information on which is the environmental attribute of the product and its positive impacts on the natural environment thus reinforces consumers' PCE. In fact, it helps them in quantifying the real contribution they are making to environmental protection through their purchase, reinforcing their PCE.

Additionally, the provision of environmental information allows consumers to recognize a product's positive environmental virtues. It also strengthens consumers' attitudes toward products with stronger environmental attributes, especially when the positive virtues are quantified. When purchasing these products, consumers often experience a positive feeling of "doing the right thing", making a positive contribution to common societal challenges. Providing consumers with information about a product's environmental virtues, therefore, allows them to feel more confident about the contribution they are making, thus reinforcing their PCE in line with their values and beliefs. For these reasons, the provision of environmental information can enhance consumers' perceived product value and their WTP.

Similarly, the consumers' WTP for circular products also increases when provided with information about these products' environmental virtues. However, in this case, the higher WTP for the environmental attributes is counter-balances by consumers' lower quality perceptions associated with the fact that these products are recycled or second-hand. The net effect is that consumers' overall WTP for a circular product is still lower than their WTP for the conventional alternative, even if it is higher than if no environmental information was provided.

Additionally, it has been emphasized by various research scholars on how distrust is a barrier that prevents consumers from purchasing products with environmental attributes, even when these consumers are predisposed to purchase the product. Distrust neutralizes consumers' positive effect and decreases a product's perceived value because decision-making risk is introduced and consumers worry that they are not getting their money's worth. Likewise, consumers elevate their trust for a product's environmental attributes if the product's environmental information is certified by an independent third party. This is because independent third-party verification is an important information cue that enhances the consumers' perceived legitimacy of product claims. Verification lowers consumers' perceived risk of purchasing products with environmental attributes, thus reassuring them that the product offers intrinsic value and meets their quality expectations.

Third-party verification is therefore likely to enhance consumers' WTP for products that have environmental attributes. In relation to circular products, third-party verification may help to diminish the consumers' negative perceptions about recycled and second-hand products. As a consequence, a higher WTP is expected for circular products when the environmental information is provided by a third-party independent verifier.

6.6.2.2 Environmental Concern

Environmental concern plays an important role in shaping consumers' attitudes and influencing consumers' purchasing choices. Consumers' motivations and knowledge influence how they interpret, realize and analyze any attempt of persuasion deriving from product labeling. Consumers with high concern tend to have greater knowledge about environmental issues and should be able to recognize and positively interpret a product's environmental claims based on functional information. Low concerned consumers tend to develop their opinions to visual ass paying low attention to additional information. Moreover, they may consider a green claim based on specific and quantitative information as exaggerated and, therefore, as a form of green-washing. An increase of WTP requires an additional effort in a consumer that shall solve a potential conflict between financial and environmental logic. Basically, the environmental benefits derived from the purchase of a second-hand product are less evident because a few consumers think about the avoided adverse environmental impacts from the production of a brand new product by purchasing a second-hand product. So, in the case of manifest environmental attribute, the effect of additional information on environmental benefit should not be influent on WTP since the role of high environmental concern should work already when basic information on the presence of recycled material in the product is provided. On the contrary, in the case of hidden environmental attribute, by providing additional information, low environmental consumers could overcome an initial skepticism and increase their ability to recognize and interpret the environmental benefit related to a product.

6.6.3 MODEL FORMULATION FOR PRICING AND RECYCLING INVESTMENT DECISIONS

In this section, since we are considering the impact of recycling on pricing and recycling investment decisions of a firm, we then define the following dynamics:

- **Recycling rate:** How recycling rate changes over time. Greenness refers to the recycling rate of a product made by a firm.
- **Demand:** How demand changes with prices and recycling rate.
- **Production cost:** How production cost changes with the recycling rate.
- **Profit:** Combining the previous two dynamics, how price changes with price and recycling rate are determined.

We write the inter-temporal profit of the firm, and then we examine its dynamic optimization problem.

6.6.3.1 Recycling

Consumers are increasingly more environmentally conscious, resulting in firms investing in greener processes like a higher recycling rate. In other words, a higher recycling rate (the fraction of recycled resources) used in the production process satisfies green consumers. Investments allow continuous enhancement of recycling over time. Yet, the recycling rate, like any quality process, may degrade slowly over time if not maintained. Given that the recycling rate is the fraction of recycled resources used – due to inventions, new developments, technological progress, regulation, etc. – over time, the notion of what constitutes a recycled product changes (compared to other firms and underlying standards) leading to a natural degradation of a firm's recycling rate if it stops investing in its greenness. Relative greenness is popular in published studies available in extant literature but not explicit as usually two products are used and the greenness of one product is normalized to zero. For example, in Denmark, due to the operating conditions and requirements for the operation of car-dismantling companies, the firms that generate recycled products fundamentally changed from the mid-1990s to the mid-2000s. From a modeling perspective, the degradation of the recycling rate equates to the degradation/depreciation of the model's state variable, an approach commonly used in the green economics literature. Thus, the recycling rate increases with investment and decreases otherwise.

With a general function, we develop a model for the relationship between recycling rate investment, $u(t) \geq 0$, and the corresponding recycling rate, $r(t) \in [0,1]$. Investment expense in recycling, $u(t)$, recycling rate, $r(t)$ are control and state variables, respectively. The recycling dynamics indicates that for all t in $(0,T)$ is stated as:

$$\frac{dr(t)}{dt} = R(u(t), r(t)), \text{ with } r(0) = r_0 \qquad (6.1)$$

We assume the recycling dynamics function, (1), $R: R^+ \times [0,1] \to R$ to be twice continuously differentiable.

Integrating (1) related the (cumulative level of) recycling rate to the flow of current investment in greater recycling $r(t) = r_0 + \int_0^t R(u(s), r(s)) ds$. Hereafter and when no confusion exists, we omit notational arguments for simplicity. Especially, we often omit the temporal notation in subsequent equations.

Investment, u, increases the recycling rate, r, with diminishing returns. Also, investment loses its effectiveness over time, translating into autonomous decay, $u \geq 0, r \in [0,1]$;

$$\frac{\partial R}{\partial u} > 0, \frac{\partial^2 R}{\partial u^2} < 0, \frac{\partial R}{\partial r} \leq 0 \qquad (6.2)$$

A parametric example of the structural formulation (6.1) together with (6.2) is $\frac{dr}{dt} = \gamma u^{\frac{1}{\gamma}}(1-r) - \delta r, r(0) = r_0$ in $[0,1]$, in which the recycling rate increases with the efficiency of the investment, $\gamma > 1$, and depreciates at a constant proportional rate, $\delta > 0$. Its dynamics are similar to model with $\frac{dx}{dt} = \gamma u(1-x) - \delta x$, where the change of the rate of sales depends on the advertising effort u and the fractional market potential $x, x \in [0,1]$.

6.6.3.2 Demand

Here, we look at the demand of consumers. The majority of related literature use a linear demand function of price and product greenness such as, $p \geq 0, r \in [0,1]$,

$$D = a_0 - a_1 p + a_2 r \qquad (6.3)$$

Sustainable Supply Chain Operations in the Circular Economy

with $a_0 > 0$ the market potential, $a_1 > 0$ the sensitivity of demand to price, and $a_2 > 0$ the sensitivity of demand to product greenness. We then generalize the parametric demand function to a structural demand function.

The price $p \geq 0$ is a control variable. The price does not influence a state variable, making price *a static* control variable. The (current) demand function $D: R^+ \times [0,1] \to R^+$ is twice continuously differentiable. The demand, D, depends on the price, p, and the recycling rate, r, which is a proxy for the greenness of the product. Consumers prefer products with higher recycling rates, meaning consumers value the environment and purchase products that reflect their values. Consequently, investment indirectly affects future demand via the recycling rate. Formally, we write the demand as, $p \geq 0, r \in [0,1]$,

$$D = D(p,r) \tag{6.4}$$

The *direct price effect on demand*, the *direct recycling effect on demand*, and the *cross effect of price and recycling on demand* are given by $\frac{\partial D}{\partial p}, \frac{\partial D}{\partial r}$ and $\frac{\partial^2 D}{\partial p \partial r}$, respectively.

Demand decreases with the price and increases with product greenness, known as recycling rate. Further, customers are marginally less sensitive to price with greener products. We account for three demand assumptions above with $p \geq 0, r \in [0,1]$,

$$\frac{\partial D}{\partial p} < 0, \frac{\partial D}{\partial r} \geq 0, \frac{\partial^2 D}{\partial p \partial r} \leq 0 \tag{6.5}$$

To repeat, in this model, product greenness is proxied by the recycling rate, r. Also, the demand function is assumed not to be "too" convex in the price, $p \geq 0, r \in [0,1]$,

$$2 - D \frac{\frac{\partial^2 D}{\partial p^2}}{\frac{\partial D^2}{\partial p}} > 0 \tag{6.6}$$

This assumption is technical and useful for the maximization of profit; it guarantees a unique maximum of the profit function, which will be defined later. Such an assumption of demand convexity is popular in dynamic pricing literature using structural demand functions. Equations (6.5) and (6.6) are satisfied with the linear demand function (6.3) and the Cobb-Douglas (iso-elastic) demand function $D = a_0 p^{-a_1} r^{a_2}$ with $a_0, a_1, a_2 > 0$.

6.6.3.3 Production Cost

Until production cost of virgin resources $c_v \geq 0$ and unit production cost of recycled resources $c_r \geq 0$. We assume that virgin resources are more costly than recycled material, $c_v > c_r$. This assumption characterizes, for instance, the case of carbon fiber and of wood-plastic composites. That's also the case when virgin resources are taxed by administrative authorities to make it more expensive than recycled material. Plus, recycling provides an alternative source of material when few virgin resources are available. For completeness, we explore numerically the alternative case of recycled resources being more expensive than virgin resources, $c_r \geq c_v$. The firm uses a mixture of recycled and virgin resources to make a product. The fraction of recycled material used is the recycling rate, r, and the corresponding fraction of virgin resources used $1 - r$. The unit cost is, therefore, the weighted average $rc_r + (1-r)c_v$. As virgin resources are more expensive than recycled one, $c_v > c_r$, we normalize $c_r = 0$. Consequently, the unit production cost simplifies to $(1 - r)c_v$.

6.6.3.4 Profit

The current profit function $\pi : R^+ \times R^+ \times [0,1] \to R$ is assumed twice continuously differentiable. The profit per unit is the retail price minus the cost per unit, $p - (1-r)c_v$. The firm sets the recycling investment, u, before demand is realized, and thus is a fixed cost. Putting the fixed and variable costs together, we obtain the profit function, revenues less costs, $p, u \geq 0, r \in [0,1]$,

$$\pi(p(t), u(t), r(t)) = \left[p(t) - (1 - r(t))c_v\right] \cdot D(p(t), r(t)) - u(t) \quad (6.7)$$

6.6.3.5 Firm's Optimization Problem

The firm maximizes the inter-temporal profit (or present value of the profit stream) over the planning horizon by simultaneously choosing the investment in recycling and pricing policies, accounting for the dynamics of the recycling rate. For simplicity, the salvage value of the recycling rate is null. The interest rate is $\alpha \in R^+$ and the objective function of the firm is:

$$\max_{u(\cdot), p(\cdot) \geq 0} \int_0^T e^{-\alpha t} \pi(p(t), u(t), r(t)) dt \quad (6.8a)$$

Subject to

$$\frac{dr(t)}{dt} = R(u(t), r(t)), \text{ with } r(0) = r_0 \quad (6.8b)$$

We then present the conditions derived from solving the mathematical program (6.8).[1] In the dynamic setting, with continuous-time, t, there is a potential unique value of the co-state variable $\lambda(t)$ (the counterpart of the Lagrange multipliers in the dynamic setting) for each time t. The Hamiltonian, H, of (6.8) with the current-value ad-joint variable (or shadow price) $\lambda(t)$ for recycling dynamics is[1]:

$$H(p, u, r, \lambda) = \left[p - (1 - r)c_v\right]D(p, r) - u + \lambda R(u, r) \quad (6.9)$$

The Hamiltonian, H, measures the inter-temporal profit, summing the current profit, $[p - (1-r)c_v]D(p,r) - u$, and the future profit, λR. We confine our interest to interior

---

[1] Schlosser R., Chenavaz R.Y., and Dimitrov S. (2021). Circular economy: joint dynamic pricing and recycling investments, International Journal of Production Economics, *236*, 108117.

solutions for u and p, assuming their existence. The Hamiltonian, H, is assumed strictly concave in investment, u, and price, p. It immediately follows that all optimal decisions must satisfy the first- and second-order conditions of the Hamiltonian Eqs. (6.10a)–(6.10e). Plus, following the maximum principle, we derive Eq. (6.10f). not that all conditions for $t \in (0,T)$.

Hence, we obtain

$$\frac{\partial H}{\partial u} = 0 \Rightarrow \frac{\partial R}{\partial u} = \frac{1}{\lambda}, \qquad (6.10a)$$

$$\frac{\partial H}{\partial u} = 0 \Rightarrow p - (1-r)c_v = -\frac{D}{\frac{\partial D}{\partial p}}, \qquad (6.10b)$$

$$\frac{\partial^2 H}{\partial u^2} < 0 \Rightarrow \lambda \frac{\partial^2 R}{\partial u^2} < 0 \qquad (6.10c)$$

$$\frac{\partial^2 H}{\partial p^2} < 0 \Rightarrow 2 - D\frac{\frac{\partial^2 D}{\partial p^2}}{\frac{\partial D^2}{\partial p}} > 0 \qquad (6.10d)$$

$$\frac{\partial^2 H}{\partial p^2}\frac{\partial^2 H}{\partial p^2} - \left(\frac{\partial^2 H}{\partial u \partial p}\right)^2 > 0 \Rightarrow -\lambda \frac{\partial^2 R}{\partial u^2}\left(2 - D\frac{\frac{\partial^2 D}{\partial p^2}}{\frac{\partial D^2}{\partial p}}\right) > 0, \qquad (6.10e)$$

$$\frac{d\lambda}{dt} = \alpha\lambda - \frac{\partial H}{\partial r} \Rightarrow \frac{d\lambda}{dt} = \left(\alpha - \frac{\partial R}{\partial r}\right)\lambda - c_v D - (p - 1(1-r)c_v)\frac{\partial D}{\partial r} \qquad (6.10f)$$

with the transversality condition $\lambda(T) = 0$.

6.7 SUMMARY

The circular economy focuses on protecting the environment and conserving resources and hence, significantly supporting green supply chain management implementation. Therefore, within the circular economy, green supply chain management should integrate the 3R principles of reuse, reduction and recycling in each supply chain cycle to achieve the goals of economic and environmental performance improvements.

Reverse logistics is regarded as a major issue for enterprises due to the necessity of managing every single stage in which products are handled and distributed toward producers, with multiple recovery options, which has led to a considerable number of uncertainties for companies.

A circular economy relies on collaboration between accountable stakeholders and this is enabled by close supply chain collaboration with partners within and beyond their immediate industrial boundaries, including suppliers, product designers and regulators.

The importance of collaboration is also to increase transparency and create joint value internally within organizations. The collaboration between a firm and its customers and suppliers, jointly referred to as "vertical collaboration" and, in most cases, focuses on dyadic customer-supplier collaborations, is considered very popular.

The packaging industry significantly impacts on the costs and environmental efficiency of the overall supply chain beginning from packaging material procurement and packaging design and development phases to logistics and end of life handling phases.

Circular products typically are defined as having one or two important features. Either they are produced with recycled materials (and thus help close the production loop), or they have an extended life cycle because they are more durable or can be resold as second-hand.

WTP is defined as the maximum price a buyer accepts to pay for a given number of goods or services and is a direct measure of consumers' real valuation of the product for his utility. It differs from a products' actual price because WTP does not account for the amount of money required by the seller to conclude the transaction.

Third-party verification is likely to enhance consumers' WTP for products that have environmental attributes. In relation to circular products, third-party verification may help to diminish the consumers' negative perceptions about recycled and second-hand products. As a consequence, a higher WTP is expected for circular products when the environmental information is provided by a third-party independent verifier.

DISCUSSION AND REVIEW QUESTIONS

1. Define green supply chain management in the context of circular economy.
2. Mention some of the supply chain operations that integrated with the circular economy.
3. What is reverse logistics and why is it considered important in the circular economy?
4. Discuss the role of collaboration in reverse logistics.
5. What is sustainable packaging?
6. Mention some of the theories that are considered useful in sustainable packaging research.
7. What is a circular product?
8. Can you differentiate between products with environmental attributes and circular products?
9. Explain the consumer's WTP for circular products.
10. Mention and explain the factors that considered important in the consumer's WTP for circular products.

SUGGESTED MATERIALS FOR FURTHER READING

Dussimon, K. (2017). *The world of packaging.* Checkout.
Economic Times (2017). November 16. Changing world of packaging: Past, present and the future, *The Economic Times*, 1–24. Retrieved from https://economictimes.indiatimes.com/tetra-pak/tetra-pak-articles/changing-world-of-packaging-past-oresent-and-the-future/articleshow/61101823.cm.

Ellen MacArthur Foundation (2015). Towards a circular economy: Business rationale for an accelerated transition, https://www.ellenmacarthufoundation.org/assets/downloads/publications/TCE_Ellen-MacArthur-Foundation_26-Nov-2015.pdf.
FoodBev (2018). November. New research reveals consumer demand for green packaging, 1–2. Retrieved from https://www.foodbev.com/news/new-research-reveals-consumer-demand-for-green-packaging/.
GAIA (2018). A burning plastic: Incineration causes air pollution, Dioxin Emissions Cost, Retrieved October 10, 2021, from https://www.no-burn.org/burning-plastic-incineration-causes-air-pollution-dioxin-emissions-cost-overruns/.
Original Unverpackt (2018). Retrieved October 10, 2021, from https://original-unverpackt.de/.
Peters, A. (2018). April. Can online retail solve its packaging problem?: FastCompany, vols 1–8, Retrieved from https://www.fastcompant.com/40560641/can-online-retail-solve-its-packaging-problem.
Rogoff, M. (2014). *Solid waste recycling and processing, Planning of solid waste recycling facilities and programs* 2ed. Elsevier.
Smirthers Pira Group (2016). Packaging material outlooks – Towards a $1 Trillion milestone 2020, Retrieved October 10, 2021. http://www.smitherspira.com/news/2016/februart/global-packaging-material-outlooks.
UNEP (2018). Single-use plastics: A road map for sustainability, Retrieved from https://wedocs.unep.org/bitstream/handle/20.500.11822/25496/singleUsePlastic_sustainability.pdf?

Part 4

7 Facilitation of Circular Supply Chains with Digital Technologies

7.1 INTRODUCTION

Recently, a significant focus is given on disruptive technologies such as Industry 4.0 and circular economy. In fact, within the last decade, many companies have begun exploring how to use digital technologies like internet of things (IoT), big data analytics, cloud computing and artificial intelligence (AI) in the management of their supply chains. In the era of digitalization, digital technologies, including the IoT, cloud computing, blockchain, additive manufacturing (3D printing) and big data analytics, are the most commonly cited in the literature. Many of these digital technologies are being piloted, deployed or implemented by companies in other to improve their data-processing capabilities and their supply chain management and control activities. The deepening of technology implementation in supply chain systems has been disruptive to traditional operational methods in areas such as product development, production efficiency and customer service. Indeed, digital technologies can aid to realizing connectivity, communication and automation. As such, these technologies are regarded as promising means to improve supply chain functions; for instance, IoT has been applied in factories to monitor production operations and also trace logistics processes. Additionally, the real-time data sourced from IoT devices are usually combined with the data from other supply chain functions and this has the potential to actualize critical business value through integrating big data analytics and AI.

Furthermore, digital technologies are not only revamping operations and products but also transforming supply chains, revitalizing business models and influencing industrial structures. In fact, companies can benefit from the integration of digital technologies for a better forecast, resource allocation optimization and supplier relationship management. Moreover, the improvement of circular economy capabilities of various companies can be influenced through supply chain relationship management and sustainable supply chain design, thereby encouraging circular economy transitions in their underlying supply chains. The circular economy concept has become integral to the main business agenda and firms have begun to realize the urgency of the development of circular strategies due to stakeholders' requirements coupled with social and environmental aspects. In a similar vein, the goal of sustainable supply chains is to meet stakeholder specifications regarding environmental practices while achieving anticipated economic performance and maintaining elevated social and ethical standards.

In addition, the production and consumption systems are designed and evaluated using sustainability performance such as resources and energy usage efficiency, manufacturing effectiveness and reliability, transportation and consumption carbon footprints, waste management and reverse logistics variations. Companies have also developed and implemented performance measures to evaluate supply chain sustainability by managing sustainable practices and their consequent related circular strategies. Hence, the ultimate goal is not just to improve environmental performance and social benefits but also to actualize increased competitiveness through implementing digital solutions in the circularity concept. For instance, IoT is deployed to measure the fill level of waste bins while optimizing routes for scrap metal bins' transportation as an extension of a Smart Waste Management platform that provides waste monitoring and optimizes supply chain procedures related to resource allocation and planning. Within the automotive sector, the implementation of 6R's (recycle, reuse, reduce, refuse, rethink and repair) practices, the eco-design of products and life cycle assessment and the supply chain digitization are the top raked propositions to overcome the challenges to supply chain sustainability. Additionally, within the food industry, IoT supply chain solutions enable sustainability and have the ability to reduce waste generation, costs, emissions and social impacts. Thus, effective circular supply chains are the "end goal" for sustainable supply chains of the future.

7.2 DIGITAL-ENABLED STRATEGIES FOR CIRCULAR SUPPLY CHAINS

Nowadays, globalization has increased the complexity of supply chains with greater interdependence and interconnections than previously. This calls for investments in information and communication technologies in developing digital-enabled strategies for maintaining and enabling interdependence and interconnection. For instance, effective supply chain management relies heavily on the utilization of well-analyzed data and also, data-driven decisions lead to better results in complex business environments. Moreover, since the primary goal of organizations is to maintain and strengthen their core competencies in a dynamic market environment, companies are required to maintain interactions with their partners through digital supply chains for improved operational efficiency. The introduction of information and communication technologies in supply chain management can significantly improve process-oriented performance, reduce energy consumption and provide supply chains with a ubiquitous information infrastructure.

Traditionally, the literature on information technologies has considered four critical measures for IT-enabled supply chain systems, namely: *cost, flexibility, time* and *quality*. Although these measures are widely agreed by various authors, other critical requirements must also be taken into consideration when referring to information flow across supply chains like *accuracy, visibility, data volume, reliability* and *availability*. *Flexibility* can ensure that companies will succeed in dynamically changing environments. There are two important information requirements, namely *reliability* and *visibility*. On the one hand, *visibility* also referred to as *availability* is an important information attribute that can be achieved through an appropriate coverage service, thereby enabling product traceability and tracking. The absence of visibility is believed to result in costly administrative decision-making processes. The effectiveness of such decision-making processes is increased when

Facilitation of Circular Supply Chains with Digital Technologies 131

vertical information systems exchange information efficiently so that resource costs can be minimized. Information *reliability* is needed to improve information flows by removing non-value-adding activities. Likewise, the *availability* of relevant, accurate and timely data from external parties is defined as an attribute of success. *Data volume* is another significant factor since different data sources are required to transmit information using various formats and protocols, thereby leading to an unprecedented data volume and variety across the supply chain. Data generation is predicted to reach zettabyte per year in a few years and as such, these massive data volumes should be processed at high velocity in real-time using data analytics to minimize costs related to decision-making approaches. Due to the added value associated with the data, there is a huge necessity for high technological capabilities for the management of these data. Additionally, *timeliness* is believed to be the attribute with the greatest impact on improved supply chain performance, while cost plays a critical role during information management in supply chains for increased competitiveness, with the potential to predict or react quickly to changes also giving companies a competitive advantage.

Furthermore, information technologies can be utilized in supply chains to reduce information asymmetries and actualize effective supply chain management. In fact, there has been an unprecedented application of emerging information technologies such as AI, big data analytics, blockchain, machine learning, etc., for developing digital-enabled strategies in various domains. This has ushered in the digital era – a new industrial transformation – that has resulted in some potential benefits. Particularly, within the manufacturing context, this new era of industrial revolution has triggered the development of smart factories, intelligent manufacturing system architectures and intelligent manufacturing technology systems. Various researchers have provided perspectives on the application of digital technologies for improving quality, efficiency, cost, customer service and overall manufacturing competitiveness. Likewise, the digital transformation has been felt across supply chains as well as resulted in facilitating the implementation of digital supply chains – this is the key to undergoing this rapid revolution.

7.2.1 Defining Digital Supply Chain

The digital supply chain is defined as an intelligent, value-added, novel network that utilizes new approaches, specifically, digital transformation with technologies to create competitive value and network effects. This is highly significant as market forecasts indicate that 76% of global population have access to the internet and about 50% are actively using social media features. For instance, social media features using pictures and videos have a significant effect on alerting the masses on malpractices and other sharp practices. Likewise, the internet of things (IoT) is becoming increasingly popular and over 26 billion "things" under IoT are predicted to become operational. Also, 90% of internet users are online buyers and about 43% apply advanced big data technologies. In essence, digital supply chain is an intelligent best-fit technological system that is based on the capability to store massive data and excellent cooperation and communication for digital hardware, software and networks. Digital supply chains exist to support and synchronize interactions within and between organizations by making services more valuable, accessible and affordable with consistent, agile and effective outcomes. Some of the notable features of digital supply chains include speed, flexibility, global connectivity, real-time inventory, intelligence, transparency, visibility, scalability, innovation, proactive and eco-friendly. Digital supply chains can enable the efficient management of supply chains to become more responsive and responsible and thereby actualize sustainable development.

In fact, available published studies in the extant literature indicate that "digital supply chain" and "Supply Chain 4.0" are used interchangeably, often with similarities in theoretical underpinnings. As such, the concept of the digital supply chain is still developing and specifically entails digital transformation with core technologies to create value in the entire supply chain network. The core technologies that drive the digital supply chains include augmented reality, cloud computing, sensor technology, IoT, nanotechnology, self-driving vehicles, 3D printing, robotics, big data and unmanned aerial vehicle. Insights can be provided on the benefits of digital supply chains via the application of these core technologies, which can be laden with complexities. Currently, the literature on digital supply chains is in its nascent stage and as such, the impact of digital supply chains on sustainability performance and its potential gains remain under-explored in theory and practice. Digital technologies are considered to be relevant to environmental management and essential for better communication, joint decision-making and the co-creation of plans and plan alternatives.

7.2.2 Industry 4.0 Solutions for Circular Supply Chains

Industry 4.0 is one of the emerging techniques since its introduction in 2011. It is the integration of smart technologies such as blockchain, big data analytics, IoT, cyber-physical system (CPS), cloud computing and other associated technologies to enable digitalization in the supply chain process. Particularly, the IoT is one of the fundamental pillars of the rise of digitalization that is transforming our society in terms of data storage, availability, management, analytics and transmission. Since its inception, the IoT research has widened its scope with Wireless Sensor Networks (WSN) being deployed not only in consumer domains but also in a growing number of industrial applications including energy, healthcare or transportation. Asset tracking and logistics are growing in importance due to the reduced deployment cost for most connected devices and the expected impact on the performance of traditional systems as a result of providing decision-makers with real-time information. Due to the rapid expansion of the IoT market, standardization led by organizations such as IEEE, IETF and 3GPP is important. Given the heterogeneous nature of the IoT ecosystem, seamless connectivity is a huge challenge, with an increasing number of communication standards being adopted (Garrido-Hidalgo et al., 2020). Some of the most representatives are Wireless Fidelity (Wi-Fi), Bluetooth Low Energy (BLE), Radio-Frequency Identification (RFID), Long-Term Evolution (LTE), Zigbee and the so-called low-power wide-area networks (LPWAN), enabling long-range communication under a power-aware procedure. Additional IoT standards have emerged to minimize energy consumption and achieve efficient transmission according to different end-application requirements.

Ultimately, Industry 4.0 has been considered as a concept to facilitate product quality and decentralize the process of decision-making through ensuring green flexibility. Additionally, the implementation of Industry 4.0 can aid in increasing transparency and visibility and thereby enable data capturing in real-time. Consequently, Industry 4.0 can be utilized to track manufactured products throughout the supply chain network and allow the circular economy model to fit properly, thereby addressing issues like supplier availability and authenticity. Furthermore, Industry 4.0 technologies like the CPS, IoT, big data analytics and others have the capability to stay connected and provide critical information throughout the product lifecycle. The convergence of circular economy and emerging technologies as a smart circular can become effective in reducing the implementation gap of circular economy through smart remanufacturing, smart reuse, smart recycling and smart maintenance.

Circular economy models and solutions assisted by Industry 4.0 technologies have been developed to transform products at the end of their life cycle into new products with different use. Notably, advanced data analytics, the IoT, forecasting techniques and blockchain applications are some of the popular tools utilized to address the needs of modern supply chains, which require flexibility, methods and processes to increase productivity, reduced or zero waste generation, resource optimization and more sustainable production and consumption practices. A key success requirement that benefits productivity, resource efficiency and waste reduction is the digitalization of processes and the implementation of practices that utilize smarter machines. Consequently, integrating Industry 4.0 technologies in supply chain solutions is regarded as critical strategy for the successful advancement of circular economy. In fact, several models exist in extant literature that tend to synergize the circular economy and Industry 4.0. For instance, a prior published study in extant literature analyzed the impact of blockchain – an Industry 4.0 technology – on the transition to circular economy. Yet another published research presented a framework that links circular economy and industry. Likewise, other academic researchers investigated Industry 4.0 practices, cleaner production and circular economy and inferred that supply chain traceability along with reuse and recycling are some of the critical practices for manufacturers that aspire for sustainability improvements. As such, Industry 4.0 practices, such as the blockchain technology, result in improved circular economy performance by minimizing transaction costs and strengthening supply chain communication and simultaneously minimizing carbon footprint.

Indeed, past published studies available in extant literature have identified the significance of Industry 4.0 technologies by utilizing technologies like big data and IoT to positively influence the implementation of circular supply chains. As such, operational efficiency and material management that can result in cost savings coupled with increased utilization of resources are the critical success factors of the adoption of circular supply chain management. Other critical success factors for the adoption of circular supply chains include information exchange and forecasting methods that are prominent for providing reliable results and minimizing waste production. In a similar vein, pressures from stakeholders like regulatory authorities, non-governmental organizations (NGOs), supply chain partners and competitors, as well as the low levels of adaptability and delayed market entry, have indicated that firms need to concentrate on the simultaneous consideration of economic, environmental and social issues. The complexity and dynamic characteristics of these critical success factors increase the uncertainty in supply chains. To address these uncertainty challenge, Industry 4.0 solutions have been developed to assist in redesigning supply chains toward the development of digital supply chain networks. For instance, there is a huge need to employ big-data-driven analysis in evaluating trust, behaviors and cultures within supply chains and cross-industry networks in other to achieve sustainability improvements. Nevertheless, studies are scarce that analyze the nexus between Industry 4.0 solutions designed for circular economy progression and performance improvements in terms of sustainable development.

Moreover, a smart collection application for waste management with the aid of IoT has been proposed within the city logistics context. Also, in the industrial domain, IoT is deployed to estimate the fill level of waste bins while also optimizing pathways for transporting scrap metal bins. This has the potential to offer a solution through extending a smart waste management platform that, besides the functionality of wastes' distance monitoring, provides a series of analytics services that optimizes supply chain procedures related to resource allocation and planning. Additionally, some issues that pertain to sustainability have been explored within the context of shipbuilding supply chain. Likewise, the key enabling technologies (IoT, AI, Big Data, Autonomous Robots, Cyber-security, etc.) has been linked with supply chain approaches (Lean, Agile, Resilience and Green). In the automotive sector, the applications of Industry 4.0 and circular economy have indicated that the implementation of 6Rs (recycle, reuse, reduce, refuse, rethink and repair) practices is one of the top-ranked measures to overcome the challenges to implementing sustainable supply chain management. Other top-ranked propositions to overcome the challenges to implementing sustainable supply chain management include the product green design and life cycle assessment and supply chain digitization.

Likewise, a web-based platform for supplier and product traceability along the entire product supply chain has been proposed. This highlights that the platform is a useful decision-making solution that improves supply chain sustainability. Indeed, the deployment of Industry 4.0 technologies can improve sustainable performance in the firm level and in the supply chain level. Furthermore, a prior published research proposed a taxonomy for establishing business operations models in circular supply chains. The proposed taxonomy is based on two areas, namely the customer value proposition and the way to interact with upstream suppliers to reengineer the internal corporate functions. Also, some academic researchers opine that even though big data tools are very popular and expected to aid in developing a circular supply chain, there are still gaps in actualizing the real-data-driven optimization solution. In yet another research, the academic researchers proposed a research pathway for actualizing circular supply chains with the aid of Industry 4.0 technologies. Their study reveals the mutual benefits between Industry 4.0 technologies like big data and circular supply chains. Also, some academic researchers in their published study, applied system of systems approach to show how big data can be essential in actualizing global supply chain management objectives. Other academic researchers in their study examined the factors that connect circular supply chain management and Industry 4.0 technologies and thereby identify enabling and challenging factors. Additionally, some research scholars in their published work analyzed the circular supply chain practices and the performance of circular supply chain agents and thereby reveal how big data analytics and tools play a critical role.

In sum, the implementation of Industry 4.0 technologies can facilitate environmental commitment and green economic goals coupled with circularity concepts like product life cycle thinking.

7.3 INDUSTRY 4.0 AND SUSTAINABLE DEVELOPMENT IN THE CIRCULAR ECONOMY

In times of industrial digitization, the linkage between Industry 4.0 and circular economy has clearly and persistently enabled the exploration of various ways through which the objectives of ecological sustainability can be achieved. Industry 4.0 has accelerated the process of overcoming the barriers to achieving circularity, and digitization has increasingly emerged as a facilitator for design and adoption of cleaner production. The principles of Industry 4.0 contribute toward vertical and horizontal integration of smart production systems through enablement of cutting-edge information and communication technology (ICT) and data accumulation techniques, which make it simple for utilization in collaborated supply chain business models needed for maintaining inventories based on real-time consumption and demand expectations. Industry 4.0, which includes concepts such as cloud manufacturing, additive manufacturing and disruptive technologies such as big data analytics, cloud computing, AI and the IoT, plays a pivotal role in sustainable business development. These technologies can enable efficient plans of action for allocation of resources by gathering real-time information from the smart production system needed for coordinating with the supplier for sustainable production decisions.

In fact, the Industry 4.0 was coined to assist in shaping the future of the German economy by German researchers and utilizes fundamental technologies, such as CPS and the IoT, to connect humans, machines, and other resources as well as products and services in real-life situations. These technologies can enable efficient plans of action for resources allocation by gathering real-time information from the smart production system needed for coordinating with the supplier for sustainable production decisions. The modern world is concerned with the emergence and use of Industry 4.0; a modern manufacturing system that is driven by information technology (IT) and achieving a sustainable society. In manufacturing, Industry 4.0 has brought new technologies that deliver maximum outputs using effective resource utilization. New technologies like the IoT, CPS and others open pathways for industrial development that can assist in improving productivity and efficiency in various organizations. For instance, Industry 4.0 integrated big data, IoT and AI for leveraging manufacturing operations.

The potential of Industry 4.0 is therefore remarkable for achieving sustainable industrial value creation across economic, environmental and social dimensions by resource efficiency improvements. The basic concept of sustainability in the Industry 4.0 context challenges traditional methods to solving problems and thereafter demands more systemic methods of addressing change. In essence, the current progression of sustainability and green economies needs a shift from homogenic systems of "doing better things". In the era of fast globalization and industrialization, consciousness about sustainability issues is rising among organizations, creating a higher need for implementing ethical and sustainable business practices in supply chains to mitigate social, environmental and economic problems.

Sustainability is described by the World Commission on Environment and Development as "development that meets the desired of the present generation without compromising future generations to satisfy their needs by knowing the scarcity of natural resources". Nevertheless, sustainability in any form can assist in establishing optimal conditions for tackling 21st-century issues in business and the environment among others. The Brundtland Report (1987) provides a well-known broad definition of sustainable development as "development that meets the needs of the present without compromising the ability of future generations to meet their own needs". The concept of sustainable development does imply limits – not absolute limits but limitations imposed by the current state of technology and social organization on environmental resources and by the ability of the biosphere to absorb the effects of human activities. In essence, sustainable development addresses diverse and complex problems that alter alongside human societies and natural ecosystems around the world coupled with a wide range of environmental concerns.

The definition of sustainable development has a broad spectrum characterizing human progress, resource utilization and business interactions. The most current and relevant interpretation of sustainable development is the triple bottom line (TBL). The TBL entails three pillars: *economic sustainability*, which focuses on securing liquidity and ensuring profit; *environmental sustainability*, which refers to the consumption of those resources that can be reproduced from living and non-living things; *social sustainability*, which contributes to the development of human and societal capital. There are three main pillars/dimensions that constitute the concept of sustainability, namely economic, social and environmental. Specifically, these pillars/dimensions build up the TBL concept of sustainability with objective to meet the resource needs of the current and future generations without hampering the environment.

The concepts of sustainability and sustainable development have increased in popularity around the globe due to their proposed solutions for problems that are associated with the environment, energy, rural development and climate among others. Some authors opine that these two concepts can be used interchangeably due to their inherent similarities. Other scholars consider sustainability and sustainable development as distinct terms and thereby describe sustainability as a conceptual term and a policy vision to hinder natural resource depletion and tackle issues that pertain to conservation, biodiversity and ecological integrity. Contrarily, sustainable development is defined as a multidimensional collective societal process that entails multiple interested parties.

The social, economic and environmental dimensions for sustainability and their relative significance have varied over time. Managing all the aspects of sustainability within an organization challenging as it demands overall organizational restructuring, with an explicit focus on adoption of Industry 4.0 technologies, sustainable cleaner production and circular economy practices. To address the challenges emanating from a paradigm shift toward ethical and sustainable business, the concept of circular economy has gained tremendous attention all over the world and is being increasingly proposed as a modern approach for creating sustainable business. The principle aim of circular economy is to achieve sustainable consumption and production levels through cleaner production and product life cycle management in order to create harmony between economic development and environmental protection. Sustainable cleaner production, which integrates several eco-design strategies, is one of the critical manufacturing concepts that can be considered as a potential contributor toward circular economy or zero waste programs. Likewise, Industry 4.0 holds huge potential in grasping sustainable industrial value creation in the TBL. In addition, businesses can develop models that encompass the TBL sustainability dimensions and also account for multiple parties alongside the environment and society at large. Such models can be significant to direct and implement innovative business operations for sustainability objectives by adopting circular economy strategies like slowing and closing the resource loop and as such, becoming critical drivers of increased competitiveness and overall sustainable development.

Furthermore, there is a growing research about circular economy as a sustainable development tool for meeting the interests of the society at the macro level. The circular economy is regarded as an emerging mindset that is geared toward the sustainable utilization of natural resources, necessitating a transition from the linear model of "take, make, use and dispose/waste" to the circular model of "reduce, recover, remanufacture, reuse, recycle and redesign". Notably, the sustainability paradigms that influence human beings and society alike have led to the increased popularity of business models that include the TBL and also account for multiple parties alongside the environment and society at large. The sustainable development process demands systemic changes and innovation in lifestyles, processes, structures and ecologies, which shows that an integrated sustainable development system must correspondingly encompass the TBL, circular economy and business models. Globally, there are social, economic and environmental challenges coupled with difficulties that are associated with abrupt technological advancement, automation and digitalization. In response to these problems, Industry 4.0 – a system that is driven by emerging IT – impacts on organizational economic aspects like productivity, competitiveness and efficiency, as well as environmental and social constraints that pertain to sustainability.

Moreover, there is a rising agreement that the use of Industry 4.0 technologies can enable a transition from the linear model of economy to a circular economy through building visibility and traceability of products post-consumption required for recovering components and rare earth materials. Hence, the principles and practices of Industry 4.0 will open up maximum possibilities of integration and practical associations for a sustainable society and world-class sustainable manufacturing. This is conceivable since the improvement of any innovation is recognized in terms of its contribution toward nation's sustainability and cleaner production technologies can lead to an improved environmental quality index. Additionally, the Paris Agreement and Sustainable Development Goals (SDGs) are necessitating innovative and diverse business initiatives which integrate business goals with those of the environment, society and economy. Nevertheless, the world is not on track to meet these goals and we are lagging behind in many areas, especially in areas such as sustainable management of water and sanitation, where water scarcity could displace 700 million by 2030. Also, in energy efficiency, where energy efficiency improvements fall 3% of needed, sustainable infrastructure and innovation where growth is declining and most importantly, sustainable consumption and production patterns where electronic waste grew by 38% in the last decade. In the last decade, only about 20% of electronic wastes were recycled, global material footprint increased by around 20% and 14% food was lost in supply chains. It becomes necessary for countries to speed up their efforts to meet sustainability goals and adopt innovative practices during the course of action. Industry 4.0 is one such practice for unlocking technology for achieving sustainability goals and even has the potential to revolutionize and handle 70% of the 169 targets underpinning these goals.

Likewise, sustainability is also regarded as a primary driver of Industry 4.0. Thus, the Industry 4.0 technologies can be incorporated with value chains by collecting and actively sharing data to ensure that real-time information about productions, equipment, machines, components flows are provided. This will assist managers in various industrial sectors to effectively tracking, monitoring and making decisions that are considered as sustainable about product recoveries in the post-consumption stage. These recovery-based methods usually replace the traditional linear "take, make, use and dispose" philosophy with a circular one that is beneficial to organizations and supply chains in social environmental and economic aspects. There is research evidence that circular economy-based models are the most competitive operational tools for achieving sustainable development in the Industry 4.0 environments. Generally, Industry 4.0-based business models are based on the IoT's connectivity, whereby "companies" products and processes are interrelated and incorporated to achieve higher value for both customers and the companies' internal processes. Industry 4.0 provides businesses with sustainable longevity, recovery and efficiency by making a contribution to their social, economic and environmental values even though many industries have long been stuck in unsustainable but financially viable business models. Particularly in small and medium-sized enterprises (SMEs), Industry 4.0-based business models can be strengthened when companies focus on their absorptive capacity toward new technological innovations and their respective innovation strategies.

Furthermore, among the Industry 4.0 technologies, the most popular for achieving sustainable development in the circular economy include big data, IoT, cloud computing and CPS. Industry 4.0 applies IoT to implement a wide range of digital manufacturing involving sensors and networked technologies. The IoT offers a connectivity that links entire environmental networks, saves resources and minimizes expenses on smart grid systems, transportation and water monitoring. Big data is a revolutionary IT that can aid in assessing environmental risks and optimizing resource use by analyzing large data pools. Cloud computing can consolidate large-scale cloud infrastructure to minimize negative environmental impacts and CPS can connect digital and physical worlds and promote sustainable solutions by making optimal reactive and proactive decisions. But then, these technologies play a lesser role when compared with IoT during developing sustainable solutions. In sum, smart products, CPS, IoT and smart processes add to value proposition and support sustainable business.

7.3.1 THE SMART CIRCULAR ECONOMY

The circular economy is attributed to the ability to avoid, reduce and negate value loss and destruction through, for instance, lower emissions, reduced pollution levels and loss of biodiversity and habitats associated with resource extraction. Consequently, circular economy practices are strongly linked to SDG 12 (responsible consumption and production) and can have an additional beneficial impact on related goals, such as SDG 6 (clean water and sanitation), SDG 7 (affordable and clean energy) and SDG 15 (life on land). At present, the adoption of circular strategies in industry is somewhat modest. Moreover, this also holds true for manufacturing firms; although they play a vital role in the creation of value, there are few improvements to decouple from the linear consumption of finite resources. There are multiple reasons for this. First, the circular economy is an emergent concept, implying a lack of tools for conducting circular economy-oriented innovation or circular-oriented innovation. Second, the link between circular economy and possible enabling digital technologies is not yet well established.

Digital technologies could be critical enablers of circular economy by tracking the flow of products, components and materials and making the resultant data available for improved resource management and decision-making across different stages of the industry life cycle. As such, digital technologies can play an important role in positioning information flows that enable resource flows to become more circular. For instance, the IoT can enable automated location tracking and monitoring of natural capital. Big data facilitates several aspects of circular strategies, such as improving waste-to-resource matching in industrial symbiosis systems via real-time gathering and processing of input-output flows. Moreover, data analytics can serve as a tool to predict product health and wear, reduce production downtime, schedule maintenance, order spare parts and optimize energy consumption. These examples illustrate that digital technologies' contribution to the circular economy include a range of circular strategies and business processes: from recycling to reusing and designing new offerings to managing maintenance.

Although there are real and theorized examples of information flows enabling circularity, there remains a gap between the expected and largely unrealized potential to use digital technologies to leverage circular strategies. So far, the answers to questions such as *in what areas* and *in which ways* digital technologies support for implementing circular strategies for manufacturing companies have been insufficiently systematized. However, there is a lack of support for improving the existing and new ways in which digital technologies can support the circular economy through *smart circular strategies*. A Gartner survey of 1374 supply chain leaders supports this premise. The results show that 70% of the respondents are planning to invest in the circular economy; however, only 12% have so far linked their digital and circular strategies. In other words, there is a lack of guidance on how to leverage digital technologies to maximize resource efficiency and productivity for a specific circular strategy. Thus, we provide some guidelines on developing the *Smart Circular Economy framework*.

7.3.2 Developing Smart Circular Economy Framework

The proposed smart circular economy framework addresses the shortcomings of the existing digital circular economy frameworks. The framework consists of three main elements: *data transformation levels, resource optimization capabilities,* and a layer linking these elements together, *data flow processes*.

7.3.2.1 Data Transformation Levels

The data transformation levels draw on the Data-Information-Knowledge-Wisdom (DIKW) pyramid. The DIKW hierarchy presents the terms *data, information, knowledge* and *wisdom* to illustrate the computer processes involved in transforming raw data into insights. Inspired by the physical layer in the Open Systems Interconnection (OSI) model, the traditional DIKW model is modified to include a fifth layer named "connected resources". Each of the five layers is discussed below:

- **Connected resources** are products, components and materials connected through, for instance, an IoT device. This enables to collect data across different stages of the resources' industrial life cycle.
- **Data** are merely raw, elementary symbols based on the observation of objects, events and/or their environment. On their own, data lack interpretation and need contextualization to offer direct value or usability.
- **Knowledge** represents the transformation of information into actionable instructions, know-how and valuable insights and answers questions such as *how* and *why*. As such, knowledge can be considered as the refinement of information with inherent rules and increased understanding.
- **Wisdom** connects actionable instructions of knowledge to autonomous decisions and actions. Wisdom combines knowledge with *interactive processes* and *adaptive judgment*. Interactive processes are the sequence of actions and reactions, while adaptive judgment is the actual decision made based on the evaluation of interactive processes and their current status.

For instance, consider an IoT device for measuring temperature in a machine with the objective of extending its life cycle. Then, the raw temperature readings form the data. Thus, information is interpretation of this temperature is represented by an average over the operating hours or a description of the machine overheating. This could be an indication of an impending failure of the machine, for which a reactive maintenance scheme is created. Perhaps, knowledge can identify the possible reasons for the machine's abnormal temperature readings. Known as condition-based maintenance, this could give insights into the machine's actual condition and schedule maintenance. Finally, wisdom could then identify a specific trend in the temperature readings and project this across future operational planning and provide an optimal service window to correct the problem based on these predictions known as predictive maintenance.

7.3.2.2 Resource Optimization Capabilities

Building on the analytics capabilities and generic interpretations, the analytic capabilities, resource-specific interpretations and supplementary questions are provided to conform to circular-oriented innovation and circular economy resource management. The resulting resource optimization capabilities present five levels of *descriptive, diagnostic, discovery, predictive* and *prescriptive* analytics.

- **Descriptive** is the preliminary step that answers the question "what happened" or "what is happening". As such, it can be considered as the process of describing, aggregating and adding context to raw data from an IoT device, this transforming it into information.
- **Diagnostic** builds on the information obtained from the descriptive level to understand "why something happened". It tried to unravel the cause and effect of events and behaviors and augments knowledge to the information. As a bridge to business models and intelligence, both descriptive and diagnostic levels provide *hindsight value* of what happened and why.
- **Discovery** addresses the acute problem of high volumes in the IoT and big data. It employs inference, reasoning, and detection of non-trivial knowledge from information and data. It attempts to build a deeper understanding of why something happened by discovering additional trends and clusters or something novel. As such, discovery provides *oversight value*.
- **Predictive** provides *foresight value* by identifying future probabilities and trends to determine "what is likely to happen". Predictive methods convert past knowledge to forecast events and behaviors, thereby obtaining wisdom.
- **Prescriptive** draws actions and judgments from the forecasts provided by the predictive level, allowing for investigation of future opportunities or issues, and provide the best course of action. As such, the prescriptive level considers the inherent uncertainty of predicting the future and combines this with advanced optimization to answer the question "what if".

These capabilities can, for example, be observed in organizations adopting three levels of analytics: aspirational, experiences and transformed. Aspirational organizations use analytics in hindsight as a justification of actions. Experienced organizations apply analytics to gain insights to guide decisions, while transformed organizations can achieve foresight and prescribe actions in advance of decision-making. Likewise, for the circular economy, these capabilities represent the organizational potential to increase resource efficiency and productivity.

7.3.2.3 Data Flow Processes

Similarly, data flow processes represent a hierarchical structure. Nonetheless, this is not necessarily always the case in practice. For instance, all three processes of data collection, integration and analytics may be employed to perform a descriptive analysis of what has happened. However, the rationale underlying this structure is emphasizing where the different digital technologies typically interconnect.

- **Data collection** is the process of generative and gathering data from various heterogeneous sources for analysis by preprocessing and aggregation. It relies on interoperability and context-awareness, which are typically included by big data, cloud computing and fog computing.

- **Data integration** is the process of contextualizing and curating these disparate data sources for analysis by preprocessing and aggregation. It relies on interoperability and context-awareness, which are typically included by big data, cloud computing and fog computing.
- **Data analysis** is the process of understanding the data for underpinning or deriving actionable decisions. It includes deployment and application of data with associated insights and foresight, facilitated by techniques such as AI, machine learning and deep learning.

Furthermore, storage and computing are abstract processes involved in each of the above steps. Overall, data can be piped from one step to another, thus, do not necessarily require physical storage in separate locations. Similarly, computation can be done on a physical device or in transit (e.g., fog computing) and a separate computing component is not required.

7.3.2.4 Maturity Levels

Building on maturity thinking, the upper levels of the hierarchical structure represent a greater potential of strategies to support or unburden human decision-makers and increase the efficiency and productivity of the systemic resource. In other words, the structure illustrates different levels of operational maturity in implementing digital technologies for decoupling value creation from the consumption of finite resources. Moreover, the hierarchical structure of increasing maturity also indicates the aggregation of digital technologies as "Lego" blocks for the application of autonomous functions. Hence, when a company matures and implements more advanced digital technologies (IoT, cloud computing, big data and analytics, respectively), it can leverage self-sensing, self-adaptive, self-organizing and self-deciding functions. Based on this, a correlation between increasing industrial automation and expanding systemic resource efficiency and productivity in a circular economy can be theorized. Support for this can be seen in the automatic production processes of smart manufacturing, enabling improved quality, productivity and flexibility of large-scale production for sustainable resource consumption.

7.4 THE ROLE OF SHARING ECONOMY IN THE CIRCULAR ECONOMY

Most companies collaborate in industrial symbiosis, which goes beyond immediate supply chain members to broadening circular resource loops by enlarging relationships. This entails open loop resource flows are developed among companies within the same industrial sector or across different industrial sectors, which overcomes the disadvantage if closed loop supply chain management to maximize value recovery. One approach is to create a business-to-business (B2B) sharing platform economy. The sharing platform transcends the existing vertical model to a horizontal model, which develops an extra relationship between industry peers to increase the capacity of circularity. Subsequently, there is a high level of involvement of third parties in developing the industrial clusters, comprising governments and logistics/technology service providers. The issue about direct competition is a major obstacle in creating a partnership between industry peers, such as in group buying. Government agencies are effective and powerful stakeholders in managing conflicts of interest and encourage resource circularity. For instance, the "Courtauld Commitment" is a public-private partnership that encourages pre-competitive collaboration of the supports "pre-competitive collaboration" of the grocery industrial sector in other to tackle the packaging and food waste in the United Kingdom. The Government of Britain made investments and tasked a specialist firm to coordinate grocery retailers and suppliers in waste minimization. In another instance, "Kalundborg Symbiosis" is a local public-private partnership in Denmark, where public sector companies collaborate with private sector firms to provide, share and reuse energy, water and material resources in industrial symbiosis.

Indeed, the sharing of products (as a service), specifically through digital sharing platforms, is increasingly seen as an enabler of a circular economy. Within a few years, digital sharing platforms have already outgrown analogous business practices. The sharing economy is commonly connected to the temporary and collaborative use of products and services, including, for instance, "sharing, bartering, lending, trading, renting, gifting, or swapping". Theoretically, reuse through sharing is one of the least resource, information and labor-intensive ways to increase the efficiency of a product and prolong its lifetime. As such, the practice of sharing products (as a service) not only represents the circular economy's principle of reuse but also underpins several goals of a circular economy, such as stewardship instead of ownership and resource efficiency. In practice, however, there is a wide variety of sharing practices and business models. Likewise, digital sharing platforms' economic, social and environmental effects are expected to be either mostly beneficial not detrimental.

Currently, there is no clear definition of the sharing economy. Some people attribute it to collaborative consumption for reasons of saving money, space and time, making friends and building offline communities and peer-to-peer trust. Technological development and Web 2.0 have stimulated the rise of digital sharing platforms supporting these long-existing offline practices. Terms such as "sharing economy", "peer economy", "collaborative economy", "on demand economy", "collaborative consumption" and "gig economy" are often used as synonyms, although they do not refer to the same thing. We may define sharing economy as the temporary use of products and services since it is actually characterized by *sharing* and *collaboration*. In this context, the sharing economy is less likely to be understood as a revolution for the purpose of abandoning or replacing private capitalism, but it is simply about establishing "collaborative consumption" as an additional, cooperative kind of economy. Basically, sharing economy always requires a classical economic system, i.e., a system based on exchanging private property on the market. Constitutive of the sharing economy is the idea of a better utilization of products and goods ("idling capacity") – if this happens free of charge or in return for payment is of minor significance. More significant instead are the philosophies of enterprises and private actors contributing to the sharing economy: *The company is expected to have a clear value-driven mission and be built on meaningful principles including transparency, humanness and authenticity that inform short and long-term strategic decisions. The providers on the supply-side should be valued, respected and empowered and the companies committed to making the lives of*

TABLE 7.1
Some Business Models of the Digital Sharing Platforms and Examples

		Type of Provider	
		Business-to-Peer (B2P)	Peer-to-Peer (P2P)
Digital sharing platform orientation	Non-profit	E.g., Makerspaces	E.g., TimeBanks
	For-profit	E.g., Zipcar	E.g., Airbnb

these providers economically and socially better. The customers on the demand side of the platforms should benefit from the ability to get goods and services in more efficient ways that mean they pay for access instead of ownership. The business should be built on distributed marketplaces or decentralized networks that create a sense of belonging, collective accountability and mutual benefit through the community they build.

Hence, on the one hand, we refer to the positive attitude of enterprises offering their goods and services. On the other hand, the advantages for consumers (supposedly) resulting from sharing economy are pointed out to rather utilization instead of ownership. How these market relations are implemented must now be determined in more detail: e.g., between peers known as peer-to-peer (P2P), business-to-consumer (B2C) and B2B. Table 7.1 presents the matrix of the different orientations of the common business models. For example, Airbnb is probably the most famous example of sharing economy, where people make their housing space available to others for a short period of time and are paid a certain amount of money, billed via the digital sharing platform, which keeps a percentage of the rent, thus financially participating in the realized swap. Zipcar is an international car-sharing provider which, after online registration, allows for the flexible use of cars by way of a card. In contrast to other non-stationary offers (e.g., DriveNow), which also fall under the business model category, this is a stationary offer, i.e., cars must be fetched at a certain place and must be given back there again. Utilization is billed on a daily, hourly or minute basis. Provider of the fleet is a commercial enterprise. Thus, in contrast to Airbnb, which does not own one single apartment but just connects private persons for the purpose of sharing, Zipcar is both the provider of the brokering digital sharing platform and the owner of the cars to the rented out.

The distinction between for-profit and non-profit is the second dimension of the matrix in Table 7.1. TimeBanks is about people making their own leisure time available to other people. Neither these private persons nor the brokering digital sharing platform makes profit from their activities. Makerspace collects digital sharing platforms supposed to support DIY, for e.g., craftwork at workshops. For this purpose, experienced craft men share their knowledge and skills for free. These digital sharing platforms are mostly provided by associations, which is why they are listed under business to peer (and not P2P). Also, they, however, do not make money from their brokering and are thus non-commercially (non-profit) organized.

Moreover, collaborative consumption is realized both among private individuals and among enterprises. By enterprises offering goods (or services), thus intensifying their utilization by many consumers, they contribute-just like private individuals to a better utilization of individual goods, thus implementing a core idea of sharing economy. It is also emphasized that sharing among peers as the most innovative and most interesting variant of the sharing economy goes as far as to no longer counting commercial sharing among the sharing economy. Moreover, the reasons why the sharing economy has rapidly become more significant in recent years are manifold. Six core points must be identified as driving forces which include:

1. The possibilities offered by the Internet.
2. The development and trying out of new business models.
3. The rediscovery of social values and the renewed joy of cooperative working.
4. The growing environmental awareness.
5. The trend toward cost efficiency and cost optimization.
6. The decreasing importance as a status symbol.

7.4.1 Consumption Work and the Circular Economy

In this sub-section, we will discuss the concept of consumption work (CW) in and its relevance to the circular economy and the CW of the sharing economy.

7.4.1.1 The Concept of Consumption Work and Its Relevance to the Circular Economy

CW denotes forms of labor "necessary for the purchase, use, reuse and disposal consumption of goods and services". Such non-ubiquitous labor includes, for example, cleaning, sorting and removing household recyclables; scanning barcodes at a self-service checkout; building flat pack furniture; or self-installing home broadband. As such, CW is now often a non-negotiable component "to complete and complement an economic process", thus highlighting how the seemingly private domain of the home and of household consumption is actually an integral part of the successful functioning of macro-economic systems. CW is thus not about any form of domestic labor. Specifically, it concerns the work that householders "regularly perform", which "is integral to the completion of a process of production or service provision".

New forms of CW include practices that are a pivotal part of circular economy. The labor required for domestic recycling – cleaning, sorting and putting items on the curb, or taking them to a recycling station – is vital to the successful functioning of contemporary waste management industries and systems, with their incorrect execution being one of the main challenges for the modern recycling industry. In addition, the other consumer/user practices that circular economy foregrounds (e.g., repairing, reusing and sharing) highlight the consumers' roles in the circular economy that is far beyond that of "acceptance" of novel products and business models. Hence, it is arguable that without the widespread adoption of the forms of CW that the circular economy necessitates, the entire project becomes untenable, particularly given comments that current circular economy framings and policies fail to resonate with citizens. The concept of CW is hereby deployed as an intervention to shed new and important light on the reconfiguration of divisions of labor presupposed by circular economy visions and models, which includes the possibilities for their successful realization and for unintended consequences.

7.4.1.2 The Consumption Work of the Sharing Economy

The "Sharing Economy" is argued as playing a pivotal role in circular economy and for this reason, it is employed as a key probe through which to explore the implications of CW within the circular economy. Here, new practices and platforms deploy "underutilized assets, monetized or not, in ways that improve efficiency, sustainability and community". This can take the form of renting out of one's spare rooms or properties (as with Airbnb), or sharing surplus food in the local community (e.g., City Harvest London). Such initiatives are argued to potentially create 570 billion Euros worth of transactions by 2025, as well as fostering novel forms of consumption and new emotional and motivational engagements while creating environmental benefits through reducing resource use. Nevertheless, research has shown that some sharing initiatives do little to address the social and sustainability issues they claim to overcome. For example, prior published studies has illuminated sharing endeavors, whilst temporarily diverting some waste from landfill, can also see shared resources ultimately ending up there, with added CW for intermediaries. As such, there is a need to cast a critical eye over the actual outcomes and impacts of forms of sharing, including the role that new forms of CW play. And in further understanding the dynamics of circular economy CW, there is arguably an important distinction to be made between access-based and ownership-based forms of circular economy consumption practice, outlined in Table 7.2.

Access-based circular economy consumption is where "no transfer of ownership takes place". That is, goods can be leased, which may involve individual and unlimited access (e.g., the private leasing of a car); or limited and sequential access (e.g., joining a car-sharing club); or pooling, which necessitates simultaneous access (e.g., car-pooling with shared ownership). By contrast, ownership-based circular economy practices can involve sequential sharing, such as passing along unwanted items from one owner to the next: or co-owning assets such as housing co-ownership cooperatives. Although "individual ownership" presented in Table 7.2, in reality, falls outside the purview of sharing economy, it does form a key component of consumer-focused circular economy practices, e.g., the care and repair of owned goods to elongate

TABLE 7.2
Circular Economy and Sharing Economy Modes of Provision

Consumption	Individual	Sequential	Simultaneous
Access	Individual access (e.g., product-service system, leasing, pay per use)	Sequential access (e.g., renting, borrowing)	Simultaneous access (e.g., pooling)
Ownership	Individual ownership (e.g., product-service system repair, maintenance, reduce)	Sequential ownership (e.g., second-hand, gift, reuse, repeat exchanges)	Simultaneous ownership (e.g., co-owning)

product life spans. Consequently, Table 7.2 aims to capture various circular economy and sharing-related spheres of practice such as the P2P economy, the second-hand economy, the collaborative economy, and PSS to show examples of them in terms of consumer involvement.

All of the above practices require distinct and overlapping forms of CW. For practices in the Individual Ownership category of Table 7.2, some argue they involve less CW by eliminating inconveniences caused by the current poor quality and obsolescence of owned goods. That is: "For the customer, overcoming premature obsolescence will significantly bring down total ownership costs and deliver higher convenience due to avoiding hassles associated with repairs and returns". At face value, this statement appears unproblematic. However, little is known about the CW involved in buying long-lasting products: what one assumes is being referred to in the phrase "overcoming premature obsolescence" consumer behavior – across the stages of product acquisition, use and disposal – is currently characterized by a lack of consumer knowledge and skills in identifying longer-lasting products. In turn, research into specific consumer practices of product care (including repair and maintenance) shows that these require time, effort and competences, which limit the involvement of some individuals. For others, however, new forms of CW encourage participation, particularly when it is framed and felt as challenge and/or fun. As such, assuming longer-lasting products equate with less CW overall is unproven and requires further scrutiny if it is to a pillar of the circular economy.

Claims of greater convenience are also made for the access-based forms of sharing economy. Forms of leasing, renting, borrowing or pooling are facilitated digitally and are thus argued by advocates to relieve consumers from the "burden of ownership". However, some academic researchers have turned attention to the "burden of access" where it has been found that while not having to repair, maintain or buy new privately owned goods is looked upon favorably by some, an equal number find it time consuming to borrow or rent goods. There are also feelings of added responsibility and, at times, anxiety about being in possession of non-owned products, which some users feel a need to take greater (not less) care of. In terms of sequential access, research on renting and borrowing has identified various forms of CW that users need to do, along with how these are experienced. For example, while car-sharing reduces the labor (and cost) of appropriating and caring for a car, there is notable planning and logistical work involved in participating in car-sharing. The notable planning and logistical works can include the following:

1. Scheduling use of the car;
2. Potentially re-arranging plans due to the relative inflexibility of car sharing;
3. Returning the car;
4. Reporting issues with vehicles and
5. Dealing with dirty cars or low fuel.

For other forms of P2P borrowing and renting, it has been remarked that "renters need to browse, find and request their wanted items, contact the seller for available times and places to meet for pick-up and drop-off, arrange payment, return the item in the same condition as originally rented and also leave feedback for the provider".

Additionally, the forms of CW can be deterrent to users due to the efforts required to take part in P2P sharing. It has also been found that members in car-sharing cooperatives found the social aspects encouraged by the service provider to be burdensome and thereby preferring instead more impersonal consumption.

7.4.2 SHARING ECONOMY PLATFORMS AND GREEN CONSUMPTION VALUES

The emergence of online second-hand P2P platforms such as eBay and Facebook Marketplace helps to facilitate the supply and demand of unused or rarely used products online. Consumers rely on second-hand P2P platforms during either reselling or purchasing process. In this context, the second-hand P2P platforms may support consumers' green consumption practices and sustainable resale behavior by extending the life cycle of unused products through taking or giving a transfer of ownership from one to others. Accordingly, the online second-hand P2P platforms have been growing in popularity, especially during the COVID-19 pandemic. For instance, in the domain of resale apparel, it is projected that the current market value of $36 billion will be doubled in the next five years, reaching $77billion in the year 2025. In Nordic countries, the second-hand P2P platform has been playing an essential role in shaping sustainable consumption behaviors and habits among young consumers for over a decade. To date, in Finland, apart from global brands' P2P marketplaces (e.g., Facebook Marketplace, eBay), there are at least five independent, fashion-related second-hand P2P providers that are available to raise consumer awareness about the importance of making more sustainable consumption voices via online platforms.

Over the last decades, green consumption values phenomena have been studied, especially its antecedents and consequences, based on the theory of consumption values (TCV). Basically, TCV is employed to explain why and how consumers decide to acquire a specific product or brand from a range of available selections. Five types of generic consumption values that influence consumer choice and behavior can be identified: functional, social, emotional, conditional and epistemic values. Importantly, the use of the TCV should be based on three fundamental axiomatic propositions and these include the following:

1. The consumption value is a predictor or independent variable.
2. Consumer choices and behavior, such as brand love and purchase intentions are functions of various consumption values.
3. The consumption values differ in different contexts and contribute to distinct consumer behavioral outcomes; for instance, in the context of online travel agencies, the functional aspect is referred to as *monetary and quality-of-benefits values*, whereas the epistemic aspect is related to *information value* when examining the consumers' purchase intention.

Furthermore, in line with the notion of previous studies on TCV research, academic scholars need to identify a set of context-specific consumption values while adopting the TCV framework since it is a generic conceptualization of values. Generally, an ethical consumer is referred to an individual who conforms to the values of green consumerism. Consumers' green consumption values are related to consumer'

Facilitation of Circular Supply Chains with Digital Technologies 149

tendency to express environmental protection behavior values through their purchases and consumption. Usually, second-hand P2P platforms serve to empower consumers' green consumption values by reducing their environmental footprint and enabling the sustainable transformation of the current consumer markets. For instance, second-hand P2P platforms redefine the life cycle of a sold product by allowing consumers to resell a rarely used or unused item online without requiring them to search for a potential buyer. In this context, consumers nowadays have an effective option to transfer the value of unused items to the next owner without directly disposing of the item, and at the same time as being consistent with their environmental protection values, they are incentivized by the financial reward.

Consumers perceive second-hand P2P platforms as part of a bigger social change that provides opportunities to improve societal well-being outcomes, as well as providing a practical and sustainable solution to waste disposal. In particular, it has been identified that six distinctive perceived utilities for using second-hand P2P platforms that are associated with consumers' green consumption values include: recreational, generative, societal benefit, protester, economic and practical values. In this regard, Table 7.3 shows the operational descriptions of the specific consumption values as identified in the context of the second-hand P2P platforms and mapped to

TABLE 7.3
Generic TCV Values Linked to Specific Consumption Values among Ethical Consumers in the Context of Second-Hand P2P Platforms

Generic TCV Values	Specific Consumption Values	Operational Description
Functional value	Economic value	Consumers' perceptions of the utility of enjoying economic gain while executing exchange for a product on the second-hand P2P platforms.
	Practical value	Consumers' perceptions of the utility of easily getting rid of unused or rarely used products while using second-hand P2P platforms.
Epistemic value	Protester value	Consumers' perceptions of the utility of enabling others to circumvent conventional marketing systems and to avoid new purchases while using the second-hand P2P platforms.
Conditional value	Generative value	Consumers' perceptions of the utility of extending the life cycle of the unused product by making it available for others while using the second-hand P2P platforms.
Emotional value	Recreational value	Consumers' perceptions of the utility of gaining the inherent pleasure of engaging with second-hand P2P platforms.
Social value	Societal benefit value	Consumers' perceptions of the utility of improving societal well-being within an online community of the second-hand P2P platforms.

the generic consumption values. Consequently, there are five specific consumption values, namely:

1. Recreational value (emotional value),
2. Generative value (conditional value),
3. Societal benefit value (social value),
4. Protester value (epistemic value) and
5. Economic and practical value (functional value).

Certain types of egoistic-related values, such as economical and practical values (functional values), that drive maintaining and enhancing the self-centered benefits of consumers' desires may result in a negative impact on consumers' green consumption values. The *economic value* is related to consumers' perceptions of the utility of enjoying economic gain while executing an exchange for a product on the second-hand P2P platforms, whereas the *practical value* relates to consumers' perceptions of the utility of easily getting rid of unused or rarely used products while using the second-hand P2P platforms. Consumers' self-focus on financial gains and the ease of the disposal of unused items outweigh their green consumption values when performing transactions on second-hand P2P platforms. In this sense, the economic and practical values activate consumers' focus on cost-benefit assessments (perceived value and price fairness); they may defend their conspicuous and impulsive consumption by *rationalizing* that the purchased items could effortlessly be sold to others in the second-hand P2P platforms for monetary returns. Thus, both the economic and practical values for using second-hand P2P platforms may encourage consumers to purchase more hedonic and unnecessary items, which undermines the consumers' green consumption values. This could be further explained by individuals sometimes exhibiting behaviors (e.g., environmentally unfriendly consumption) that are inconsistent with their values (e.g., ethical consumerism) for the purpose of achieving certain goals.

The *epistemic value* (protester value) refers to consumers' perceptions of the utility of enabling others to circumvent conventional marketing systems and avoid new purchases while using second-hand P2P platforms. To pursue a protester value, consumers utilize second-hand P2P platforms as a protest against environmentally unfriendly consumption and retailing practices. The reason given is that second-hand P2P platforms empower consumers to attenuate the need for new products and directly decrease the chances of labor exploitation, toxin waste, and the abuse of environmental resources during the production process. in this sense, the protester value is related to altruistic value as it emphasizes solving overconsumption behavior and nurturing pro-environmental purchase patterns.

The *generative value* is related to religious and spiritual beliefs that drive sustainable behavior. It also represents the consumers' perceptions of the utility of extending the life cycle of the unused product by making it available for others while using the second-hand P2P platform. The generative value of using second-hand P2P platforms is related to altruistic-related value as it demonstrates an unselfish concern for the welfare of others by extending the life cycle of unused products to others who cannot afford new products. The generative value is associated with two sequential objectives: increasing the unused items' life cycle, so the items are available for people who are in need of them and practicing green consumption values to accomplish things that make the world a better place and to demonstrate their care to others through ethical consumption.

The *recreational value* (emotional value) refers to consumers' perceptions of the utility of gaining the inherent pleasure of engaging with second-hand P2P platforms. Additionally, once consumers perceive the environmental benefits of using second-hand P2P platforms, they should maintain their attitude behavior consistency by experiencing positive emotions – feeling proud of practicing green consumption values to achieve ecological goals – while trading their unused items on the second-hand P2P platforms.

The *societal benefit value* (the social value) refers to consumers' perceptions of the utility of improving societal well-being within an online community of the second-hand P2P platforms. In the context of second-hand P2P platforms, consumers are motivated to adopt green consumption values as they enjoy the sharing practices that could contribute to a greater level of benefits to society. From an environmental perspective, the societal benefit value of using second-hand P2P platforms aims to preserve natural resources and develop a sense of community. For instance, it has been found that the engagement of socially motivated consumers on second-hand P2P platforms has significantly fostered a zero-waste society, lowered carbon footprints and minimized negative environmental impacts. Accordingly, when buying and selling on second-hand P2P platforms, consumers associate themselves with socially and environmentally friendly practices; this practice not only creates social links between them but also enhances their green consumption values.

7.5 INTERNET OF THINGS AS AN ENABLER OF CIRCULAR ECONOMY

Effective implementation of circular strategies requires not only innovation in product design but also a focus on business models that incentivize companies to keep products and materials at their highest value for as long as possible while ensuring minimal environmental impact. Designers aiming at developing circular offerings need to have the ability to integrate the design of both products and business models. Research into circular and sustainable business models has shown that service-oriented value propositions have the potential to decouple profit from production volumes and thereby reduce resource use. Such business models have been studied extensively within the research field of product-service systems (PSS). PSS are combined product and service offerings designed to fulfill specific customer needs. Compared to a traditional product manufacturer, a PSS provider has a stronger incentive to deliver on aspects such as quality, efficiency, durability and reusability. Moreover, business models based on product access rather than ownership can lead to reduced resource use through increased utilization of products since one product can satisfy many peoples' needs for a certain function that they only use occasionally. Examples are car sharing services and tool rental services.

In parallel to the increased focus on sustainability, many companies find themselves in a race against competitors to seize new opportunities in the digital era.

Resulting from the fast development in sensing and communication technology, more and more products are being equipped with digital capabilities. A simple example is that of RFID tags, which allows for identification and location tracking of unique items. Now, an IoT is emerging in which "smart objects" can sense their local situation, process information and interact with their users. The IoT has been defined as a *"system of uniquely identifiable and connected constituents capable of virtual representation and virtual accessibility leading to an Internet-like structure for remote locating, sensing, and/or operating the constituents with real-time data/ information flows between them, thus resulting in the system as a whole being able to be augmented to achieve a greater variety of outcomes in a dynamic and agile manner"*. The IoT is thus closely linked to other digital technologies, such as cloud computing and big data analytics. In order to reap the benefits of the IoT, organizations will need to develop digital maturity and find ways to "create value from data", ensuring that the collected data can effectively inform actions and decisions.

Some academic researchers have pointed out the enabling effects of digitalization and IoT on the design and implementation of circular strategies. Nevertheless, the opportunities of IoT for circular economy have yet to be realized in practice. As such, more research is needed to understand what is hindering the uptake of IoT-enabled circular strategies. In all, prior published studies have emphasized the role of IoT to support the implementation of circular strategies and business models in companies, often in the context of PSS. For example, case studies have shown that IoT can support companies in extending the scope of value creation beyond design and manufacturing to "use solutions" and "operations services". IoT has also been pointed out as a supportive technology for improved maintenance and repair in PSS. Specifically, sensor-enabled prognostics can improve operational reliability and allow for preventive and predictive maintenance, which can extend the service life of products and systems. Moreover, by collecting data from the use phases, companies can continuously improve the design of their products, for example, to enhance durability.

Another aspect that has been investigated in extant literature is that products with digital elements can more easily be upgraded with additional functionality, something that could increase their lifetime. In relation to the circular strategy of increased utilization, IoT can support sharing of products between multiple users by allowing for monitoring of product condition, status, location and usage. Product-in-use data can also be used to improve product recovery strategies such as reuse, remanufacturing and recycling. In remanufacturing literature, specifically, uncertainty about the type and condition of products available for remanufacturing at a certain time has been acknowledged as a persisting challenge. Inspection and testing of products entering a remanufacturing process could benefit from more information about, for example, original design specifications and repair history. Nevertheless, such information flows are not yet well established. Moreover, accurate estimations of remaining lifetime could support decisions about when to optimally remanufacture a product and thereby improve the profitability of remanufacturing activities. In relation to recycling, prior published studies has mentioned opportunities for RFID tags in products to increase recycling efficiency and for improved information about material composition of used material to make a recovery process more profitable.

TABLE 7.4
Opportunities for IoT to Support Circular Strategies in PSS of a Company

Opportunity Type	Specific Areas
Internet of things (IoT) supports servitized business models	• IoT allows for monitoring of system performance, enabling performance-based service contracts. • IoT makes service models more attractive through adding digital services.
IoT supports reuse and/or remanufacturing	• IoT enables better estimations of remaining lifetime. • IoT enables tracking of used products, parts and materials.
IoT supports maintenance	• IoT enables detailed record keeping of manufactured products/parts that are installed, thereby facilitating maintenance and adaptations. • IoT enables condition-based and predictive maintenance.
IoT supports design for durability	• IoT can enable data about products' condition in the field, which can assist in providing information for product redesign to reduce faults.

Indeed, IoT offers a range of opportunities to support circular economy strategies in PSS of a firm as presented in Table 7.4. As presented in Table 7.4, firstly, IoT can assist in supporting servitized business models since it allows the manufacturer to more accurately measure the actual performance of the manufactured product systems, thereby supporting a performance-based service contract. Secondly, the IoT can help the form to develop and offer new data-enabled services coupled with the traditional product function. Consequently, such services could imply a closer relationship between the service provider and the manufacturer and likewise make the PSS a more attractive agenda. In the food retail segment of the company, for example, the data-enabled services include advice on how to redesign the store in order to optimize sales and evaluation of the effect of events in the store on sales number. Thirdly, there is an opportunity for the IoT to collect and store data about the composition and condition of products over time. This situation could improve the maintenance and adaptations of the system since the service provider, as well contracted installers, would have an idea of all the products/parts that are installed coupled with their performance. Additionally, there is opportunity in using IoT for predictive maintenance in different companies. If failure prediction can occur and actions can be taken before breakdown occurs, the number of maintenance visits required could be minimized and it could be ensured that the service technicians were always well prepared for the job, including the right spare parts. Fourthly, IoT could support reuse by allowing the firm to track and trace used products/parts and to more accurately estimate their remaining lifetimes after one use cycle by monitoring the condition of products over time. Since the remaining lifetime affects the residual value of a product, this could reduce some of the risks related to reuse strategies. Fifthly, IoT could assist in providing insights into the condition of products could be used to support redesign of products, making them more durable and thereby avoiding failures in the first place.

TABLE 7.5
Challenges Associated with the Implementation of Internet of Things (IoT) for Circular Economy Opportunities

Challenge Category	Specific Challenge	Particular Areas
IoT-specific challenges	Design for interoperability, adaptability and upgradability	• The uncertainty of future technological developments makes it difficult to design for interoperability over time. • Design changes might lead to the need for new models for failure prediction and remaining lifetime estimation for every new product version.
	Data quality and management	• Lack of data about which luminaries actually failed in the field (labeled data). • Parameters known to influence the condition of the product not collected. • Lack of data from products that have actually failed. • Not always clear which data set originated from product.
General challenges	Customer preferences and behavior	• The product-service system (PSS) has to stay relevant over time even if the customers' needs keep changing. • The companies are familiar with a transactional way of buying product function, and might not the willing to accept a service-based business model.
	Financial risk and uncertainty	• The value of used products depends on future market developments that are difficult to predict, especially since IoT might speed up the development.

On the other hand, the challenges associated with the use of IoT to support circular strategies and, more generally, the challenges to circular business model implementation as presented in Table 7.5. As presented in Table 7.5, firstly, there are generally a lack of data on the actually failed products, which make it difficult to develop a reliable model. The lack of data describes actual failures in the field that can be explained by the fact that smart function systems are relatively new and data gathering just started a couple of years back. Additionally, the long time that is required to produce a reliable model is considered a challenge with respect to subsequent product generations. It is not certain that a model that works for one version of the product also produces reliable results for a new version. Secondly, the collected datasets are usually missing parameters regarded as important for describing the condition of manufactured product, and it might not be clear which data originated from each product. The origin of the data is important since the expected lifetime of product depends on the product version and configuration. Thirdly, there is a need for information about which products actually failed in the field in order to appropriately label the sensor data. This information is not usually sufficiently structured, which tends to hamper the model development.

Facilitation of Circular Supply Chains with Digital Technologies   155

Furthermore, there is a challenge of developing both hardware and software to be adaptable, interoperable and upgradable, as would be required to fit the envisioned circular PSS. Specifically, there is a challenge in translating failure prediction models between product versions. This challenge might be reduced if products were intentionally designed for interoperability. Nevertheless, there is usually a large uncertainty about what kind of IoT technology will be available and demanded by customers in a few years. It is also possible that both hardware and software will be outdated quickly, which could reduce the lifetimes of smart lighting products rather than prolonging them. There is also practical challenge in designing products that could continuously be upgraded with the latest hardware over time since it would be difficult to combine an aesthetically appealing product design with a requirement to leave space in the product for a range of potential new sensor modules. Apart from the IoT-specific challenges, there are a number of general challenges to the implementation of a circular PSS. Firstly, there is an uncertainty in how the buying preferences of the manufacturers will develop and if they would accept a service contract instead of the transactional sales model that they are used to. The challenge would be to really make the service model attractive for the manufacturers. Moreover, there is a challenge of designing a functional system that could stay relevant to the manufacturer over the full duration of its technical lifetime accommodating for changes in the manufacturer's needs and wants over time. Finally, there is also a challenge/barrier related to the financial uncertainty of reuse. Even if IoT could enable more accurate estimations of the remaining lifetime of used products, the profitability of reuse also depends on the market demand for the products in the future, which is difficult to predict.

7.6 BIG DATA ANALYTICS – AN EMERGING PARADIGM FOR CIRCULARITY IN FUTURE SUPPLY CHAIN

In the past decade, the concept of the circular economy has become a much-talked-about topic because natural resources are becoming increasingly scarce. Furthermore, the world is more concerned with issues such as waste disposal and global warming. In parallel, the emergence of new digital technologies that are mainly operated by big data also makes the implementation of circular economy concepts possible. The role of big data in transitioning to the circular economy has received much attention from the scientific community. These digital technologies are seen as one of the key enablers for a wide adoption and accelerated transition to the circular economy. As an important method of digital technologies, data mining can extract useful information from data through decision support systems to identify patterns in the data. For circular economy companies, data can be transformed into insights based on data mining, which provides the basis for better decision-making. Thus, data mining can positively advance management toward the circular economy by feeding sustainability-oriented decision-making processes that require information.

Moreover, as compared to linear economy (take-make-dispose), the circular economy focuses on closing the raw material cycle and minimizing its use. Raw materials are collected, transformed and used until they are discarded as waste in the linear economy and value created through the production and selling of as many items as possible. On the other hand, the circular economy follows the reduce, reuse and recycle (3R) model. Resource usage is minimized (reduce), re-usage of products and components is maximized (reuse) and materials are reused (recycle) with high standards. Overall, the circular economy changes the philosophy of an organization with regard to value creation and how it is preserved along with sustainable business models. For instance, instead of producing music CDs, businesses are creating subscription-based licenses to preserve value. The objective of maintaining sustainability in the circular economy is different compared to the linear economy. In the linear economy, the objective of sustainability is to reduce the ecological impact with the same output, whereas, in the circular economy, the focus is on the environment as well as economic and social aspects. The focus, therefore, shifts from eco-efficiency changes to eco-effectiveness when the circular economy is adopted.

Besides focusing on core circular economic principles, firms today are influenced by multiple sources of information characterized by volume, veracity, velocity, value, variability and visualization of data. Firms are therefore utilizing big data originating from a large set of stakeholders (decision-makers) to harness internet, social media and cloud computing capabilities and preserve value. Big data helps to integrate multiple aspects of the circular economy through physical, cyber and stakeholder interactions. For instance, the ReSOLVE model consists of six elements: regenerate, share, optimize, loop, virtualize and exchange. "Regenerate" entails the shift in focus toward renewable materials and energy to allow the ecosystem to regenerate and the return of recovered natural resources to the biosphere. This helps in reclaiming, retaining and restoring the health of natural systems (recover). "Share" highlights the concept of maximizing use via sharing among multiple users and opting for a design that supports maintenance and repair. For example, sharing of cars, furniture and appliances. It emphasizes reuse and secondhand products to minimize the use of fresh materials (repair, reduce and reuse). "Optimize" emphasizes the productivity and efficiency of products and removes waste from the supply chain. Here, firms should use automation, big data analytics and remote sensing to steer circular economy more effectively (reduce, rethink, refurbish and remanufacture). "Loop" involves keeping a closed circuit and working on inner loops such as remanufacturing/refurbishing and recycling at the end of life of a product (refurbish, remanufacture and recycle). Firms' supply chains should be capable of recycling and digesting material anaerobically as well as extracting biochemical from organic waste. "Virtualize" means converting products to service-based systems and automating them. For instance, books can be converted into e-books, and CDs can be converted into online content (refuse). "Exchange" encourages the ultimate replacement of old material with advanced renewable materials compatible with technologies such as 3D printing (repair and reuse). Figure 7.1 shows the ReSOLVE and big data-enabled model of the circular economy.

When decision-making changes from a simple group of limited members to a large-scale group decision-making challenges may arise in terms of knowledge distribution, cost and behavioral changes. Due to the multiple stakeholders in large-scale group decision-making, it is important that the dimensions of the decision-makers be reduced through clustering analysis, assignment of weights to sub-groups is complex in this context since the opinions of decision-makers vary greatly. Therefore,

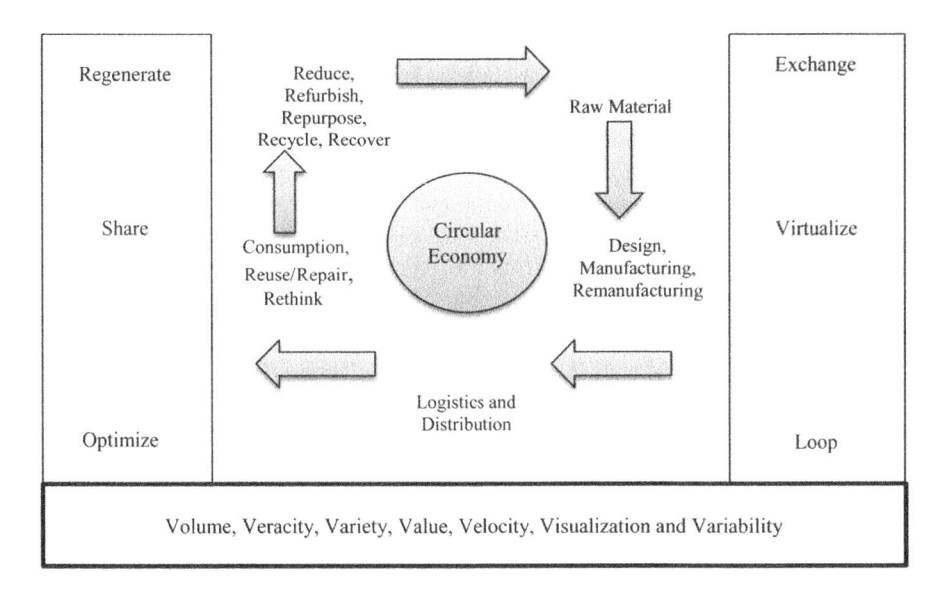

Facilitation of Circular Supply Chains with Digital Technologies 157

FIGURE 7.1 Big data and ReSOLVE model enabled circular economy.

the classical approaches of weighted or arithmetic averages may not be suitable in large-scale group decision-making. Due to diverse backgrounds and aptitudes, the complex behavior of large stakeholders can make it challenging to reach a consensus for effective decision-making. Furthermore, due to differences in expertise, status and education, it may result in intra-group conflicts in decision-making. In large-scale group decision-making, it becomes extremely critical and costly for a moderator, who is responsible for effectively implementing the consensus reaching process, providing suitable alternatives and ensuring an adequate feedback system to finalize the decision. In large-scale group decision-making, as compared to group decision-making, knowledge distribution is a challenge. Additionally, in classical decision-making, there are few decision-makers and they are considered independent, whereas in large-scale group decision-making, stakeholders may be associated on the basis of their social status or trust built over a period of time.

7.6.1 Business Intelligence and Data-Driven Insights

Business intelligence is an important resource for acquiring and assimilating intelligence on customer opinions and needs, leading to the identification of new business opportunities. It refers to the "techniques, technologies, systems, practices, methodologies and applications that analyze critical business data to help an enterprise better understand its business and market and make timely business decisions". Business intelligence identifies the patterns whereby a firm is able to use different ways to scan and absorb information as a basis for predicting opportunities to reduce uncertainty. Business intelligence can enable firms to leverage a specific type of new knowledge to provide insights about the common base of organizational knowledge and process in order to understand how a particular task takes place. This implies that improved levels of business intelligence enhance tasks and lead to improving the data-driven insights among decision-makers. To effectively collaborate and search for new knowledge from multiple points in time, firms rely on business intelligence to realize value from the technology to generate diverse data insights. Conversely, although there exists some evidence that business intelligence is evenly distributed across firms and encourages the pursuit of data insights, some firms might not benefit from such insights, given their weak data-related capabilities.

The concept of data-driven insights has recently gained attention by virtue of its potential to generate deep data insights. Moreover, the use of big data analytics reduces the complexity of generating insights from the data and increases the understanding of the optimal set of actions based on descriptive, prescriptive and predictive data insights. Data-driven insights are hence linked to three approaches: descriptive, predictive and prescriptive insights. Descriptive insights focus on the importance of the relationship between historical (past data) and current tasks to gain insights into tasks, whereas predictive insights emphasize predicting possible future outcomes resulting from data and information originating from business intelligence and prescriptive insights emphasize the decision-making process carried out to improve future outcomes. Nevertheless, knowledge embedded in IT requires the managers to apply business intelligence to deliver insights into what happened in the past and how to integrate new insights into existing resources to improve future outcomes. This calls for managers and key workers to have greater learning capabilities and helps to foster more effective data-driven insights. Thus, business intelligence can build capabilities, leading to building data-driven insights.

Consequently, big data analytics plays an important role in shaping circular economy. Data management insights shape analytics capabilities and encourage managers to make quick decisions in real-time to solve problems and deliver innovative solutions. Business intelligence allows faster decision-making based on past material use and collection trends; in turn, the manager uses it to design a system to support recycling, reuse and remanufacturing activities. Hence, the use of business intelligence allows an organization to enhance the existing stock of knowledge resources – which, in turn, promotes the design of new services and products with better recyclability features. Indeed, business intelligence is a pre-requisite for circular economy performance in extracting new insights about the material recovery rate and generating value from end of life products. As such, business intelligence can be positively associated with a firm's circular economy performance.

7.6.2 Big data Analytics and Data-Driven Insights

Big data analytics comes from big data analytics infrastructure flexibility, big data analytics management capabilities and big data analytics personnel expertise. Big data infrastructure emphasizes the importance of the relationship between historical (past data) and current tasks to gain insights into tasks. Big data analytics management capabilities emphasize predicting possible future outcomes resulting from data and information originating from business intelligence. Big data analytics personnel expertise emphasizes the decision-making process carried out to improve future outcomes. For instance, big data capabilities enable managers to quickly develop, deploy and support firms' resources. Big data analytics personnel capabilities serve as catalysts to mobilize management to the understanding of different business functions to address changing needs in the big data environment. By fostering big data analytics management capabilities, firms can transform big data analytics for strategic use. As such, the analysis of the impact of big data has become a priority for executives who wonder how it can be used to generate insights from structured and unstructured data for better decision-making.

Firms with a high level of big data analytics tend to have more focus on the generation of useful knowledge. Through using big data analytics, firms can improve internal processes, operations and organizational efficiency, allowing them to identify opportunities from different kinds of data that could be used for decision-making. In data-driven insights, organizational big data analytics can be an explanatory factor to learn from past behaviors and understand their impact on future outcomes. Organizational big data analytics is considered an important capability that impacts organizational performance. Big data analytics is a knowledge-based capability, and it is important for the effective utilization of business analytics to better plan and adapt to changing conditions. Hence, enhancing the level of learning capabilities within organizations can help managers to improve their understanding of past and present trends and predict future trends.

Technological infrastructure such as sensors and RFIDs are increasingly being employed with electronics equipment that may enable a product to be traced for recycling. Also, the effective utilization of new technologies can support remanufacturing, recycling and reuse of parts or components at the end of the product's life. By integrating technological infrastructure, enhancing management capabilities to trace real-time material in the product life cycle and integrating personal skills, several benefits can be generated in terms of material reuse – improving material efficiency and circularity of product design (reduction of waste from the production process and reuse of the material), among other sustainability-related benefits. Big data capability can improve tangible and intangible organizational productivity. For instance, big data capability can assist organizations in aligning resources with long-term and short-term strategies; this is because big data analytics is acknowledged as an essential enabler of the circular economy. The effective utilization of big data analytics is important for the enhancement of the circulation of resources – increasing the effectiveness of the material and thereby increasing the effectiveness of business operations. Big data analytics capabilities enable firms to successfully utilize infrastructure and manage personal expertise to develop processes and products compatible with reuse and recycling.

7.6.3 DATA-DRIVEN INSIGHTS AND DECISION-MAKING QUALITY

The effective utilization of resources and effective decision-making among managers are sets of actions to be performed in relation to tasks. Decision-making quality ensures that managers understand what to do and what they are trying to achieve. Decision-making in a digital environment is embedded in a better understanding of data or key information. Knowledge resources may lead to making better decisions inside organizations. Decision-making quality can be defined as a decision-maker's ability to make correct decision, referring to it as the quality of the decision made by the decision-maker. In contrast, decision-making effectiveness focuses on decision outcomes. The acquisition of data resources sets the direction and action to be performed in relation to minimizing waste and recycling of the products. In addition, the acquisition of different types of data resources and knowledge could help a firm to extract the right insights on the design out of waste from processes and products and enable products to be reused. The authentic and valuable insights generated from the data are important for the firm, as they can be chosen to formulate appropriate decisions to create new courses of action. Valuable insights generated from diverse data sources to understand past and present trends, as well as predict future trends, can positively influence decision-making quality.

Data-driven insights create a good understanding of effective decision-making. For instance, an organization's learning capabilities integrate and leverage good insights into the best course of action to improve decision-making because a large amount of information is utilized to solve existing problems and generate innovative solutions. Selecting the best course of action involves learning about the optimal courses of action and may require the use of efficient technologies for the reuse and redesign of products and services to improve material recovery. By effective decision-making, value is created for the organization by redesigning products, improving material efficiency and effectiveness for end of life products. The circular economy-related decisions are based on correct and valid data insights derived by discovering certain relationships and if rigorously implemented, firms will be in a better position to discover new patterns from using visualization tools to adapt to changing environmental challenges, thereby improving productivity and efficiency.

7.7 SUMMARY

Digital technologies can also act as triggers for innovating new business models for circular economy. The development of emerging digital technologies is driving a shift toward circular economy practices and innovation. Furthermore, a simultaneous transformation toward the implementation of digital technologies in industrial businesses is ongoing alongside the emergence of circular economy.

In industrial businesses, digital technologies are considered to be part of the fourth industrial revolution, called Industry 4.0 or the Industrial Internet. These terms refer to the industrial transformation in which data gathering and storing transform products into value-creating systems that form connected networks of people, products and systems.

In terms of the digital technologies applied in Industry 4.0, these technologies have been categorized into three based on function: *data collection*, *data integration* and *data analysis*. Data collection technologies include sensors (e.g., RFID) and devices that connect products and users to the internet (e.g., IoT). Data integration technologies store and format data and enable the use of data analysis technologies, which produce and develop information.

In a similar vein, technologies have been categorized by digitalization capabilities: intelligence capability, connective capability, and analytical capability. Intelligence capability refers to upgrading key hardware with digital components that gather data. Connective capabilities refer to linking products wirelessly to one another and the Internet. Analytical capabilities perform knowledge development functions, generating intelligence from the abundant data provided by the sensors and systems. Data collection technologies include RFID, IoT and CPS. Among data integration technologies, cloud and blockchain technologies are the most frequently discussed. Big data analytics and AI also emerge as key data analysis technologies.

Industry 4.0 – a system that is driven by emerging IT – impacts on organizational economic aspects like productivity, competitiveness and efficiency, as well as environmental and social constraints that pertain to sustainability. The use of Industry 4.0 technologies can enable a transition from the linear model of economy to a circular economy through building visibility and traceability of products post-consumption required for recovering components and rare earth materials. The smart circular economy framework provides some guidelines on how to leverage digital technologies to maximize resource efficiency and productivity for a specific circular strategy. The three main elements in developing a smart circular economy framework include data transformation levels, resource optimization capabilities and a layer linking these elements together, data flow processes.

Moreover, the sharing economy is commonly connected to the temporary and collaborative use of products and services, including, for instance, "sharing, bartering, lending, trading, renting, gifting or swapping". Theoretically, reuse through sharing is one of the least resource, information and labor-intensive ways to increase the efficiency of a product and prolong its lifetime. As such, the practice of sharing products (as a service) not only represents the circular economy's principle of reuse but also underpins several goals of a circular economy, such as stewardship instead of ownership and resource efficiency. The emergence of online second-hand P2P platforms such as eBay and Facebook Marketplace helps to facilitate the supply and demand of unused or rarely used products online. Consumers rely on second-hand P2P platforms during either reselling or purchasing process.

The IoT is defined as a system of uniquely identifiable and connected constituents capable of virtual representation and virtual accessibility leading to an Internet-like structure for remote locating, sensing, and/or operating the constituents with real-time data/information flows between them, thus resulting in the system as a whole being able to be augmented to achieve a greater variety of outcomes in a dynamic and agile manner. Big data infrastructure emphasizes the importance of the relationship between historical (past data) and current tasks to gain insights into tasks. Big data analytics management capabilities emphasize predicting possible future outcomes resulting from data and information originating from business intelligence. Big data analytics personnel expertise emphasizes the decision-making process carried out to improve future outcomes. For instance, big data capabilities enable managers to quickly develop, deploy and support firms' resources. Big data analytics personnel capabilities serve as catalysts to mobilize management to the understanding of different business functions to address changing needs in the big data environment.

Business intelligence refers to the "techniques, technologies, systems, practices, methodologies and applications that analyze critical business data to help an enterprise better understand its business and market and make timely business decisions". Its intelligence identifies the patterns whereby a firm is able to use different ways to scan and absorb information as a basis for predicting opportunities to reduce uncertainty.

Decision-making quality can be defined as a decision-maker's ability to make correct decision, referring to it as the quality of the decision made by the decision-maker. In contrast, decision-making effectiveness focuses on decision outcomes.

DISCUSSION AND REVIEW QUESTIONS

1. Mention the four critical measures for an IT-enabled supply chain.
2. What is Industry 4.0? Outline some key Industry 4.0 technologies.
3. How can Industry 4.0 enable the shift to circular economy?
4. Define sustainable development.
5. Discuss circular economy as a sustainable development tool.
6. Outline the key pre-requisites for effective development of smart circular economy framework.
7. What is sharing economy?
8. Explain the role of sharing economy in the circular economy.
9. Define business intelligence.
10. Discuss the role of business intelligence in giving data-driven insights for achieving circular supply chains.
11. Define the IoT.
12. Outline some opportunities for the IoT to support circularity strategies in PSS.
13. What are the challenges to the use of the IoT in implementing circular economy?

SUGGESTED MATERIALS FOR FURTHER READING

Garrido-Hidalgo C., Olivares T., Ramirez F.J., Roda-Sanchez L. (2019), An end-to-end Internet of Things solution for reverse supply chain management in Industry 4.0, *Computers in Industry*, 112, 103127.

Nakamoto, S. (2009). Bitcoin: A peer-to-peer electronic cash system, Retrieved December 12, 2019, from 2009. www.bitcoin.org.

Shyam, G. K., Manvi, S. S., & Bharti, P. (2017). Smart waste management using Internet-of-Things (IoT), 2017 2nd International Conference on Computing and Communications Technologies (ICCCT), *IEEE*, 199–203.

Social Accountability International (2014). SA8000: 2014. International Standards.

Swachhcoin Foundation (2018). *Whitepaper v1.2#May 2018*.

Symbiosis, K. (2017). Effective industrial symbiosis, *Ellen MacArthur Foundation Case Studies,* https://www.ellenmacarthurfoundation.org/case-studies/effective-industrial-symbiosis.

Wrap (2017). Wastes & Resources Action Programme, United Kingdom: Bringing industry together to tackle food packaging waste, *Ellen MacArthur Foundation Case Studies*, https://www.ellenmacarthurfoundation.org/case-studies/untied-kingdom.

8 Application of Blockchain Technologies in Circular Supply Chains

8.1 INTRODUCTION

As an emerging topic arising at the intersection between digitization and sustainability, the concept of blockchain for the circular economy is defined as "a technology for a sustainability transformation of the linear paradigm". On the other hand, the circular economy is regarded as a mature domain, in which most of the dynamics are highly specified and with a wide of valid critical performance indicators to utilize, thereby providing the inputs that are right for smart contract coding. Additionally, the circular economy ecosystem is a multi-layered combination of material streams from suppliers, manufacturers, logistics service providers, distributors and retailers producing a considerable amount of data. Beyond facilitating traditional business and services, blockchain technologies have also supported the transition to a circular economy. Nevertheless, the transition to circular economy in the manufacturing sector can be hindered by various barriers. Such barriers include lack of standard policy, higher complexity leads to resistance to changing the traditional linear economy and industry models, protection of intellectual property, high costs and lack of quality assurance for recycled/reused products, low awareness on circular economy. Blockchain technology has received particular attention for reasons such as its rapid growth is supporting supply chain traceability, sustainability and information security over the last decade and its potential to cope with multiple circular economy challenges simultaneously. Likewise, smart contracts can deal with a massive quantity of data in few seconds, and in that situation, avoid intermediaries and reduce the transaction costs. Also, a huge amount of information and data are exchanged among parties due to the frequent cooperation and communications that exist in the circular economy network. In addition, the relationship between distributors and consumers is rapidly changing and a new dynamic process of distributor-to-consumer underlines the need to clarify the significance of a smart contract-based framework that may enhance the efficacy of distributor-to-consumer transactions and prevent counterfeiting.

8.2 THE BACKGROUND AND ROLE OF BLOCKCHAIN TECHNOLOGIES

The concept of blockchain technology was firstly proposed by Nakamoto in 2009, who defined it as a technology using data mining and bitcoin techniques to develop data structure and encode the transaction of information. Blockchain is the central and underlying technology of cryptocurrencies, is one of the examples of innovations that is pivotal to the business management revolution movement. It is also an emerging and utilitarian technology that has the potential to have a significant impact on the functioning of a large number of business organizations. The conceptualization and use of blockchain technology were vital to the start of the cryptocurrency revolution Bitcoin in 2009, which emerged as the world's first digital currency, which didn't require and warrant a trusted authority. Additionally, the blockchain refers to a technology of distributed ledger in which every transaction and related information is encrypted by hashing, and all network members have access to the same. The main characteristics of blockchain technology include decentralization, distrust, transparency, traceable and un-forgeable transactions, anonymity and credibility. The information within a blockchain will be stored online permanently, with high transparency and security. Indeed blockchain technologies can be applied in different platforms and are not limited to cryptocurrency and capital markets. With the development of the Internet of Things (IoT), the application of blockchain can assist organizations to develop collaborative services. In such a context, the architecture of service has been updated because of the fast development of blockchain technologies.

Ultimately, the role of blockchain technologies in bridging trust, traceability and transparency is discussed below:

8.2.1 Traceability

Traceability can enable product tracking and provide product tracking information in the process of production and distribution. There is growing research attention being paid to areas related to supply chain visibility and traceability. In this context, customers need greater traceability and knowledge of the origin of products by manufacturers and retailers. Hence, the real economic and social problem is to bridge the gap in the supply chain traceability related to control in spite of the production being ethical, safe or have respect for sanctions. Defining the products' origin is often problematic due to the supply chain complexity and products' flow over extended networks. This complexity needs that products are monitored throughout their entire life cycle, beginning from raw material purchasing to production, distribution and consumption.

A notable example of traceability architecture in the supply chain is the OriginChain which currently utilizes several private blockchains that are distributed geographically to the traceability service provider. The main purpose is to establish a reliable traceability platform that comprises other organizations, including government-certified laboratories, large suppliers, and retailers with a strong relationship with the company. When compared to a public blockchain, this traceability platform has better performance and lower costs. OriginChain usually stores two kinds of data on the chain as variables of smart contracts to be preserved: the hash of traceability certificates and the necessary traceability information that is required by the regulatory framework.

8.2.2 Trust

Trust is one of the key characteristics of blockchain technologies which indicates an exchange of partner expectations that the other party relies on, behaves as expected and acts reasonably. The main feature of blockchain protocols is to provide an immutable recording of transactions, integrating a distributed database whose transaction blocks are connected chronologically and cryptographically through decentralized consensus mechanisms. This structure prevents the diffusion of wrong/counterfeit information and self-regulates the behavior of agents without central authorities' need. Through the use of smart contracts, blockchain technology has gone up to exceed the level of cryptocurrencies and has been applied in various industrial and commercial sectors. High energy and time are required to verify blocks in public and permissionless blockchain, while in private networks, there is a reduction in the risk of Sybil attacks.

In practice, the proof of work (PoW), proof of stake (PoS) and Byzantine Fault Tolerance (BFT) mechanisms develop costs for including blocks and hence, discourage potentially harmful nodes from interference. Likewise, the energy, time and scalability rise, and as such, the system efficiency is affected. If the participants are known in the private network, there is usually no threat of attacks, and hence the costs related to security issues decrease. Hence, identity-based authentication (e.g., hash-based users) presents more efficient alternatives that allow for different levels of privacy. The data structure consists mainly of two parts, namely the block header, which contains the previous block hash where the hash value is utilized to connect the previous block and meets the integrity needs of blockchains. The other part instead comprises of the basic information of the block and related transactions (e.g., ID, status and position). Since cyber-attacks have risen and become sophisticated, solutions are required to preserve the nodes' reliability without requesting for excessive energy and time costs.

8.2.3 TRANSPARENCY

Transparency is the extent to which information is easily accessible to both counterparties in exchange and external observers. It is a primary parameter to assist in accessing the supply chain performance, given the emerging secure environment associated with the blockchain. Even before reaching the final consumer, products travel through a vast network in which different actors are present (e.g., extractors, producers, retailers, distributors, conveyors and storage facilities). In this context, it becomes possible to manage transparent and accurate information for each phase, thereby guaranteeing compliance, safety and accuracy, focusing on the requirements for sustainable and social responsibility. Current markets need supply chain information transparency and sustainable economic dynamics for both the environment and society. Likewise, many industries are adopting these practices coupled with emerging technologies in order to improve supply chain transparency, especially in highly competitive, scattered and complex markets. Blockchain technologies have the potential to increase system transparency, thereby resulting in fewer failures. Changes in the current system are highly essential to improve the speed and processing times of network even though no great hardware investments are necessary for blockchain upgrading. Greater transparency can enhance the ability for increasing productivity, providing better customer services and reducing expenses. Hence, transparency is a highly significant to increase supply chain performance.

8.3 BLOCKCHAIN AND CIRCULAR ECONOMY

Within the circular economy domain, blockchain technologies can enable new decentralized systems and applications to improve data managing, sharing, transparency and control level costs. For example, the different authorities can combine the benefits while making efforts to maintain control over the blockchain application costs. In this context, it becomes possible to control all related potential assets and smart contracts, which represent an attractive and more efficient alternative to a more centralized circular economy asset monitoring system for environmental regulators. During the implementation of blockchain technologies, smart contracts are utilized to make transactions between different users faster and more effective. Smart contracts are automatically and independently carried out on each network node, based on the data contained in the transaction. There are many applications of blockchain technology in the circular economy domain. For instance, the implementation of blockchain solutions would simplify energy supply procedures, reduce request volatility, and allow to manufacturing in real-time the quantity required by the market. In this context, it would be possible to optimize and save natural resources.

Additionally, there is the research evidence on developed frameworks to guide the implementation of blockchain technologies in assessing how the product lifecycle can have better environmental performance. Industry practitioners and academic scholars have applied a number of methods to overcome these barriers. Indeed, blockchain technology provides some practical support for the transition to circular economy. Firstly, blockchain technology can assist to integrate and share information along the whole supply chain process and consequently, the material and products exchange can be smooth. Additionally, blockchain technologies offer higher security with regard to keeping and managing information online and this characteristic can prevent the confidential information leaking and assist to protect organizational intellectual property. Lastly, all the relevant supply chain partners, particularly consumers, can access more information quickly from the upstream aspects (relating to design, raw materials and manufacturing processes). Blockchain technologies can facilitate consumer understanding of the broad supply chain and therefore improve the integration and cooperation between supply chain partners.

Furthermore, blockchain technologies can cause disintermediation of the supply chain in which a lower number of levels entails reduced transaction costs, time and waste in the supply chain. First and foremost, blockchain technologies can assist in guaranteeing safety and authenticity by reducing resource consumption. For example, traditional energy systems have a centralized management model with high-pressure drops in very extended networks. On the other hand, a peer-to-peer network that is based on blockchain technologies can result in network amplitude reduction and thereby drastically decrease the resulting energy waste over long distances and storage facilities. Consequently, there are various platforms based on blockchain with the potential to decrease the waste that accrues from supply chains (e.g., ECOChain, ElectriCChain, SunContract). Secondly, blockchain technologies can aid in guaranteeing that manufactured products sold as environmentally friendly are authentic/real. For instance, the approval of the forest certification program can help in tracking the origin of around 740 million acres of certified forests worldwide using blockchain technologies. Thirdly and lastly, blockchain technologies can assist in recycling performance improvements. For example, people in Northern Europe are encouraged to recycle by providing them with rewards in the form of cryptographic tokens. In this context, blockchain-based project Social Plastic has shown how it is possible to reduce plastic waste by changing it into money.

The manufacturing industry is one of the most significant industries across the world. Nevertheless, it has also been illustrated that it could be one of the most harmful to the environment and therefore has faced constant pressure to transition to circular economy. Subsequently, from the initial stages of design through to manufacturing and to the final stages, the ideas on circular economy compel the manufacturing industry to prioritize sustainability in terms of emphasizing long-life products, using and reusing materials and giving consideration to end of life products. During transition to a circular economy, upcycling and recycling concepts are paramount and a major difficulty pertains to the alignment of values across the supply chain, particularly with those of the consumer. As consumers become increasingly concerned with sustainability issues, such practices as upcycling or recycling are growing in popularity. Nevertheless, consumers in the manufacturing industry are generally knowledgeable about the retail stage and have limited information about how their decisions influence other parties in the supply chain. Blockchain technologies provide a practical means of increasing the alignment between consumer values and demand with the interests of other parties in the supply chain, prompting transition to a circular economy model. The traditional sustainable supply chain management concept focuses on minimizing waste but not the reuse and refurbishment of raw materials. There are five common strategic objectives in traditional supply chain management and blockchain technology can provide potential support to help to achieve these objectives effectively.

A discussion of the potential support of blockchain technology in supporting such objectives is detailed below:

8.3.1 Cost

Blockchain technologies can generate a unique code for each financial transaction and can thereby facilitate a comprehensive check of the financial flow within the whole supply chain process.

8.3.2 Speed

Blockchain technologies can increase process speed by reducing physical interactions and communications.

8.3.3 Risk Control

Transactions using blockchain technologies can only occur when all the relevant parties accept it in specific touch-points within the blockchain network. This function assists to control the risk of data for all supply chain transactions.

8.3.4 SUSTAINABILITY

Blockchain technologies can assist to develop measurable and meaningful performance measurement indicators for environmental, economic and social sustainability.

8.3.5 FLEXIBILITY

Blockchain technologies can assist customer to track and trace their orders from upstream to downstream. This helps consumers to effectively make required changes in an easy manner and for suppliers to likewise adjust to the changes immediately.

8.4 BLOCKCHAIN AND CIRCULAR SUPPLY CHAIN MANAGEMENT

8.4.1 KEY AREAS OF BLOCKCHAIN-ENABLED CIRCULAR SUPPLY CHAIN MANAGEMENT

The concept of circular supply chain management incorporates circular thinking and the significance of circular economy into supply chain management with the goal of developing a zero-waste supply chain through all supply chain functions and within each stakeholder's realm. The key areas of applying blockchain technologies in circular supply chain management include data management resource deployment, supplier selection and development, procurement, production and operations, materials management in the logistics process, reverse logistics, supply chain control, green product management, reuse of waste across various circular supply chains. These key areas are presented in detail below:

8.4.1.1 Supplier Selection and Development

Blockchain technologies can develop platforms and databases by storing the historical performance data of all the suppliers. Consequently, customers can quickly find the most suitable suppliers. Additionally, blockchain technologies can assist customers and suppliers to create smart contracts in order to trace and benchmark supplier performance.

8.4.1.2 Procurement

Blockchain technologies can help in tracking and analyzing products' life cycle so that all the stakeholders in circular supply chain management can simultaneously create resource efficiency and material supply resilience in the procurement process.

8.4.1.3 Data Management Resource Deployment

Effective data management can help the relevant stakeholder in the circular supply chain management to make the required changes in a speedy manner. Additionally, blockchain technologies can assist in enhancing the resilience and flexibility of circular supply chains.

8.4.1.4 Materials Management in the Logistics Process

Blockchain technologies make products and materials to be highly traceable, thereby reducing the amount of products and materials that are lost through handling in the logistics process. Consequently, the lead time can be shortened and resource efficiency improved in the logistics process.

8.4.1.5 Production and Operations
Blockchain technologies can fully integrate the data that arise from internal production and operations and that of external supply chain requirements. Hence, all the relevant stakeholders in circular supply chain management can align and audit their production and operations to satisfy the 3R rules of the circular economy concept under precision.

8.4.1.6 Green Product Management
The information about green products is usually difficult to obtain and manage, and as such, blockchains can be applied to obtain and store green product data. For instance, blockchain technologies can effectively monitor gas emissions, thereby enabling customers to have information on whether a product is considered green or not.

8.4.1.7 Reverse Logistics
The characteristics of reverse logistics indicate that there is a close resemblance to recycling, recovering, and reusing materials, products and waste. Nevertheless, the traditional reverse logistics suffers from a setback in obtaining accurate information that pertains to the time, location, quality and condition of the materials, products and waste. The basic cause of such setbacks is due to the complicated nature of the multi-tier supply chain processes. Blockchain technologies can effectively track all the supply chain transactions. Hence, the stakeholders in circular supply chain management can effectively monitor and control the entire reverse logistics process to reuse and refurbish wastes and return components.

8.4.1.8 Reusing Waste Across Various Circular Supply Chains
Blockchain technologies can help in developing a platform to encourage the integration of the concept of circular economy across various circular supply chains and the respective stakeholders. For instance, when two organizations from different circular supply chains require each other's waste or used components, such organizations can make transactions and free exchanges without the use of a middleman.

Hence, blockchain technologies can be of benefit to multiple circular supply chains simultaneously.

8.4.2 STAKEHOLDERS IN THE BLOCKCHAIN-ENABLED CIRCULAR SUPPLY CHAIN MANAGEMENT

Within the context of circular supply chain management, all the relevant stakeholders are involved, namely supplier, manufacturer, distributor, retailer and consumer (see Figure 8.1). As illustrated in Figure 8.1, the stakeholders are linked through logistics activities. The solid line signifies the forward logistics while the dashed/dotted line shows the backward logistics/reverse logistics process such as product recycling and recall. Contrary to the traditional supply chain, the circular supply chain includes reverse logistics, which pertains to recycling operations and recall of the product for reuse and considered as the reverse process of forward logistics.

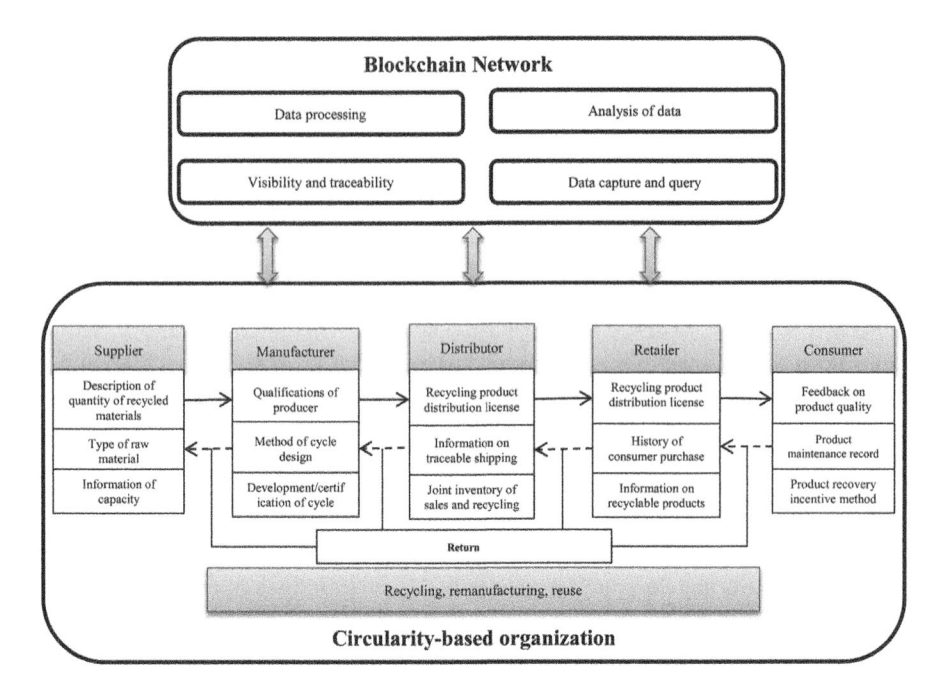

FIGURE 8.1 Stakeholders in a blockchain-enabled circular supply chain.

Moreover, in a blockchain-enabled circular supply chain, four entities play a critical role: (i) *certificate authority* (responsible for providing unique identities to the supply chain partners), (ii) *network administrators* (responsible for defining standard schemes, such as blockchain policies and technological requirements for the network), (iii) *membership service provider* (responsible for providing certifications to the partners for participating in the supply chain network), and the other *supply chain partners* (manufacturers, reverse logistics service provider, selection center, recycling center and landfill, that must be certified by a registered auditor or certifier to maintain the system trust). These supply chain partners ensure the blockchain nodes and processes are entirely authentic. When a new partner is included to the network, the certificate authority creates a temporary account with limited functions after conducting an initial verification of the new users' suitability for the tasks which have been included to the network. At the point of adding a new user, this information is shared on the network via smart contract and the certifiers definitively authenticate the new user through historical analysis of his business behavior by membership service provider. If the newly added user turns out to be truthful, this definitively unlocks permissions granted by the certificate authority within the initial phase. In a similar vein, network administrators are in operation to develop new processes and policies.

In fact, with the support of blockchain technologies, all the relevant partners can directly access the information on manufactured products. With limited access, it becomes possible to guarantee a security level through a digital key exclusively for the parts involved. All the information tag associated with the product connects physical products to their virtual identity in the blockchain. Each of the different partners will have a critical role obtain authorization to enter new information in product's profile or start an exchange with another party, where obtaining authorization can require smart contracts and consensus. Both parties can sign a digital contract to authenticate the exchange before a product is transferred or sold to another partner. The blockchain ledger is subsequently updated by the details of the transaction. Blockchain technology can highlight and detail at least five critical product dimensions, namely nature, quality, quantity, location and ownership. In this manner, blockchains simultaneously offer an organization the ability to identify responsibilities for the product or service quality and customers the possibility to inspect the product history from raw materials to the final product.

Many blockchain applications can be found in the supply chain's circular model, and many are found in the waste sector as well. For instance, Swachhcoin is a blockchain-based platform that is utilized in the micro-management of household and industrial waste and which converts such into useful products in an efficient and environmentally friendly manner. A wide range of raw materials with high economic value originates from treated waste. The Swachh ecosystem is a decentralized autonomous organization that is governed autonomously based on predefined instructions in the form of smart contracts. Swachhcoin utilizes a large number of innovative technologies to implement an iterative process cycle and makes the system completely autonomous, efficient and productive. This iterative process cycle focuses on the data exchanged between the various ecosystem actors, analyzes this data, and provides real-time suggestions based on predictive methods. A blockchain-based supply chain enables a new circular business model. While linear supply chains are mainly based on the take-make-dispose model, the blockchain-based supply chain allows implementing a make-use-recycle model. With the utilization of the blockchain, all the manufactured products can be traced along the entire supply chain, from origin to the market and subsequent recycling. The benefit of this model is that all the manufactured products are tracked with blockchain technology, and it becomes possible to provide a critical service to final customers, such as guaranteeing the product's origin.

8.5 ACCESS TO DATA IN THE BLOCKCHAIN NETWORK

In order to enable the integrity and the traceability of manufactured products in the whole life cycle, stakeholders are required to upload the necessary data. The manner in which data flows through and connects within the stages of supply chain management is presented in Figure 8.2.

The three stages in the supply chain management include the pre-production, production and post-production stages. Each of the mentioned stages comprises different types of product-related activities, applications or services including demand forecast, product research and development, manufacturing process control and product recycling. Each of these activities can be described using a product and enterprise information, for instance, for product R&D, there is product information that includes design instructions, 2D design drawings, and modes. Likewise, for supplier qualification certification, there is information that pertains to enterprise product output

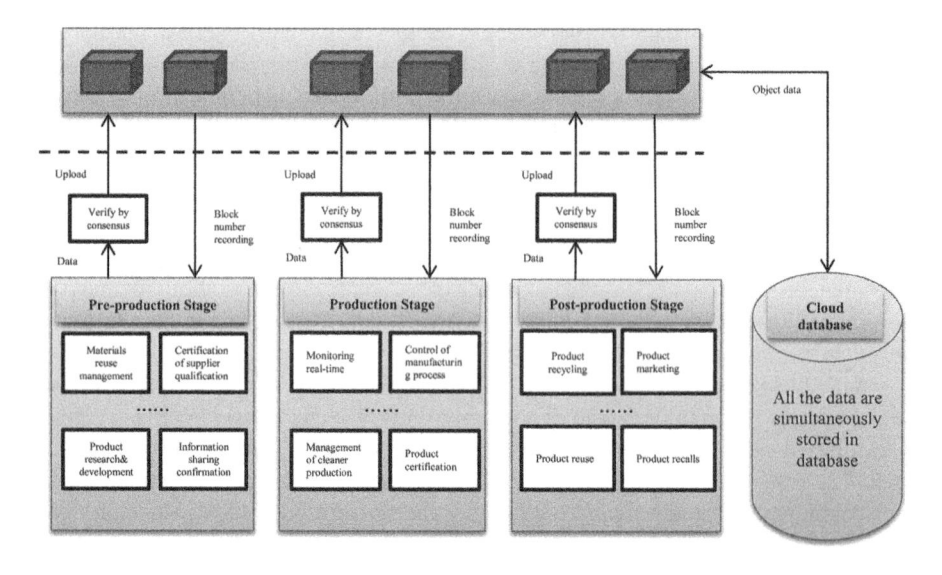

FIGURE 8.2 Data flow within the circular supply chain.

and enterprise reputation. All these information are stored in respective databases. Indeed, this does not only improve the traceability of the product in the life cycle but also ensures a transparent and credible recycling environment for the product in its further stage. Consequently, this approach maximizes the use of manufactured products and ensures the reduction of waste resources. In all, the adoption of blockchain technology can enable circular supply chains of manufacturing companies to become more sustainable and accelerate the progression of a circular economy.

Different supply chain participants have different authorizations and permissions in the blockchain-based circular supply chain management platform. Suppliers need to be accredited with qualification certifications by uploading their basic information if they consent to participating in the manufacturing activities through the platform and accessing relevant data. During the production stage, manufacturers need to upload real-time data on the manufacturing process to the cloud database. Product data may be uploaded later, in the production and post-production stages. Logistics enterprises provide logistics and reverse logistics services for the whole supply chain and likewise access some information, for example, about inventory, when authorized by retailers. Retailers are mainly responsible for selling, so they can share the product sales information with their upstream firms and cooperative partners. Manufacturers with self-established logistics systems and sales channels can obtain some benefits from a blockchain-based system because they can share information in a more secure and efficient manner. Consumers can access the information on certification of products and suppliers to check the quality and condition of products and likewise trace some product information. Such consumers can also be given some product-related environmental protection information.

All the information is encrypted and cannot be accessed without permission. For example, users can get data and information only through linkages that grant them access to large design files in the cloud databases through the predefined application programming interface (API). Also, it is through permission that the access to certain information like supplier certifications, working conditions information and data on product recycling can be gotten in order to evaluate the reliability of others and their sustainability qualifications. It should be noted that supply chain participants have no authority to tamper with data or information, either in the blockchain or in the cloud database. This is because both the blockchain and the cloud database are linked by the hash value, and any changes will result in an incompatibility in the proposed platform. In this context, a collaborative decision-making and information sharing environment will be developed in a blockchain-based circular supply chain management platform. As such, it will provide opportunities for the stakeholders in the circular supply chain to quickly respond to the market.

As earlier mentioned, the blockchain is a technology that is based in the concept of the distributed database, in which data is not stored on a centralized server but in several interconnected machines, called nodes (peer-to-peer). The blockchain makes it possible to innovate the current management of transactions through a process that connects distributed cryptographic primitives of benefit to guarantee information traceability and security. The main benefit of distributed systems in the domain of circular economy is the presence of information on all the machines connected to the network. This kind of database is based on two fundamental processes that are useful to guarantee accurate operations and limit the number of information to the basic minimal. We define these two fundamental processes below:

- **Duplication:** This is a process that is considered useful to ensure that the same data is present on each machine connected to the circular economy network. This process allows identifying a master database that will be taken as a model to be duplicated on all the other devices on the network.
- **Database replication:** This is software that has the potential to identify any logical internal change to the database; once the database has been identified, this software allows replicating the change on all the machines connected to the circular economy network.

Additionally, the functioning of the blockchain is based on the following components presented below:

- **Node:** This is a representation of a single blockchain actor and physically constituted by a server.
- **Transaction:** This is a logical processing unit that coincides with a sequence of elementary operations that need to be verified, approved, and then archived.
- **Block:** This is a logical unit that is represented by the union of a set of transactions that are grouped to be verified, approved and archived.
- **Hash:** This is a non-invertible algorithmic function that allows representing a text and/or numeric string of a variable length in a unique string of predefined length.
- **Ledger:** This is a master book in which all transactions are immutably recorded and sequentially ordered.

Within a blockchain system, a block is developed when a product supply plan is generated. A block consists of a header and body. As such, in the proposed blockchain-enabled circular supply chain management architecture, the block header contains information like a hash of the previous block, a time stamp, and version. Since the block body is of limited size, only some simple structure information is stored in it. For instance, in the pre-production stage, information about the product name, supplier name, product sales and demand and product reuse are linked to other data and stored in a block. Additionally, smart contracts with rules for sharing information among different supply participants are carried in the block. In a similar vein, other data and information including the product research and development data/information, supplier quantification certification and product demand forecast model are stored in product-related and supplier-related cloud databases. In the production stage, the block comprises of linkages to the cloud database. With respect to supplier linkage, it comprises of access to manufacturing process data, cleaner production management data and data that is monitored in real-time. In the context of product linkage, access to product certifications, namely quality certification are likewise included. Within the post-production stage, the recycling product linkage is usually stored in blocks. Additionally, this linkage is utilized to access data which in this case includes data on product recycling, sales/leasing, reuse, recall and so on, all of which can help in achieving the circular supply chain sustainability.

8.6 MANUFACTURING SUSTAINABILITY CHALLENGES AND BLOCKCHAIN-ENABLED SOLUTIONS IN CIRCULAR SUPPLY CHAINS

There are certain sustainability challenges that the manufacturing sector face that pertains to the triple-bottom-line (TBL) factors, namely economic, environmental and social dimensions. Within the economic context, it should be noted that due to streamlined operations and cost reductions that occur from outsourcing production to low-wage countries, the manufacturing sector has transited to becoming market driven. Thus, the manufacturing industry has established demand-driven flexible supply chain management in spite of the geographical distances of supply chain partners. Consequently, products are manufactured in surplus, which tends to discourage reuse and other circularity strategies. Indeed, there is a constant pursuit of emotional "highs" through emotionally additive searching, impulsive buying and a certain appeal in combining the usage with ownership of manufactured products. These attitudinal and behavioral characteristics associated the manufactured products have resulted in a correlative interaction with the lifecycle of manufactured products. Likewise, within the environmental context, the production processes involving in manufacturing products generated environmental and occupational hazards that contribute to greenhouse gas emissions and has huge environmental effects. For instance, there is a high incidence of industrial water pollution as a result of the production processes of manufacturing products. Also, wastes from manufactured products reach millions of tons yearly. In addition, manufactured products utilize quite a huge number of packaging including labels, tags and containers and these quickly amount to wastes since the product lifecycle is very short. Indeed, the manufacturing is regarded a hugely destructive industry to the environment.

Furthermore, since manufacturing operations are usually outsourced to low-wage countries for cost reduction, related environmental problems have worsened as a result. Firstly, the cost of resources, namely water, energy and land is really very low, and that is easily ignored or subsidized by the local government. Secondly, most low-wage countries are lacking in terms of concern for environmental quality and have lesser or non-existent environmental requirements/standards. Thirdly and lastly, since the consumption market is usually far from these low-wage manufacturing countries, the harmful impacts on the environment are not often seen by the public at the sites of consumption. Within the social context, most employees work in poor working conditions in the low-wage countries where manufacturing processes are outsourced to. For instance, women in countries like Cambodia can only afford to sleep on the shop floor of companies that manufacture products for use in Europe and North America. Also, in Dhaka, Bangladesh, there are child laborers who work for 10 hours per day to earn just $1, even under threatening conditions. Additionally, in China, there are thousands of workers who toil around the clock in order to meet up with the production demands even though dust from production plants constitutes a heavy irritant to the lungs. There is also the risk that manufacturing workers face during the process of manufacturing such as risk of sustaining injuries due to building collapse. Furthermore, low-wage countries are generally characterized by a lack of consistent government monitoring of manufacturing factories for compliance with laws and regulations. In sum, there exist a lot of social sustainability issues in the manufacturing sector that pertains to child labor, poor working conditions, exploitative wages, human rights, long working hours, etc.

The economic, environmental and social challenges in the manufacturing sector are known to be related. Given that the industrial production technology and mode of operations management cannot make any disruptive change, increased rate of production leads to pollution of the natural environment and as such, workers suffer the risk and harm. Likewise, blockchain technologies present potential solutions to these sustainability challenges in the manufacturing sector, as illustrated in Table 8.1.

Indeed, blockchain can be adopted in supply chain operations to make transactions safer and more transparent, traceable and efficient. Due to the increasing popularity of sustainability needs in the manufacturing sector, more and more manufacturers and retailers have recently invested in sustainability strategies, a trend that is projected to continue to accelerate. A circular economy can engineer the macro-trend toward adopting sustainability strategies as a proactive philosophy rather than an afterthought, disruptive technologies like blockchain can be employed to enable circularity objectives in the pre-production, production and post-production stages. As earlier mentioned, overproduction of products remains a key challenge for manufacturing companies, which can have environmental and social consequences. Blockchain technology can be utilized to mitigate these consequences through enhancing sustainable manufacturing, fair labor practices and extending the product lifecycle by reusing and recycling the materials involved.

Firstly, blockchain technologies can be utilized to reduce overproduction of products. Most manufacturing companies operate a linear model of

TABLE 8.1
Manufacturing Sustainability Challenges and Potential Blockchain Solutions

Sustainability Challenges	Potential Blockchain Solutions
Economic challenges in the pre-production, production and post-production stage	• In the pre-production stage, blockchain solutions can enable supply chain partners to cooperate successfully to forecast demand and minimize the bullwhip effect. • Also, blockchain technologies can assist in enabling the creation of a decentralized, trustworthy network to share the asset database peer-to-peer. • In the production stage, blockchain technologies can furnish a supply chain with security, speed and scale of data exchange in a distributed manner across all the relevant supply chain partners. • In the post-production stage, blockchain technologies can be effective in reducing fraud and errors, time, costs and waste of manufactured products in the transit process.
Environmental and social problems in the pre-production and production stages	• In the pre-production stage, blockchain technologies can aid in programing to automatically trigger actions (including supplier verification and certification) once certain conditions are met and thereby can accelerate the flow of data between nodes. • Also, blockchain technologies can assist in providing a better option for evaluating and selecting the right suppliers. • Additionally, blockchain technologies can enable supplier verification to be conducted, recorded and assessed in a quick manner by all the blockchain nodes. • Consequently, a blockchain-based supplier selection process can be regarded as being much easier, efficient and effective within the pre-production stage. • Blockchain record and traceability system can support the TBL sustainability factors through monitoring and tracing real-time occurrences with regard to environmental and social responsibilities. • Also, blockchain technologies can help in detecting working conditions and workers' status by collecting environmental data such as light, humidity and temperature and man-hours/working hours. • Such data can be utilized to evaluate, analyze, certify and recertify whether the suppliers have met the ethical standards and requirements. • Additionally, blockchain technologies can enable auditing the quality and safety of the use of chemicals, water and land during manufacturing, besides auditing manufacturing from biological sources and technical fibers that are derived from non-renewable chemical resources. • In the post-production stage, blockchain technological solutions can help in verifying, recording and authenticating the production and usage history of the manufactured product. Consequently, products can be resold, rented and donated to extend lifetime after washing, sanitizing and quality. Brand auditing. • Through blockchain verification and authentication, materials are acknowledged at the end of life can be reused and remanufactured into other products, hence maximizing the utilization of manufactured products and minimizing landfill waste amounts as well.

design-manufacturing-sale-disposal, causing bull-whip effect. The linear model entails that only two adjacent nodes can have proximity to share information partially. As such, information shared about demand from end-customers experience distortion when going to upstream suppliers. Hence, the linear system can result in a vast amount of waste from overproduction and transit inventory. A basic solution has been to seek centralized information on customer demand to minimize bullwhip effect, but this requires free communication among supply chain partners. Nevertheless, this is considered problematic to achieve in a system that is laden by different problems, including lack of trust, lack of shared vision between supply chain partners and lack of complete information sharing in multi-tier supply chains. Since blockchain can assist in the creation of a decentralized, trust-free network to share the asset database peer-to-peer and furnish a supply chain with security, speed, and scale of data exchange in a distributed manner among all supply chain partners obviating the need for trust building. Hence, blockchain technologies can assist supply chain members to cooperatively and successfully forecast demand and thereby minimize the bullwhip effect in the pre-production stage. Additionally, blockchain technologies can aid in reducing fraud and errors, reducing the time, costs and waste from manufactured products in the transit process. Also, blockchain technologies can help in removing the need for double verifications and by so doing reduce the inventory amount of production and related packaging in the whole supply chain network. Hence, the waste that accrues in the production stage can be drastically reduced. Furthermore, the decentralized, trust-free network can share the security, speed, and scale of data including sales, stock, and transition after production in a distributed manner. This tends to enable all supply chain partners to adjust their individual operations, inventory, delivery and sales and reorder schedules in an orderly manner. As such, the whole supply chain network can possibly minimize inventory in the whole channel within the post-production stage.

Secondly, blockchain technologies can be utilized to meet the environmental and social sustainability challenges through the process of supplier selection and supplier management tracking. Sustainable supplier selection is considered as one of the most critical decisions for achieving supply chain sustainability in the pre-production stage. Since most production activities have been outsourced to developing countries that are characterized as low-wage countries, it becomes important for manufacturing companies to identify reliable and ethical suppliers with relevant sustainability certifications. Basically, multi-criterion selection system which consists of environmental, social and economic factors/considerations is used for the process of sustainable supplier selection. Within the context of environmental protection, the recycle/reuse/reduce option has been found to be the topmost criterion for supplier selection. Likewise, the Social Accountability 8000 (SA8000) standard certification deals with child/forced labor, health and safety, freedom of association, discrimination, disciplinary practices, working hours, remuneration and management systems. It is highly essential that suppliers are able to comply with these basic requirements/expectations in order to achieve certification. As such, the process of supplier evaluation and selection is considered to be complex and time-consuming, involving a variety of partners/actors, operations and a plethora of information.

However, blockchain technologies can be effective in providing a better means for the process of supplier evaluation and selection. It is expected that a potential supplier is effectively verified before being permitted to access the blockchain. Due to the inherent characteristics of automation, blockchains can be programmed to automatically trigger actions (including supplier certification) once it becomes certain that the required conditions are fulfilled and can effectively accelerate the data flow between nodes. Consequently, the verification can be successful quickly conducted, recorded and also assessed by the blockchain nodes. As such, a blockchain-based process of supplier evaluation and selection will become a lot easier, more effective and efficient and also be able to set the pace for circular supply chain management in the pre-production stage. The blockchain record and traceability system can support the three pillars of sustainability by monitoring and tracing real-time occurrences in terms of environmental and social sustainability since blockchains can record, trace and monitor peer-to-peer transaction of all assets accurately. For instance, blockchain technologies are essential for auditing manufacturing from biological sources and technical fibers that gotten from non-renewable chemical resources. Also, blockchain technologies can detect the working conditions and the status of employees by collecting data from worksite that pertains to light, humidity, temperature and working hours. These data can be utilized to analyze, evaluate/re-evaluate, certify/recertify whether the suppliers have abided by ethical requirements/standards to engage with their employees in a fair manner in the production stage.

Within the post-production stage, most manufactured products are treated as waste and discarded, even though still in reusable condition. Blockchain technologies can help in facilitating the recycling and reusing of such manufactured products through appropriate procedures. The production and usage history of manufactured products can be easily tracked and authenticated since blockchain has verified and recorded the information of such products (namely brand, model, manufacturer, component, technology for processing and data of purchase) and even the consumers. Such manufactured products can still be resold to extend their active lifespan after relevant processing procedures. This exemplifies the critical role of blockchain technologies in circular supply chain management. Furthermore, products regarded as being in their end of life stage can be repurposed to manufacture other products through blockchain verification and authentication. As a result, blockchain technologies can assist in minimizing the amount of product waste that can end up in landfills and with saving on the resources utilized for products and production lines.

8.7 SUMMARY

Blockchain technology has received particular attention for reasons such as its rapid growth is supporting supply chain traceability, sustainability and information security over the last decade and its potential to cope with multiple circular economy challenges simultaneously. The role of blockchain technologies in business operations includes bridging trust, traceability and transparency.

There are five common strategic objectives in traditional supply chain management and blockchain technology can provide potential support to help to achieve these objectives effectively. These strategic objectives include cost, risk control, speed, sustainability and flexibility.

Due to the increasing popularity of sustainability needs in the manufacturing sector, more and more manufacturers and retailers have recently invested in sustainability strategies, a trend that is projected to continue to accelerate. A circular economy can engineer the macro-trend toward adopting sustainability strategies as a proactive philosophy rather than an afterthought, disruptive technologies like blockchain can be employed to enable circularity objectives in the pre-production, production and post-production stages.

In a blockchain-enabled circular supply chain, four entities play a critical role: (i) certificate authority, (ii) network administrators, (iii) membership service provider (responsible for providing certifications to the partners for participating in the supply chain network) and (iv) the other supply chain partners.

The blockchain makes it possible to innovate the current management of transactions through a process that connects distributed cryptographic primitives of benefit to guarantee information traceability and security. The main benefit of distributed systems in the domain of circular economy is the presence of information on all the machines connected to the network. This kind of database is based on two fundamental processes that are useful to guarantee accurate operations and limit the number of information to the basic minimal. The fundamental processes include duplication and database replication.

DISCUSSION AND REVIEW QUESTIONS

1. Briefly define the concept of blockchain.
2. Enumerate the role of blockchain technologies.
3. Mention some challenges to implementing sustainability objectives in the manufacturing industry and some potential solutions of blockchain technologies in solving such challenges.
4. Outline the entities in a blockchain-enabled circular supply chain and their critical role.
5. Mention and briefly explain the key areas of blockchain-enabled circular supply chain management.

Part 5

9 Circular Economy and Sustainable Business Performance

9.1 INTRODUCTION

Globally, organizational concern regarding business environmental management has been growing. Environmental improvement in businesses have been encouraging firms to think and act toward reducing the negative effects from ill environmental performance, from both production and consumption ends. In this context, companies have a responsibility to defend the environmental and sustainable values of society and need to show it to their stakeholders. The circular economy has been increasingly seen as a possible solution to pursue a more sustainable development. The new economic system, called circular, aims to include practices such as reducing, reusing, recycling and recovering to traditional systems. Nevertheless, the circular economy is an approach that seeks to have been brought up only more recently in the organizational and research environments, but its theoretical foundation derives from older schools of thought, such as Industrial Ecology, Biomimicry, Natural Capitalism, cradle-to-cradle, performance economy and others. The definition of circular economy considers both the environment and economic benefits simultaneously under the notion of a regenerative performance requiring circulation of technical nutrients while ensuring safe entry and exit of nutrients in and out of the biological sphere. The circular economy also demands a shared conscience, responsibility and performance involving the entire life cycle and all the stakeholders of both the organization and the product. The circular economy has advanced a great deal in the last decade and the exploration of alternatives in support of the circular economy in industries has been observed to bring consistent benefits not only to the literature but also to the business sector. On those grounds, the organization that appears to be most proactive in accelerating the transition to a more circular economy around the world is the Ellen MacArthur Foundation. This organization stands out by helping to pave the way to the adoption of circular initiatives by both the public and private sectors. Many companies seem to struggle to view the circular economy as a revenue-making paradigm rather than risky and costly. Likewise, more sustainable business models have been discussed in the last few years, especially embracing the concept of circular economy toward circular business models. Therefore, in this chapter, a discussion of the circular business models and the main contributions of the circular economy on sustainable management in businesses are presented in detail. Additionally, we present some pressing issues to consider with respect to the environmental impact of circular economy business models. Also, insights are provided concerning the relationship between firm's dynamic capabilities and circular economy development. Additionally, the different aspects of circular economy rebound (CER) in circular business are discussed.

9.2 CIRCULAR BUSINESS MODELS

Circular business models manifest in organizational structures that span the gamut from for-profit organizations to social enterprises and non-profit social ventures. The latter two social purpose organizations provide a socioeconomic sustainable bridge between economic growth, environmental stewardship and social progress. In a similar vein, the complexity of social and economic value creation requires social purpose organizations to work with a broad set of stakeholders representing social and commercial interests, which often creates adaptive tensions and frictions that need to be better orchestrated. In aiming for a better future – not only for a specific group in their ecosystem but also for the ecosystem (i.e., our society) at large – social purpose organizations provide inspiring examples of the implementation of a circular mindset.

In line with growing interest from environmental activists, politicians and business practitioners, work on circular business models in the academic literature has increased significantly over the last five years. In the circular economy, business models and business model innovation are discussed as tools for fundamentally changing the way business is done and driving it toward sustainable and social innovation. The business model concept has, starting with the proliferation of Internet-based businesses in the late 1990s, received increasing scholarly attention. Business models have traditionally been viewed as value creation processes of firms, as descriptions of how the parts of business systems fit together and as sets of decision variables. These allow firms to use and coordinate their resources to create and deliver value to customers for appropriate monetary compensation. Most commonly, circular business models are conceptualized as holistic descriptions of how organizations create value for their stakeholders, optimize material loops and thereby capture value. More specifically, the existing circular business model literature describes four distinct logics for value creation as presented in Table 9.1: (1) Efficient material-technical loops, (2) effective product-service loops, (3) social-collaborative loops and (4) symbiotic ecosystems.

9.2.1 Efficient Material-Technical Loops

Value creation in efficient material-technical loops works by closing, slowing and narrowing biological and technical lifecycles. Closing loops refer to maximizing material and energy efficiency by reusing material through recycling and collecting. Slowing loops are about prolonged use and reuse of goods over time, through the design of long-life goods, repairing, refilling, refurbishing and upgrading. Lastly, narrowing loops is about reducing resource use associated with the production process, resulting in efficiency improvements. Material-technical loops support the use of fully renewable, recyclable or biodegradable resources. Furthermore, new technologies, such as smart materials, 3D printing and blockchains, can increase the efficiency of such loops. Efficient material-technical loops are characterized by forward-and backward-integrated processes. That is, they are set up to deliver sustainably produced goods to customers and retrieve end of life (EoL) goods for the

TABLE 9.1
Circular Business Models

Circular Value Creation Logic	Efficient Material-Technical Loops	Effective Product-Service Loops	Social-Collaborative Loops	Symbiotic Ecosystems
		Content		
Changing and creating (new) activities	Maximizing material and energy efficiency • Developing and building for durability • Repairing, refilling and refurbishing • Recycling and collecting • Upgrading	Deliver functionality rather than ownership: • Paying for use • Leasing • Renting • Maintaining • Servitization	Proactively engage all stakeholders: • Sharing • Diffusion of sustainable practices • Slowing down consumption	Driving systemic change: • Re-purposing the role of business for the society and environment • Restoring and reincarnating • Scale-up solutions
		Structure		
Liking activities, resources and actors in new ways	Circular supply chains, vertical (forward and backward) integration	Service solutions, vertical (forward) integration	Collaborative consumption platforms, network integration	Open associative and collaborative networks, network integration
		Governance		
Ways of governing/ managing the activity system	Supply chain management, firm-centered contractual models	Service management, firm-centered with contractual models	Platform orchestration, decentralized with collective contractual models	Collective entrepreneurship, multi-organizational governance, decentralized with collective authority

recycling process. The governance mechanism – the way activities are managed and actors are coordinated – consists of well-defined contract models that ensure coordination of the circular supply chain. When closing and slowing material loops, it is essential to include all parties, from design and raw material suppliers to end users, service providers and recyclers, in the associated information flows. Furthermore, the social relationships between supply chain partners are considered to be essential in creating closed loop supply chains.

9.2.2 Effective Product-Service Loops

Effective product-service loops create value by replacing product ownership with access to the products and services, for example, through renting, leasing and pay-for-use approaches. In the exiting circular business models literature, these product-service loops are commonly discussed under the rubric of product-service systems (PSS). The underlying impetus of PSS is to reconsider how material and service needs are being met and work toward goods and parallel services that more environmentally benign and materially/energetically efficient. Since the 1990s, PSSs have been discussed as effective instruments for moving society toward higher resource efficiency and close product-service loops. Sustainability in PSS can be further enhanced through dynamic and continuous upgrades of the goods integrated in the service offering. On the other end of the PSS spectrum, sustainability researchers have suggested to "dematerialize" or "servitize" goods and to consider fundamental needs rather than products when developing circular business models (e.g., providing transportation services rather than selling cars). The proposed governance mechanisms (similar to the previously described efficient material-technical loops) are firm-centric and follow the logic of one focal firm managing the PSS.

Taking together, much of the literature discussing value creation in circular business models is thus narrowly focused on the efficiency and effectiveness of circular lifestyles and fundamentally rooted in the causal relationships of the value chain. This literature thus calls back to Porter's structure-conduct-performance approach centered on competitive advantage and profitability. While the Porterian view of the value chain is broadened and the engagement of versatile actors is getting more consideration, the underlying value creation logic of many circular business models is still focused on competitive advantage and profitability. Sustainable and environmental goals are byproducts of creating higher economic value for the focal firm – a value creation mechanism that does not fully align with the triple-bottom-line and the systemic nature and complexity of the circular economy.

9.2.3 SOCIAL-COLLABORATIVE LOOPS

Collaboration, rather than competition, is regarded as a central practice for transitioning toward a well-functioning circular economy. The emergent academic debate revolving around the collaboration of interdependent actors in circular systems directs sustainable and circular research toward a more systemic perspective, which is more suitable for addressing the complex challenges of the circular economy. That is, value creation in social-collaborative loops is focused on linking actors to perform sustainable practices effectively. This approach is compatible with the idea of "sweating idle assets" in the sharing economy, which reduces demand for new manufacturing. Hence, the consumption cycle is slowed down and underutilized resources become activated. Social-collaborative loops keep assets in the economy and create new opportunities for actors in the ecosystem. Customers, for example, engage in alternative consumption systems based on sharing, which use the idling capacity of already produced but rarely used goods or individuals' spare time and skills. Following the logic of social-collaborative loops, customers are no longer seen as passive recipients but active performers co-creating new consumption systems. Realizing the full potential of social-collaborative loops requires that their governance mechanisms are set up to take advantage of open and collaborative infrastructures. On sharing platforms, for example, review mechanisms help to collectively govern the practice of versatile actors.

9.2.4 Symbiotic Ecosystems

Symbiotic ecosystems create value by closing resource loops (similar to recycling). However, differing from the above-described logics of circular business models, symbiotic ecosystems build on collective action and collaboration of various actors in their value creation logic. Sustainable challenges are so vast that a real transition toward sustainable development demands joint efforts and collective entrepreneurship and that the sustainable efforts of a single firm hardly lead to success. Symbiotic ecosystems consider broader institutional structures and horizontal network integration and acknowledge that the success of sustainable innovations depends to a large part on the structure and dynamics of their environment. The governance of such circular business models is decentralized, with a certain degree of collective authority held by multiple organizations and entrepreneurs. This emergent circular business model logic points toward a more holistic and systemic perspective built upon business models. It draws upon an entrepreneurial ecosystem framework, which has contributed to a deeper understanding of the context of agglomerations of individuals, businesses and other regulatory bodies. This emergent circular business model logic recognizes the interplay of collective action and the environment and promotes the study of their interdependencies and connections.

9.3 DRIVING BUSINESS MANAGEMENT SUSTAINABILITY THROUGH CIRCULAR ECONOMY

The influence of the circular economy toward more sustainable businesses can be seen across a range of business areas. In some areas, this influence is more evident, seen as an underlying issue, in others, there is some blur on the real implications of circular economy practices to businesses. However, many practices toward circularity might not have been pinpointed as such, hence having received other names, even though many have been in practice since long. Some of the business areas where circular economy can act as a driver toward more sustainable practices include strategic planning, cost management, circular supply chain management, quality management, environmental management, process management, logistics and reverse logistics service management and research and development. These practices can comprise mutual, multi-directional changes among the areas previously mentioned, and others, as well as one, might exert direct unidirectional influence over another. Or even yet, they can cause a chain of events where an area "A" influences another area "B", which in turn influences another area "C" and even goes back to influence area "A". Moreover, this circle of influences may even involve more than three agents in a single iteration.

A detailed discussion on the key impacts of the circular economy toward a more sustainable conduct in various business areas shown in Figure 9.1 is presented as follows.

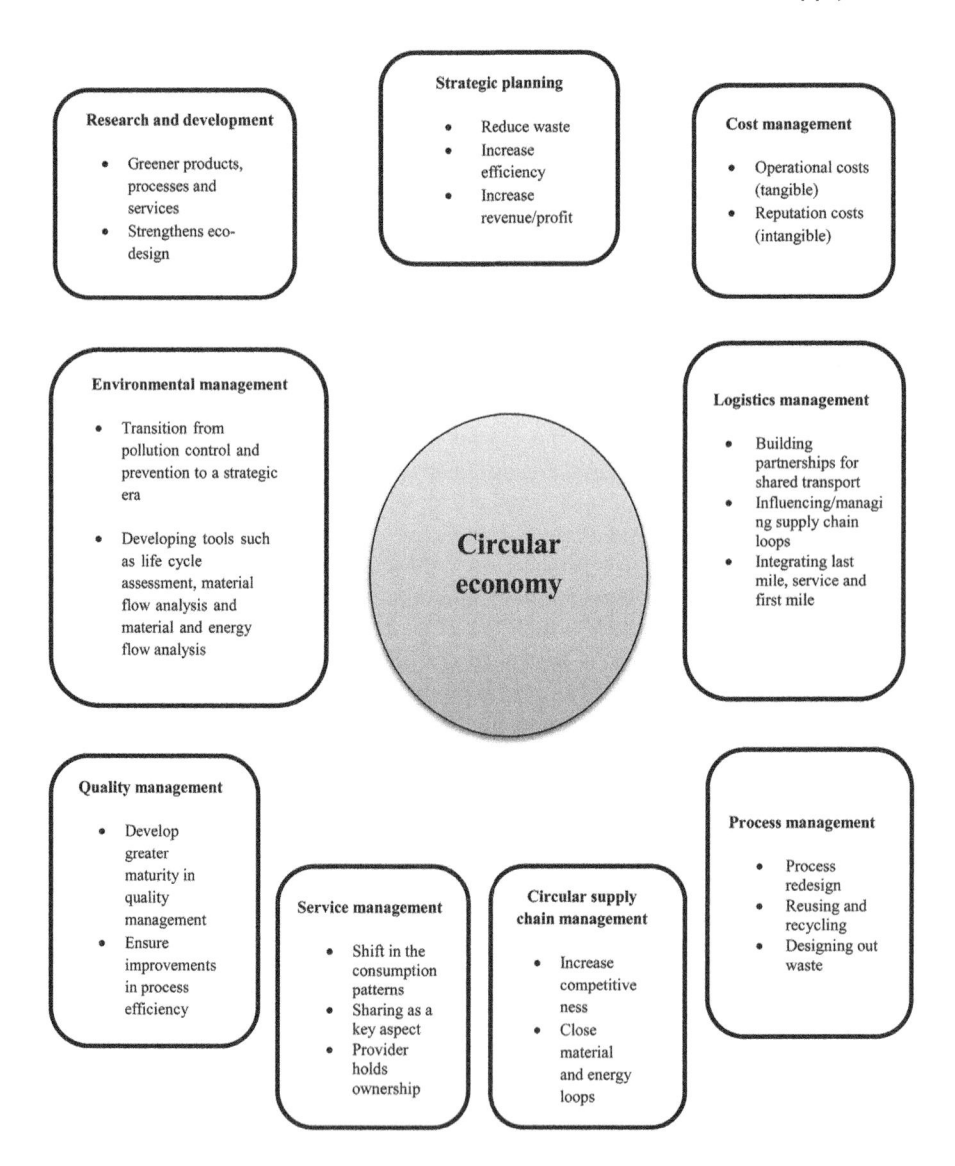

FIGURE 9.1 Key business areas with impact from circular economy.

9.3.1 Strategic Planning

The circular economy contributes to greater resource efficiency and a more sustainable economic development by means of using its main principles to gain strategic advantage, where companies seek to lower the environmental burdens and improve the economic aspects of their operations. In the current environment, circular economy is considered a strategic and relevant issue for the profitability of companies and for creating values. Thereupon, managers want to subsidize better environmental alternatives.

Circular Economy and Sustainable Business Performance 189

As for the environmental aspects, the adoption of circular economy principles enables companies to close resource loops, providing ways to align the company's strategic planning with more circular principles. Circular economy functions, therefore, as a motivator for companies that desire to adopt more sustainable business models. A company may, for instance, outline its supply chain management practices to maximize resources efficiency through the reduction, reuse and recycling of waste and attaining environmental goals. Furthermore, the adoption of circular economy principles as the main philosophies for strategic planning provides companies with the means to identify and tackle different sources of revenue. Companies that follow this path are able to create means to reduce operational costs through resource recycling and reuse and also reach different audiences. Organizations may strategically develop their business models to be fully viable.

9.3.2 Cost Management

In the context of cost management, the adoption of circular economy principles and practices plays a critical role since it allows companies to convert products that are at the end of their life cycles into resources for the conception of other/new products. This allows for waste minimization and simultaneously decreases the need for inputs of virgin material. In addition, resource scarcity causes price increase and volatility, negatively impacting a company's value creation and capture. Undoubtedly, changing from linear to circular business models, both efficiently and sustainably, may require investments from all parties involved in the company's network.

In recent times, the European Union recognized the circular economy as a high-impact strategy to help society to be aware of the limits of economic growth. Although the barriers to adopting such practices are to be considered (such as potentially high upfront investment costs for circular economy projects and low prices of virgin material caused mainly by greater offer), there are several cases in which the results of its implementation turn out to be favorable in more than one expected way. A practical example of applying circular economy percepts into cost management can be seen in Alcatel's adoption of monitoring and treatment of the electronic wastes it generates. As Alcatel tackles the Chinese market, it identifies clear economic advantages provided by this practice, such as the cost reduction provided by the reuse of components and, simultaneously, the reduction of possible tangible costs that are to be expected from poor environmental performers. In Alcatel's case, not only did the company create a clear economic advantage by recycling and reusing the waste it generates, but it also avoided an intangible cost of reputation damage, which might be expected from companies that are not perceived as environmentally friendly.

Other examples of cost-affecting strategies are shown in Ikea's and Waitrose's (a British supermarket) practices. Ikea offers consumers the inconvenience of having to assemble their furniture themselves, but it comes at a lower price compared to traditional furniture purchases. Waitrose, in turn, offers the possibility of buying products (such as pasta and wine) in the quantities the consumer wants, using their own containers or "borrowing" a container from the store until their next purchase, which reduces food waste at the end of its life cycle. Both strategies are subtly attached to traditional business approaches but contribute to more circular systems. In those cases and others, slight changes are observed in the revenue patterns, thus affecting the companies' cost management strategies. It should be noted that traditional cost management strategies might even hinder company development, where the financial value of recovery is merely one condition for the creation of a circular flow in supply chains.

9.3.3 CIRCULAR SUPPLY CHAIN MANAGEMENT

The circular economy is often regarded as a provider of opportunities for companies to stretch the economic life of goods, joining efforts along the chain of supply and also engaging consumers, seeking to recover the value of such products throughout its lifecycle. Hence, the potential for value recovery offers good opportunities for the creation of circular supply chains. In the context of supply chain management, circular economy provides means for integrating its main concepts within the existing management principles. Circular supply chain management encompasses the configuration and coordination of organizational functions within and across business units in order to slow down, close or narrow energy and material flows. This results in the minimization of resource input into the system and also prevents waste and emissions from leaking out of the system, hence improving operational effectiveness and increasing competitiveness. In order to adopt a more circular supply chain management, companies are required to align their strategies in order to successfully attain specific goals, where economic, environmental and social bottom lines must be considered and proactive action from multiple stakeholders is required. It is necessary that the company achieve a balance in the environmental, economic, logistics, organizational and marketing performances in order to integrate a circular economy to supply chain management. As such, more circular supply chains have the potential to be more independent and also to avoid volatile and high prices. Companies may attain social goals, for instance, by orienting their business models to create local jobs, while others may declare commitment to customers and communities as a social-oriented action. In all, a circular economy offers companies opportunities for systematic thinking and allows such companies to integrate it to a more sustainable development of their supply chain. In a similar vein, an organization is able to proactively manage its stakeholders either by engaging their partners in making their business models viable or pushing their partners toward the adoption of input materials that are made mostly by recovered materials/resources, thus enabling the market of such materials to grow.

Examples of actions that can be taken to increase the circularity of a supply chain include expanding urban collection points, including incentive programs to encourage customers to return the capsules or take them to a pick-up point, cultivating a culture of civic responsibility and awareness around waste reduction and association with specialized recycling companies to explore each waste separately. A long-term perspective with short-term actions can be observed from building economically viable businesses in order to disseminate circular economy principles or to use certain materials in order to show that they may not need to end up in landfills. Nonetheless, a more circular practice might rearrange a supply chain altogether if compared to a traditional chain. Circular economy, therefore, presents itself as a philosophy that is adaptable and has the capacity to be integrated to supply chain management.

9.3.4 Quality Management

During implementing of circular economy practices, there is still an inherent need for quality products and processes. Companies need a shift in policy that enables protecting the environment while promoting business models that assure manufacturing/production quality and also allow maintaining business competitiveness, customer-oriented and differentiation strategies. Nevertheless, the shift from a linear to a circular economy leads to issues previously inexistent or unperceived in terms of product and process quality. Organizations should address the issue that its customers might perceive the products that have been made with the use of recovered input materials as lower quality products. This consequently drives organizations into developing quality management practices in order to keep their reputation out of harm. Hence, it is important to pinpoint the main material flows in quality management and the need to have a quality management system that is both more integrated with circular economy and more mature. The circular economy can foster quality improvement in processes. For the performance of closed loop systems to be considered to be of high quality, relevant materials must be selected and approved based on certain quality standards.

9.3.5 Environmental Management

There has been growing concern regarding the environmental aspect of sustainable and circular business models. Rather than proposing that organizations should manage the environment, which inherently implies ownership of the natural resources it has access to, organizations should adopt environmental stewardship. The principles of circular economy have a close relationship with a company's environmental management and performance, and on the one hand, it is argued that more circular systems are able to help to prevent negative impacts on the environment. Nevertheless, on the other hand, one must not neglect the consequences of rebound effects, which, if not accounted for, might offset the impacts prevented by the intended strategy and ravage the sustainable efficacy of more circular systems. Likewise, the development of products/processes with greater environmental awareness charges companies with the adoption of more sustainable measures. Hence, it raises the need to utilize tools that can evaluate processes from an environmental standpoint in order to quantify potential environmental impacts. Potential reductions in primary energy use and environmental and toxicological impacts can also generate satisfactory results in terms of adopting a circular economy approach.

One of the environmental assessment tools that can support the circular economy is the life cycle assessment. The International Organization for Standardization (ISO) refers to life cycle assessment as a tool aimed at raising environmental awareness of potential impacts associated with products, aiming to evaluate the environmental aspects and potential impacts of the life cycle of a whole process, product or service. It can be characterized as the most important tool for assessing potential environmental impacts in modern environmental management. The tool may guide improvements on the environmental performance of products by assisting in decision-making and selection of environmental performance indicators and marketing strategies. It can be used in selection, classification and management decision support and also be used to encourage environmentally friendly practices and assist in sustainable decision making. The evaluation is performed by a compilation of inputs and outputs, assisting environmental management in identifying opportunities for improvements in production systems. Hence, the use of life cycle assessment allows evaluating the system as a whole in order to quantify the potential environmental impacts.

Likewise, an integrated management approach is proposed in order to solve existing conflicts between industrial development and environmental protection through adopting circular economy concepts, particularly in the China context. This might be attributable to the rapid development of China's economy, and industries have caused increasingly high rates of pollution and resource depletion. The strategic transition from end-of-pipe control to pollution prevention sets an example of improved environmental management. The notion of circular economy marked the change in the Chinese model of pollution treatment from end-of-pipe to a structural change toward a more circular economy. Moreover, sustainable business models have focused on recovering products and resources and creating value from waste. This is in line with the concept of circular economy for providing political guidance for a more sustainable transition and presenting a positive vision for the future in terms of climate change, ecosystem degradation and increasing the risks of raw materials scarcity. Quite unlike industrial approaches, circular economy approaches have not been the subject of education for sustainability which has been slow to adopt circular systems in the curriculum. Due to the need for further assessment and adoption of circular systems, which might not always have an ideal performance throughout the entire product life cycle, businesses usually build cases for a more circular conduct and even experiment with such approaches.

9.3.6 Process Management

Within the circular economy, processes might be reengineered so as to extend product life, reduce environmental impacts, or increase financial results. On those grounds, much thought is put onto strategies for product and resource recovery; hence, many waste management processes/strategies are based on the circularity concept. To internalize circularity, many processes have been going through a redesign to facilitate aspects of (e.g.,) reusing, recycling and transporting as for logistics and reverse logistics. The management of processes might be affected with respect to reengineering production processes in order to make them more circular (e.g., restructuring facilities), or even switching from one set of operations to another (production based on virgin inputs versus production based on non-virgin inputs). Generally, existing business models for the circular economy have limited application and there is no comprehensive framework supporting every kind of company/process in designing a circular business model. In this sense, the processing or manufacturing phase of a product is one that lacks a fair share of the resources consumed and the environmental impacts caused by a product hence it is rendered a key spot for managing and promoting or fomenting circularity.

One of the central changes in process conception and redesign is the elimination or reduction of waste and even if/when waste is produced, it should be planned to have its value recovered. Circular economy principles have driven strategies and changes in processes in a range of fields, such as in the area of chemical or biological processes and a myriad of industrial processes. Besides waste management strategies (including reduction, reuse, recycling, final disposal) and even partnership deals to either provide or receive waste, changes toward greater circularity may affect factors such as energy consumption rates and types of raw materials. Furthermore, all of these interactions among processes might lead to industrial symbiosis. This might happen among processes within the same industrial facility (internal recovery), as well as it may happen among related or non-related companies (external recovery). One process' outputs might be another one's inputs and this interaction/relationship may happen philanthropically or be based on financial or economic incentives. Such interactions, whether designed environmental wise or not, influence the environmental profiles of processes, leading organizations through a more sustainable path.

9.3.7 Logistics

The application of the concepts of circular economy to the field of logistics incurs a few implications. Some of the highlighting issues are sharing transport means so as to increase load factor and avoid unnecessary transport, and strengthening and stimulating industrial clustering, thus, industries are able to share services. It all contributes to lowering transportation costs, besides lowering environmental impacts and connecting with one underlying key aspect of a circular economy-sharing. Reverse logistics has been stretching out around the world, involving all layers of supply chains in various companies and sectors, and this area of research has become a key competence in modern supply chains and also a profit generating function. In the context of the circular economy, logistics and reverse logistics management assists in closing, slowing and narrowing supply chain loops. Hence, it is also highlighted the importance of building partnerships to promote reverse logistics practices in order to enable recovery strategies such as recycling and remanufacturing. Indeed, reverse logistics is a major component of the functioning of a circular economy. Based on the concern that post-use wastes must be transferred back upstream so that they can be re-processed, thus recovering their value, which builds on the concept of take-back systems. In this context, whether wanted or not, the final consumer is the agent who controls the flows of EoL processes. This kind of agent can make or break such reverse systems, hence the importance of sensitizing customers and encouraging a change in culture in order to embrace a circular behavior. Additionally, last mile delivery service and first mile reverse logistics can be integrated so as to increase circularity. Deliveries, pickups and intermediary logistics services have the potential to increase transport efficiency and circularity if merged or shared. Indeed, such interactions lead to both environmental and financial benefits, which invariably improve business sustainability.

9.3.8 Service Management

The research on circular economy has gradually expanded from government policy to the management of the value chain and material flows but now has a more business-oriented perspective. In this regard, service companies are in a strategic place between manufacturers and end users; hence, they play a significant role in the transition to a circular economy. Many times, efforts are devoted to major changes in the processing of products in order to attenuate some sort of negative impact, while in parallel, potential in services is often neglected. The circular economy is considered holistic and adaptive; in this context, the use of PSS, a model that uses eco-efficient services with the potential to replicate and compete with the "fast-fashion" industry, has been increasingly observed and these systems have been highlighted as great enablers of the circular economy. Moreover, PSS have been signaled as a path for greater sustainability. In fact, offering services rather than products is one of the most effective ways of walking toward a circular economy and decoupling profits from massive resource consumption since, in the standard pattern of consumption, products have been prematurely aged.

Likewise, the offer of PSS has implications to the development of effective take-back systems and the design of more durable products that also facilitate recovering value at the end of their use cycle (e.g., for recycling, remanufacturing, etc.). Two notable companies that offer PSS are MUD Jeans and RePack. One good example is posed by the company MUD Jeans, which instead of selling jeans, rents them. One can rent a pair of jeans for a year and have free repairs if it be the case. This kind of practice makes producers seek to make long-lasting products instead of speeding its obsolescence to produce new ones and increase sales. When the provider holds ownership, more of the company's interests are invested in it. Another company is RePack that provides packaging services for e-commerce. The company promises to remove package waste and design packages to last at least 20 cycles. Notwithstanding, much thought is usually put into medium and large organizations and more so, the micro/small companies also have the potential to contribute to such a circularity model involving both upstream and downstream partners. This is in spite of the presence of barriers, majorly economical, to be overcome or else the small companies might struggle with changes in the short term. Furthermore, the idea that offering services and sharing are major steps toward achieving the circular economy is very popular in industries and academic fields. Indeed, PSS contribute to increasing circularity, regardless of whether product-oriented, user-oriented or result-oriented. Such practices may provide consumers with the products/services they want and would otherwise not be able to afford, economically or even time or space-wise, for instance. It does, nonetheless, slow the pace of consumption that, at times, ravages resources.

9.3.9 Research and Development (R&D)

Research and development has been addressed as an attempt to explore competitive advantages and innovation in order to compete in an increasingly globalized environment. In this context, eco-design and lifecycle assessment-based research

Circular Economy and Sustainable Business Performance 195

and development allows selecting alternative materials, seeking better economic and environmental performance throughout the whole lifecycle of products. In this context, the design stage of a product can ferment a more circular performance. By means of designing long-life goods and extending the life of the products (by offering services to extend product life such as remanufacturing and repairing), the use phase of those products is extended, thus slowing the flow of resources.

Furthermore, the role of product design to some extent differs from that of businesses based on a linear economy (based on throw-away products), and it is argued that a thoughtful design of products can provide competitive advantages for organizations. Hence, one could observe the importance of investing in R&D activities as it influences economic performance. It is important to observe that eco-design does not apply exclusively to product development or even to product-oriented organizations. Service-oriented companies employ eco-design to their business models in order to implement circular economy into their daily practices. Product design implications reach a range of fields, contributing to greater economic sustainability in production chains by improving product life cycles, making them more manageable and bringing innovation.

9.4 SYNERGIZING THE BUSINESS AREAS FOR CIRCULAR ECONOMY IMPACT

All the business areas in which circular economy can impact have different effects on one another, and some might be more impacted by circular economy initiatives than others. Considering an entire supply chain, there might be trade-offs between areas relating to circular practices. An example would be seeking to reduce costs (cost management) and environmental impacts related to logistics (logistics and reverse logistics). This is by using local bio-resources to produce products with higher added value (where the resource could have at least one more cycle before being sent for energy recovery), thus addressing research and development but transporting it by a longer distance so it could be processed. These trade-offs will be specific to the resource/region/system under consideration but should be accounted for when deeming the sustainability of the business. However, the synergies among those business areas could also yield further business opportunities. The impacts of circular economy practices on each of the areas presented here will indirectly impact the entire value chain of the business. Collaborations among different actors along the supply/value chain are necessary for making better use of resources being dealt with, and they can help to reveal and also boost opportunities for new businesses. A few examples of business opportunities are presented as follows:

- Integrating a more circular thinking into strategic planning can help companies to value the local economy and reduce environmental impacts from logistics by working with suppliers that are located nearby, which also saves time and money with transportation.
- Investing in more circular economy-driven research and development for designing products and revenue streams can assist companies to reduce environmental impacts and close, slow down and narrow resource flows

while reducing waste and improving their reputation both among consumers and business partners.
- Another approach in terms of research and development is to think about the entire production chain including the product's EoL routes. Developing a product with a circular tendency can help gauging benefits in the supply chain, logistics and production/manufacturing by reducing the inputs of virgin material, among other measures.
- Closing the cycle in terms of material and energy can be an interesting strategy for organizations working in cooperation networks. When the use of resources/products is cascaded into a circular system, it can be interesting for areas such as strategic planning, cost management and environmental management. Reducing costs, reducing the extraction of raw materials from nature and generating energy with waste are key points that also help to shape emerging models.

Although it might seem that environmental management and circular supply chain management stand out within the areas being influenced by the circular economy, many other opportunities might arise from bringing a circular thinking into the organization and internalizing flows of resources. The opportunities herein are generic examples, hence, further and more concrete opportunities can be spotted for specific systems.

Moreover, circular businesses are a branch of sustainable businesses. Although not necessarily sustainable on their own, circular business models help to achieve greater sustainability. However, designing a sustainable business or turning an existing business more sustainable by implementing circular practices might incur a range of managerial implications. These implications entail management issues and changes to a business model and operations that managers need to cope with and communicate throughout the entire organization and also the chain of supply when going circular. This may also imply changes in the company's organizational culture. Changes in the way products are consumed, disposed and managed demand a change in culture. The concern with the behavior toward circularity has been observed since the 1990s, even if not under that name at times. Pursuing a circular economy implies a fundamental transition in society.

One of the challenges is to shift the company's as well as the customer's views, sensitizing them to stand from a cleaner viewpoint, thus detaching benefits and experiences from purely economic aspects. To that end, companies might have to adapt existing capacities to build new ones. All of it leads to a change in behavior, both the company's and customers'. The company might want to or have to deploy actions to encourage circular behavior, as its own culture can play a critical role in enabling the implementation of a circular economy. Additionally, it will also need coherent changes in government policies and, thus, all the change embedded in it. Furthermore, besides the market culture, even more importantly, the company's culture needs a shift from commonplace practices to be able to maintain its activities, facing constant challenges and adaptation within a market dominated by linear strategies. Accordingly, circularity happens differently depending on the context. In fact, aspects such as social, organizational, structural and political have to be taken into consideration, and they all involve cultural traits, thus, being context-driven.

All the nine business areas that were found to be affected by the implementation and management of circular initiatives have changes and barriers to overcome. One highlighting reason for the need of identifying the impacts in different areas is that, on the one hand, across an organization, different stakeholders might have to deal with the different impacts (or even the same impacts but in different places), each one in a particular way. They can and should interact in order to develop integrated visions and action plans, as they are all part of the same overall strategy. Nevertheless, those actions need to be deployed on a daily basis and will be ultimately broken down into operational tasks. On the other hand, on a more hierarchical perspective, directors (or any other agent with the role of integrating and harmonizing the work of all those different areas) need to be aware of the bigger picture and be knowledgeable of the more general implications that increased circularity might have. Furthermore, a few areas might be more impacted than others, which will also depend on the strategy for circularity, thus the circular business model and also the type of company and the segment. In this context, barriers are amplified in developing countries, as the fact that they are seeking to fit into the market quickly results in a low interest in adopting circular economy practices and organizations still lack structure and information when aiming at circular practices. This is due to the fact that the circular economy requires a structural change that reshapes the manufacturing and the organizational culture. Therefore, the implementation of circular initiatives needs to be analyzed beforehand so that barriers and expenses are foreseen.

Furthermore, as a further managerial implication, life cycle thinking can support the environmental, economic and social aspects that may be linked to circular economy actions. Understanding the circular economy and being able to, in fact, apply it in different areas within companies may be a key point for organizations to move forward with material and energy recirculation, recycling, reuse, remanufacturing and other circular economy deployments. Also, new interactions between resource consumption and revenue models have been established in order to increase the sustainability of businesses. In this context, researchers and practitioners have been finding ways to decouple the consumption of resources from the revenues of businesses. How far on this road businesses will go remains to be seen. However, it will very likely impact production and consumption patterns, and companies need to be up for those changes if they want to remain in business. Moreover, currently, there are standards that help guide companies toward achieving a more circular and more environmentally friendly conduct. Examples of those are the first standard on circular economy, the BS 8001 and the ISO 14000 series, where one can find in ISO 14001 the requirements with guidance for the use of environmental management systems.

9.5 ENVIRONMENTAL IMPACT OF CIRCULAR ECONOMY BUSINESS MODELS

Here, we firstly define circular business model experimentation and then classify the companies that experiment toward circular business models into two broad categories with examples. Secondly, we present a review of some examples of the environmental impacts and rebound effects that can result from circular business models. We then discuss the different types of environmental impact and list some environmental impact assessment tools currently available for use to academics and practitioners.

9.5.1 Experimentation Toward Circular Business Models

Circular business models present a viable alternative to the current linear systems for production and consumption. Some examples of such business models include rental, subscription or leasing, refurbished, remanufactured and secondhand products. These types of business models have the potential to significantly reduce the environmental impact if actively designed to do so. While many definitions exist, we define a business model as the basic plan of how a business proposes, creates, delivers and captures value. Circular business models are business models that specifically target environmental and economic resource savings through narrowing, closing, slowing and regenerating resource loops. Businesses do not necessarily need to close resource loops by themselves, within their own internal system boundaries, they can also be part of a system of business models that together close a material loop and work toward a "circular" goal. Companies typically test and validate these new business model opportunities through experimentation. Business model experiments can help reduce uncertainty, manage risk and test organizational capabilities in a controlled environment. This early trial phase tends to involve multiple iterative rounds of testing and pilots. Previous studies in product design literature have suggested that 80–90% of a product's environmental impact is decided in the design phase. The same is true for business models since circular business models are not sustainable by default. Hence, it is important to forecast the potential environmental impacts of new business models at an early stage to maximize their impact reduction potential.

Companies that experiment with circular business models can broadly be classified into two categories. First, there are "linear" firms that are experimenting with circularity. These are traditional established firms with linear business models that are trialing new circular business models. These firms still exploit their linear business experiments to trial new ways of doing business to reduce their environmental impact. Some recent examples of this include IKEA's Buy-Back Program, Volvo's car sharing and subscription initiatives and Adidas's rental platform trial in France. The second category of companies are those that are "born circular" that started out with circular business models as their core business strategy, but their business experiments can lead them in two directions. In the first case, experimentation could lead to new circular; revenue streams, value propositions and market niches. An example of this is Fairphone, a company that sells modular phones and encourages repair, has recently tested a new phone-as-service initiative where the company retains ownership of the phones. Another example is the packaging reuse company Loop that has trialed new zero-waste e-commerce systems. In the second case, some born circular companies can also conduct business experiments that lead them in the direction of linearity. This might be the case because there is increased demand for their product offerings, and they are exponentially growing in size, resulting in higher environmental impact. Another reason may be the pressure to create new revenue streams and stay ahead of competition. These "linear" ventures and resulting increased environmental impact may be temporary or permanent, and they might be intentional or accidental. Such companies could be put in this situation because they are unaware of the environmental impacts of their new business ideas before implementation. An infamous example of such a case includes the Mobike bicycle graveyards created from exponential growth and oversupply. So, business experiments conducted by companies that may have started out as "circular" or sustainable could either create new "circular" business opportunities or move them toward linearity through unintended rebound effects.

The abovementioned examples illustrate that business strategies can change quickly and iteratively with every step of the experimentation process. And with every step, they may make implicit or explicit decisions on the environmental impact that follows. It is important to measure the environmental impact of these decisions during the experimentation phase itself in order to prevent design lock-ins.

9.5.2 Environmental Impacts of Circular Business Models

As mentioned earlier, circular business models might not be more environmentally sustainable. Perceived savings from circularity can sometimes lead to rebound effects by increasing the consumption of other resources. Moreover, consumers can sometimes be careless toward rental products, diminishing their potential lifetimes. It has been demonstrated that rebounds of consumers who were given access to wastepaper recycling are beneficial for the environment, consumers were later shown to use more paper towels compared to the control group when given the option to recycle them. This might be due to consumers being unaware of the true costs of recycling and that *making recycling readily available at all times could actually boomerang such that in some cases people consume more than they otherwise would.* This indicates that recycling can only be a means to an end and that overall resource consumption needs to be reduced to derive environmental benefits. Likewise, a peer-to-peer boat sharing platform, as shown in both the boat lessees and the lessors, experienced rebound effects. In the case of some participants, the rebound effect contributed to losing about one-fifth of potential emissions reduction obtained from the resource sharing. Many study participants reported increased consumption of resources, enabled through economic savings. In some cases, more air travel was undertaken because of financial savings. In some cases, higher personal use of the boat than usual was reported. This resulted in a net increase of most of the participants' annual emissions, despite being part of a resource sharing business model. Such field experiments can be crucial in showcasing whether a perceived "green" activity actually has the intended environmental benefits. Hence, it is important to keep track of environmental impacts while trialing new circular business ideas.

9.5.3 Present State of Environmental Impact Assessment

Environment impacts can be created at the micro, meso and macro-levels. The micro-level is the level of the product or company, the meso-level refers to the level of industrial networks, and the macro-level is at the level of cities, nations or society in general. Environmental impact assessment tends to be specifically tailored to one or more of these levels. Moreover, the word "tool" is used as an overarching term to describe frameworks, assessment methods, indicators, strategies and tools that can be used by a company to determine the environmental impact of its business model. Many types of tools exist in both academia and practice for assessing the environmental impact of business models. Nevertheless, most of these existing methods focus on the product or material-flow levels. Some examples of commonly used impact assessment tools are input-output analysis, life cycle assessment (LCA), material flow analysis (MFA), recycling efficiency rate, Global Reporting Initiative (GRI), greenhouse gas (GHG) indicators and internal reporting guidelines. Environmental impact assessment tools can be divided into two categories: ex-post or ex-ante. Ex-post methods measure the environmental impacts of the final outcomes after certain actions have been carried out by the company. They can use lagging indicators or reactive indicators like "amount of waste generated" and "total water consumption" to quantify the impact. Many environmental impact assessment tools such as the LCA and GRI fall into this category. Ex-ante assessment methods, on the other hand, aim to predict the impact before the events have occurred. They can use leading or proactive indicators such as "industrial efficiency levels" and "types of vehicles used for transport" to provide guidance and warning about proposed actions, hence giving companies the opportunity to improve on their strategies.

9.6 FIRM'S DYNAMIC CAPABILITIES AND CIRCULAR ECONOMY DEVELOPMENT

The circular economy is conceptualized as an economic model for closed loop production and consumption systems, where waste is designated a valuable resource. Compared to the traditional linear economic model, which has a *"take, make, dispose"* model of production, the circular economy model is based on product maintenance, reuse, remanufacture and recycling which implies switching the production's and consumption's concepts of *EoL* for restoration. This is because more efficient use and reuse of resources and the resulting lower overall resource inputs, energy, emissions and waste leakage could reduce negative environmental impacts. This can occur without jeopardizing growth and prosperity, all while achieving a better balance between the economy, environment and society. The circular economy is a cyclic system that aims to eliminate waste by turning goods that are at the end of their life cycle into resources for new ones. Closing material loops in industrial ecosystems can create a continual use of resources. This can be achieved through long-lasting design, proactive maintenance, recycling, repairing, refurbishment and remanufacturing. Hence, the circular economy model is an economic system of recycling and reusing of resources where the reduction of the elements is imperative; that is, reducing the production to the minimum and opting for the reutilization of the elements that, because of their properties, cannot be returned to the environment.

The circular economy's premise is the transformation of the way resources are utilized by shifting from existing open production systems (i.e., traditional linear systems where resources are used to produce finished products and become waste after their consumption) to closed production systems (i.e., circular systems where resources are reused and kept in a loop of production and consumption). As defined above, the aim of this kind of closed loop cyclic system is to eliminate waste by turning goods that are at the end of their life cycle into resources for new ones. By maximizing the efficient use of resources, this fundamental redesign of materials, products and value creation systems should ultimately reduce the negative environmental effects of emissions and resource waste that naturally accompanies the consumption of physical goods. The circular economy is often facilitated by means of product-life extension, redistribution/reuse, remanufacturing, and recycling. The notion of the circular economy has been approached in the scientific literature from several interdisciplinary perspectives, including industrial ecology, product design practices and environmental, political and social science. The implementation of circular economy principles often requires new visions and strategies and a fundamental redesign of product concepts, service offerings and channels toward long-life solutions. This is in line with the reassessment of suppliers and partners as well as value chains that focus on long-term instead of short-term efficiency.

Dynamic capabilities consist of a set of higher-level activities that allow firms to orient their ordinary activities to high-payoff endeavors. This requires managing and coordinating firms' resources to address rapidly changing business environments. Dynamic capabilities encompass two important elements for achieving competitive advantage: dynamic and capabilities. The term "capabilities" refers to the capacity of firms to deploy resources, usually in combination, using organizational processes to achieve an objective. Firms' capabilities result from learning, organizational resources and organizational histories. Learning is an outcome of practice and experimentation, permitting tasks to be performed more effectively. The term "dynamic" refers to the changing nature of the environment and highlights the role of innovation in the context in which timing is critical. Thus, dynamic capabilities refer to the ability of firms to change their own capabilities, for instance, by developing new products to deal with changes in the external environment. Dynamic capabilities not only encompass capabilities but also firms' processes and routines. In a similar vein, dynamic capabilities are considered as the firm's ability to integrate and reconfigure capabilities to address rapidly changing environments.

The creation and development of circular economy skills constitute an example of the development of dynamic capabilities. First, the circular economy and environmental management require the integration of a number of if resources and competencies such as information systems, technical systems or tacit knowledge that resides in the organization. Second, the growing pressure from consumers for environmental stewardship has pushed firms to increase their responsiveness as well as their flexibility and ability to change quickly. Finally, path dependencies and continuous improvement are inherent in tasks that characterize the circular economy and environmental management. Proactive environmental strategies such as the development of circular economy models constitute dynamic capabilities, which are linked to product-focused and process-focused practices. Product-focused practices refer to the development of products that are compatible with the circular economy. The circular economy advocates the use of biodegradable materials in the production of consumer goods so that once consumes, they can return to nature without harming the environment. In those cases in which eco-friendly alternative materials are available, for example, for electronic and metallic components or batteries, the circular economy business calls for the production of easy-to-disassemble pieces that can be reused and incorporated into new products. When this is not possible, the circular economy model envisions an environmentally respectful and friendly recycling process of those parts of the product that are neither biodegradable nor reusable. Therefore, firms face important challenges such as the innovation of circular economy products. Process-focused activities refer to the circular economy model's pillar of closed loop production and consumption systems. As compared to the traditional linear economic model, circular economy models comprise not only the design, production, distribution and usage phases but also the phases of collection of the product at the EoL and feeding of materials back into the cycle. This spans not only producing organizations and users but also third parties (e.g., waste management organizations or raw material suppliers). Hence, a condition for the implementation of closed loop systems is the establishment of collaboration and cooperation among organizations, with the aim of facilitating the development of circular economy products. The establishment of collaboration and cooperation agreements poses important challenges for the organizations in terms of the introduction of innovations in their processes, such as new managerial modes or creation of information channels.

For exploring how the circular economy-related dynamic capabilities influence the decision to implement circular economy product-focused and circular economy process-focused activities, we consider three factors. The first factor is the organizations' level of competencies to implement the circular economy model. Competences refer to the collective learning in the organization, especially how to coordinate diverse production skills and integrate multiple streams of technologies. Hence, competences are the potential to be effective, or the ability of an organization to achieve its goals. Capabilities and competences are related in the sense that "capability" is the condition of having the capacity to do something, and "competence" is the degree of skill in the task's performance. Capabilities and competences are related in a bidirectional process: an organization with capabilities can acquire a new skill set or knowledge by learning and doing, which increases the organizational competences. Moreover, the competences are antecedents of the capabilities since having knowledge and skills in carrying out an activity predisposes to its realization. In the context of environmental studies, it has been found that eco-efficient dynamic capabilities depend upon the integration and coordination of competences, innovations and new routines. Thus, the tenure of circular economy competences fosters the development of circular economy capabilities and thus circular economy product and process-related practices.

The second factor refers to the possession of national and international standards that determine the acquisition of processes and organizational routines to develop the circular economy business model. The possession of standards is an example of path-dependent learning, which comprises an important aspect of the dynamic capability model. Moreover, the possession of standards by the organization is the result of demonstrating an ability to plan and organize tasks. The path dependency in new process standards (e.g., ISO certifications) influences the ability of firms to improve environmental performance by reducing toxic emissions. Therefore, the possession of circular economy standards enables the circular economy-related capabilities, demonstrating knowledge and skills in the development of organizational routines.

Finally, the third factor is the possession of *knowledge* and *communication channels* that facilitate cooperation with external actors and promote organizational competences for the implementation of the circular economy business model. A proactive environmental strategy involves stakeholders at multiple levels of the organization. For example, product stewardship requires integrating the perspective of both internal and external stakeholders into the product design and product development processes. In the context of environmental sustainability, the integration of stakeholders has been considered as a sensing capability, one of the three basic components of dynamic capability.

9.7 CIRCULAR ECONOMY REBOUND IN CIRCULAR BUSINESS

Although the circular economy sounds intuitively beneficial for the environment, care should be taken when assessing the true environmental benefits of circular business: companies that operate within the circular economy paradigm and are based on circular business models. One of the recently emerging reasons for the potential failure of circular economy practices to deliver on their environmental promises is called *Circular Economy Rebound* (*CER*). The original, more thoroughly researched "classic" rebound effect typically occurs when increases in production/consumption efficiency are canceled out due to absolute increases in production/consumption, also known as Jevons paradox. A common example concerning this type of rebound can be found relating to energy: when energy improves, prices lower and usage/demand rises in response leading to a higher net use of energy (and a worse environmental outcome). Rebound may occur in the context of circular economy and significantly diminish hypothesized environmental benefits, as the theory on circular economy places too much focus on material resource flows and lacks the inclusion of behavioral economics and market forces. If *CER* is occurring, it could have implications for reaching GHG emission reduction targets, and even change the preference order of EoL practices. CER can allegedly manifest itself in two main ways:

1. through imperfect or insufficient substitution (microeconomic) and
2. through price or re-spending effects (micro- and macroeconomic).

Nevertheless, narrowing down on and quantifying particular manifestations of rebound effects in the circular economy can be problematic and lead to undesirable mitigation strategies. In explaining the CER, we discuss important aspects, namely as follows.

9.7.1 THE ENVIRONMENTAL REBOUND EFFECT

Since the "classic" rebound effect relates to energy efficiency, there is a need to broaden the scope to include a wider, more comprehensive understanding of the effect in an environmental, sustainability or circular economy context. There are available practical insights on how the debate on rebound effects has "outgrown" the energy efficiency domain and can now be understood as a set of economic (and behavioral) mechanisms. In doing this, the separation to distinguish the classic rebound effect in the early energy literature from the broader *environmental rebound effect* (*ERE*) has been created, which is rooted in "lifecycle thinking". The *ERE* perspective allows the study of technological innovations beyond energy efficiency improvements to include a wider array of environmental consequences while it avoids to become a substitute, term for any economic cause-effect mechanism.

Apart from cases in which the ERE detracts from or diminishes the realized environmental benefits of a certain technological improvement, there are also cases in which a "negative rebound effect" can be observed (with an actual positive effect). During investigating the ERE of electric cars, it was observed that in some cases, high capital costs can actually generate a decline in net environmental pressures, thereby reversing the rebound direction. This occurs when a consumer buys a car that has clear environmental benefits and is relatively more expensive than its alternatives, binding more income otherwise spent on high impact goods (re-spending effect), and therefore "reinforcing the environmental benefits". This means that producers might also be underestimating achieved environmental benefits following a technological innovation.

9.7.2 Rebound in the Circular Economy

CER occurs when circular economy strategies fail to deliver on their environmental promise in ways very similar to the ERE. Generally, circular economy strategies consist of recycling, remanufacturing, refurbishing and reusing of materials. The net environmental impact of these strategies is determined by the difference in Impact 6 between primary and secondary production in combination with the accompanying change in production quantity. The environmental benefits of these secondary production strategies can thus only fully materialize if and when they actually displace or at least significantly lower primary production. A lack of displacement/substitution can be the result of the inferior quality of secondary goods (e.g., recycled plastics and paper) or when a new market is opened up due to the vastly different price at which the new good is being sold (e.g., refurbished smartphones). Therefore, only in some cases circular economy strategies will displace primary production through superior performance in competition. As a result, assuming that every unit of secondary production achieves environmental benefits directly proportional to the difference between the secondary and primary good's impacts seems a premature conclusion. Nevertheless, this assumption is often implicitly made in circular economy strategies, as rebound effects continue to be omitted from life cycle analyses (LCAs), and corporations benefit from this lack of disclosure through promoting inflated environmental achievements. Therefore, to recognize and account for the rebound effect is essential to safeguard both environmental and market integrity in the circular economy.

9.7.3 Circular Business Models and Circular Economy Strategies

Basically, a circular business model is how a company creates, captures and delivers value with the value creation logic designed to improve resource efficiency through contributing to extending the useful life of products and parts (e.g., through long-life design, repair and remanufacturing) and closing material loops. Furthermore, resource efficiency strategies, which often equate to circular economy strategies, do not by definition lead to increased resource efficiencies or environmental benefits. Rather, innovating the business model toward a circular business model can help create an offer that embeds a circular strategy and successfully operates it.

9.7.4 Mitigation Effects

Drawing upon the early literature mainly focused on the classic and ERE, several historic and current mitigating approaches have been explored. For instance, an accumulation of suggested pathways has been described, even though no binding act or policy currently exists that explicitly mentions the rebound effect was observed/noted, and thus there is no enforced policy on the subject yet. In a small yet significant amount of different legal acts by the European Commission, the term is mentioned, though remaining suggestive. In the academic world, mitigating strategies have often revolved around changing consumer behavior, stressing the need to consume more efficiently, differently and less in general. Also, market-based instruments centered on carbon and energy pricing have been discussed. The European Commission produced the most substantive and comprehensive report on rebound effects, including a wide range of suggested policy pathways. The need for simplified measuring tools is also mentioned, as well as the potential for smart meters to mitigate direct rebound and attentiveness toward perverse green advertising that promotes moral licensing and compensation behavior following innovations. Despite the absence of the circular economy concept in these mitigation approaches, they could possibly be applied to the current paradigm and prove useful in the transition.

Threefold of contributions has been presented that, when adhered to, can aid in minimizing CER. The conditions are as follows:

1. Firstly, products and/or materials from secondary production need to be presented as true alternatives for primary production, with comparable quality, price and marketing efforts. If a product from secondary production cannot seriously compete with its primary alternative, meaningful substitution – as well as the accompanying environmental benefits – will likely not occur.
2. Secondly, circular substitutes should at least have no effect on the total demand or decrease total demand for the given good on the macro scale. Therefore, markets with a somewhat satiable demand or low-price sensitivity would be less vulnerable to rebound effects (e.g., home appliances would be more satiable than clothing or electronics).
3. Thirdly, even in the case that the first two conditions are met, it needs to be made sure that introducing a new product from secondary production to the market indeed diverts buyers away from primary production. This is especially difficult since the usual methods to draw consumers (searching niche markets or lowering prices) should not be used to ensure the environmental benefits by avoiding *CER*. Therefore, although theoretically attainable, fostering business circumstances that reduce the creation of CER will prove difficult for businesses that try to transition toward circular practices as they are competing with other businesses that do not.

9.7.5 REBOUND AND INEQUALITY

Mitigating rebound effects could have detrimental outcomes for the income group of society. As illustrated in a case study of smartphone reuse, this happens because the low prices of refurbished smartphones enabled a whole new group of consumers to purchase them, significantly increasing the total demand of smartphones. Placing too much value on the attempts to reduce re-spending and macroeconomic rebound would therefore exclude consumer groups from the option to purchase a certain good. Jarringly, enabling the new consumer group access to a good often is exactly the point in such cases, often making rebound mitigation strategies socially undesirable. To illustrate how this problem manifests in rebound quantifications, consider again the "negative rebound effect", which occurs when the rebound effect reverses, and causes extra environmental benefits. This effect could be observed when a good is both a better alternative environmentally and more expensive, binding extra income that could otherwise be spent on high-impact goods. The *ERE* model, and specifically the re-spending effect, captures this tendency. Likewise, the ERE model describes how income that was liberated or bound due to cost changes will or will not be re-spent over the various consumption categories. Based on this logic, increasing the price of environmentally friendly goods would be more beneficial for the environment because it would stop people from consuming other goods. By extension, it also means that the poorer people are, the better it is for the environment. Therefore, when discussing rebound mitigation options based on calculations with a model that captures this effect, especially in relation to policy, these considerations concerning what is (socially) desirable for society should be taken into account.

9.7.6 MITIGATING REBOUND IN THE TRANSITION

A key insight is that rebound is not bound to any particular circular economy strategy or business model. Indeed, the CER manifests in multiple ways. This means that no circular economy strategy or practice is inherently void of rebound, as the source of rebound often does not reside in the strategy. However, some areas are more prone to generate rebounds than others. This has more to do with the market form of the industry or sector that the organization operates in than the strategy it applies, as well as demand and price elasticity of the goods. The reason for this is that the rebound effect is, in its nature, a relativistic measurement indicator, dependent on the price and impacts of alternatives and the level of competition in the market. Additionally, there is a wide range of identified causes or drivers of CER, while the differences in circular economy strategies remain minimal and mutually exclusive. Some causes were clearly psychological (moral licensing), others economic (high competition/insufficient substitution) or technological (automation). Whether a company employs a certain strategy does not necessarily influence the risk of generating CER. Only for secondary production, there is an increased vulnerability to unnecessary down-cycling (leading to insufficient substitution), emphasizing the need for smart recycling practices. Although this list of potential rebound manifestations is certainly non-exhaustive, it does not indicate that seeking relations between circular economy strategies and CER will likely not deliver significant results.

Some rebound effects are direct causes of the transition toward circularity. This includes the need for infrastructure and transportation between organizations that can now benefit from each other's waste streams and the increased necessity for disassembly practices due to modular design. This type of rebound is inherent to the transition, as it embodies the energy required to move from one system to the next. It could be seen as the "necessary evil" of the transition, retaining its "evil" aspect only as long as energy consumption/production still has the large environmental impact that it has today. Although perhaps still blurry, there appears to be a distinction between rebound that is inherently caused by the transition toward a circular system and rebound caused by other factors (economic, psychological). Separating *transitional* CER and *strategic, design* or *behavioral* CER could be useful. This is an important distinction to make when confronted with a potential rebound effect to prevent the implementation of ultimately counterproductive measures.

Consequently, the role that rebound and the mitigation of it should most definitely not have is the one of obstacle or barrier to positive change or reason for inaction. On a more practical level, producers of circular products need to be aware of the substitution potential of products in order to reach the desired environmental benefits. The quality, comfort and security of a product need to be safeguarded for it to compete with its alternatives and to avoid becoming too much of a niche product. Furthermore, rebound mitigation measures that could exclude customer groups are not acceptable, as it interferes with the core ideas of the circular economy. The existence of rebound relating to transportation and infrastructure in the transition emphasizes the critical importance of clean energy sources and the realization that there will be no effectively functional circular economy without it. Setting up the circular economy requires financial, material, logistical and infrastructural investments, which are accompanied by an inevitable increase in energy use. This increased energy use is, in fact, a rebound effect of the transition that will bring about tremendous environmental benefits and can and should therefore not be avoided altogether. Identifying rebound as such will constitute a powerful argument for the acceleration of the energy transition as a precursor to the transition toward a circular economy. Some specific suggestions for mitigation of rebound causes are presented in Table 9.2. Another consideration for organizations to mitigate rebound is to re-calculate environmental performance metrics when certain demand or sales benchmarks have been exceeded. To avoid a direct rebound effect resulting from a rise in sales and thus production (for example, through lowering prices), perhaps sales cannot be allowed to exceed a certain number in order for the initial environmental assessment to hold.

Moreover, in discussing the rebound effect and how to avoid it, a new approach toward design is critical. The "traditional" designer often works as a self-contained entity within the production process, focusing mainly on aesthetics, cost-efficiency and acceptance by the consumer. The "new" designer needs to have a more comprehensive approach to design, seeing through the whole supply chain, taking away the heavy burden of complex EoL practices from the recycler by anticipating the continuous cycling of materials and resources in the system. In this way, systems can be intelligently constructed from the outset, as opposed to current practices in which responsibilities are simply transferred when goods/materials switch hands,

TABLE 9.2
Rebound Causes and Mitigation Strategies

Rebound Cause	Suggested Mitigation Strategy
Insufficient substitution – competition	Maximize displacement potential, e.g., quality
	Government intervention in markets, e.g., subsidies and eco-taxes
Moral licensing	Sustainability communication and awareness
Strategic/design decisions, unnecessary down-cycling	New design approach
Automation	Use renewable energy
Increase in transportation	

and recyclers end up with the often impossible task of retrieving valuable resources from monstrous hybrids. Diving into what this means opens up a wide range of possibilities and implications. The first and foremost aspect of this new design approach concerns the realization that value chains need to become more collaborative, open and transparent. This entails, among others, the need to know the origins and composition of the materials that designers work with and more scientific involvement in the process to approach higher technical effectiveness in product design and recycling. The realization that a lot of contemporary recycling technologies are actually solutions to problems that can be averted in the first place by taking a new approach to design is extremely important.

Furthermore, there is a need for systems thinking and a change in the notion of value, as without a more comprehensive view on both transition-enhancing policy and rebound mitigation policy, the efforts will be in vain. This entails reshaping design and business models, rethinking consumption and ownership practices and eliminating perverse incentives or value drivers among many more. Optimizing the current system through endless incremental efficiency increases rebound effects and actually becomes an inhibiting barrier for real meaningful change. While circularity is a broad concept that can be approached through different lenses, the way in which goods and services are valued and how value is created and extracted lies at the heart of the shift between linear and circular economies.

9.8 SUMMARY

Circular business models are conceptualized as holistic descriptions of how organizations create value for their stakeholders, optimize material loops and thereby capture value. Four logics for value creation in the circular business model include: (1) Efficient material-technical loops, (2) effective product-service loops, (3) social-collaborative loops and (4) symbiotic ecosystems. Some actions that can be taken to increase the circularity of a supply chain include expanding urban collection points, including incentive programs to encourage customers to return the capsules or take them to a pick-up pint, cultivating a culture of civic responsibility and awareness around waste reduction and association with specialized recycling companies to explore each waste separately.

The influence of the circular economy toward more sustainable businesses can be seen across a range of business areas. Some of the business areas where a circular economy can act as a driver toward more sustainable practices include strategic planning, cost management, circular supply chain management, quality management, environmental management, process management, logistics and reverse logistics service management and research and development.

Collaborations among different actors along the supply/value chain are necessary for making better use of resources being dealt with, and they can help to reveal and also boost opportunities for new businesses.

Moreover, circular business models are business models that specifically target environmental and economic resource savings through narrowing, closing, slowing and regenerating resource loops. Companies typically test and validate these new business model opportunities through experimentation. Business model experiments can help reduce uncertainty, manage risk and test organizational capabilities in a controlled environment.

Capabilities and competences are related in a bidirectional process: an organization with capabilities can acquire a new skill set or knowledge by learning and doing, which increases the organizational competences. In the context of environmental studies, it has been found that eco-efficient dynamic capabilities depend upon the integration and coordination of competences, innovations and new routines. Thus, the tenure of circular economy competences fosters the development of circular economy capabilities and thus circular economy product and process-related practices. The possession of circular economy standards enables the circular economy-related capabilities, demonstrating knowledge and skills in the development of organizational routines.

A proactive environmental strategy involves stakeholders at multiple levels of the organization. For example, product stewardship requires integrating the perspective of both internal and external stakeholders into the product design and product development processes. In the context of environmental sustainability, the integration of stakeholders has been considered as a sensing capability, one of the three basic components of dynamic capability.

CER occurs when circular economy strategies fail to deliver on their environmental promise in ways very similar to the ERE. Rebound may occur in the context of circular economy and significantly diminish hypothesized environmental benefits, as the theory on circular economy places too much focus on material resource flows and lacks the inclusion of behavioral economics and market forces.

DISCUSSION AND REVIEW QUESTIONS

1. What are circular business models?
2. Mention and briefly explain some of the distinct logics of circular business models.
3. How do symbiotic ecosystems differ from the other logics of circular business models?
4. List the key business areas with impact from the circular economy.
5. Briefly discuss some business opportunities in synergizing the business areas for circular economy impact.

6. What are some of the strategies for improving circularity in supply chains?
7. Define experimentation within the context of circular business models.
8. What is circular economy rebound?
9. Briefly explain some important aspects of circular economy rebound.
10. Mention the ways in which circular economy rebound can manifest itself.
11. Mention some of the conditions for minimizing of circular economy rebound in business.
12. List some of the causes of the rebound effect and corresponding mitigation strategies of such listed causes.
13. Briefly discuss the factors to be considered when exploring how the circular economy-related dynamics capabilities influence the decision to implement circular economy product-focused and circular economy process-focused activities, we consider three factors.

Part 6

10 Enablers and Associated Risks to Implementing Circular Economy

10.1 INTRODUCTION

In this chapter, we provide a detailed discussion on the key aspects of the shift toward circular economy coupled with the driving factors of the circular economy paradigm. Additionally, we give some insights on the enablers of circular supply chains and some challenges that firms are bound to encounter during implementing circular economy principles.

10.2 THE CIRCULAR ECONOMY PARADIGM AND DRIVING FACTORS

The circular economy represents a paradigm to decouple growth and resource consumption. It calls for new models of production that prescribe a set of actions and strategies aimed at reducing resource consumption, improving efficiency and reducing waste. However, although it is profoundly connected to the broader concept of environmental practices, overlapping the two definitions and considering them as synonymous is misleading. In other words, producing a "green product" does not necessarily mean producing a "circular product". For instance, looking at the requirements for obtaining the EU Ecolabel – the most famous and internationally recognized label for green products – for textiles, there are several criteria linked to resource efficiency (e.g., minimum content of recycled PET, nylon and filament fibers) and product durability (e.g., criteria on textile washing resistance). These are all criteria that are perfectly in line with circular economy principles and objectives, which means that a "circular product" could probably be labeled as green. However, there are other criteria that are typical of a "green product" but not necessarily of a "circular" one: for instance, the absence of dangerous substances in wastewater or the requirements on air emissions limits. On the other hand, a circular product may also be less green. In fact, the use of recycled resources may increase the overall environmental footprint of a product if the recycling process generates a high environmental impact. Taking into account the circular economy paradigm, we present in detail the four main factors which potentially affect companies' propensity to adopt circular economy principles: (1) economic drivers – gaining competitive advantage through resource efficiency (optimization), (2) regulatory drivers – ensuring law compliance and preventing future law requirements, (3) environmental value drivers – reducing a company's environmental impacts due to ethical motives and (4) resource-related risk drivers – reducing a company's dependence on scarce raw materials.

10.2.1 WIN-WIN STRATEGIES

There has been a huge emphasis on the economic benefits of adopting environmental practices. Driven by a business case framing, several managers decided to reduce the environmental impact of their products and production processes in order to differentiate their products and target environmentally sensitive consumers. Other managers decided to reduce production costs through more efficient use of raw materials, energy and other resources. Economic motivations maybe even more important in explaining the adoption of circular economy practices. The circular economy is based on the concept of resource efficiency – "produce more with less" – which is inherently linked to materials, and thus, cost savings. This relationship is dues, for instance, to the substitution, reuse or recycling of production inputs, the better use of by-products, the conversion of waste into products and reduced waste disposal costs. Resource efficiency also depends upon the adoption of production optimization strategies: reducing scrap, optimizing energy, water and resource usage, adopting lean production principles, etc. The successful implementation of a resource-efficiency strategy leads to lower production costs, and thus cost reduction-oriented companies are more likely to adopt it. In other words, the need to reduce production costs can be effective for adopting circular economy practices.

10.2.2 THE ROLE OF REGULATORY INITIATIVES

The role of regulatory pressures has been extensively investigated in environmental management literature. On the one hand, regulatory initiatives can impose coercive pressures on organizations that are forced to comply with new environmental prescriptions. On the other hand, environmental regulations work as an external signal that focuses managers on latent issues and determines their reactions. In the EU, the Circular Economy is at the heart of a recent strategy aimed at combining economic growth and preserving the environment. The circular economy strategy represents the final output of a long series of EU policies aimed at decoupling economic growth from resource consumption and waste production. According to this view, products need to be reconceived from the very beginning with a life-cycle approach that takes into consideration all the production phases from raw material extraction to the products' end of life. The EU circular economy package contains an ambitious action plan of EU regulations in relation to different key circular economy aspects: eco-design, waste, food waste, packaging waste, secondary raw materials, by-products, plastics, critical raw materials, biomass and bio-based materials, etc.

10.2.3 ENVIRONMENTAL VALUES AS A KEY ISSUE

The adoption of a circular economy business model can generate environmental benefits in terms of reduced raw materials and natural resources together with waste prevention and minimization. Thus, a company can be motivated to adopt a circular economy business model by the willingness to reduce its adverse environmental impacts. The adoption of environmental practices can, therefore, be explained by ethical reasons, i.e., reducing the environmental impact of industrial production.

Managers sometimes pursue environmental protection through their business development practices, even if this limits their profits. There is strong empirical evidence that the environmental attitudes, expectations and motivations of top managers are an important factor in explaining the environmental proactivity of a company. For instance, when managers have a high commitment and are aware of the advantages, disadvantages and tools of environmental management, they tend to give more formal importance to environmental issues within the organization. The importance of managements' attitudes toward environmental stewardship in the adoption of corporate environmental management practices. In fact, according to the value belief norm (VBN) theory, personal attitudes and moral norms are both antecedents of pro-environmental behavior in organizations. Moral norms influence individual beliefs and when violating a moral norm, individuals feel the responsibility for the related negative consequences produced by their actions. This means that companies are led by environmentally conscious leaders tend to adopt pro-environmental behaviors. Thus, the adoption of a circular economy business model represents a valid strategy to reduce a company's overall environmental impact.

10.2.4 SUPPLY RISK-RELATED DRIVERS

According to the EU Commission, the global demand for resources is increasing, driven by population growth and improving standards of living. Almost all predictions suggest that the demand for resources will continue upwards: the world's population is growing by 200,000 people a day and is expected to exceed 9 billion by 2050. By 2030, there will be three times the current number of people with "middle class" consumption levels in the now-developing world. As a consequence, after decades of growth based on declining prices of real resources, there are indications that the world has entered a new phase where the prices of real resources are rising. The overexploitation of resources due to mass production and consumption coupled with resource scarcity is the basis of the concept of the circular economy. Because the EU is poor in terms of natural resources – the EU consumes eight billion tonnes of materials per year, of which one-fifth is imported – and has to face a constantly increasing demand for products and services, it is fundamental to develop a strategy aimed at decoupling growth from resource consumption. According to the natural resource dependence theory (NRDT), all organizations depend directly or indirectly on natural resources because the natural capital or the resulting ecosystems are the source of the raw materials for all physical assets. This, coupled with the growing scarcity of natural resources, could put supply chains at risk if managers fail to address the pending scarcity issues, especially in conjunction with the growing demand for goods and services.

10.3 THE SHIFT TOWARD CIRCULAR ECONOMY

An examination of the conceptual origin of circular economy reveals that some decades ago, Kenneth Boulding and others contemplated the biophysical limits of the present linear economic system and increasing ecological deficit. In 1966, Boulding introduced the concept of closed systems and envisioned a future economy that would operate by regenerating existing finite resources. Many attempts have been made at the definition of circular economy emphasizing various aspects of the model. Some academic researchers claim that the circular economy is based on the redesign of production systems at various levels, where the focus is on value preservation in closed loops throughout the lifespan of raw materials and goods. Circular business models are characterized by (1) closing the raw material chains, (2) a transition from ownership to the provision of services and (3) more intensive utilization of the functionality of products. In this sense, such business models are based on the five recognized building blocks: (1) closing loops, (2) creating (multiple values), (3) choosing an appropriate strategy, (4) designing an entity that fits with organizing between parties and (5) developing circular earnings models. Ultimately, the circular economy is an industrial system that is restorative or regenerative by intention and design. The circular flow of income in any industry is a simplified yet significant aspect of its functioning. The flow, however, illustrates how businesses interact with other economic participants within the key macroeconomic markets that coordinate the flow of income or goods throughout the system. This aspect is critical to understand, especially for every business professional, because it provides everyone with a valuable tool for understanding the economic environment in which businesses operate.

The development of the concept of circular economy has been revolving around principles of 3R/4R such as Reducing, Reusing, Recycling and Renewing. There are indications in the extant literature that emphasizes that the circular economy model will get developed further and refined as there is a wider application in different industries. The rise of Big Data has helped circular economy by providing insights into the regeneration of resources, reuse of waste resources, redesign of business model, collaboration for a joint venture and product forecasting. Additionally, concepts such as product sharing platforms have begun to reemerge and so have different success metrics which were previously criticized. Large organizations such as Unilever are pushing forward with the circular economy movement by producing design guidelines such as "Design for Recyclability" which represents a new business model for better recycling and expanded use of refills. The path to a sustainable future will always reflect several principles of the circular economy and institutions such as EMF have helped to standardize the understanding of the circular economy, i.e., Redesign, Redistribute, Reuse and Recycle. Even though the concept of the circular economy and its benefits are beginning to be understood, the actual implementation and change toward a circular economy is an obstacle for its wider application. Some of the drivers of circular economy are factors such as extending the life cycle of products through 3R, ecological balance and protection, data-driven analytics, government policies and behavior of consumers.

10.3.1 Extending the Life Cycle of Products Through 3R

The objective of 3R (i.e., reduce, reuse and recycle) practices are to reduce create-use-discard and move toward create-use-reuse, and the cycle continues. It has a direct impact on society, ecology, economy and the environment. The enabling factors that help in promoting 3R are Product-as-a-Service (PaaS), consumption patterns, collection of used goods, repair and then finally, an efficient distribution and material handling system.

10.3.1.1 Product-as-a-Service

The concept of Product-as-a-Service, also popularly known as PaaS, has been a major enabler of life cycle extension of the product. Though not a very new thought, it has been well established and discussed in various research that focuses on presenting products as service to customers will increase the resource efficiency through reuse but also increase jobs related to the economies that support this service model. It is also widely recognized that a service-related model for products will increase efficiency in utilization of resources and thus reduce consumption which in turn reduces waste generation. As adoption of 3R practices increases, it also influences the migration to the serviced model of companies and value creation for the customer.

10.3.1.2 Sustainable Consumption

Sustainable consumption involves avoidance of wastage and reduction of the consumption in perishable natural resources and energy. According to the United Nations, sustainable consumption is about promoting efficient resource and energy use while providing access to basic services and better quality of life for all.

10.3.1.3 Collection

Generally, collection of used products is driven by efficiency gains and lower costs. However, if there is a need to increase 3R practices, the emphasis should be toward value creation at every step of the transaction. The different material collection mechanisms that will move from a collection of waste to take back model by producers will help reduce the use of virgin resources, thereby reducing the impact on ecology.

10.3.1.4 Repair

Given the economic conditions of most countries, repair has always been on the agenda of the general population. It extends the life of the product, and a parallel economy caters to the demand. Innovative technologies such as 3D printing can also extend the life of products that are well beyond their intended lifespan. Not just plastics, but through innovation, metallic parts can also get repaired, and the additive life of the products increased. Even developed economies are moving toward maintenance/repair and reuse, as seen by an increase in smartphone repair services in Denmark.

10.3.1.5 Distribution and Material Movement

Material flow and distribution of resources are very important to close the loop and hence create a cycle. There is a need for a sustainable and integrated supply chain to achieve efficiency 3R for circular economy. Green material movement and distribution are needed to balance industrial development in the traditional sense and for environmental protection. Integration of supply chain to form a closed loop between upstream and downstream partners will also play an important role. Reverse logistics increases the relationship between the consumer and the producer by closing the loop as the customer will not get tempted and willing to try out old and refurbished goods without fear of return or refund.

10.3.2 ECOLOGICAL BALANCE AND PROTECTION

The core concept behind circular economy in nature is cyclical. It uses its resources and reuses them again once its use is complete. At the current rate of the population growth, the consumption stands at 1.7 times its capacity, which is not sustainable in the long run. The drivers to achieve ecological balance are to work on energy/resource efficiency, clean and renewable energy sources, waste management to reduce what goes into our landfills and waste to energy (WTE) to harness the energy lost.

10.3.2.1 Energy and Resource Efficiency

The more efficient utilization of resources on product creation means less wastage. Process efficiency also reduces wastage and allows harnessing waste energy and letting it flow back into the system. Energy efficiency can get integrated into green housing. The movement to electric vehicles from fossil fuel-driven ones is a remarkable step toward energy efficiency and zero-emission.

10.3.2.2 Clean and Renewable Energy

The continued use of fossil fuels after the industrial revolution has resulted in global warming. Thus, the use of clean and renewable energy sources that do not produce noxious waste is a major contributor to circular economy ecology. However, the challenges are presented due to the shortage of renewable energy sources and the rising environmental pollution caused by fossil energy. This is further compounded by the ever-increasing burden of growth of the economy is a challenge. Nevertheless, globally there have been advancements in harnessing clean energy sources such as wind, thermal and solar, which will help drive circular economy.

10.3.2.3 Waste Management

Waste can be in any state (solid, liquid, gas) and normally gets discarded. They make their way into the environment and landfills. Toxic waste, if not disposed properly, are hazardous to the environment and health and well-being of society. Plastic waste is threatening our marine life and ecology. Waste management and recovery is a very important step toward having ecological balance and protection. Electronic waste (e-waste) is another problem that the world is facing now more than ever, and efforts are on to harness the value in them and reduce pollution. Methodologies to locally manage e-waste and infrastructure network needed to facilitate these are also taking place.

10.3.2.4 Waste to Energy

WTE completes the cycle of the flow of energy within the system with minimization of loss of energy in the system and environment. It also reduces the burden on landfills. The use of waste from one process for the creation of energy for another completes the cycle. Food waste from the food processing industry could get harnessed for energy generation.

10.3.3 Big Data and Information Flow

The proliferation of intelligent systems and tracking, data and information flow play an important role in developing a sustainable economy. Hence, data-driven insights play an important role as an enabler for circular economy adoption and evolution. The major factors that have fueled Big Data and analytics are cloud computing, internet of things (IoT) and artificial intelligence (AI)-driven data analytics.

10.3.3.1 Cloud Computing

Cloud computing is a technology that has the capability of executing powerful and complex calculations and analytics but eliminates the cost associated with maintaining hardware resources by the consumers. It has allowed even small and emerging economies to use the services of cloud service providers. Cloud computing is providing "Computing as service" and competitive economics to harness the power of big data.

10.3.3.2 Internet of Things (IoT)

To capture the data needed for analysis, IoT plays an important role. The proliferation of intelligent devices and coagulating the data over the internet is integrating different aspects of our life and ecology. The role of IoT in the industry can never get underestimated for efficiency and sustenance through meaningful data gathering, processing and analysis.

10.3.3.3 Data-Driven Analytics and Artificial Intelligence (AI)

The data captured and stored through IoT devices needs analysis in real-time to predict usage patterns and hence efficiently utilize our resources. The application of data-driven insights is significant in the context of managing resources and waste for sustainable business development. AI-driven data analytics is providing new insight for decision-making for business managers. AI is beginning to play an important role in the prediction and estimation of waste produced in society and this information can be used for planning efficient management and increasing 3R applicability. AI is able to have a pivotal role in accelerating and adopting circular economy principles. For example, AI-generated product concept designs can be utilized to change how materials are developed for consumer electronics. Also, AI-enabled predictive maintenance, which is extensively used in industrial machinery and installations environment, could be adapted and applied to consumer electronics. In doing so, enhancing the product life cycle, and reducing the design cycle and waste material.

10.3.4 Government Policies

Policies in an economic environment play an important role in the adoption of sustainable methodologies. It is achieved sometimes by incentivizing innovative approaches or by enforcing regulations. Policies in terms of capacity building, proper urban planning, asset management and legislation and regulations are the major elements.

10.3.4.1 Government Policies Promote Capacity Building

Handling of waste, energy requirements of society and eco-efficient industrial parks play a major role in kick-starting sustainable industrial development. Capacity-building activities where institutions and communities come together to engage in activities toward sustainable society actively get initiated by the government. Capacity building for proper educational outreach is a necessity for social upliftment.

10.3.4.2 Urban Planning

Resource management with efficiency is dependent on proper urban planning that helps in efficient waste management. Sustainable development is mainly possible through urban planning, which can also result in a healthier society. Urban planning is important to tackle the enormous challenges that developing countries face due to rapid growth in economy and population and wish for a better quality of life.

10.3.4.3 Legislation and Regulation

Regulations play an important role in the adoption of policies and abidance. A strong regulation can guide the development toward the desired level. Regulations and policies dictate how businesses get conducted, be it supply chain management or energy efficiency. Policies create an ecosystem where firms collaborate toward innovative alliances and promote sustainability.

10.3.5 Consumer Behavior

Consumer behavior is an important psychological attitude toward circular behaviors. The individual behavior attitude or the collective attitude of a community has an important role in influencing circular behavior. The collective attitude can affect society and can even influence the regulating authority toward enforcing regulations and can also lead a movement toward circular behavior. Education, communication and economic factors have a major impact on the behavior of the population toward the adoption of circular economy at all levels.

10.3.5.1 Education

Education has a direct effect on consumer behavior and attitude. Education is related to knowledge, and it affects the perception of the consumers and their attitude toward the environment and other social causes. Knowledge acquired also affects what they buy and how they perceive the value. With education, consumers become more concerned toward the welfare of the ecology with consumer behavior. Psychographic profiling also known as the study of personality, values, attitudes and lifestyles has shown that conscious consumer behavior toward ecology is dynamically related to the level of education they receive.

10.3.5.2 Persuasive Communication

Proper and effective communication on a cause and its effects can induce and influence consumer behavior be it a brand or a social cause. Consumer behavior shift can be achieved through effective advertisement, promotion, etc. effective

CSR communication also helps effective participation of individuals in a cause during a crisis. With social media being widely used, it has become an effective channel in influencing consumer, individual and social behavior and attitude.

10.3.5.3 Cultural Factors

Consumer behavior is driven through cultural ideologies. A consumer is often influenced by their culture, social class and peer groups. Consumer behavior varies by ethnicity and society as a while. Even attitude toward activities such as sports get influenced by culture. Consumer ethics and culture have even influences how they utilize products over their life and extend their use through 3R. Consumer behavior, specifically in emerging markets, is driven by culture and often leads to the sustainable use of materials. Cultural factors affect the way consumers dress, eat and buy products which in turn has an impact on the business economy.

10.4 TOE CLASSIFIED ENABLERS OF CIRCULAR SUPPLY CHAIN

The enablers of circular supply chains were identified through an extensive search of journal contributions, abstracts and keywords available in SCOPUS using keywords such as "enablers", "manufacturing", "circular supply chains", "circular economy" and "sustainability". The identified enablers of circular supply chains were classified using technological, organizational and environmental contexts/perspectives based on the Technology-Organization-Environment (TOE) theory. The TOE theory posits that there are broader contexts that significantly impact innovation adoption and use in addition to the quality of technological innovation. The TOE theory, when compared to other frameworks for innovation adoption, provides a more holistic approach by considering all three aspects, namely technological, environmental and organizational. The technological aspect describes both the internal and external technologies relevant to the firm, including the ones existing inside the firm, as well as those available for possible adoption by the firm, i.e., are available outside but have not yet be adopted. Technologies could be material like equipment or immaterial like data and methods. Thus, the technological context tends to focus on how the technological attributes can affect the firm's decision to adopt innovations. The organizational aspect relates to the firm's resources and assets such as the firm size, hierarchy, procedures, administrative structure, human resources, extra resources and the connection between works. This context includes organizational features such as number of employees, resources, hierarchy, annual revenue/sales and so on. Finally, environmental context comprises of the "arena" in which a firm conducts its business activities, including its industry, competitors, suppliers and relations with governmental entities.

Prior published studies are available in extant literature on innovation adoption, thereby pinpointing a wide and successful application of TOE theory in various domains. For example, a past published a study in extant literature study proposed a multi-layered TOE-based risk management framework to identify and manage the risks associated with smart city governance. Likewise, some academic researchers applied the TOE theoretical framework to study the effects of relative advantage, complexity, top management support, cost, market dynamics, competitive pressure, cost and regulatory support on blockchain adoption for operations and supply chain management among small and medium-sized enterprises (SMEs) in Malaysia. In yet another instance, some research scholars in their study employed the TOE theory to propose and validate a research model for a better understanding of the critical success factors of adopting service platforms for organizational performance using data from 228 Chinese catering organizations. Some academic researchers explored the use of e-booking systems in the maritime supply chain and, in particular, the factors influencing the adoption of such systems at the organizational level. Their study reveals that adoption is influenced by several factors, including pressure from trade partners, pressure from leading organizations, as well as organizational compatibility and so forth. Additionally, some research scholars in their study conducted a chain-level analysis of information systems and technologies adoption within the maritime transportation context. Their results suggest that the adoption of inter-organizational information systems is largely affected by factors such as industry characteristics, governmental power and supply chain trade partners' power among others.

We present in detail the enablers of implementing circular supply chains below:

10.4.1 Technological Enablers

Technological enablers include availability and access to technological infrastructures, sufficient security and privacy, positive perception to digital technologies, quality data and technology maturity. The availability of technological infrastructures is a critical determinant of implementing circular supply chains. Indeed, access to enabling infrastructures for a smooth transition to digitalization is considered critical to the success of circular supply chains. The implementation of information technologies for circular supply chains requires sufficient security and privacy. As such, sufficient security is considered critical for firms to effectively deploy digital tools like big data analytics and IoT to improve supply chain functions and actualize sustainability objectives. Positive perception is considered a significant factor to the effective implementation of circular supply chain practices since this variable plays an important role in technology adoption in different contexts. For instance, the employees' positive perception of emerging technologies for circularity solutions could aid in a smooth transition to the use of such emerging tools. Access to quality data is highly significant since substantial efforts are required to standardize input-output values in different purposes. In fact, since all supply chain operations are usually not managed through technology, it requires a great effort to collect and manage data effectively from the operations. Moreover, as the ownership of data is mostly controversial, clearly stating the ownership will enable companies with data accessibility.

10.4.2 Organizational Enablers

The organizational context encompasses the internal characteristics of firms that can facilitate the effective implementation of circular supply chain innovations in the supply chains. The organizational enablers include sufficient budgetary allocations, top management support, effective organizational policies, high-skilled employees and organizational change culture. Given the high cost of implementing technologies including cost of employee training and installing necessary hardware and software, it becomes essential that there is sufficient budgetary allocation to enable offsetting such costs. Top management support refers to the degree to which managers comprehend and embrace the technological capabilities of a new technological innovation system. And this can be significant in firms' decision to implement circular supply chain solutions for actualizing sustainability goals. Highly skilled personnel are highly essential for the success of technological innovations. As such, firms can aspire to invest in employee trainings on digital issues so as to improve employee competence and enable an effective implementation of circular supply chains. Organizational culture can aid the readiness for implementing circular supply chains for improved performance and increased competitiveness. In fact, a shift to IT-oriented culture is highly essential to circular operations for expected performance gains. Likewise, the congruence of values facilitates supply chain operations including adoption of circular supply chain innovation.

10.4.3 ENVIRONMENTAL ENABLERS

This context concerns the external environment of the firm that can facilitate the implementation of circular supply chains for sustainability improvements. The environmental enablers include customer awareness of digital supply chain technologies, government regulatory framework, presence of reward and incentives, effective supply chain collaboration and industry and stakeholders' participation. Government regulations may be prohibitive, but sometimes, these regulations can encourage firms to adopt technological innovation. In fact, government rules in terms of technological standards, encouragement and legislation can aid in increasing the implementation of circular supply chain innovations. Additionally, receiving external support from suppliers/vendors as a result of effective supply chain collaboration is a key ingredient to facilitate the implementation of circular supply chain. Public awareness on the benefits of digitalization can also facilitate the decision for implementing circular supply chains for sustainability objectives. Moreover, robust reward and benefit system can serve as an incentive for employees during the transition to a low-carbon economy through implementing circular supply chain.

10.5 RISKS ASSOCIATED WITH CIRCULAR SUPPLY CHAINS

Globally, firms are struggling with environmental issues and making efforts to find effective procedures for possible solutions. As such, firms are becoming more interested in adopting circular supply chain strategies in their business operations to develop sustainable supply chain. Although the circular supply chains have numerous economic and environmental advantages, the implementation of circular supply chains is regarded as challenging due to the many risks/obstacles. In fact, the rate of implementation of circular supply chains is considerably low due to considerable risks associated with it. Despite the numerous eco-friendly objectives of circular supply chains, firms' managers are still not quite enthusiastic toward implementing due to the risks that tend to serve as deterrent to the environmental benefits. Risks associated with circular supply chains tend to inhibit it from its proper functioning since such supply chains become unstable and create many problems that deter the quality and performance, thereby resulting in negative environmental consequences as well. Thus, risk-based circular supply chains are bound to fail to achieve their intended value and result in negative mishaps. To enable circular supply chains for function effectively for expected value and gain, it becomes impediment to identify risks that need to be addressed in such supply chains. Such risks should be effectively controlled using the principles of risk management so as not to continue to prevent the entire circular supply chain framework. The principles of risk management are highly significant to ensure risk-based circular supply chain operations are effectively analyzed in terms of risk recognition, risk assessment and risk control/mitigation. Additionally, it is important to leverage insights into the risks associated with linear supply chains so as to understand the risks associated with circular supply chains. For example, there has been a research that presented an evaluation and ranking of strategies to reduce circular supply chain risks. The descriptions on supply chain risk and supply chain risk management differ and comprise both company and customer perspectives.

Companies are bound to face risks during implementing circular supply chain concepts. The risks can impact negatively on the companies' performance, quality and overall motivation and also be categorized as technological, organizational or other relevant aspects. Consequently, the risks associated with circular supply chain implementation need to be identified and effectively addressed for improving circular supply chain initiatives across the supply chain. Moreover, there is a huge requirement to utilize a structured systematic method during evaluating risks associated with any complicated system problem. In response, there are prior published studies in extant literature that involves investigating risks associated with circular supply chains. For instance, there has been a research that discussed risk assessment in a circular supply chain for critical risk mitigation. Also, a case study has been provided to create value from circular supply chain related to fast-moving consumer goods in which there is a discussion on the minimization of system risks. Likewise, a procedure has been offered based in weight assessment ratio analysis and multi-criteria decision analysis for analyzing risks in agriculture using circular supply chain concepts.

Indeed, numerous governments have recognized the importance of the implementation of a circular economy by promoting institutional frameworks that regulate environmental risks and promote the adoption of environmental technologies. In this sense, laws and regulations to promote circular economy have motivated companies to pursue circular economy principles. Some researchers classify the motivators for the adoption of circular economy into the following groups: economic, financial and market groups; institutional and regulatory organizations; social and cultural groups and technical organizations. In a similar vein, circular economy motivators are systematized into three categories: (i) consumer preferences, which place more emphasis on access to services than the possession of products; (ii) recent technological advances with the stimulus of adopting more circular practices (e.g., IoT, RFID and advanced manufacturing) and (iii) government regulations that have stimulated and rewarded the adoption of circular economy practices. Likewise, the new consumer preferences and more sensitive markets for sustainable products are important motivators of the adoption of circular economy. New technologies labeled as "Industry 4.0", such as the IoT and additive manufacturing, are fundamental to meeting the needs of firms and clients who are more inclined toward greener choices. The availability of these new technologies has motivated companies toward circular economy principles because such technologies more easily enable firms to track their environmental impacts and waste, contributing to firms' sustainability performance.

On the other hand, it is recognized that firms face barriers/risks to adopting circular economy practices since it requires changes in the processes of production and development of new products, consumer behavior, governmental policies and business practices. The challenges for circular economy adoption range from the societal level to the organizational, creating barriers to implementing circular economy principles at the firm level. Some of the barriers to circular economy adoption include:

1. *Financial* – i.e., difficulty in measuring the financial benefits and the potential profitability derived from the adoption of circular economy because the low price of many virgin materials prevents circular economy products from out-competing their linear equivalents. Thus, financial barriers are mainly related to uncertainty in financial benefits and potential profitability of circular concepts. It has been found that financial barriers, especially related to financial risk and uncertainty, can partly explain the current reluctance amongst companies to adopt circular business models. Circular business models often imply a larger operational risk for the provider than a pure sales model as use-phase services such as maintenance are taken on by the provider. In business models where the provider keeps the ownership of the product, the "capital tied up" also adds financial risk for the provider. Furthermore, in the case of remanufacturing, an important financial uncertainty is the *product attractiveness at a certain remanufacturing cost compared with competitors and substitutes* at the point in the future when a product leaves one use cycle to enter the next. In order to calculate the total business case of several use cycles of a product in a remanufacturing model, both the remanufacturing cost and the customers' future willingness to pay for the remanufactured product need to be estimated.

    The value of a remanufactured product depends on how the market for a certain product category develops over time. Several academic scholars have emphasized the barrier of "fashion vulnerability", which means that if the market demand change quickly, it can be challenging to propose business models that favor long and multiple use cycles. Such changes in market demand can be fashion driven, or due to fast technological developments. Products that are sensitive to changing fashion or that are undergoing fast technological changes are thus extra challenging.
2. *Structural* – i.e., communication difficulties between departments and across the supply chain, as well as lack of clarity regarding the responsibilities of different departments.

3. *Operational* – i.e., a lack of the required operational capacity and infrastructure to adopt circular economy. For instance, operational bottlenecks to adopting circular economy exist, such as difficulties in updating logistics and manufacturing equipment and facilities. It also concerns infrastructure and supply chain management. In relation to this, "return flow challenges", i.e., challenges related to effectively managing product-take-back systems in circular business models have been discussed. In particular, many remanufacturers are struggling with low predictability in quantity and quality of incoming products to be remanufactured, which often leads to inefficiencies in the remanufacturing system.
4. *Attitudinal* – people have a shallow understanding of circular economy and do not realize how important it is because they tend to avoid change (risk aversion). Indeed, attitudinal barriers relate to actors' perception of sustainability and level of risk aversion. Attitudinal barriers can relate to different actors in the supply chain. These barriers relate to leadership and attitudes of employees coupled with low customer acceptance caused by factors such as long-standing procurement habits or the perception that reused products are inferior to new ones. Also, "customer type restrictions" have been mentioned by research scholars meaning that not all types of customers are receptive to all types of circular business models.
5. *Technological* – i.e., difficulty in integrating circular economy into product design and production processes or lack of access to appropriate technology, such as a lack of technology to track waste and emissions from products. Indeed, technological barriers concern product design and production processes. Some research scholars discuss "product category restrictions", stating that some types of products are more suitable for circular business models than others. Examples of product features that the authors mention as beneficial for a circular business model are that it fails functionally rather than by dissipation. That is, the value added of the returned components is high relative to market value and original cost, and that the product technology is stable.

Furthermore, it has been opined that barriers to circular economy are related to a lack of skilled people, administrative processes, regulations, technical solutions and capabilities and a lack of financial resources. A common finding is that government actions have an important role in framing institutional policies toward circular economy adoption.

Hence, based on a taxonomy of circular economy barriers derived by various studies in extant literature, the main barriers/risks to implementing circular economy can be categorized into six groups: (1) government and regulatory, (2) economic and financial, (3) technological, (4) societal, (5) organizational and managerial and (6) infrastructural, supply chain and market as shown in Table 10.1. A detailed discussion of the barrier categories is presented in Table 10.1.

TABLE 10.1
Circular Economy Risks/Barriers

Categories	Specific Barriers
Governmental and regulatory	Lack of standardization
	Failure of waste management policy to result in high-quality recycling
	Obstructive laws and regulations
	Unsupportive laws on waste management
Economic and financial	Lack of funding for circular business models
	Non-consideration of environmental cost (externalities)
	Tremendous upfront investment costs
	High costs coupled with low economic benefits in short term
Technological	Challenges in tracking recycled materials
	Difficulty in ensuring product quality throughout its lifetime
	Difficulty in delivering high-quality products made from recovered materials
	Difficulty in designing reused and recovered products
	Difficulty in sorting and recycling used textiles
	Lack of advanced green process technologies
Societal	Lack of trustworthy public information
	Lack of social awareness
	Difficulty in finding qualified personnel and expertise
	Insufficient customer demand for circular products
Organizational and managerial	Unclear vision about circular economy
	Hesitant company culture and poor leadership toward circular economy
	The appearance of other tasks with a higher priority
	Organizational structures that result in difficulty for circular economy implementation
	Difficulty in setting a reasonable process of circular products
	Increasing production cost
	Existence of other solutions that are better than circular economy implementation
Infrastructural, supply chain and market	Lack of high-quality recycling materials
	The price of recycled materials higher than virgin materials
	The absence of information exchange system
	Lack of successful circular business models
	Challenge of collaborative innovation among supply chain partners

10.5.1 GOVERNMENT AND REGULATORY ISSUES

The barriers/risks classified under the government and regulatory category include lack of standardization, waste management policies that fail to result in high-quality recycling, obstructive laws and regulations, and unsupportive laws on waste management. The absence of refurbishment and recycling guidelines and standards results in mixed product quality. Weak government accountability often fails policy makers to develop appropriate industrial policies, thus impeding circular economy progress.

This problem is rooted in the fragmented regulatory systems of most regions, which results in the lack of effective collaboration mechanisms. Insufficient human resources and institutional capabilities further resulting in not clear responsibilities of various authorities charged with implementing circular economy. Innovation policies should be upgraded to effectively implement circularity, including effective taxation policy, financial supports, training, public procurement standards and stricter laws and regulations.

Furthermore, the regulatory (institutional) barriers include inconsistent policy messages and poor institutional infrastructure. An often-cited barrier is that the institutional infrastructure is path-dependent and favors a linear economy. Since many supply chains are highly internationally integrated, the consistency of policies between countries is crucial for circular economy adoption in large firms. Heterogeneity in policies between countries is the main hindrance. By-products are often legally classified as waste before the end of their life cycle, which switches ownership from private to public. High administrative costs of reporting waste streams, complex waste legislation and poor implementation of existing circular economy policies are also considered as barriers. Too little R&D, lack of support with training, poor physical infrastructure for reversed logistics and lack of circular economy management tools for small and medium-sized enterprises are problematic. Unintentional effects of policies also create problems. Stimulating the use of energy-efficient appliances may also be inconsistent with a circular economy since existing products are replaced earlier, sometimes not compensating for the saved energy. The North-South trade of goods for reuse, recovery and recycling from the Basel Convention of hazardous waste from 1992 fails to recognize the value of waste.

10.5.2 Economic and Financial Issues

Economic barriers are financial barriers for circular economy adoption and include difficulties for funding circular business models, high up-front investment costs and low virgin material prices. Enterprises and industries face numerous economic and financial barriers to circular economy related to benefit, cost and capital. In this category, risks identified as lack of funding of circular business models, environmental costs (externalities) are not considered, tremendous upfront investment costs, high costs but low economic benefits in the short term. The transition from a linear to a circular economy requires changes in almost all value chain activities that require much time and upfront investment. Moreover, additional costs regarding collaborating with external parties and managing environmental impact are factors that harper movement of companies toward circular economy. These costs and the insufficient market demand obstruct the survival of novel circular business models. Also, external financing is often difficult to access by small- and medium-sized companies.

10.5.3 Technological Issues

The development of related technologies supports the circular economy transition. The barriers in terms of the technological issues include challenges in tracking recycled materials, ensuring product quality throughout its lifetime, difficulty to deliver high-quality products made from recovered materials, difficulty to design reusable and recoverable products, difficulty to sort and recycle used textiles, and lack of advanced green process technologies. Technical barriers include factors regarding the technological thresholds of related technology, for example, gaps between invention and production. Improper and overly complicated product designs constitute a problematic task for remanufacturers and recyclers. Designing circular products must use environmentally friendly technology. Implementing circular economy requires new sustainable technologies in terms of environmental-friendly design, green production, and life cycle assessment; it also requires competent professionals to manage the transition.

Moreover, the design-for product-life extension or design for opportunities for repair is crucial, as opposed to, e.g., fast fashion. Some current product design is a major obstacle for remanufacturing, reuse and recycling. Life cycle cost analysis suggests that a large share of cost reduction opportunities for a project or product pertains to the early stages in its development. The same is true for environmental impacts. In many countries, separation of waste is limited, which causes real or perceived problems with the quality of recycled goods and materials. One issue is hoe recycled goods can be of lower quality or less flexible than virgin material. Another issue is the reliability of supply of recycled goods making virgin material more preferred by many producers. The infrastructure for effective waste management is lacking in many places. Many recyclables are not separately collected. Food waste is especially difficult to separate. There is not always the capacity to handle all the collected recycled goods which are instead placed in landfill. The goods that are recycled, however, may lack proper standards, and therefore, customers are willing to purchase what is recycled. This is only partly due to insufficient separation.

Historically, the circular economy literature has been more focused on availability of technological enablers. Although various necessary technologies have been developed, several studies cite the lack of know-how among the practitioners of these solutions. Circular economy technologies may involve niche technologies that differ from the expertise within the firm, especially evident in SMEs. Lacking IT systems for measuring and monitoring progress is an obstacle. Although specific software for detecting waste may exist, it appears not to have spread to all businesses or not been used die to the lack of waste stream data. IT systems are also necessary for the shift from a physical-goods dependent economy to a serviced economy and less resource-intensive immaterial satisfiers of human needs.

10.5.4 Societal Issues

Circular economy barriers/risks in society include the lack of trustworthy public information, lack of societal awareness, difficulty to find qualified personnel and expertise, and low consumer demand for circular products. The implementation of circular economy programs requires public participation. Not knowing the benefits of circular economy and not sharing of past data regarding technical knowledge subsequently lead to the companies' and customers' lack of awareness and urgency to circular economy. Furthermore, the lack of widely distributed expertise has resulted in the inability to diffuse technical knowledge on circular economy, institutions and governments to society. Also, public demand for circular products is still low causes insufficient pull forces to stimulate the design and innovation of circular products.

Likewise, three categories of social (and cultural) barriers to circular economy adoption are resistant company culture, lack of consumer awareness and weak cooperation throughout the supply chain. The circular economy-resistant company culture plays out on three levels: resistance from managers, circular economy initiatives in isolation from main operations and low engagement in management strategies. Top and mid-management resisted initiatives in a circular economy direction as change may not be in line with their incentive schemes. While circular economy initiatives may be happening within a larger firm, all divisions are not aware of the changes. Some firms report that a circular economy is not a part of their current innovation strategy and they do not have any measurable goal related to a circular economy, indicating low strategic engagement. A framework to explain the low consumer awareness and interest in a circular economy has been provided and in conclusion, psychological ownership of products, strong status quo bias, consumerist culture to satisfy needs and status were key factors behind negative attitudes toward circular economy goods. Circular economy has been found to be of lower priority in consumers' decision process and many reported lacking awareness both about the meaning of the concept and about the circularity of their purchased goods.

Confidentiality about processes and volumes in production hampers industrial symbiosis and exchange of by-products. Cooperation across the supply chain is viewed as intrusive on business models, not economically beneficial and hampering the competitive nature throughout the supply chain.

10.5.5 Organizational and Managerial Issues

The identified barriers/risks classified under the organizational and managerial category comprise unclear vision about the circular economy, hesitant company cultural and poor leadership toward circular economy, the appearance of other tasks with a higher priority, organizational structures that result in difficulties for circular economy implementation, difficulty in setting a reasonable price of circular products, increasing production cost, and the existence of other solutions that are better than the implementation of circular economy. There is huge emphasis by various researchers on the importance of top managers' appreciation of new approaches as a factor that influences companies in designing their supply chains. Because of circular economy's high complexity, its implementation cannot be handled by a single department in an organization. Yet, the question of how to manage the responsibility of circular economy within an organization remains unanswered. Furthermore, recent research has indicated that integration within an organizational structure remains low. Firms have yet to mainstream the implementation of circular economy into their vision, goals, strategy and key performance indicators.

10.5.6 Infrastructural, Supply Chain and Market Issues

This barrier/risk category comprises the lack of high-quality recycled materials, the price of recycled materials higher than virgin materials, the absence of an information exchange system, a lack of successful circular business models and a challenge in collaborative innovation among supply chain partners. The unavailability of quality circular materials and the relatively cheap virgin material are critical market challenges. That undermines the affordability of circular products when the cost of virgin materials is much less than that of environmentally friendly materials. Moreover, the complexity of supply chain management might increase because a company operates a circular business model, which, in turn, affects the way of production, processing, and service offering in the value chain. Infrastructural issues regarding the lack of reliable information and the absence of successful business models make the path toward circular economy unclear and risky.

Particularly, market barriers are obstacles to a circular economy adoption due to non-existent or ill-functioning markets. The barriers concerning lack of market are twofold. The market mechanism for product recovery is not in place, which is particularly evident in the market for recycled goods, which fails due to a combination of factors including quality standards (leading to the classic lemons problem in resale markets), perceptions of quality, supply uncertainties and lack of economic incentives. It can also be the case that an actor has a clear mission statement and is not allowed to or lacks incentives for branching out. For example, wastewater plants receive possible valuable phosphate or other minerals from the sewage water, they might, however, not have the expertise or scale to make use of the by-product. The perceived quality of recycled materials makes the price-performance ratio insufficiently beneficial to switch to circular economy operations. One reason for low perceived benefits (and another example of poorly internalized externalities) is low virgin material prices. The lower perceived prices of raw materials are due to the fact that externalities are not internalized through taxes or economic incentives.

The supply of virgin materials adapts more easily to price changes than the supply of recycled material since new mines can start as material price rises. Recycled materials are dependent on previous consumption patterns and therefore have an inelastic supply. Thus, the price volatility of recycled materials is larger, which creates uncertainty. Uncertainty decreases willingness to invest in recycled material markets, and the substitution to recycled material markets stays low. High up-front investment costs have often being mentioned as the second most important barrier (after lack of awareness and sense of urgency). Any major shift in a society requires switching costs and these costs can vary. Reversing the supply chain, renegotiating contacts, adapting technology to suit new inputs or high development costs for new product design are just some examples.

10.6 SUMMARY

The circular economy represents a paradigm to decouple growth and resource consumption. The four main factors which potentially affect companies' propensity to adopt the circular economy paradigm include (1) economic drivers, (2) regulatory drivers, (3) environmental value drivers and (4) resource-related risk drivers.

The enabling factors that help in promoting 3R are PaaS, consumption patterns, collection of used goods, repair and then finally, an efficient distribution and material handling system.

The challenges for circular economy adoption range from the societal level to the organizational, creating barriers to implementing circular economy principles at the firm level.

The drivers to achieve ecological balance are to work on energy/resource efficiency, clean and renewable energy sources, waste management to reduce what goes into our landfills and WTE to harness the energy lost.

Consumer behavior is an important psychological attitude toward circular behaviors.

Risks associated with circular supply chains tend to inhibit it from its proper functioning since such supply chains become unstable and create many problems that deter the quality and performance, thereby resulting in negative environmental consequences as well. Thus, risk-based circular supply chains are bound to fail to achieve their intended value and result in negative mishaps.

DISCUSSION AND REVIEW QUESTIONS

1. In the shift toward circular, mention some of the recognized building blocks of circular business models. State the key characteristics of circular business models.
2. Outline and briefly explain the main factors that have the potential to affect firm's decision to adopt the circular economy principles.
3. Enumerate the key aspects of the shift toward circular economy.
4. Mention and briefly explain the challenges to implementing circular economy principles at the firm level.
5. In extending the life cycle of products through 3R, there are certain factors that need to be taken into consideration. Outline and briefly discuss these factors.
6. The individual behavior attitude or the collective attitude of a community has an important role in influencing circular behavior. What factors can influence consumer behavior in adopting circular economy principles?
7. Government policies are regarded as a key aspect of the shift toward circular economy. How can government policies influence the shift toward circular economy?

11 Behavioral Perspectives to Implementing Circular Economy

11.1 INTRODUCTION

In this chapter, we provide a detailed discussion on the behavioral perspectives to implementing the principles of the circular economy. By so doing, we present insights on the role of purchasers in the circular economy and the eco-labeling schemes as a behavior change tool to influence the adoption of the circular economy paradigm. Additionally, we describe organizational citizenship behavior for the environment (OCBE) and the driving factors to adopting labeling schemes among consumers and businesses.

11.2 THE ROLE OF PURCHASERS IN THE CIRCULAR ECONOMY

Purchasing in a circular economy implies seeking to purchase work, goods or services that close the energy and material loops within the supply chain and minimize or eliminate waste. Purchasing in the circular economy requires more than just waste management. A broader system perspective is needed that encompasses the entire life cycle of products and processes and the interaction of this system with the environment and the economy. The circular economy is concerned with the creation of self-sustaining production systems. Circular purchasing and sustainable purchasing both increase the level of complexity of purchasing. Yet, sustainable purchasing is related to creating value for society, economy and the environment, which could include minimizing material use. In contrast, circular purchasing is more related to closing the material loop and minimizing waste by, for instance, reducing, recycling and reusing materials. Hence, circular purchasing is more narrowly defined than sustainable purchasing. Moreover, the role of the purchaser is critical in the transition toward a circular economy. Purchasing is the linking pin between suppliers and the production – or service – processes of the organization. Several factors make the transition toward circular purchasing challenging: the complexity of the organization, the multiple stakeholders that are involved in the purchasing process, the flexibility required to work together in networks and the innovation needed to create circular products.

Circular purchasing activities are not standard activities for purchasers. For example, standard procedures may not be effective for circular purchasing, new alliances may need to be formed, and internal resources may need to be utilized. Indeed, purchasers in the circular economy need to have an entrepreneurial skill set, i.e., they need to be intrapreneurial. Several characteristics are considered relevant to purchasers when they have to deal with sustainability issues. These characteristics and competences include aspects of intrapreneurship, for example, taking initiatives and exploring the market. Employees are acting as change agents usually increase the level of sustainable purchasing by advising and facilitating project teams oriented at sustainable purchasing. Purchasing professionals are the gatekeepers to the supply chain; their activities are aimed at controlling and tracking incoming materials and products. Purchasers are able to connect the goals of their organization to the goals of the suppliers and internal and external end users. In collaboration with suppliers, they have a role in decreasing supplier risks and in increasing product innovation. They provide the connection between suppliers and internal business functions such as production and R&D. Their important role and strategic position within the organization means that they can contribute to the bottom-up transition toward circularity. For instance, purchasing professionals and supply chain managers can collaborate with suppliers to gain access to required materials and end users in order to ensure that the products or services can be reused or recycled and that value is created. The pricing, time and value for product principles that purchasers use in their daily work are constantly evolving due to the transition toward a circular economy.

Currently, the human side of the transition toward a circular economy is still not well-known, even though quite much is known on technology developments related to circular economy. Certain green human research practices can increase the sustainable performance of organizations. It can increase the employees' motivation to become part of environmental projects. The importance of individual employees in the transition toward a circular economy cannot be over-emphasized. Employees can have the role of ambassadors and are able to identify and implement circular initiatives. Nevertheless, they need to feel engaged in order to be an ambassador. Employee engagement and empowerment are found to be related to circular initiatives. In fact, many employees are willing to play a role in sustainable projects, but given that employees also have other responsibilities, the key is to engage them. Hence, implementing an engagement strategy by communication and training is critical. Moreover, organizations are slow in providing their employees with the opportunities to be involved in green activities and therefore limit the effectiveness of their environmental efforts. This could also be the case for a specific type of employee, namely the purchaser.

The role of the purchaser is becoming more complex due to the increasing focus on environmental issues and the circular economy. Purchasers not only have to take cost and quality into account but also sustainability. Some of the competences of purchasers in relation to sustainability include the application of tools (use of tools to understand data from suppliers and identify the risks); demand management, which relates to the ability to explore the market opportunities; sustainability compliance, which includes knowledge about sustainability and commitment to change. The skill set of the purchasers dealing with the challenging environment has been described as an *entrepreneurial* skill set, and have identified the following skills: making decisions, using interpersonal communication, applying influence, being internally motivated and finding creative solutions. The future purchaser can be described as someone who has expertise, self-confidence and good leadership skills. These descriptions of purchasers show several commonalities with the description of an intrapreneur. Demand management and finding creative solutions could be translated into innovativeness and opportunity recognition. Taking the initiative and applying influence could be related to the intrapreneurial dimension of being proactive. Furthermore, knowledge and motivation are significant future purchasing skills for dealing with environmental complexities and are also regarded as important aspects of intrapreneurship.

The ability of a purchaser to actually take action and become successful depends on the situational enablers. It is thus essential to investigate not only the behaviors and characteristics of the purchaser but also the drivers and constraints, i.e., contextual factors. Some of the drivers of purchasing and supply chain sustainability efforts include involvement of top management, government regulation, financial benefits and competitive advantage, ISO certification, customer demands, trust between buyers and suppliers, market performance, awareness and reputation of the organization. Figure 11.1 shows a framework of intrapreneurship to illustrate the role of the purchaser in relation to circular purchasing. Organizational factors that influence the intrapreneur include management support, organizational structure, rewards, work discretion and resources.

There are similarities on the influence of the context on circular purchasing and the influence of the context on intrapreneurship. Management support is a factor that influences circular purchasing and also influences intrapreneurship since it refers to the willingness of management to facilitate and promote intrapreneurship. It develops a norm within the organization and encourages employees to undertake intrapreneurial activities. Additionally, other organizational factors may influence circular purchasing as well as intrapreneurship. For instance, organizational structure refers to the flexibility of the organization. The rules and regulations in place can negatively influence intrapreneurship. Likewise, open channels of communication allow for ideas to be evaluated, selected and implemented. Rewards can increase

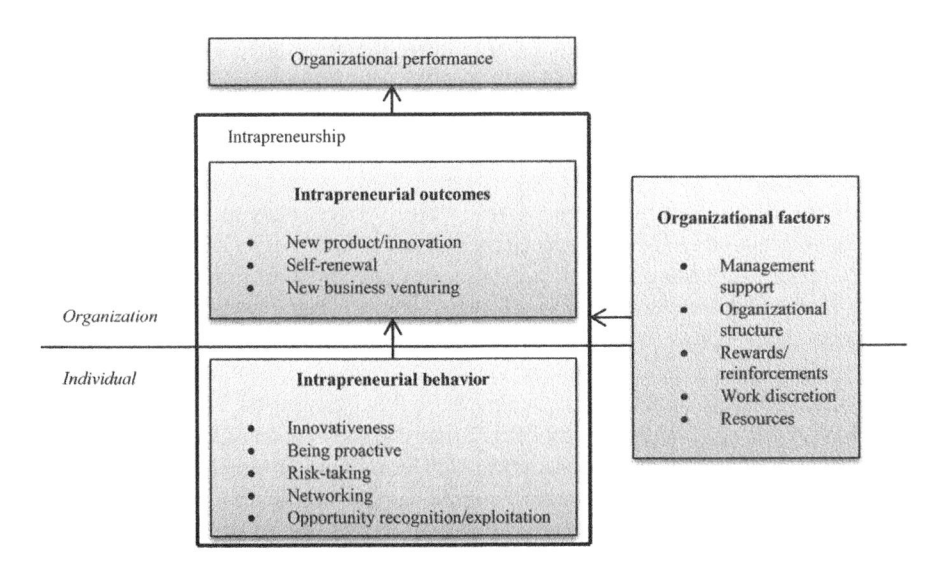

FIGURE 11.1 Framework for intrapreneurship.

the willingness of employees to participate in innovative projects or, in the case of purchasers, can increase the willingness to participate in circular projects. These rewards should be in line/corroborate the goals of the organization. Work discretion gives the intrapreneur freedom in the decision-making process. It is also important for intrapreneurship – and arguably also for circular purchasing – that the employees receive certain resources that can be used to increase circular activities. These resources mostly refer to time and financial resources. These contextual and organizational factors could thus increase circular purchasing. Since circular purchasing can be regarded as an innovation in purchasing, the contextual factors that influence the purchaser n the transition to circular purchasing can be similar to those that influence the intrapreneur.

11.3 ORGANIZATIONAL CITIZENSHIP BEHAVIOR FOR THE ENVIRONMENT AND CIRCULAR PURCHASING

The circular economy concept entails a new way of looking at products and requires a different organizational design in which the principles of reuse, recycle and reduce are included and in ways of purchasing. Nevertheless, regulations and/or reward systems for supporting circular activities are still being developed, which creates few external incentives for organizations to implement circular activities. Therefore, developing circular activities including circular purchasing is largely dependent on internal initiatives. Consequently, purchasers play a critical role in this transition to a circular economy. They are responsible for selecting suppliers and therefore have a direct impact on an organization's interactions with the supply chain. Hence, circular purchasing is determined by OCBE. OCBE is defined as voluntary and unrewarded environmental actions that go above and beyond the job requirements in an organizational setting. Some of the examples include opting for solutions to make services and products more sustainable or giving co-workers advice about environmental issues. Indeed, the purchasers showing high levels of intention toward OCBE are more likely to engage in circular purchasing.

There are several barriers to OCBE in the workplace. Such barriers include personal barriers such as personal attitudes and lack of supervisor support and lack of resources. Furthermore, circular purchasing is likely to be part of a new strategic direction for an organization, one which requires purchasers to be proactive and take risks to act on OCBE. In order to overcome these barriers, OCBE is associated with circular purchasing through purchaser intrapreneurship. Intrapreneurship can be defined as a process whereby employees recognize and exploit opportunities by being innovative, proactive and by taking risks in order for the organization to create new products, processes and services, initiate self-renewal or venture new businesses to enhance competitiveness and performance of the organization. Given that circular purchasing is a new, innovative process, intrapreneurship is considered to be a critical behavior in the relationship between OCBE and circular purchasing. Likewise, when other factors that are critical to circular purchasing, such as regulations, are not introduced in the organization, purchasers are required to engage in additional proactive and risk-taking behaviors to, for example, gain supervisory support and obtain additional resources to facilitate the process toward circular purchasing.

Furthermore, OCBE are discretionary acts by employees within the organization that are directed toward environmental improvement; these actions are not rewarded or required by the organization. OCBE is related to the concept of organizational citizenship behavior (OCB) which refers to voluntary behavior that improves the functioning of the organization but is not rewarded. While OCB is directed toward individual persons (OCBI) or organizations (OCBO), OCBE is directed toward the environment. Individuals who score high on OCBE have a willingness to engage in actions that are positive for the environment. OCB is also found to increase job satisfaction, which is believed to support circular economy. Nevertheless, it is unknown if OCBE also increases circular purchasing. Circular purchasing is a complex form of pro-environmental behavior, where purchasers need to overcome certain hurdles within the organization and they need to convince other colleagues, such as the budget holders, to purchase in a circular manner.

11.4 ECO-LABELING AS A BEHAVIOR CHANGE TOOL

Product labeling schemes, and particularly third-party certified labels, are regularly offered as a solution to support circular economy outcomes by making informed purchasing decisions easier for consumers and providing an incentive for producers. Product labeling schemes aim to provide credible information to persuade and inform consumers without the need for individuals to exert significant cognitive effort to interrogate the green credentials of products. Eco-labels, just like other signs and prompts, are a way of informing the consumer about more sustainable product choices and advising them on how to use the product more sustainably by, for example, communicating its reusability, reparability or recyclability attributes. Eco-labels are thus a tool for changing behavior by guiding the consumer toward more environmentally friendly purchase decisions. For producers, labeling schemes can provide incentives to improve the environmental performance of products. For example, consumers' higher willingness to pay for green products than for non-labeled products, as well as the opportunity to differentiate a firm's products from other competitors through labeling, can motivate producers to adopt eco-labels. The criteria of labeling schemes can influence R&D activities, procurement, and standards for product development and manufacturing. Due to this relation of labeling with the implementation of cleaner production methods and the emergence of new products, eco-labels have been described as "a visible manifestation of an eco-innovation process".

However, labels can only promote circular economy outcomes if producers and manufacturers employ them and comply with the requirements and expected outcomes promised by the label. This is important to reduce the risk of greenwashing – i.e., making inflated or misleading environmental claims about a product to conceal the lack of effort in improving the environment. Thus, the regulations and practices around labeling schemes and their governance structures are critical for fidelity, legitimacy and trustworthiness of the labeling scheme. Over the last decade, there has been an increase in eco-labels worldwide. As of May 2020, 458 eco-labels across 199 countries and 25 industry sectors have been listed in the global directory of eco-labels, the Ecolabel Index.[1] Besides long-established and longstanding labels focusing on environmental friendliness of products such as the Blue Angel in Germany or the EU-flower, newer labels focus more specifically on circular economy outcomes like the durability and reparability of products. France has been one of the forerunners in this regard and has recently introduced a voluntary reparability and durability labeling scheme, part of which, a reparability label, will become mandatory in 2021.

While recycling is a lower-order circular economy objective, the Australasian Recycling Label is noteworthy in this chapter. Launched in 2019, it is a voluntary scheme that aims to reduce recycling contamination by providing consistent on-package labeling to guide correct predisposal treatment and sorting and, in the long term, encourage the purchase of products with more recyclable packaging. It was recently favorably highlighted in a global review of recycling labels and standards. Nevertheless, these new applications of labeling schemes require extensive behavior change across producer-consumer interactions to achieve their goals, and whether the intent of such labels is being realized in practice is yet to be established. Likewise, the second important trend, the mainstreaming of behavioral public policy, seeks to critically apply evidence and behavioral insights to optimize the impact of policy on behavior. There has been a substantial increase in the application of behavioral science to public policy since 2010, with over 250 governments establishing behavioral science teams. Behavioral public policy is contested and rapidly evolving but fundamentally involves adopting a behavioral lens in a pluralistic and non-deterministic way across the policy process. It is suited to responding to complex problems that involve behavioral and structural dimensions. The drivers to adopting or supporting product labeling schemes among consumers or businesses are presented below:

11.4.1 Drivers to Adopting Product Labeling Schemes

11.4.1.1 Knowledge and Awareness

Labels can only influence purchasing behavior when consumers are aware of a label or have some knowledge about it. In other words, awareness is one key factor for an eco-label to be effective and a prerequisite for impacting consumer behavior. Indeed, knowledge and awareness are critical influencers on label effectiveness. Knowledge and awareness can stem from a combination of information and communications about the label, the consumer's capability to understand the environmental benefit of purchasing an environmentally friendly product, as well as visibility (e.g., on products, in stores, in business or government policies). In Denmark, campaigns aimed at increasing the recognition and knowledge of eco-labels have been shown to be effective. The evidence on mass consumer behavior suggests that label knowledge and awareness is somewhat limited to "greener" consumers, where eco-labels typically provide information and/or "nudges" to already convinced audiences of the need to consume more sustainably. This can have implications for the overall market share of eco-labeled products and interested consumers, which will remain limited if only a small proportion are sensitized to the information conveyed by the label through aligned values and preferences.

---

[1] http://www.ecolabelindex.com/ accessed on 31/12/2021.

11.4.1.2 Trust

In the context of eco-labels, trust can be achieved through third parties where the certification criteria are perceived as transparent, accurate and uses well-established methodological approaches (e.g., life cycle assessment). Trust is found to be greater toward main (certified) eco-labels, particularly when the guarantee body was a non-governmental organization (NGO) or consumer organization and not related to the producer or retailer as a source of environmental information. In fact, the credibility of the eco-label source can influence the purchase decision. On the other hand, trust decreased when there was no clarity about who sits behind the schemes, how the schemes are organized, the environmental relevance of the product and in what ways the labeled products are superior to non-labeled products. Consumer distrust, in general, makes it hard for consumers to understand the meaning and content of eco-labels. In addition, terms like "green" or "bio" have been overused by companies to state their supposedly green product's attributes because these terms are not protected by the law and thus can be applied widely. This diminishes the credibility of environmental product declarations, particularly if not certified through third-party schemes. A balance needs to consider offering enough information to consumers and businesses to demonstrate credibility, accuracy and transparency without becoming too cognitively or administratively burdensome. In the absence of trust, eco-labels will have little or no impact on consumer choices, including willingness to pay a premium for certified eco-products. Similarly, businesses' perception of the costs of complying with the obligation (in terms of process and verification/reporting) outweighing the benefits may also be driven by trust – in consumers' behavior (e.g., that there is a market for eco-labeled products), in third party or government enforcement of obligations and the behavior of competitors (e.g., concerns of level playing fields, greenwashing and undercutting).

11.4.1.3 Consumer Preferences and Perceptions

Support and purchase of eco-labeled products are more widespread among consumers with altruistic, social and/or environmental values. They may also appreciate the public "visibility" that eco-labels offer (e.g., desire to be seen as a green consumer). However, it was also apparent that the criteria applied within labeling schemes may create tension with other product qualities that consumers value. For example, while a product might possess sound environmental credentials (e.g., in terms of recycled content; energy and water use), consumers may question what implications this might have on the quality and durability of the product. In addition, well-entrenched purchasing habits (where consumers have purchased the same product time and time again without the need for conscious deliberation) reduce the effects of eco-labels. While consumers' environmental values, product values as well as purchasing habits influence their support for eco-labeled products, price perception and willingness to pay to play a role too. Eco-labeled products are often perceived to be more expensive, but consumers report a willingness to pay a premium.

11.4.1.4 Business Influences

While many of the drivers to adopting eco-labels described so far focus on consumers, the evidence also discussed a range of influencers that might impact businesses supporting, adopting or producing new products and services to qualify for eco-label certification.

These influences are summarized as follows.

11.4.1.4.1 Societal and Consumer Influencers

Eco-labeling can improve a brand's reputation. Research shows that the introduction of eco-labels can increase the value of supermarket brands. However, for well-known brands or products that already have a nutrition label, eco-labeling does not increase the product value. Labeling thus can increase a product's value, which may be associated with a sales increase.

Producers may also introduce eco-labeling to react to societal and customer demands for environmentally sound products. Pressure from customers, shareholders, neighborhood and community groups can influence a firms' view toward green labeling.

11.4.1.4.2 Economic Influencers

A range of factors influences a company's economic decisions to adopt eco-labeling. These include considerations of whether eco-labels and certified products have sufficient market penetration (and differentiation from mainstream products and services) to justify costs of ongoing certification processes and to invest in different material streams and production processes to deliver products that qualify for certification.

Eco-labels may also provide opportunities to enter new markets if they extend beyond specific jurisdictional boundaries or maintain a presence in existing markets under new (mandatory) circular economy requirements.

11.4.1.4.3 Operational Influencers

These refer to whether businesses have sufficient influence or control over their supply chain to ensure they continue to meet the requirements of the labeling scheme (while protecting brand reputation). Conversely, businesses may benefit from encouraging or requiring suppliers to participate in a given labeling scheme, provided it aligns with their needs.

11.4.1.4.4 Environmental Influencers

These refer to judgments based on whether specific labeling schemes actually deliver on what they promise (e.g., based on circular economy outcomes) and are not simply a form of "greenwashing" that encourage less environmentally focused competitors to adopt. This can be complicated by the multi-faceted and undefined nature of circular economy and sustainability more broadly. Different consumers and different businesses may disagree about what circular economy attributes and outcomes a given label should or does guarantee.

11.4.1.4.5 Government Policy Influencers

Finally, businesses may not be interested in meeting voluntary or environmental targets outlined in certification programs unless they are linked to mandatory (legislated) labeling requirements or supported through green procurement policies.

11.4.2 Impacts and Outcomes of Labeling Schemes

In this section, we discuss the impacts and outcomes of labeling schemes under various categories, namely: behavioral impacts and outcomes, environmental impacts and outcomes and business impacts and outcomes.

11.4.2.1 Behavioral Impacts and Outcomes

An intention-behavior gap has been identified that indicates that while eco-labels might be successful in raising awareness and creating intentions to purchase more environmentally sustainable products, this will not always translate to actual purchases in real shopping situations (where other factors such as costs become more tangible). The existing studies suggest that eco-labeling schemes are more likely to have an influence when consumers perceive a clear connection between the certified product and an environmental (or other) outcome that they value. Despite the observed gap between intention and behavior, there is some evidence of actual changes in consumer behavior as a result of environmental product information and labeling. For example, the comparative information that eco-labeling schemes can provide at the point of sale can influence purchasing decisions by making more expensive, environmentally sound products more competitive. There is empirical evidence that comparative life cycle cost information increases the purchase likelihood for green products with higher initial costs and lower operating costs (e.g., refrigerators, cars). By making the life cycle costs salient at the point of purchase, such information can provide an alternative reference point to the purchase prices, making the product more competitive.

11.4.2.2 Environmental Impacts and Outcomes

There is tangible evidence of measurable improvements to the environment stemming from the adoption of eco-labeling schemes albeit scare. In fact, there are problems with poor environmental impacts of voluntary certification in some industries, which could result in eco-labels masking the environmental harms of products. Eco-labels are more likely applied to easily make changes, and as a result, they tend to effect only small or no changes in production practices or environmental improvements. Further research is required to demonstrate the contribution of eco-labeling schemes to circular economy outcomes.

11.4.2.3 Business Impacts and Outcomes

There is little evidence or reliable data to suggest that sufficient market penetration of eco-labeling schemes and associated products (beyond environmentally conscious consumers) has occurred to result in widespread market shifts or changes to product portfolios. Instead, there is a suggestion that labeling schemes can be manipulated for competitive advantage, to increase product prices and to increase demand for products by alleviating consumer guilt for purchasing products that may have negative environmental implications. For many companies, gaining competitive advantages or increasing their market shares is the main driver to adopt eco-labeling schemes. Still, there are few ways in which eco-labels could wield an influence. For example, they could indirectly force producers to redesign their products to be able to offer eco-labeled products, and the negotiation of criteria for eco-labeling schemes could improve the environmental performance of an entire sector.

11.4.3 Interventions to Support the Adoption of Labeling Schemes

In behavioral science, interventions can be described as a set of activities or strategies designed to change behaviors, oftentimes by increasing an individual's, organization's or population's capability, opportunity or motivation to undertake a behavior. Example interventions include increasing knowledge and understanding through education, persuading through communications (e.g., images, messages), providing incentives, or making changes to the environment to facilitate certain behaviors. Eco-labels on their own are an information-based intervention tool and are therefore unlikely to create significant shifts in consumer choices or production without other complementary policy tools. Two categories can support the adoption of product labeling schemes.

The first involves *holistic marketing strategies* (and associated certification and assurance) to communicate the meaning, intentions and value of a label and certified products, which must be visible and relevant to a broad cross-section of consumers and businesses (not just those that are eco-orientated). Such marketing strategies need to be ongoing and adaptable, as labeling schemes may evolve and innovate based on technological advancements. There is evidence that suggests that comprehensive marketing and education endeavors have been successful in raising awareness of labeling schemes and sales of some labeled products. Awareness and intentions to purchase labeled products can improve when issues of personal benefit, negative environmental outcomes and known decision-making biases are incorporated into communications, e.g., loss aversion, status quo bias, social norms, hyperbolic discounting. For example, "negative labels" (that signal harms the environment) tend to be more effective at influencing consumer preference, beyond an eco-conscious market, than "positive labels" (that signal benefits the environment). Specifically, while positive labels tend to appeal to people with strong environmental interests, those with less environmental concern are more sensitive to negative labels.

The second category of interventions that can assist in the adoption of product labeling schemes involves *regulatory* or *policy approaches*, where mandatory labeling laws and/or procurement standards are imposed, including legal and enforceable definitions of key certification criteria. Other regulatory tools can involve the restriction or banning of "polluting products" and taxes and subsidies that support the production and purchase of greener products and services. However, mandatory labeling has also been known to have unintended consequences, such as signaling to consumers a lower quality product (e.g., recycled content is used in production) or impeding entry into the market of smaller but innovative enterprises. Providing financial or expert support for undertaking product certification processes may assist in overcoming such barriers.

11.5 ECO-LABEL AND CIRCULAR ECONOMY

The proliferation of labeling schemes and their application to a circular economy transition is based on a belief that they can inform and empower consumers and encourage behavior change in consumption and production based on widely accepted and desired societal and environmental goals. Although labels can increase awareness and intentions, this does not necessarily affect consumers' purchasing behaviors unless there is a clear connection between the certified product and an environmental outcome. This connection is, however, difficult to prove, and often, there is little evidence about the environmental impacts, excerpt for instances where the impact is a result of easily made changes with only minimal or small environmental improvements. Eco-labels on their own are an information-based communication tool that is unlikely to create significant shifts in consumer choices (or production). This aligns generally with behavioral science, where it has been found that information alone is typically unlikely to change behavior.

Transitioning to a circular economy requires a variety of changes in consumption and production behaviors and outcomes from reduced consumption to resource recovery. Increasing attention on "sufficiency" and "de-growth" business models and branding suggest labels could play a role in reducing consumption and extending the life and value chain of products and services. Furthermore, a circular model requires extended consumer-product responsibility over the product lifespan to its end of life. For example, maintenance behaviors to prolong product lifetimes or the return of products to specialized recycling programs. Labeling could play a role here, for instance, in the form of product care or recycling instructions (beyond the scope of packaging waste, as the Australian Recycling Label). While labels and certification with post-purchase behavioral and business model implications are emerging, to what extent labeling schemes could play a role in this context remains to be answered.

Apparently, a number of conditions should be in place for a labeling scheme to have a chance of making a difference and thus work as an effective behavior change tool. Below, we reflect on six conditions and provide further advice on how behavioral science may improve a label's effectiveness:

1. *Labeling schemes should be **trustworthy** and **transparent**, involving **accurate** and **defensible** product evaluations based on agreed criteria and methods.*

    The behavioral sciences provide evidence that credible sources increase the acceptance of messages and their persuasiveness. Research has shown that written communication such as those provided in eco-labels will be most credible from sources with technical expertise. Therefore, labeling schemes should think carefully about the sender of the information to be most effective on consumers' purchase decisions. Swift and comprehensive detection of the misuse of labeling schemes, alongside harsh but fair and proportionate punishment or cost, could deter organizations and businesses from poor behavior, reward compliance, and again help to foster trust on the consumer side. This approach could extend to "budges" – behavioral science informed regulations aiming to protect consumers' ability to enact desirable behaviors by preventing firms from making misleading or overly complex claims and offers.

2. *Information on the labeling schemes should be **disseminated** and **visible** to consumers and producers, particularly at key decision-making moments (e.g., points of sale; start of a new production process).*

Following research on the effectiveness of signage, the clarity of the sign's purpose predicts the perceived effectiveness of signs and prompts. Balancing the complexity of information presented on labels with consumers' ability to process information in a quick and meaningful manner is critical for the design of effective labels. For eco-label designers, this suggests that the written instructions should be clear, easy to read and understand and that the requested behavior (e.g., reuse, recycle, repair) is straightforward to perform. Considering the first and second points, holistic marketing strategies and regulatory approaches can support behavioral public policy interventions aiming to "boost" the capacity and quality of citizen's decision-making by assuring trustworthy, timely and relevant information.

3. *Product labeling criteria **should be associated with tangible environmental credentials** that distinguish them from other products (otherwise, any differences between certified and non-certified products may be marginal at best).*

    If consumers could experience the tangible environmental credentials of eco-labeled products sooner rather than later, the support for labeling schemes is likely to increase. This relates to the present bias, where people are motivated by costs and benefits that can be experienced immediately compared to those delivered over time. Prominent examples of the present bias highlight people's difficulties in saving for their retirement, which represents a future benefit but a present cost. For eco-labels, more direct experiences of how the lifetime of the labeled products reduces resource depletion (e.g., communicating that a product is made out of recycled PET bottles) may lead to more tangible environmental credentials.

4. *Consumers and producers need to understand and value the intention and objectives of labeling schemes to encourage informed (and potentially different) production, purchasing and post-purchase choices.*

    With this in mind, labeling schemes should appeal to a multitude of consumer and business values. Similarly, economic and operational influencers affect business adoption of labeling. The behavioral sciences provide ways to personalize communication to cater for different audiences such as audience segmentation approaches. Compared to more generic approaches, bespoke communication efforts that consider different consumer and business values have been found to increase engagement. Similar results have been reported for eco-labels, which indicate that highlighting personal benefits in communications are an effective strategy. Behavioral science can provide insights on alternative ways for labels to personalize communication. For example, evidence from environmental communication suggests that communicating how the product (or longer use/recycling of products) can make a difference to the local or regional area of the message's effectiveness.

5. *Labeling schemes and certified products need to achieve sufficient market penetration to remain sustainable and viable.*

    To support the implementation of labeling schemes on the business and producer sides, changes in the regulatory and legislative context are needed. Incentivizing businesses to participate in third-party certified labeling schemes may reduce the risk of "greenwashing" and enhance consumers' trust in labels while also supporting higher participation in more demanding, performance-based schemes. Similarly, reforms around eco-labeling schemes can reduce the plethora of existing labels to a smaller number of more effective mandatory or third-party certified labeling schemes.

6. *Labeling schemes are unlikely to work in isolation and should be implemented in conjunction with other policy tools (e.g., competing product restrictions, procurement standards, taxes/subsidies).*

By themselves, labeling schemes are likely to have little impact on consumption or production decisions beyond the environmentally inclined. In behavioral science terms, labeling schemes are one of many tools to support circular economy outcomes. On their own, they are unlikely to achieve big changes. However, in combination with other tools, such as government regulations and restrictions, their impact can become visible over time. Similar findings are reported in other fields. For example, health warnings on cigarette packaging were one of a series of tobacco control strategies (e.g., point-of-sale bans, advertising bans in print media, etc.) that lead to a significant reduction in smoking in Australia over time. For policy makers, this highlights the need to combine eco-labels with other instruments that support circular economy outcomes. These findings align with broader literature that critique voluntary and "beyond-compliance" approaches to environmental policy, and the call for integrated, tailored mixes of policy tools.

In the absence of any of these conditions, it is believed that the impact of product labeling schemes on circular economy objectives will be limited. However, behavioral science techniques can improve the effectiveness of eco-labels more broadly.

11.6 SUMMARY

Transitioning to a circular economy requires a variety of changes in consumption and production behaviors and outcomes from reduced consumption to resource recovery. Increasing attention on "sufficiency" and "de-growth" business models and branding suggest labels could play a role in reducing consumption and extending the life and value chain of products and services.

The future purchaser can be described as someone who has expertise, self-confidence and good leadership skills. These descriptions of purchasers show several commonalities with the description of an intrapreneur. Organizational factors that influence the intrapreneur include management support, organizational structure, rewards, work discretion and resources.

Some examples of OCBE include opting for solutions to make services and products more sustainable or giving co-workers advice about environmental issues. The purchasers showing high levels of intention toward OCBE are more likely to engage in circular purchasing.

The ability of a purchaser to actually take action and become successful depends on the situational enablers. It is thus essential to investigate not only the behaviors and characteristics of the purchaser but also the drivers and constraints, i.e., contextual factors.

Eco-labels on their own are an information-based intervention tool and are therefore unlikely to create significant shifts in consumer choices or production without other complementary policy tools. Trust is found to be greater toward main (certified) eco-labels, particularly when the guarantee body was a NGO or consumer organization and not related to the producer or retailer as a source of environmental information.

DISCUSSION AND REVIEW QUESTIONS

1. Mention some of the competences of purchasers in relation to sustainability in the circular economy.
2. Describe the role of the purchaser in relation to an intrapreneur in the circular economy.
3. Eco-label is a behavior change tool. Briefly discuss.
4. Mention and briefly explain the key conditions that must be met for a labeling scheme to effectively work as a behavior change tool.
5. Define organizational citizenship behavior for the environment. Give some examples.
6. Outline some of the notable barriers to organizational citizenship behavior for the environment.
7. Enumerate the driving factors of adopting eco-labeling schemes among consumers and businesses.
8. Define interventions in the context of behavioral science and list some notable examples.
9. Eco-labels are unlikely to create significant shifts in consumer choices or production without other complementary policy tools. However, two categories can support the adoption of product labeling schemes. Mention and explain these categories.

SUGGESTED MATERIALS FOR FURTHER READING

Ayres, R. U., & Ayres, L. W. (1996). *Industrial Ecology*. Edward Elgar Publishing.

World Economic Forum (2019). Platform for accelerating the circular economy, World Economic Forum, https://www.weforum.org/projects/circular-economy.

Part 7

12 Deployment Considerations for Implementing Reverse Logistics

12.1 INTRODUCTION

The proximity in meaning and essence between reverse logistics and circular economy can lead one to consider both terms to be synonymous. To be sure, reverse logistics is not the same as circular economy, but a part of circular economy in the same way a tire is part of a truck. Simply put, reverse logistics is one of the instruments or strategies for achieving a circular economy because of its role of facilitating the return of used products to manufacturers. In other words, reverse logistics is a key enabler of the circular economy because of its role in coordinating the flow of material and information. This is essentially a departure from the classic linear (forward) logistics that supports procurement, production logistics and distribution of new parts and products from manufacturers to consumers. Here, trucks used to deliver new products and parts will not return empty but will take back used parts (including packages, etc.) and products from consumers and redistribute these to manufacturers. Understood this way, one is able to clearly see how both terms intersect and how reverse logistics fits into circular economy. This removes the confusion that one may come across when analyzing the various definitions for circular economy and reverse logistics out there. For these definitions and the historical development of both terms may appear to overlap.

The widespread assertion of reverse logistics as a pivotal tool to recoup value, obtain sustainability and even ensure repeat customers (Chan & Chan, 2008) have led to its adoption by companies and have attracted the attention of scholars in the last decade. The significance of product recovery and disposition in reverse logistics has been on the increase due to environmental issues, economic reasons, and socio-corporate responsibilities (Niknejad & Petrovic, 2014; Selvi & Kayar, 2016). Different authors have offered insights into the subject of reverse logistics and most of them agree that not much academic work has been carried out as in the case of forward logistics. They argue that reverse logistics should not be viewed as a "costly sideshow" to standard business operations. Instead, they propose that reverse logistics – including the disposition process such as remanufacturing, refurbishing, recycling, reuse or disposal of goods – should "be seen as an opportunity to build competitive advantage". Genchev et al. (2010) are of the view that a resource-based approach to reverse logistics can strengthen the capability of the firm's reverse logistics. Generally, a significant component of the work related to reverse logistics is performed in the designated warehouses. Just as in the case of forward logistics where product distribution is planned and implemented, there is a marked degree of unpredictability associated with returns in reverse logistics since most returns are unplanned. This, in turn, leads to difficulties associated with labor, equipment and truck capacity requirements, and the routing of movement according to transport modes. In its many definitions, reverse logistics can be described as the process of collection, inspection, sorting and disposition of returned or/and used products from the consumers to a retailer or manufacturer. In a modified form of the definition of reverse logistics by the Council of Supply Chain Management Professionals (CSCMP), reverse logistics is that part of returns management that plans, implements and controls the efficient, effective flow of goods and related information between the point of consumption and the point of origin in order to recapture value or properly dispose of the goods. From the perspective of business logistics, therefore, reverse logistics focuses on the role of supporting product returns. Govindan, Soleimani and Kannan (2015) assert that the reverse logistics process commences at the end users where used and unused products are collected, sorted and decisions are then made on the different disposition options. Disposition refers to the final process in reverse logistics, which explains the exit route that the returned product will take (Bernon, Rossi & Cullen, 2011). Disposition plays a crucial role in the determination of the revenue streams and recovery level of the returned products.

The forward logistics is represented by the five sequential blocks, which starts with raw materials (upstream) and ends at the final consumer (downstream). The structure suggests that forward logistics is based on marketing and sales forecasts planned to achieve optimal distribution of products from the manufacturing sites to retail outlets through distribution centers. Right from the onset, the routing to the retail outlets is known prior to distribution, and product flow is quite transparent. By contrast, reverse logistics is reactive and involves less visible flow of products since it follows no forecasts and returns could be unpredictable. While the forward logistics follows a one-to-many distribution pattern, the reverse tends to follow a many-to-one distribution network which culminates in difficult routing and planning at higher transportation costs. While there is only one option for the forward logistics, which is to move the product down to the final consumer through the different channels of distribution, reverse logistics requires different return and disposition options due to the state of the returned products. The part of Figure 12.1 immediately below the forward logistics blocks shows the disposition process and its components including the supply chain partners involved in the process. As an illustration, a returned unused product from a consumer due to poor satisfaction is very likely going to be subjected to the reuse option, which invariably may be returned to inventory or repackaged and resold, thus, recouping the most value from the return (Hazen, Hall & Hanna, 2012). However, in the event that the returned product is used or defective, any of the product upgrade options – repair, reconditioning, refurbishing, re-manufacture, or some combination of them may apply at the manufacturing stage, which by-passes the retailers/wholesalers (Khor & Udin, 2012). A returned product in its end of life (EoL) stage may be subjected to recycling to initial material (at the raw material stage) or confined to a landfill (which is certainly located away from the manufacturing or raw material stage). Other factors that may aid disposition decisions are discussed under

Deployment Considerations for Implementing Reverse Logistics 251

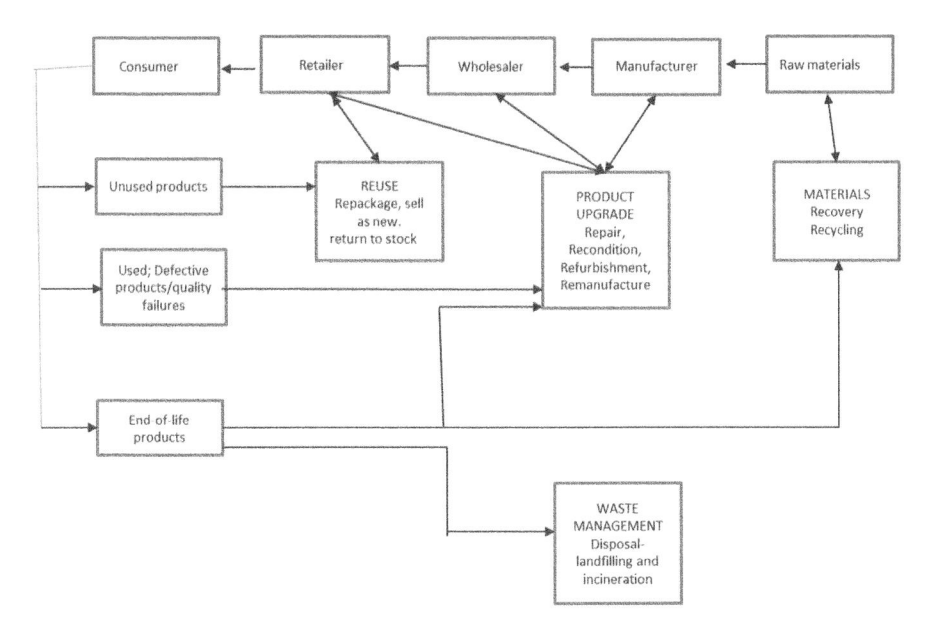

FIGURE 12.1 Interdependence between forward and reverse logistics.

economic issues related to return on investment (Hall et al., 2013; Matar, Jaber & Searcy, 2014); market-related issues such as competition, brand image and protection; supply chain drivers such as legislation and value-adding (Gobbi, 2011) and the third-party supply chain partners. Other factors include environment-related issues (Badenhorst, 2018).

12.2 THE STAGES IN THE REVERSE LOGISTICS PROCESS

Typically, the reverse logistics process can be broken into two general areas based on whether the reverse flow consists of products or packaging materials. For product returns, the bulk is represented by customer returns, while for packaging materials, the returns are for reuse many times before disposal. Damaged packages may be refurbished and returned for reuse. Transportation and warehousing are significant portions of the physical movement and work associated with reverse logistics. However, there are five sub-processes that unfold when products are returned to a warehouse. The stages include receipt; inspect, sort and stage; returns processing; returns analysis, and other support activities (Stock, 2004). Some basic reverse logistics activities are shown in Table 12.1. The point where products are inserted into the reverse flow determines the resulting reverse logistics setup. Each of the stages requires different resources and capabilities to be effective. As an illustration, some organizations may set aside a separate goods return warehouse (receipt stage) from the one where finished goods are handled for forward logistics. Furthermore, the return analysis stage requires properly trained and remunerated staff since important disposition decisions such as repackaging or refurbishing are taken at this stage.

TABLE 12.1
Basic Reverse Logistics Activities

Type of Material	Reverse Logistics Activities
Products	Return to supplier
	Sell via outlet
	Resell
	Salvage
	Recondition
	Remanufacture
	Refurbish
	Reclaim
	Recycle
	Landfill
Packaging	Refurbish
	Reuse
	Reclaim materials
	Recycle
	Salvage

Source: Adapted from Going backward: reverse logistics trends & practices, 1998.

Some industries exhibit an interesting supply chain that attempts to combine the forward and reverse activities into a single system in order to integrate returned products and/or packaging materials back into the production and distribution network (Pienaar & Vogt, 2012). The concept is demonstrated by the life cycle of a glass bottle in a beverage bottling company supply chain and it is generally known as a closed loop supply chain (CLSC). In this context, the bottle is sourced or made by the company and filled with the beverage at the factory. The product is transferred to the sales store for sale. However, the customer takes the product away but deposits some cash which is refunded to him upon the return of the empty bottles. The sales store returns the empty bottles to the manufacturer, where the bottle is reused. After several reuses, the bottle is withdrawn from circulation and crushed into input raw materials for making more bottles. The interesting feature of the CLSC is that the manufacturer is responsible for the ultimate disposal of the product in an environmentally friendly manner. The peculiarity of some packaging materials suggests the need to plan for the returns. This will be illustrated in the case study for returnable plastic containers for tomatoes from the retailers to the farm.

The role of logistics in the returns' management process includes the planning, implementation and execution of avoidance, gatekeeping and product disposition. Much as "avoidance" refers to early control of the reasons for returns, and "gatekeeping" focuses on the screening of return requests, "disposition" refers to the evaluation of the various options to which the returns could be subjected. Consequently, benefits can only be realized if the correct combination of disposition options is made and the entire process executed effectively (Agrawal, Singh & Murtaza, 2016b). In fact, countries and organizations that subscribe to reverse logistics philosophy and implement its core principles are considered to be forward-thinking. Ravi and Shankar (2015), using a nationwide questionnaire-based survey to assess reverse logistics practices in India, found that the implementation of reverse logistics is a strategic level decision with long-lasting financial and economic effects on firms. In line with Ravi and Shankar (2015), Kaviani et al. (2020) assert that reverse logistics enables efficient resource management. Agrawal, Singh and Murtaza (2016a) and also Khor et al. (2016) have demonstrated that economic benefits can accrue from revenue generation and value reclamation through returned products. Environmental advantages can equally be realized through product recovery that prevents returned products from being dumped in landfills, thereby reducing damage and waste (Ravi & Shankar, 2015; Shaharudin, Zailani & Tan, 2015). Managed efficiently, the disposition option of product recovery can also lead to market expansion opportunities and customer satisfaction. These are encouraging insights because they show that reverse logistics can indeed yield excellent results for all stakeholders. Moreover, the fact that reverse logistics is yielding good results may convince more organizations to implement it in their supply chains, especially toward the achievement of sustainable development goals.

Nevertheless, studies and the experiences of companies also reveal that the implementation of reverse logistics requires more than goodwill or good intent of organizations because of the technicalities such as provision of an effective and efficient collection, sorting treatment and segmentation, among others involved. Ho et al. (2012) explain that the swift developing practice of returning products in large volumes overwhelms the handling capacity of some companies. At the macro-level, Ambekar et al. (2021), using Interpretive Structural Modeling and Matriced Impacts Croises Multiplication Appliquée à un Classement (MICMAC) approach, found that macro-level barriers such as insufficient government policies and unavailability of standard codes influenced other barriers. Using yet another method, the Delphi Method and Structural Equation Modeling, Waqas et al. (2018) discovered that companies with insufficient capital, skilled personnel, new technologies and information systems and operating anti-reverse logistics policies have found it hard to successfully implement reverse logistics. These findings are important because they show that implementing reverse logistics needs time, adequate planning and resources in order to reduce the development of reverse logistics success impediments. However, not all companies, particularly those in developing countries, have embraced the philosophy of reverse logistics let alone implemented it vigorously (Badenhorst, 2016).

While it is useful to know reverse logistics offers great benefits and has been successful in some organizations, it would also be helpful to understand the factors that are important for organizations planning to implement reverse logistics to consider in order to achieve success. Therefore, we will focus on the deployment considerations for implementing reverse logistics. Knowledge of reverse logistics deployment considerations is essential before implementation. Generally, companies consider cost, human resources and government policies in implementing reverse logistics. According to this classification, the considerations are grouped as financial and economic, return loops, social, environmental, infrastructure and technology, management and organizational and customer awareness and incentive.

12.2.1 Financial and Economic Consideration

Literature provides sufficient evidence to show that organizations that seek to implement RL and also want to succeed in it cannot afford to overlook or exhibit a laissez-faire attitude toward the financial and economic elements of RL deployment. In most cases presented in literature, the financial and economic position of organizations was the most significant factor that determined the success or failure of RL. Interestingly, this conclusion is not specific to one country or continent despite the level of development; company notwithstanding the industry; or even specific research in spite of different methods (González-Torre et al., 2010; Jindal & Sangwan, 2011; Ho et al., 2012; Abdulrahman, Gunasekaran, & Subramanian, 2014; Chileshe et al., 2018; Waqas et al., 2018; Kaviani et al., 2020). RL involves general administration, remanufacturing, disposal and landfills, reliability tests, secondary markets and so on (Dowlatshani, 2010), which require a relatively high investment (Waqas et al., 2018). Therefore, in analyzing the cost-benefit of implementing RL, companies must take great care to not only consider the remanufacturing cost but also associated costs – training, monitoring mechanisms, storage and others – that come along with it (Dowlatshani, 2010; Abdulrahman et al., 2014) in order to have a complete and realistic picture of the financial and economic demands involved in implementing RL. According to Ho et al. (2012), a company's financial strength and support has a positive impact on the implementation of reverse logistics because having sufficient capital has a higher likelihood of encouraging companies to improve their service and look for new business strategies.

12.2.2 Return Loop Consideration

As companies think of venturing into RL, they need to determine the loop to focus on and study it in order to understand what financial, economic, technological, environmental, social and regulatory consequences it is associated with. In this regard, the Ellen MacArthur Foundation Circular Economy model diagram, which has four loops for the technical side, is a good place to start:

a. The outermost loop, recycle, is the loop of last resort. Here, a product or its component is returned to the materials that it is made of. This is so because it no longer offers any useful consumption value in its present condition. Hence, extra value like labor, energy or materials that went into creating such a product or component is stripped away. Ohimain (2013) offers us an example of recycling by describing how the defunct Delta Steel Company in Nigeria depended on recycling scrap iron to make new products for reuse due to the shortage of iron ore. In considering this aspect of the return loop, companies are obliged to consider the means of obtaining this end of life and end of use products – whether they would do it themselves directly or depend on third parties to gather end of life products and deliver to them. Factors that can help them make an informed decision include the capacity to gather, transport and store end of life products and process them for reuse (Li et al., 2018) in relation to cost and performance efficiency (Anttonen et al., 2013; McCarthy, Silvestre, & Kietzmann, 2013).

b. The next is the remanufacturing loop, in which manufacturers restore a product to its original position or better new standard by replacing obsolete or worn-out or degrading parts affecting the performance of the product. This follows steps such as disassembly, sorting and cleaning, scanning, refurbishment or substitution, reassembly and testing for quality before its introduction to the market (Singhal, Tripathy & Jena, 2020). For example, companies such as Svelitus, a company that uses remanufacturing as its main business model, buys return products from other companies, remanufactures them and sells them in the open market, Scania truck company remanufactures components such as the gearbox, and Volvo has a remanufacturing plant where worn-out engines of heavy-duty trucks are remanufactured following the steps we highlighted previously in this paragraph.
c. The inner loop, reuse, is used to denote the selling of old products to be directly reused by a new customer. Reuse items are usually not subjected to repair work. Rather, they undergo surface work such as cleaning to erase marks, replacing broken handles and so on (Cole, Gnanapragasam & Cooper, 2017). In this way, they do not require much regarding energy and labor. Usually, manufacturers, in collaboration with retailers, design "take-back schemes" that enable consumers to return products that meet reuse requirements to retailers, who in turn sell them to other consumers.
d. The innermost loop, maintenance, means that the life of a product is prolonged through activities like intentional product design by manufacturers that ensure a product can be used more intensively as a way to reduce the overall quantity of the item demanded. This is by far the most efficient loop in a circular economy.

In addition, companies also have to consider how these loops will function. That is, whether the return loop will be closed whereby the materials, products or components are recovered for use by the same company in the same product or a different product; open, same sector, which means the recovered materials will be used by another company in the same sector; or open, cross sector whereby recovered materials flow to a different industry or sector (Weetman, 2016).

To conclude, it is very important for companies to consider the return loops to effectively know the requirements of reverse logistics in the recovery of products. We do not here imply that companies must necessarily choose one. Rather, our aim is to point companies' attention to the possible demands of each return loop type so that they are better prepared to design long-lasting products, take-back schemes, remanufacture worn-out components, or recycle EoL or end-of-use products.

12.2.3 Social Consideration

As the final goal of RL is sustainability, it is not surprising that social factors, a crucial aspect of Elkington's (1998) triple bottom line approach to sustainability also features as a deployment consideration in implementing reverse logistics. Manufacturing firms also implement RL based on the pressure from communities, their concern for the social wellbeing of communities and promotion of their corporate image among various community groups. Govindan and Bouzon (2018) unequivocally affirm that higher public awareness on environmental issues like waste disposal, loss of biodiversity, natural resource depletion, increasing landfills and others drive communities and even NGOs to apply pressure on manufacturing firms to implement RL. Thus, it is the case that implementing or failing to implement RL will affect the corporate image of manufacturing firms as the study of Hong and Huang (2021) on the relationship among reverse logistics, corporate image and social impact in the medical device industry reveals.

Implementing RL may also be the result of the social consideration of communities as regards the creation of large numbers of jobs and career opportunities, provision of disadvantaged people with workforce skills and business ownership opportunities (Chini & Bruening, 2003; Leigh & Patterson, 2006; Denhart, 2010). Using an example from deconstructing buildings, Denhart (2010) explains that where it takes a single worker with heavy machinery to demolish a 2000 sq. ft. building in one day, deconstruction requires four workers and about two weeks with the opportunity of recovering reusable building materials. According to Afum, Sun and Kusi (2019), manufacturing firms that consider these things exhibit good corporate citizenship, which constitutes a key factor for RL adoption and implementation by manufacturing firms. This claim is backed by the findings of Abdullah and Yaakub (2017), who discovered that very low corporate citizenship among Malaysian firms accounted for an insignificant influence on these firms to implement and enhance their RL operations. In addition, companies like Svelitus focus on remanufacturing as its main business model. In the future, it is probable that this will give many other businesses the impetus to adopt remanufacturing and perhaps, other aspects of the return loop as their main business model in various countries.

Further, trust in the quality of recovered materials or products often determines consumer acceptability or patronage of the product. Patronage of recovered products by consumers plays a significant role in encouraging or discouraging RL activities (Jiménez-Parra, Rubio & Vicente-Molina, 2014; Kaviani et al., 2020). For, if consumers are not predisposed toward purchasing recovered products or materials, it becomes a serious barrier regardless of an excellent technical and operational design (Guide & Van Wassenhove, 2009). To mitigate this barrier, manufacturing firms should establish a consumer profile that include consumers that have a favorable attitude toward recovered products, has a clear motivation of respect for the environment, and a positive consideration of the opinion of their close social environment (family, friend, etc.) when making a purchase (Jiménez-Parra et al., 2014).

12.2.4 Environmental Consideration

Authors, activists and various countries substantially cite environmental issues such as reduction of carbon footprint, prevention of pollution, waste management, and reduction in the use of raw materials as one of the principal reasons for the adoption of circular economy and by extension, RL. According to Pearce, Turner and Turner (1990), western literature first used the term "Circular Economy" to depict a closed system of economy-environment interactions, which may have been inspired by the Brundtland report of 1987 that called for the formulation of long-term environmental strategies for achieving sustainable development by the year 2000 and beyond. Examining the history of CE, Winans, Kendall and Deng (2017) constantly highlights environmental consideration as a crucial reason for CE adoption by countries such as Germany, which intended to address raw materials and natural resource use issues; China which emphasized on post-consumer waste recycling just as the United Kingdom, Denmark, Switzerland, and Portugal have done. The essence is to encourage and promote environmentally friendly industrial activities. Thus, the formulation of expressions like eco-industrial park, eco-industry network and industrial symbiosis to capture this particular essence of CE to leave the environment undamaged from economic activities.

Reverse logistics has become a crucial aspect of CE and supply chain management with the increased emphasis on environmental responsibility and sustainability. As mentioned earlier in this chapter, RL facilitates the recovery of materials and products for reuse, remanufacture or recycle. Studies agree that it is undoubtedly one of the most effective solutions to decrease environmental pollution and waste of resources by capturing the values of used products. However, in what might appear to be a contradiction, studies also strongly suggests that the transportation, processing and production of recovered materials and products comes with certain environmental challenges that can undermine the very same environment RL activities are designed to protect, sustain and improve. Gao (2019) asserts that the employment of different vehicle types to transport recovered materials and products results in different vehicle-based carbon emissions. Due to the energy-efficient and environmentally friendly approach of remanufacturing, firms may overlook emission influencing factors like size of manufacturing, vehicle loads, collection and inspection center facilities, vehicle type and the travel distance of vehicles. Ali et al. (2018) measured the impact of reverse logistics performance indicators (cost, recycling efficiency, time, quality and waste on sustainability performances (economic, environmental and social) in fast moving consumer goods (FMCG) industries. They found out that cost, recycling efficiency (recycling time, time of product arrival at collection centers and volume of power, water and gas consumption) and waste due to poor manufacturing, improper recycle or recovery affect the environment. Trochu et al. (2020) provide insight from RL activities in the construction, renovation and demolition industry. According to these researchers, quality uncertainty related to RL operations may deteriorate the overall supply chain environmental performance and profitability if not considered during the design stage of RL network. These findings reveal how important it is for manufacturing firms or third-party firms involved with RL to thoroughly evaluate the means, processes and procedures for undertaking RL in order not to frustrate the very same environmental objectives that compelled them to implement RL.

Thus, scholars have proposed different approaches and models to minimize the impact of RL activities like transportation, recycle, remanufacture and others on the environment to make it safe and friendly (Table 12.2).

12.2.5 Infrastructure and Technology Consideration

Infrastructure and technology like storage facility, handling equipment, vehicles and systems to monitor and track product lifecycle and returns perform a cardinal function in RL implementation (Abdulrahman et al., 2014; Waqas et al., 2018). The

TABLE 12.2
Approaches, Designs and Models Developed by Scholars

	Author (Year)	Approach or Model
1.	Moslehi, Sahebi and Teymouri (2021)	A multi-objective stochastic model for a reverse logistics supply chain design with environmental considerations
2.	Zohal and Soleimani (2016)	Developing an ant colony approach for green closed loop supply chain network design: A case study in gold industry
3.	Trochu et al. (2019)	A carbon-constrained stochastic model for eco-efficient reverse logistics network design under environmental regulations in the CRD industry
4.	Gao (2019)	A novel reverse logistics network design considering multi-level investments for facility reconstruction with environmental considerations
5.	Zhang et al. (2018)	A stochastic reverse logistics production routing model with environmental considerations
6.	Kannan et al. (2012)	A carbon footprint-based reverse logistics network design model
7.	Choudhary et al. (2015)	A carbon market sensitive optimization model for integrated forward-reverse logistics
8.	Safdar et al. (2020)	Reverse logistics network design of e-waste management under the triple bottom line approach
9.	Shuang, Diabat and Liao (2019)	A stochastic reverse logistics production routing model with emissions control policy selection
10.	Ren et al. (2020)	A genetic algorithm for fuzzy random and low-carbon integrated forward/reverse logistics network design
11.	Guo et al. (2017)	Forward and reverse logistics network and route planning under the environment of low-carbon emissions: A case study of Shanghai fresh food e-commerce
12.	Reddy et al. (2019)	A three-phase heuristic approach for reverse logistics network design incorporating carbon footprint
13.	Wang, Hao and Li (2020)	Reverse logistics network design considering customer convenience and low carbon emissions
14.	Dutta et al. (2020)	A multiobjective optimization model for sustainable reverse logistics in Indian e-commerce market
15.	Kannan, Pokharel and Kumar (2009)	A hybrid approach using ISM and fuzzy TOPSIS for the selection of reverse logistics provider
16.	Rabbani and Saravi (2017)	Design of forward/reverse logistics with environmental consideration
17.	Bazan, Jaber and Zanoni (2016)	A review of mathematical inventory models for reverse logistics and the future of its modeling: An environmental perspective
18.	Chen et al. (2021)	Third-party reverse logistics provider selection: A computational semantic analysis-based multi-perspective multi-attribute decision-making approach
19.	Shaik and Abdul-Kader (2018)	A hybrid multiple criteria decision-making approach for measuring comprehensive performance of reverse logistics enterprises
20.	Govindan et al. (2020)	An integrated hybrid approach for circular supplier selection and closed loop supply chain network design under uncertainty

availability of infrastructure enables a manufacturing firm to effectively track individual products and handle returns or recalls without jeopardizing its economic, social and environmental objectives. The availability of RL infrastructure can function as a profit center because it can enable substantial cost reduction and even be a source of competitive advantage (Stock, Speh & Shear, 2006). Conversely, unavailability of infrastructure can make return management clumsy and burdensome and may thus increase the cost for firms (Jack, Powers & Skinner, 2010). Tibben-Lembke and Rogers (2002) highlight the situations that make the availability of competent infrastructure and technology expedient. According to them, RL is difficult to plan and forecast because of the great uncertainty involved, has many origins unlike forward logistics, return is more susceptible to damage due to improper and lack of uniform packaging, unclear points of origin, inconsistent inventory management due to random return of products, lower visibility of entire RL process among others. This reveals why the presence or absence of infrastructure can significantly enable a firm's economic, social and environmental objectives as long as RL is concerned or otherwise frustrate them.

The criticality of infrastructure and technology consideration is evidenced by the fact that it features as a remarkable barrier to the implementation of RL in various studies. In the study of Waqas et al. (2018), it was one of the overall top five barriers to the implementation of logistics in the manufacturing sector. Abdulrahman et al. (2014) highlight it as one of the five most critical barriers of RL in the Chinese manufacturing sectors. Likewise in South Africa, Meyer et al. (2017) uncovered a lack of information systems and infrastructure as the main internal barriers for orgnizations' RL practices. Al Zaabi, Al Dhaheri and Diabat (2013) label it as one of the five main barriers of RL in their paper. Bouzon, Govindan and Rodriguez (2018) also identify it as one of the five key barriers to RL from an organizational perspective. Dashore and Sohani (2008) consider it to be one of the seven prominent barriers in his study. This, however, does not mean that infrastructure and technology is a critical barrier in every industry or country as revealed by the studies of Chinda (2017) and Moktadir et al. (2020), where it is found to have the least influence in reverse logistics implementation. Notwithstanding, infrastructure and technology are a crucial element in RL infrastructure. In fact, without infrastructure, it would be almost impossible to implement RL efficiently as many manufacturing industries have experienced.

12.2.6 Management and Organizational Consideration

The deployment of RL in organizations is firmly hinged on certain indispensable management and organization factors which, if not appropriately considered, will weaken the RL activities of an organization or in the worst-case scenario, prevent RL from being implemented (Abdullah et al., 2011; Jindal & Sangwan, 2011; Luthra et al., 2011; Gardas, Raut & Narkhede, 2018; Moktadir et al., 2019). At the heart of management and organizational consideration lies management awareness, and in fact, studies reveal that awareness is the first stage in the stages of the adoption of ideas, products or services. Awareness does not imply an automatic implementation as management has to consider other factors. Rather, it is the door that leads to the consideration of other factors. Management and organizations can become aware of RL by sourcing information about it or by trial as in the sense of a test drive. Also of great importance is the level of interest, support and commitment by top management. For instance, authors have found that in the leather footwear industry in Bangladeshi, and the automobile service sector's effort to reduce exploration and production of oil, a lack of interest, support and commitment has been a major obstacle hampering RL implementation (Moktadir et al., 2019). Management and organizational support and commitment entail encouragement of employees to learn RL (Luthra et al., 2011), the establishment of proper organizational structure to support RL (Sirisawat & Kiatcharoenpol, 2018), provision of resources and staff training, integration of RL into supply chains of the firm, leading strategic planning sessions for RL implementation (Prakash & Barua, 2017), and modification of company policies to accommodate RL (Gardas et al., 2018).

12.2.7 CONSUMER AWARENESS AND INCENTIVES

Manufacturers' awareness and adoption of RL depends on the consumer's level of awareness to be effective as the collaboration of individual consumers with manufacturing firms is necessary for the manufacturing firm to efficiently undertake reverse logistics activities. As mentioned before, awareness precedes acceptance or adoption. Therefore, to be effective, firms have to ascertain the level of their consumer awareness in relation to reverse logistics and design strategies to educate and persuade consumers to return their old products for reuse, remanufacture, or recycle. Zaccaï (2008) considers consumers as the central players from the standpoint of environmental activities because they are the ones who buy green products, use and maintain products to reduce environmental impacts and correctly dispose of or return products. Findings strongly indicate that awareness is essential if consumers will engage in this process (Saphores et al., 2006; Nnorom, Ohakwe & Osibanjo, 2009). Saphores et al. (2006), using multivariate models, found that education was one of the effective factors affecting participation in e-waste recycling in Canada. Similarly, Nnorom et al. (2009) undertook research to estimate and explain consumer willingness to pay a premium for green cell phones in Nigeria and discovered that awareness constitutes one of the most important predictors of willingness to pay. In essence, manufacturing firms should not assume that their consumers are aware of their RL activities but actively endeavor to educate and inform them about their RL activities.

In addition to considering awareness, manufacturing firms should also consider incentives as findings show that consumers' willingness to return their old products depend, to a great extent, on discount or reward offered by manufacturing firms and retailers, especially in developing countries where executive agencies do not give enough attention to appropriate laws (Abdulrahman et al., 2014; Dixit & Vaish, 2015). This was the case in Massachusetts, where the willingness of consumers to return their old ink cartridges was driven by incentive the retailer offered in exchange (Bai, 2009), and in India, where economic benefits were a significant factor that affect consumers' willingness to take part in recycling e-waste (Dwivedy & Mittal, 2013). Hence, considering the key role consumers play in reverse logistics, it behoves companies to consider how aware consumers are about their RL activities and also determine what incentives will encourage them to willingly and actively participate in their different RL programs.

12.3 CURRENT TRENDS AND FUTURE DEVELOPMENTS OF CIRCULAR SUPPLY CHAINS IN THE RETAIL INDUSTRY

There is no gainsaying that the retail industry plays a pivotal role in facilitating circular supply chains when we consider how it enables forward logistics (from the manufacturers to consumers) and reverse logistics (from consumers back to manufacturers) (Dias et al., 2019). In essence, the retail industry functions as a contact point for both stakeholders. The industry gets goods from manufacturers or wholesalers and sells directly to the consumers for personal or family use and also serves as a collection point for goods from consumers on behalf of manufacturers for reuse, remanufacture or recycle. Figure 12.2 illustrates the role the retail industry plays in circular supply chains.

This role of facilitating circular supply chains is crucial when the rate of consumption of goods from industries such as the cell phone, fashion, textile, food and others is taken into account. In the cell phone industry, about 1.5 billion phones are sold globally each year, according to the Statista Global Surve, 2021), while in the United States alone, over 150 million phones are thrown away annually. Chung (2016) asserts the fast-fashion industry produces 80 billion new clothes annually, generated 92 million tons of waste in 2015 alone and that consumers keep fashion clothes for 35 days on average. The rate of consumption and waste in these industries have further convinced stakeholders of the need for circular supply chains. Therefore, manufacturing firms, in collaboration with the retail industry, are finding creative ways to get back products from consumers for reuse, remanufacture or recycle (Upadhyay et al., 2021).

So far, return-policy-based coordination has been widely employed by the retail industry to facilitate circular supply chains. A customer may return a good due to defects, wrong expectations, buyer's remorse, impulse buying, product recalls, bad intent, warranty returns, or just not wanting the good anymore (Frei, Jack & Brown, 2020). And with the rise of e-commerce, the return rate has increased drastically

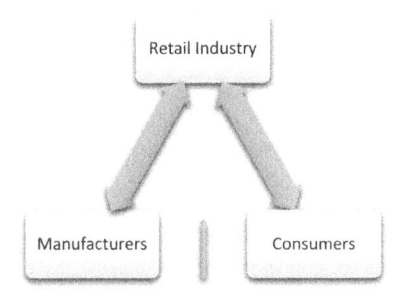

FIGURE 12.2 The role of retail industry in circular supply chains.

over the years leading to challenges such as high return handling cost for companies and (their) retail outlets (Asdecker, Karl & Sucky, 2017). The most current trends of circular supply chains in the retail industry include:

- **Establishment of Collection Centers:** Companies are establishing collection centers in retail outlets to facilitate and encourage the return of products. In contrast to forward logistics, reverse logistics is a multi-channel ecosystem and thus requires that customers should be able to return products through the same channel to enhance visibility, quick and easy returns, and refunds. For example, H&M, a fast-fashion company, installed green boxes in 3300 of its stores to collect unwanted garments to reuse them or recycle them into new clothes. It collected 3000 tonnes of garments in 2018, which was below the target of 25,000 tonnes per year. Likewise, Marks & Spencer, a multinational retailer, designed a reverse logistics solution that enables its customers to collect and return products via the same channel. Battery producers in Spain have also employed this same strategy to recover batteries from customers and retail outlets are among the network of collection points. In fact, small kiosks are being opened by top retailers to enable the return of goods that have been sold online since consolidating returns is a strategy that helps retailers eliminate the risk of a wasted carrier journey due to the defined minimum threshold of returns before they are sent to regional processing centers.
- **Hiring Third Party:** Retailers, especially e-commerce players, are hiring third-party reverse logistics providers in order to reduce and effectively handle the complexities inherent in the influx of product returns from multiple points of origin (Chen et al., 2021) so they can quickly sort them out for reuse, remanufacture or recycle them and in this way, keep customers happy (Meade & Sarkis, 2002). In most cases, third-party providers are contracted because they possess the labor and infrastructure capacity to process returned products for offline and online retailers. This may be networks and technology needed to provide real-time information of products and enhance the visibility of products for proper tracking. In selecting third-party reverse logistics providers, retailers consider factors such as cost, delivery and service, quality, efficiency and so on (Angel & Tan, 2018; Chen et al., 2021).
- **Free Returns:** Retailers like Walmart, Target, Shoprite and several others are also offering free returns to customers. Customers can take it to the store themselves after completing and submitting the return summary or drop it off at a specified location. In their view, free returns are a chance for them to make more sales and interact more with customers to help them build a loyal and satisfied customer base. To understand how free returns work for specific retailers, consumers are urged to examine their distinct return policies.

Circular supply chains in the retail industry are still a developing field. In line with scholars (Aminoff & Kettunen, 2016; De Angelis, Howard & Miemczyk, 2018) who assert that the circular supply chain is an underexplored area of research, Bernon et al. (2011) considered circularity in the retail industry as an immature and developing field while Dias et al. (2019) consider it as a field that is still under development following the result of their systematic literature review on reverse logistics for return management in retail from 2007 to 2016. Dias et al. came to this conclusion because they found only ten (10) references useful for the final analysis of their systematic review. Going forward, more research is necessary for the future development of the circular economy in the retail industry to inform, build knowledge, identify sources of complexities, understand current challenges and find realistic solutions.

One setback of circular supply chains in the retail industry has been the low visibility of products. The retail industry, in collaboration with manufacturing firms, would have to rethink how technology is currently used to facilitate the tracking and tracing of products to increase visibility across the chain. Mastos et al. (2021), therefore, opines that redesigning circular supply chains with Industry 4.0 technologies can enable efficient circular supply chain management. Additionally, for this field to further develop, manufacturing firms would need to design products that fit into the circular supply chain model of the retail industry, while governments in different countries can help with the development of regulations and policies that encourage and support circular supply chains in the retail industry.

12.4 THE OVERALL IMPACT OF CIRCULARITY ON CONTEMPORARY LOGISTICS

The adoption and implementation of circular economy principles in the logistics aspect of all industries require a remarkable shift in how the players in these industries have thought about and practiced logistics for many decades. Making this shift demands acquiring and employing sufficient information, skill and knowledge. Forward logistics has always been the common practice in the supply chains of industries where companies did not have to think about recovering goods from customers for reuse, remanufacture or recycle. However, with the emphasis on circularity, manufacturing firms must now include environmental wellbeing into their supply chains and modify their supply chain models for the recovery of goods. In fact, this is a requirement for those in countries where the governments have policies that mandate the practice of circular supply chains and also as a strategy to attract and keep those customers who are environmentally conscious. To be sure, as circularity evolves in the logistics sector, it will become a source of competitive advantage.

Manufacturing firms have also realized that the efficient implementation of circularity in logistics requires the establishment of new facilities or the adjustment of old facilities to reflect their new reality. They need new spaces for storing and sorting to determine where recovered products will go – for reuse, remanufacture, or recycle. And for every facility, they are encouraged to design their circular logistics network in a manner that will not frustrate the aim of having a circular logistics network in the first place. For instance, scholars (Kannan et al., 2012; Choudhary et al., 2015; Zohal & Soleimani, 2016; Zang et al., 2018; Safdar et al., 2020; Trochu et al., 2020) have urged manufacturing firms to design their circular logistics transport system in a way that will support low-carbon emission. Therefore, manufacturing firms are finding ways to restructure their logistics processes in an environmentally friendly way.

And while some firms understand and can do this on their one, others hire third-party logistics service providers to help them design and manage a circular logistics system.

And with the evolution and gradual spread of extended producer responsibility (EPR) across the globe, firms are beginning to integrate circularity in the design of products that are easier to reuse, repair, recycle and retain their value for as long as possible. And since firms must have some level of product visibility across the whole value chain to be able to fulfill the requirements of EPR, they are also investing in the use of technology like RFID to track and trace goods seamlessly in real-time, and big data to manage circular supply chain design and maintain a relationship with actors in the value chain (Del Giudice et al., 2020). Further, integrating circular economy into logistics has compelled firms to train employees and upstream and downstream value chain partners so that they are informed and able to participate with appropriate knowledge and skills.

Overall, rethinking logistics, redesigning logistics transport networks, establishing new facilities or adjusting old ones to reflect current realities, design of products that align with circular economy principles, investing in technologies that support circular logistics, and training employees to obtain appropriate information, skill and knowledge constitute the impact of circularity on contemporary logistics.

12.5 SUMMARY

Typically, the reverse logistics process can be broken into two general areas based on whether the reverse flow consists of products or packaging materials. For product returns, the bulk is represented by customer returns, while for packaging materials, the returns are for reuse many times before disposal. Damaged packages may be refurbished and returned for reuse. Transportation and warehousing are significant portions of the physical movement and work associated with reverse logistics. However, there are five sub-processes that unfold when products are returned to a warehouse. The stages include receipt; inspect, sort and stage; returns processing; returns analysis and other support activities.

Firms are beginning to integrate circularity in the design of products that are easier to reuse, repair, recycle and retain their value for as long as possible. And since firms must have some level of product visibility across the whole value chain to be able to fulfill the requirements of extended product responsibility, they are also investing in the use of technology like RFID to track and trace goods seamlessly in real-time, and big data to manage circular supply chain design and maintain a relationship with actors in the value chain.

The role of logistics in the returns' management process includes the planning, implementation and execution of avoidance, gatekeeping and product disposition. Much as "avoidance" refers to early control of the reasons for returns, and "gatekeeping" focuses on the screening of return requests, "disposition" refers to the evaluation of the various options to which the returns could be subjected.

The adoption and implementation of circular economy principles in the logistics aspect of all industries require a remarkable shift in how the players in these industries have thought about and practiced logistics for many decades. Making this shift demands acquiring and employing sufficient information, skill and knowledge.

There is no gainsaying that the retail industry plays a pivotal role in facilitating circular supply chains when we consider how it enables forward logistics (from the manufacturers to consumers) and reverse logistics (from consumers back to manufacturers) (. In essence, the retail industry functions as a contact point for both stakeholders. So far, return-policy-based coordination has been widely employed by the retail industry to facilitate circular supply chains. The most current trends of circular supply chains in the retail industry include the establishment of collection centers, hiring third parties and free returns.

DISCUSSION AND REVIEW QUESTIONS

1. Mention and briefly explain the key considerations for the effective deployment of reverse logistics.
2. Explain the role of the retail industry in facilitating circular economy principles in the supply chain.
3. Briefly discuss the most common trend of the circular supply chains in the retail industry.
4. Outline the stages in the reverse logistics process.
5. What is the overall impact of circularity on contemporary logistics?

SUGGESTED MATERIALS FOR FURTHER READING

Abdullah, N., Halim, N. A., Yaakub, S., & Abdullah, H. H. (2011). Reverse logistics adoption among Malaysian manufacturers. In International Conference on Management, Economics and Social Sciences (ICMESS'2011), 23–24 December 2011 (Unpublished), Bangkok, Thailand.

Abdullah, N. A. H. N., & Yaakub, S. (2017). The pressure for reverse logistics adoption among manufacturers in Malaysia. *Asian Journal of Business and Accounting*, 8(1), 151–178.

Abdulrahman, M. D., Gunasekaran, A., & Subramanian, N. (2014). Critical barriers in implementing reverse logistics in the Chinese manufacturing sectors. *International Journal of Production Economics*, 147, 460–471.

Afum, E., Sun, B. Z., & Kusi, C. L. Y. (2019). Reverse logistics, stakeholder influence and supply chain performance in Ghanaian manufacturing sector. *Journal of Supply Chain Management Systems*, 8(3), 13.

Agrawal, S., Singh, R. K., & Murtaza, Q. (2016a). Prioritizing critical success factors for reverse logistics implementation using fuzzy-TOPSIS methodology. *Journal of Industrial Engineering International*, 12(1), 15–27. https://doi.org/10.1007/s40092-015-0124-8

Agrawal, S., Singh, R., & Murtaza, Q. (2016b). Disposition decisions in reverse logistics by using AHP-Fuzzy TOPSIS approach. *Journal of Modelling in Management*, 11(4), 932–948. https://doi.org/10.1108/17465660710834453

Ajani, A., & Kunlere, I. O. (2019). Implementation of the extended producer responsibility (EPR) policy in Nigeria: towards sustainable business practice. *Nigerian Journal of Environment and Health*, 2, 44–56.

Al Zaabi, S., Al Dhaheri, N., & Diabat, A. (2013). Analysis of interaction between the barriers for the implementation of sustainable supply chain management. *The International Journal of Advanced Manufacturing Technology*, 68(1–4), 895–905.

Ali, A. H., Zalavadia, S., Barakat, M. R., & Eid, A. (2018). The role of sustainability in reverse logistics for returns and recycling. *Archives of Business Research*, 6(7). https://doi.org/10.14738/abr.67.4645.

Ambekar, S., Roy, D., Hiray, A., Prakash, A., & Patyal, V. S. (2021). Barriers to adoption of reverse logistics: a case of construction, real estate, infrastructure and project (CRIP) sectors. *Engineering, Construction and Architectural Management*. https://doi.org/10.1108/ECAM-02-2021-0112.

Aminoff, A., & Kettunen, O. (2016), "Sustainable supply chain management in a circular economy – towards supply circles", in Setchi, R., Howlett, R. and Liu, Y. T. P. (Eds), *Sustainable Design and Manufacturing* (pp. 61–72). Springer, Cham.

Angel, A., & Tan, A. (2018). Designing reverse logistics network in an omnichannel environment in Asia. *LogForum*, *14*(4), 519–533.

Anttonen, M., Halme, M., Houtbeckers, E., & Nurkka, J. (2013). The other side of sustainable innovation: is there a demand for innovative services?. *Journal of Cleaner Production*, *45*, 89–103.

Asdecker, B., Karl, D., & Sucky, E. (2017, January). Examining Drivers of Consumer Returns in E-tailing with Real Shop Data. In Proceedings of the 50th Hawaii International Conference on System Sciences. Hilton Waikoloa Village, Hawaii.

Badenhorst, A. (2018). What practice can learn from theory: "the potential impact of disposition decision factors on organisational performance". *Journal of Transport and Supply chain Management*, *12*(0), a338. https://doi.org/10.4102/jtscm.v12i0.338

Badenhorst, A. (2016). Prioritising the implementation of practices to overcome operational barriers in reverse logistics. *Journal of Transport and Supply Chain Management*, *10*(1), 1–12. https://doi.org/10.4102/jtscm.v10i1.240

Bai, H. (2009). Reverse Supply Chain Coordination and Design for Profitable Returns – An Example of Ink Cartridge. Unpublished Master Thesis. Worcester Polytechnic Institute.

Bazan, E., Jaber, M. Y., & Zanoni, S. (2016). A review of mathematical inventory models for reverse logistics and the future of its modeling: an environmental perspective. *Applied Mathematical Modelling*, *40*(5–6), 4151–4178.

Bernon, M., Rossi, S., & Cullen, J. (2011). Retail reverse logistics: A call and grounding framework for research. *International Journal of Physical Distribution Logistics Management*, *41*(5), 484–510. https://doi.org/10.1108/09600031111138835

Bouzon, M., Govindan, K., & Rodriguez, C. M. T. (2018). Evaluating barriers for reverse logistics implementation under a multiple stakeholders' perspective analysis using grey decision making approach. *Resources, Conservation and Recycling*, *128*, 315–335.

Carrasco-Gallego, R., & Ponce-Cueto, E. (2010) A Management Model for Closed-Loop Supply Chains of Reusable Articles. 4th International Conference on Industrial Engineering and Industrial Management Sept 2010. Bali, Indonesia.

Chan, F. T., & Chan, H. K. (2008). A survey on reverse logistics system of mobile phone industry in Hong Kong. *Management Decision*, *46*(5), 702–708.

Chan, F. I. S., Chan, H. K., & Jain, V. (2012). A framework of reverse logistics for the automobile industry. *International Journal of Production Research*, *50*(5), 1318–1331. https://doi.org/10.1080/00207543.2011.571929

Chen, Z. S., Zhang, X., Govindan, K., Wang, X. J., & Chin, K. S. (2021). Third-party reverse logistics provider selection: a computational semantic analysis-based multi-perspective multi-attribute decision-making approach. *Expert Systems with Applications*, *166*, 114051.

Chileshe, N., Rameezdeen, R., Hosseini, M. R., Martek, I., Li, H. X., & Panjehbashi-Aghdam, P. (2018). Factors driving the implementation of reverse logistics: a quantified model for the construction industry. *Waste Management*, *79*, 48–57.

Chinda, T. (2017). Examination of factors influencing the successful implementation of reverse logistics in the construction industry: pilot study. *Procedia Engineering*, *182*, 99–105.

Chini, A. R., & Bruening, S. (2003). Deconstruction and materials reuse in the United States. *The Future of Sustainable Construction*, *14*, 1–22.

Choudhary, A., Sarkar, S., Settur, S., & Tiwari, M. K. (2015). A carbon market sensitive optimization model for integrated forward–reverse logistics. *International Journal of Production Economics, 164*, 433–444.

Chung, S.-W. (2016). Fast fashion is "drowning" the world. We need a fashion revolution. Retrieved 23 October 2021 from www.greenpeace.org

Cole, C., Gnanapragasam, A., & Cooper, T. (2017). Towards a circular economy: exploring routes to reuse for discarded electrical and electronic equipment. *Procedia CIRP, 61*, 155–160.

Dashore, K., & Sohani, N. (2008). Green supply chain management: a hierarchical framework for barriers. *Journal of Sustainable Development, 5*, 2011.

De Angelis, R., Howard, M., & Miemczyk, J. (2018). Supply chain management and the circular economy: towards the circular supply chain. *Production Planning and Control, 29*(6), 425–437.

Del Giudice, M., Chierici, R., Mazzucchelli, A., & Fiano, F. (2020). Supply chain management in the era of circular economy: the moderating effect of big data. *The International Journal of Logistics Management, 32*(2), 337–356.

Denhart, H. (2010). Deconstructing disaster: economic and environmental impacts of deconstruction in post-Katrina New Orleans. *Resources, Conservation and Recycling, 54*(3), 194–204.

Dias, K. T. S., Braga, S. S., Silva, D., & Satolo, E. G. (2019). Reverse logistics for return management in retail: a systematic literature review from 2007 to 2016. In Mula, J., Barbastefano, R., Diaz-Madronero M., Poler, R. (eds), *New Global Perspectives on Industrial Engineering and Management*. Lecture Notes in Management and Industrial Engineering, Springer, Cham. https://doi.org/10.1007/978-3-319-93488-4_17.

Dixit, S., & Vaish, A. (2015). Perceived barriers, collection models, incentives and consumer preferences: an exploratory study for effective implementation of reverse logistics. *International Journal of Logistics Systems and Management, 21*(3), 304–318.

Dowlatshahi, S. H. A. D. (2010). A cost-benefit analysis for the design and implementation of reverse logistics systems: case studies approach. *International Journal of Production Research, 48*(5), 1361–1380.

Dutta, P., Mishra, A., Khandelwal, S., & Katthawala, I. (2020). A multiobjective optimization model for sustainable reverse logistics in Indian E-commerce market. *Journal of Cleaner Production, 249*, 119348.

Dwivedy, M., & Mittal, R. K. (2013). Willingness of residents to participate in e-waste recycling in India. *Environmental Development, 6*, 48–68.

Ecobank. (2015). Middle Africa Briefing Note, 10 August 2015.

Elkington, J. (1998). Partnerships from cannibals with forks: the triple bottom line of 21st-century business. *Environmental Quality Management, 8*(1), 37–51.

Etebu, E., Nwauzoma, A. B., & Bawo, D. D. S. (2013). Post-harvest spoilage of tomato (*Lycopersicon esculentum* Mill.) and control strategies in Nigeria. *Journal of Biology, Agriculture and Healthcare, 3*(10), 51–61.

Food and Agricultural Organisation. (1989). Prevention of post-harvest food loss: fruits, vegetables and root crops: a Training Manual, 17 (Part 2), 1–157.

Food and Agricultural Organisation (2011). Packaging in Fresh Produce Supply Chains in Southeast Asia (fao.org), 1–146.

Franklin Associates (2016). Comparative Life Cycle Assessment of RPC and Display and Non-Display Ready Corrugated Containers Used for Fresh Produce Application, Prepared for: IFCO Corporation, 1–21.

Frei, R., Jack, L., & Brown, S. (2020). Product returns: a growing problem for business, society and environment. *International Journal of Operations & Production Management, 40*(10), 1613–1621.

Gao, X. (2019). A novel reverse logistics network design considering multi-level investments for facility reconstruction with environmental considerations. *Sustainability, 11*(9), 2710.

Gao, X., & Cao, C. (2020). A novel multi-objective scenario-based optimization model for sustainable reverse logistics supply chain network redesign considering facility reconstruction. *Journal of Cleaner Production, 270*, 122405.

Gardas, B. B., Raut, R. D., & Narkhede, B. (2018). Reducing the exploration and production of oil: reverse logistics in the automobile service sector. *Sustainable Production and Consumption, 16*, 141–153.

Genchev, S. E., Landry, T. D., Daugherty, P. J., & Roath, A. S. (2010). Developing reverse logistics programs: a resource-based view. *Journal of Transportation Management, 21*. https://doi.org/10.22237/jotm/1270080120.

Genchev, S. E., Richey, R. G., & Gabler, C. B. (2011). Evaluating reverse logistics programs: a suggested process formalization *The International Journal of Logistics Management, 22*(2), 242. https://doi.org/10.1108/09574091111156569

Gobbi, C. (2011). Designing the reverse supply chain: the impact of the product residual value. *International Journal of Physical Distribution and Logistics Management, 41*(8), 768–796. https://doi.org/10.1108/09600031111166429

González, Torre, P., Alvarez, M., Sarkis, J., Adenso, & Díaz, B. (2010). Barriers to the implementation of environmentally oriented reverse logistics: evidence from the automotive industry sector. *British Journal of Management, 21*(4), 889–904.

Govindan, K., & Bouzon, M. (2018). From a literature review to a multi-perspective framework for reverse logistics barriers and drivers. *Journal of Cleaner Production, 187*, 318–337.

Govindan, K., Mina, H., Esmaeili, A., & Gholami-Zanjani, S. M. (2020). An integrated hybrid approach for circular supplier selection and closed loop supply chain network design under uncertainty. *Journal of Cleaner Production, 242*, 118317.

Govindan, K., Soleimani, H., & Kannan, D. (2015). Reverse logistics and closed-loop supply chain. A comprehensive review to explore the future. *European Journal of Operational Research, 240*(3), 603–626. https://doi.org/10.1016/j.ejor.2014.07.012

Guide, V. D. R. Jr, & Van Wassenhove, L. N. (2009). OR FORUM – The evolution of closed-loop supply chain research. *Operations research, 57*(1), 10–18.

Guo, J., Wang, X., Fan, S., & Gen, M. (2017). Forward and reverse logistics network and route planning under the environment of low-carbon emissions: A case study of Shanghai fresh food E-commerce enterprises. *Computers & Industrial Engineering, 106*, 351–360.

Hall, D. J., Huscroft, J. R., Hazen, B. T., & Hanna, J. B. (2013). Reverse logistics goals, metrics, and challenges: perspectives from industry. *International Journal of Physical Distribution Logistics Management, 439*, 768–785. https://doi.org/10.1108/IJPDLM-02-2012-0052

Hazen, B. T., Hall, D. J., & Hanna, J. B. (2012). Reverse logistics disposition decision making. *International Journal of Physical Distribution & Logistics Management, 42*(3), 244–274. https://doi.org/10.1108/09600031211225954

Hazen, B. T., Hall, D. J., & Hanna, J. B. (2013). Task-technology fit for reverse logistics performance. *The International Journal of Logistics Management, 24*(2), 230–246.

Ho, G. T. S., Choy, K. L., Lam, C. H. Y., & Wong, D. W. (2012). Factors influencing implementation of reverse logistics: a survey among Hong Kong businesses. *Measuring Business Excellence, 16*(3), 29–46.

Hodges, R. J., Buzby, J. C., & Bennett, B. (2010). Postharvest losses and waste in developed and less developed countries: opportunities to improve resource use. *Journal of Agricultural Science, 149*, Issue S1: Foresight Project on Global Food and Farming Futures, February 2011, 37–45.

Hong, S. Q., & Huang, Y. J. (2021). Relationship among reverse logistics, corporate image and social impact in medical device industry. *Revista de cercetare și intervenție socială, 72*, 109–121.

Huang, Y., & Yang, M. (2014). Reverse logistics innovation, institutional pressures and performance, *Management Research Review, 37*(7), 615–641. https://doi.org/10.1108/MRR-03-2013-0069

Idah, P. A., Yisa, Y. M., Chukwu, O., & Morenikeji, O. O. (2012). simulated transport damage study on fresh tomato (Lycopersicon esculentum). *Agricultural Engineering International: CIGR Journal, 14*(2).

Jack, E. P., Powers, T. L., & Skinner, L. (2010). Reverse logistics capabilities: antecedents and cost savings. *International Journal of Physical Distribution & Logistics Management, 40*(3), 228–246.

Jafari, A., Heydari, J., & Keramati, A. (2017). Factors affecting incentive dependency of residents to participate in e-waste recycling: a case study on adoption of e-waste reverse supply chain in Iran. *Environment, Development and Sustainability, 19*(1), 325–338.

Jiménez-Parra, B., Rubio, S., & Vicente-Molina, M. A. (2014). Key drivers in the behavior of potential consumers of remanufactured products: a study on laptops in Spain. *Journal of Cleaner Production, 85*, 488–496.

Jindal, A., & Sangwan, K. S.(2011). "Development of an interpretive structural model of barriers to reverse logistics implementation in Indian industry", J. Hesselbach and C. Herrmann (eds.), in *Glocalized solutions for sustainability in manufacturing* (pp. 448–453). Springer, Berlin, Heidelberg.

Kannan, D., Diabat, A., Alrefaei, M., Govindan, K., & Yong, G. (2012). A carbon footprint based reverse logistics network design model. *Resources, conservation and recycling, 67*, 75–79.

Kannan, G., Pokharel, S., & Kumar, P. S. (2009). A hybrid approach using ISM and fuzzy TOPSIS for the selection of reverse logistics provider. *Resources, conservation and recycling, 54*(1), 28–36.

Kaviani, M. A., Tavana, M., Kumar, A., Michnik, J., Niknam, R., & de Campos, E. A. R. (2020). An integrated framework for evaluating the barriers to successful implementation of reverse logistics in the automotive industry. *Journal of Cleaner Production, 272*, 122714.

Khor, K. S., & Udin, Z. M. (2012). Impact of reverse logistics product disposition towards business performance in Malaysian E & E companies. *Journal of Supply Chain and Customer Relationship Management, 2012*, 1–19. https://doi.org/10.5171/2012.699469

Khor, K. S., Udin, Z. M., Ramayah, T., & Hazen, B. I. (2016). Reverse logistics in Malaysia: The contingent role of institutional pressure. *International Journal of Production Economics, 175*, 96–108. https://doi.org/10.1016/j.ijpe.2016.01.020

Kitinoja, L., & Kader, A. A. (2015). Measuring Postharvest Losses of Fruits and Vegetables in Developing Countries. PEF White Paper 15-02.

Kroon, L., & Vrijens, G. (1994). Returnable Containers: an example of reverse logistics. *International Journal of Physical Distribution and Logistics Management, 25*(2), 56–68.

Leigh, N. G., & Patterson, L. M. (2006). Deconstructing to redevelop: a sustainable alternative to mechanical demolition: the economics of density development finance and pro formas. *Journal of the American Planning Association, 72*(2), 217–225.

Lewandowski, M. (2016), Designing the business models for circular economy – towards the conceptual framework. *Sustainability, 8*(1), 43.

Lewis, S. (2015). RPA Publishes New Food Safety Guidelines for Reusable Plastic Containers. Food Online 12 March 2015.

Li, Y., Kannan, D., Garg, K., Gupta, S., Gandhi, K., & Jha, P. C. (2018). Business orientation policy and process analysis evaluation for establishing third party providers of reverse logistics services. *Journal of Cleaner Production, 182*, 1033–1047.

Li, Y. L., Ying, C. S., Chin, K. S., Yang, H. T., & Xu, J. (2018). Third-party reverse logistics provider selection approach based on hybrid-information MCDM and cumulative prospect theory. *Journal of Cleaner Production, 195*, 573–584.

Luthra, S., Kumar, V., Kumar, S., & Haleem, A. (2011). Barriers to implement green supply chain management in automobile industry using interpretive structural modeling technique: an Indian perspective. *Journal of Industrial Engineering and Management (JIEM), 4*(2), 231–257.

Maleki, R. A., & Meiser, G. (2011). Managing Returnable Containers Logistics – A Case Study. Part II – Improving Visibility Through Using Automatic Identification Technologies. International Journal of Engineering Business Management, *3*(2), 1–8.

Mastos, T. D., Nizamis, A., Terzi, S., Gkortzis, D., Papadopoulos, A., Tsagkalidis, N., & Tzovaras, D. (2021). Introducing an application of an Industry 4.0 solution for circular supply chain management. *Journal of Cleaner Production, 300*, 126886.

Matar, N., Jaber, M., & Searcy, C. (2014) A reverse logistics inventory model for plastic bottles. *The International Journal of Logistics Management, 25*(2), 315–333. http://doi.org/10.1108/IJLM-12-2012-0138

McCarthy, I. P., Silvestre, B. S., & Kietzmann, J. H. (2013). Understanding outsourcing contexts through information asymmetry and capability fit. *Production planning & control, 24*(4–5), 277–283.

Meade, L., & Sarkis, J. (2002). A conceptual model for selecting and evaluating third-party reverse logistics providers. *Supply Chain Management: An International Journal, 7*(5), 283–295.

Meyer, A., Niemann, W., Mackenzie, J., & Lombaard, J. (2017). Drivers and barriers of reverse logistics practices: a study of large grocery retailers in South Africa. *Journal of Transport and Supply Chain Management, 11*(1), 1–16.

Moktadir, M. A., Ali, S. M., Paul, S. K., & Shukla, N. (2019). Barriers to big data analytics in manufacturing supply chains: a case study from Bangladesh. *Computers & Industrial Engineering, 128*, 1063–1075.

Moktadir, M. A., Rahman, T., Ali, S. M., Nahar, N., & Paul, S. K. (2020). Examining barriers to reverse logistics practices in the leather footwear industry. *Annals of Operations Research, 293*(2), 715–746.

Moslehi, M. S., Sahebi, H., & Teymouri, A. (2021). A multi-objective stochastic model for a reverse logistics supply chain design with environmental considerations. *Journal of Ambient Intelligence and Humanized Computing, 12*(7), 8017–8040.

Murray, A., Skene, K., & Haynes, K. (2017). The circular economy: an interdisciplinary exploration of the concept and application in a global context. *Journal of Business Ethics, 140*(3), 369–380.

Niknejad, A., & Petrovic, D., 2014, Optimisation of integrated reverse logistics networks with different product recovery routes. *European Journal of Operational Research, 238*(1), 143–154. https://doi.org/10.1016/j.ejor.2014.03.034

Nnorom, I. C., Ohakwe, J., & Osibanjo, O. (2009). Survey of willingness of residents to participate in electronic waste recycling in Nigeria: a case study of mobile phone recycling. *Journal of Cleaner Production, 17*(18), 1629–1637.

Ohimain, E. I. (2013). Scrap iron and steel recycling in Nigeria. *Greener Journal of Environmental Management and Public Safety, 2*(1), 1–9.

Panigrahi, S. K., Kar, F. W., Fen, T. A., Hoe, L. K., & Wong, M. (2018). A strategic initiative for successful reverse logistics management in retail industry. *Global Business Review, 19*(3_suppl), S151–S175.

Pearce, D. W., Turner, R. K., & Turner, R. K. (1990). *Economics of natural resources and the environment.* Johns Hopkins University Press.

Pienaar, W., & Vogt, J., (2012). *Business Logistics Management: A value chain perspective,* 4ed. Oxford University Press.

Prakash, C., & Barua, M. K. (2017). Flexible modelling approach for evaluating reverse logistics adoption barriers using fuzzy AHP and IRP framework. *International Journal of Operational Research*, 30(2), 151–171.

PricewaterhouseCoopers AG WPG (2011). Reuse and Recycling Systems for Selected Beverage Packaging from a Sustainability Perspective, 1–1456 reuse-and-recycling-systems-for-selected-beverage-packaging-from-a-sustainability perspective.pdf (cooplesvaloristes.ca) (Assessed on 2 May 2022).

Rabbani, M., Akbarian Saravi, N., & Farrokhi-Asl, H. (2017). Design of forward/reverse logistics with environmental consideration. *International Journal of Supply and Operations Management*, 4(2), 115–132.

Rapusas, R. S., & Rolle, R. S. (2009). *Management of reusable plastic crates in fresh produce supply chains, a technical guide*. Food and Agricultural Organisation.

Ravi, V., & Shankar, R. (2015). Survey of reverse logistics practices in manufacturing industries: an Indian context. *Benchmarking: An International Journal*, 22(5), 874–899. https://doi.org/10.1108/09564230910978511

Reddy, K. N., & Kumar, A. (2021). Capacity investment and inventory planning for a hybrid manufacturing – remanufacturing system in the circular economy. *International Journal of Production Research*, 59(8), 2450–2478.

Ren, Y., Wang, C., Li, B., Yu, C., & Zhang, S. (2020). A genetic algorithm for fuzzy random and low-carbon integrated forward/reverse logistics network design. *Neural Computing and Applications*, 32(7), 2005–2025.

Reusable Articles. (2010). 4th International Conference on Industrial Engineering and Industrial Management September 2010.

Safdar, N., Khalid, R., Ahmed, W., & Imran, M. (2020). Reverse logistics network design of e-waste management under the triple bottom line approach. *Journal of Cleaner Production*, 272, 122662.

Saphire, D. (1994). *Delivering the goods: Benefits of reusable shipping containers*. Inform Inc.

Saphores, J.-D. M., Nixon, H., Ogunseitan, O. A., & Shapiro, A. A. (2006). Household willingness to recycle electronic waste: an application to California. *Environment and Behavior*, 38(2), 183–208.

Selvi, M. S., & Kayar, Y. (2016). Reverse logistics activities in enterprises and implementation reasons. *International Journal of Research in Business & Social Science*, 5(1), 15–29. https://doi.org/10.20525/ijrbs.v5i1.46

Shaharudin, M. R., Zailani, S., & Tan, K. C. (2015). Barriers to product returns and recovery management in a developing country: investigation using multiple methods. *Journal of Cleaner Production*, 96, 220–232. https://doi.org/10.1016/j.jclepro.2013.12.071

Shaik, M. N., & Abdul-Kader, W. (2018). A hybrid multiple criteria decision making approach for measuring comprehensive performance of reverse logistics enterprises. *Computers & Industrial Engineering*, 123, 9–25.

Shuang, Y., Diabat, A., & Liao, Y. (2019). A stochastic reverse logistics production routing model with emissions control policy selection. *International Journal of Production Economics*, 213, 201–216.

Singhal, D., Tripathy, S., & Jena, S. K. (2020). Remanufacturing for the circular economy: study and evaluation of critical factors. *Resources, Conservation and Recycling*, 156, 104681.

Sirisawat, P., & Kiatcharoenpol, T. (2018). Fuzzy AHP-TOPSIS approaches to prioritizing solutions for reverse logistics barriers. *Computers & Industrial Engineering*, 117, 303–318.

Statista Global Surve (2021). Global smartphone sale to end users 2007 t0 2021. Retrieved 24 October 2021 from www. statista.com

Stock, J. R. (2004). *Product returns/reverse logistics in warehousing: Strategies, policies, and programs*. Oak Brook, IL: Warehousing Education and Research Council.

Stock, J., Speh, T., & Shear, H. (2006). Managing product returns for competitive advantage. *MIT Sloan Management Review, 48*(1), 57.

Subramanian, N., Gunasekaran, A., Abdulrahman, M., & Liu, C. (2014). Factors for implementing end-of-life product reverse logistics in the Chinese manufacturing sector. *International Journal of Sustainable Development & World Ecology, 21*(3), 235–245.

Tibben-Lembke, R. S. (2002). Life after death: reverse logistics and the product life cycle. *International Journal of Physical Distribution & Logistics Management, 32*(3), 223–244.

Trochu, J., Chaabane, A., & Ouhimmou, M. (2020). A carbon-constrained stochastic model for eco-efficient reverse logistics network design under environmental regulations in the CRD industry. *Journal of Cleaner Production, 245*, 118818.

Upadhyay, A., Mukhuty, S., Kumar, V., & Kazancoglu, Y. (2021). Blockchain technology and the circular economy: implications for sustainability and social responsibility. *Journal of Cleaner Production*, 126130.

Vigneault, C., Thompson, J., & Wu, S. (2009). Designing container for handling fresh horticultural produce. *Postharvest Technologies for Horticultural Crops, 2*, 25–47.

Wang, B., Hao, H., & Li, H. (2020, September). Reverse logistics network design considering customer convenience and low carbon emissions. *Journal of Physics: Conference Series 1633*(1), 012153.

Waqas, M., Dong, Q. L., Ahmad, N., Zhu, Y., & Nadeem, M. (2018). Critical barriers to implementation of reverse logistics in the manufacturing industry: a case study of a developing country. *Sustainability, 10*(11), 4202.

Weetman, C. (2016). *A circular economy handbook for business and supply chains: Repair, remake, redesign, rethink*. London, UK: Kogan Page Publishers.

Winans, K., Kendall, A., & Deng, H. (2017). The history and current applications of the circular economy concept. *Renewable and Sustainable Energy Reviews, 68*, 825–833.

Wood, G., & Struges, M. (2010). *Single trip or reusable packaging – considering the right choice for the environment*. Warwick, UK: Warwick Research Archive Portal.

Zaccaï, E. (2008). Assessing the role of consumers in sustainable product policies. *Environment, Development and Sustainability, 10*(1), 51–67. doi:10.1007/s10668-006-9038-3.

Zhang, Y., Alshraideh, H., & Diabat, A. (2018). A stochastic reverse logistics production routing model with environmental considerations. *Annals of Operations Research, 271*(2), 1023–1044.

Zohal, M., & Soleimani, H. (2016). Developing an ant colony approach for green closed-loop supply chain network design: a case study in gold industry. *Journal of Cleaner Production, 133*, 314–337.

Case 1: The Use of Reusable Plastic Containers in Tomato Logistics System
A Case Study in Nigeria

C1.1 INTRODUCTION

Generally, some industries exhibit an interesting supply chain that attempts to combine the forward and reverse activities into a single system to integrate returned products and/or packaging materials back into the production and distribution network. This concept is demonstrated by the life cycle of a glass bottle in a beverage bottling company supply chain, and it is generally known as a closed loop supply chain (CLSC). In the agricultural space, the drive to return the packaging materials (such as reusable plastic crates, RPC) for reuse in the same way bottles in the beverage bottling industries are returned in the CLSC has not been fully successful in most developing countries. This case explores the idea for tomato logistics system in the belief that a lasting solution would be found.

In Nigeria, the use of reusable plastic crates (RPC) is not yet widespread across the agricultural space. What is predominant in the tomato value chain is the use of raffia-made baskets for the forward logistics flows with minimal return for reuse. This contributes to the post-harvest losses experienced by tomato farmers.

C1.2 TOMATO PRODUCTION IN NIGERIA

Nigeria's tomato production has in recent times fluctuated between a high of 2.08 million tonnes in 2006 and a low of 1.49 million tonnes in 2011. The production for the year 2013 was about 1.57 million tonnes. Although Nigeria is a major producer of tomatoes, the output cannot satisfy domestic consumption and importation is used to fill the gap. One of the reasons for the inability to satisfy domestic demand is the high level of post-harvest losses.

Post-harvest losses in developing countries are at the heart of virtually every discussion on agriculture and food security in the developing world. Despite all the attention paid to the subject, experts and authorities do not seem to agree as to the exact scale of the problem and have produced conflicting figures on the subject. The Food and Agricultural Organization (FAO) opined that estimates of production losses in developing countries are hard to judge, but some authorities put losses of sweet potatoes, plantain, tomatoes, bananas and citrus fruits as high as 50%. Furthermore, it has been cautioned that estimating post-harvest losses is difficult and not very reliable. Actually, measuring what has been lost implies that it is known what was there at the outset and this is not usually the case. Quoting from the US

National Academy of Sciences, one researcher pointed out that estimates of post-harvest losses in developing countries vary greatly from 1% to 50% or even higher.

Generally, it is claimed that losses as high as 50% to 70% are common in fruits and vegetables between the points of rural production and urban consumption. The same study also reported that, in laboratory experiments, the plastic container performed better than the woven basket in reducing the mechanical damage resulting from impact and vibration while simulating the transportation of tomatoes. Other estimates of the level of losses in the local tomato industry in Nigeria include the following:

- "as much as 40% (by volume) is damaged" by the time it gets to its destination,
- "losses are staggeringly high, typically reaching around half of the crop",
- "51% due to damage" in transportation,
- "the estimated total loss is about 60%",
- "20% on the farm and 28% in transit".

It is, of course, evident that the figures do not all refer to the same thing since some refer to total losses across the entire value chain while others only deal with losses in some parts of it. Despite the differences in the results of these studies, one clear conclusion that can be drawn is that a significant proportion of the tomato harvest does not reach the dining table – an issue of serious concern to the agricultural authorities and agencies interested in food security. It follows that reduction of post-harvest losses should be an important component of efforts aimed at boosting food availability in the country.

Factors that contribute to transportation losses include the following:

- Unsuitable transport containers
- Overloading of vehicles
- Rough roads
- Irresponsible driving
- Heat accumulation or very poor ventilation within transport vehicles
- Virtual absence of refrigerated and insulated trucks

It would be correct to state that all these factors are present in the Nigerian environment. Manifestations of losses are visible at all points along the supply chain, from the farm to the final retailer.

C1.2.1 Unit of Measure in the Trade

Tomatoes, like many other food commodities in Nigeria, are sold not by weight but by volume and the unit of measure is the basket. This basket is woven from raffia, is semi-rigid, does not have a regular shape, and yet it is the receptacle most used in Nigeria for transporting tomatoes from the farm to wholesale markets. The culture has persisted over decades. This lack of uniformity of shape and poor rigidity goes against one of the practices recommended for bulk packaging for transporting farm produce on land: the use of containers of uniform shape with good stacking strength and that can be easily stacked in a vehicle without damaging the produce.

Case 1: The Use of Reusable Plastic Containers in Tomato Logistics System

FIGURE C1.1 Tomatoes in baskets at a local market in Nigeria.

Unfortunately, there are no agreed specifications for the dimensions of the basket and this absence of specifications has resulted in the concurrent use of baskets with a wide range of carrying capacities.

To add to the confusion, baskets were sometimes referred to as "small", "medium" and "big", but those terms meant different things to different people and were not tied to any generally agreed specific physical dimensions or weights. All these differences in perception and evaluation notwithstanding, tomato prices in wholesale markets are based on the basket. Both farmers and traders are said to depend on their experience and knowledge of the tomato market to negotiate prices for a given basket of products. Figure C1.1 shows tomatoes in baskets.

C1.2.2 THE NIGERIAN TOMATO SUPPLY CHAIN

The tomato supply chain features, between the farmer (more likely than not to be a smallholder) at one end and the final consumer of the product at the other end, a number of intermediaries, some of whom are major while others are minor. The chain stretches from the farmer through the northern markets and then to the southern wholesale markets, retailers and finally to the customer. In physical terms, the chain is roughly 1000 km long and the major means of north-south transportation is by road. Road quality ranges from well asphalted and smooth to cratered and barely passable. The use of the rail network is still in the exploratory stage.

C1.2.3 CURRENT PRACTICE

The woven basket is the packaging of choice from the farm right up to the major retailers. The baskets are fabricated in the south and taken up to the north for use. In theory, they are relatively cheap, single use items, but some reuse is known to occur, especially in the short-distance trade. Successful introduction of the RPC and its widespread acceptance and use will mean the elimination of the woven baskets from the tomato trade.

The major stakeholders include the following.

C1.2.3.1 Farmers

The majority of the farmers are small-scale and are fragmented across the different tomato planting localities in the north. They produce about a range of 10–20 baskets of tomatoes each within the harvesting season. There are few large-scale farmers with resources to exert considerable control over the flow of their products to the southern wholesale markets, and they produce a lot more baskets of tomatoes each within the harvesting season than the small-scale farmers do.

C1.2.3.2 Middlemen at the Northern Markets

They buy directly from the small-scale farmers and resell to the dealers in the local markets. Quite often, they reach out to the farmers and help to arrange the means of transportation to the local markets.

C1.2.3.3 Dealers at the Northern Markets

They play a very significant role in the supply chain. In most cases, they provide the small-scale farmers with funds and support and ultimately arrange for the supply of the raffia baskets to the farmers during harvest. They have a long reach to the farmers and can easily bypass the middlemen. Their relationship with the farmers is such that they practically determine the price at which a farmer's produce is purchased, and they arrange for the transportation of the tomatoes to the southern markets. Instances of interaction with large-scale farmers do exist. More often than not the dealers engage local agents for the sorting and aggregation of all products purchased from the farmers.

C1.2.3.4 Dealers at the Southern Markets

They are agents to dealers and large-scale farmers in the northern markets, and it is through them that the tomatoes are sold to retail outlets and bulk end users in the southern markets. The dealers organize the offloading of the trucks on arrival and, based on the demand and supply situation in the southern markets, they determine the prices at which the different basket sizes of tomatoes are sold and thereafter remit the revenue to the dealers and large-scale farmers in the northern market after accounting for the transport costs. It is evident that some dealers in the southern market now order their own tomatoes from the north without involving their former principals. The dealers are also known as the wholesalers. Figure C1.2 shows the wholesale market.

C1.2.3.5 Dealers' Agents at the Southern Markets

The dealers also have agents that interact with the retailers and effect the sale of the baskets of tomatoes.

C1.2.3.6 Transporters and Their Agents at Both Sets of Markets

The northern and southern markets have registered commission transport agents who organize for trucks for the transportation of the baskets of tomatoes to the southern markets for a fee of about 10% of the transport cost.

Case 1: The Use of Reusable Plastic Containers in Tomato Logistics System   277

FIGURE C1.2   Tomato wholesalers at Mile 12 Market, Lagos.

C1.2.3.7   Raffia Basket Suppliers

Alongside the tomato markets in the north are the raffia basket suppliers who sell baskets to the members of the trade that need them. The raffia basket is sourced from the south-south and south-eastern markets (about 1000 km from the northern farmlands) through a chain of stakeholders including raffia bamboo suppliers, manufacturers (weavers), dealers and middlemen, and then transported to the northern markets. Figure C1.3 shows the transportation of baskets to the north.

FIGURE C1.3   Trucks transporting baskets to the north.

C1.2.3.8 Retailers at the Southern Outlet Markets

These are those that purchase the baskets of tomatoes from the wholesale market, e.g., Mile 12 in Lagos, for resale in smaller quantities to the end users in the different market outlets within Lagos and the immediate environment.

C1.2.3.9 Supermarkets

Supermarkets like "Shoprite and Game" are also retailers. Their importance lies in the fact that they sell the tomato fruit by weight and not in baskets, and therefore, they are in a position to appreciate the need to preserve tomatoes from damage on its journey. It is evident that most of them have already embraced the use of crates.

C1.2.3.10 Suppliers of Inputs and Services to Farmers

Some non-government agencies and private organizations offer different services and inputs to the farmers. The inputs include fertilizers, improved tomato seedlings and irrigation pumps. These are arranged on terms of trade agreed with the farmers.

C1.2.3.11 Consumers

They are classified into households, hotels, schools, restaurants, hospitals and other food consuming/retailing institutions. Depending on their requirements, they buy either directly from the wholesale markets or from the retail outlets.

C1.3 REUSABLE PLASTIC CRATE (RPC)

RPCs belong to a class of goods commonly described as returnable transport items (RTI) or sometimes reusable transport items. They form part of the returned packaging materials for reuse under the reverse logistics activities. They are made in several varieties, with the main variables being material, design and size. The most common materials used are high-density polyethylene (HDPE) and polypropylene, while the most common design structures are the following:

- Stacking crates with vertical walls. Its squared design makes efficient use of space.
- Nesting crates with sloping walls that have variable nesting ratios, depending on the design features. Their use involves a trade-off between the quantity of products that can be transported in each truck space and the number of empty containers that can be fitted into the truck for the return journey.
- Stacking and nesting crates which can be stacked when loaded and can nest when empty. This design can achieve space savings of up to 57% when nested.
- Collapsible crates which typically take 3–6 times less space than assembled containers.
- Crates with attached lid.

Crates may or may not be provided with ventilation holes. Ventilated crates are preferred for the transportation of vegetables.

Case 1: The Use of Reusable Plastic Containers in Tomato Logistics System

There are no standards for the physical dimensions of crates, with companies adopting sizes best suited to their purposes. Examples of crates used in other places for transporting tomatoes:

- Philippines – 520 × 362 × 260 mm
- IFCO North America – 600 × 401 × 104 mm
- Sri Lanka – 525 × 350 × 300 mm
- Europool Model 24 – 600 × 400 × 241 mm

In Nigeria, the popular crate has the following dimensions 595 × 390 × 230 mm model made by Celplast from HDPE, which is amply supplied with ventilation holes. It is stackable, has vertical walls and is also nestable. The carrying capacity is said to be 20 kg, but measurements in the field indicated that 25 kg is a better estimate. However, this figure is subject to variation, with the degree of variation depending mainly on bulk density of the product and loading efficiency. Figure C1.4 shows the Celplast RPC while Figure C1.5 shows two nested Celplast RPCs.

C1.3.1 RPC MANAGEMENT SYSTEMS

The reuse of secondary packaging materials listed three types of management systems:

- Switch pool system, in which every participant has an allotment of containers for which he is responsible (cleaning, control, maintenance and storage) and its two variants.
- Systems with reverse logistics, in which containers are owned by a central agency and of which there are three variants.
- Systems without reverse logistics.

FIGURE C1.4 The Celplast RPC.

FIGURE C1.5 Two Nested Celplast RPCs.

Five groups of actors in the RPC system were identified:

- A central agency that owns a pool of reusable containers.
- A logistical service provider responsible for storing, delivering and collecting empty containers.
- Senders of full containers.
- Recipients of full containers.
- Carriers transporting full containers from senders to recipients.

Over the years, other modifications and refinements have emerged, but the fundamental elements of these systems remain the same:

- The system is either an open loop or a closed loop one. In the latter, crates always return to the same point of origin, whereas in the former, containers need not return to the point of origin.
- There are one or more owners of the containers and responsibilities for cleaning, control, maintenance and storage are assigned to one or more entities.
- Container flows are managed by one or more entities.
- Financial and information flows follow an agreed pattern.
- The system is either single-depot or multi-depot.

A big advantage of open loop systems is that they eliminate – the reverse logistics. Some of the features that are conducive to the reuse of shipping containers are the following:

- Frequent deliveries (rapid inventory turnover, which enhances revenue).
- Small number of parties (which streamlines retrieval of empty containers and increases their availability for reuse).

- Company-owned or "dedicated" distribution vehicles (which reduce backhaul costs, e.g., Nigerian Bottling Company and its fleet of distribution vehicles).
- Short distribution distances (reduces backhaul costs and cycle time).

In this case study, the first two features are present, the third is totally absent and the fourth is present only in the local trade but absent from the long-distance trade.

Since the use of returnable containers may bring with it some additional operational and transportation costs, efficient methods are needed to track and manage the flow of containers so as to avoid significant increases in logistics costs. Tracking methods vary, ranging from simple manual systems to expensive hi-tech systems, but the objective is the same – to improve visibility in the chain. Lack of visibility has often been cited as a major contributor to the ineffective management of returnable containers. Figure C1.6 shows the life cycle flow chart of returnable containers.

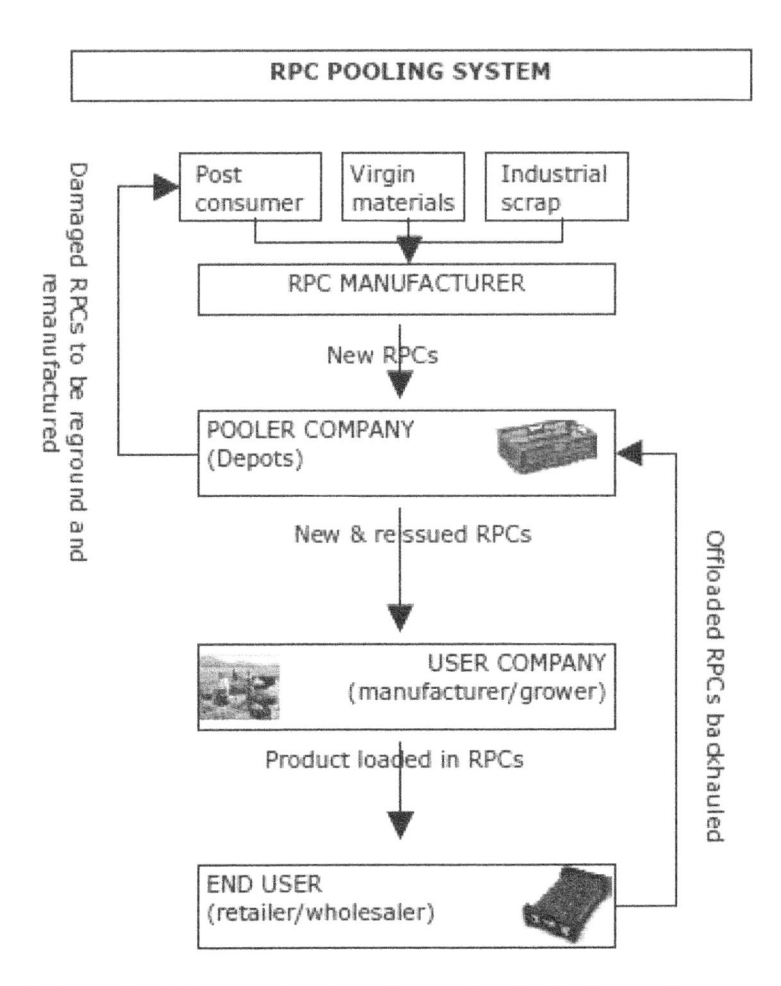

FIGURE C1.6 RPC life cycle flowchart. (Source: http://onlinelibrary.wiley.com.ezproxy.library.ubc.ca/doi/10.1002/pts.731/abstract.)

Managing an RPC rental system "requires tight organization and control for use in a regular forward and reverse service". The economic efficiency of the system "directly depends on the velocity" with which the crates travel through the supply chain. Inefficient management of the system will result in a few financial penalties including increased cycle time and the excess container inventory that results from it, a higher rate of losses and the consequent need for a higher rate of container replacement.

Some of the obstacles to the introduction of plastic crates can be removed or eased by government intervention (regulation and standardization). This intervention can take a few forms, few examples are as follows:

- Penalties for the disposal of non-reusable packaging. Charge a fee (or a higher fee if there is one already) for the disposal of woven baskets. One difficulty would be in the application of this fee to tomato baskets only (at least in the first instance) while sparing baskets used to convey other produce.
- Economic incentives to encourage the use of reusable packaging.
- Standardization of reusable packaging.
- Policies favoring reusable packaging.
- Public enlightenment campaigns.

In general, some of the principal obstacles to the introduction of RPCs are the following:

- Large initial capital requirement.
- Cost of tracking and accounting for containers.
- Cost of returning the containers for reuse.
- Cost of providing storage for empty containers.
- Resistance to change by stakeholders in the value chain.

All these elements are present in the case under consideration.

C1.3.1.1 Ownership Issues

A critical issue is that of ownership, of which various models are available. Examples of owners include the following:

- Manufacturers/producers – as is the case with glass bottles and plastic crates in the beer and soft drinks markets in the country.
- Logistics company.
- Joint pool.
- Independent company.

C1.3.1.2 Pool Size

The size of the pool is basically determined by two variables: the demand and the cycle time. Invariably disruptions in the two variables will occur during operations, and for this reason, two factors of safety (one for each variable) are used to augment

Case 1: The Use of Reusable Plastic Containers in Tomato Logistics System

the calculated pool size. Having a wrongly sized pool (oversize or undersize) incurs economic penalties and should be avoided, which implies striking a balance between operational efficiency and optimization of financial resources.

Furthermore, pool size can be increased by several factors:

- Containers staying longer at the receiver's end
- Reuse of the containers by the receiver
- Receiver passing on the containers to another user
- Failure to collect the empties and get them into a condition for reuse

In determining pool size, allowances must be made for:

- Time to return the crates to origin
- Time for cleaning and sanitizing
- Losses in the system
- Seasonal variations in demand

The pool size may shrink due to losses of the following types:

- Quality losses – crates damaged beyond economic repair or otherwise unsuitable for use
- Incidental losses – fortuitous misplacement and loss by customers
- Structural losses – due to deliberate fraud, theft, resale or conversion to alternative usage

C1.3.1.3 Return Rate

Once the size of the pool has been determined and operations commence, they can only be sustained if used crates are returned for reuse at a rate that matches the demand. The service operator must aim at attaining the highest possible return rate. A low return rate will impose a financial burden on the business that may prove unsupportable in the long run.

Estimates of return rates in the 80–99% range have been published in Europe. Experience from Grenada indicates that RPCs "are attractive and have many alternative uses and are subject to high pilferage". Pilferage rates "as high as 20% during a single harvest season" have been reported from the Philippines. A loss rate of that magnitude will be difficult to sustain in the long run. These two countries are developing countries like Nigeria and high losses may also occur here if measures are not taken to prevent them, especially in the early stages of the project. Inefficiencies in retrievals will escalate loss rates, necessitate the injection of larger than planned numbers of new crates into the system, and increase cycle times and operational costs.

Some of the recovery incentives used to prevent pool shrinkage are as follows:

- **Economic incentives**
  - *Deposits*: The amount paid as a deposit acts as a guarantee that the rented items will be returned. In the case of loss, the deposit becomes partial compensation, and therefore, for it to be meaningful, it may

equal "at least the value of the container". The deposit is refunded when the containers are returned and the customer pays a fixed service fee for the rental of the containers. This model has very high return rates, typically close to 100% because of the deposit paid. On the other hand, it requires extra administrative effort. Also, the willingness of a customer to accept it declines if the price of the product is low (which is the case with tomatoes).

- *Rental*: The customer pays a daily rental as in the case of shipping containers. Linking the amount charged to the time the RPC is in use by the customer helps to speed up cycle time by providing the customer with an incentive for the early return of crates. One major potential point of contention that must be addressed is the allocation of responsibility for making good any losses and damages which occur during the "customer use" part of the supply chain.
- *Account management with periodic payments*: Incoming and outgoing quantities of crates are recorded and periodic reconciliation (e.g., monthly) provides a basis for calculating and charging usage. Periodic inventory audits are required, and the method is highly dependent on accuracy in recording stock movements.
- **Non-economic incentives**
  - *Equal exchanges or "full-for-empty"*: The customer brings one empty crate and receives in return one full crate, as is presently the case for glass bottles and plastic crates in the local beer and soft drinks industries. In these two industries, this option represents a significant barrier to entry because of the level of investment required to acquire the initial stock of RTIs. Its principal advantage is that it offers a simple strategy for minimizing losses and does not require any extra administrative effort.
  - *Immediate retrieval or repacking*: Goods once purchased are removed from the RPC, which can then be returned to source. This option is available to supply chain partners who may not want to use equal exchanges.
- **User accountability**: The service provider relies on the goodwill of the customer for crate recovery. Monitoring of the crates during the "customer-use stage" (e.g., using manual, barcode, RFID or other auto-ID technologies) is an indispensable condition for successful application. This incentive is best suited to cases where the value of the individual rental item is high.

C1.3.2 CYCLE TIME

Cycle time is a crucial factor in the management of CLSCs. Achieving a short cycle time and thus a high utilization rate per unit promotes the economic efficiency of the system. From the point of view of the RPC service provider, it would be preferable to exercise control over as much of the supply chain as possible. This will not only shorten cycle time but also improve visibility. For this reason, the backhaul operation should be handled by the service provider.

C1.3.3 Maintenance of Crates

Several research findings have established that RPCs "have the potential to become contaminated and spread pathogens". Other studies have gone as far as to query the efficacy of existing cleaning and sanitizing procedures. In recognition of this possibility of infection, the US FDA recommends "cleaning and sanitizing any surface or equipment intended to contact fresh tomatoes at a frequency sufficient to prevent the surface or equipment from becoming a source of contamination". The Reusable Packaging Association goes further to recommend that all food contact containers should be washed, rinsed, sanitized and dried between every use, without fail.

C1.3.4 Service Life of Crates and Trip Rate

One of the principal benefits of the plastic crate is its reusability and long life compared to the basket, which has a one-time use. Since the purchase price of the crate is invariably much higher than that of the basket, the crate must make enough trips to justify this cost differential. There is no uniform standard and different figures have been reported from various places. In the Philippines, a useful life of 5 years and trip number of 300 has been reported. From North America, the IFCO reported an average trip number of 39.3 (with a minimum of 23.4 and a maximum of 72.9). A study in Europe reported that after 12–13 years, the crates covered by the study were still in operation and the expectation was for a 15–20 years lifetime. This European study may not be very helpful in the case being studied since it was based on a crate making just five trips a year and all loads were palletized.

C1.3.5 Cost of Packaging

A fundamental consideration in the introduction of RPCs is the question of cost. According to the FAO, it is clear that packaging cost must not exceed the willingness of the market to accept the added value of the product, i.e., the extra cost involved. Stakeholders in the tomato value chain are being asked to replace the existing basket with the RPC. The first question they are likely to ask is: Is the RPC cheaper for us than the basket? The answer had to be in the affirmative for the change to be embraced with enthusiasm.

The cost of a basket was about N420 and the nominal capacity had been adjudged to be 50 kg of product, i.e., the packaging cost is N8.4 per kg of product carried. Using this rate, the cost for 25 kg of product (the capacity of the RPC) will be N210. This figure represents the upper limit of what can be charged as a rental for the RPC without increasing the cost of packaging above the current basket-based level. Irrespective of other considerations, the RPC will be perceived as being "more expensive than the basket" if the rental charge exceeds this value. If this perception (whether it is factual or not) were to take hold, it is very likely to prejudice the acceptance of the RPC as well as to create an obstacle to a willingness to use it.

In making any packaging cost comparisons, it needs to be borne in mind that the carrying capacity of 50 kg assigned to the basket is frequently exceeded in the case of heavy baskets and, for small baskets, is not reached. The RPC, when widely adopted, will totally remove this "large" basket versus "small" basket issue. Whether or not this will be considered as a welcome development by the trade remains to be seen. Also, RPCs may eventually bring about a change to sales by weight rather than by volume.

C1.4 DISTRIBUTION OF THE BENEFITS OF USING RPCS

If a farmer uses RPCs to move tomatoes from the farm to the nearest local market, the distance is usually short and the potential gain in quality from using RPCs as against baskets will most probably not be on the same scale as is realized on the much longer journey to southern markets. It is by no means certain that the farmer will receive a higher price than would have been the case if baskets had been used – there are many factors that determine the market price of tomatoes at a given point in time and at a given location, and the farmer is often not bargaining from a position of strength. If the farmer is unable to see any extra revenue accruing to him through using RPCs, then it would be difficult to make a case for the rental of RPCs by the small-scale farmer. The experience reported from the Philippines is informative. Farmers in that country were said to "expect the cost of packaging innovations to be borne by traders and consolidators who they perceive to be deriving the largest percentage of profit". There is no reason to suppose that Nigerian farmers feel differently. So, it is not merely a question of if the farmer will benefit or not; it is a question of the farmer believing that he will benefit.

When the dealer buys tomatoes from a small-scale farmer, the transaction is concluded on the spot and will not be subsequently reopened, irrespective of what happens to the tomatoes as they travel down the chain. This suggests that the farmer has little or no interest in the condition in which the tomatoes arrive in southern markets and, by reason of this fact, will not usually receive any financial benefits from the improvements in quality attributable to the use of RPCs. However, this scenario might be different for large-scale farmers with resources to control the transportation to and sales in the southern markets.

Based on what is available in the literature, the bulk of the damage done to the tomatoes occurs on the road trip to the south, during which period the tomatoes are the property of the dealer. It, therefore, follows that if the tomatoes arrive in the southern market in better condition than would have been the case with baskets and command a higher price, the beneficiary is the dealer. Would a dealer, in the knowledge that using RPCs would enhance his profits in southern markets, choose to pay the farmer a higher price than he would have for the same product but in baskets? While it is true that this question cannot be answered with certainty one way or the other, the normal practices of business behavior in Nigeria would suggest an answer in the negative.

Moving produce from the southern wholesale markets to the retail outlets involves shorter journeys than the north-south trip and should therefore cause less damage to the product than the main north-south trip. The benefit to the retailer may lie more in the reduction of damage achieved on the north-south journey than that achieved on the much shorter retail run.

Going by the above analysis, it is evident that the dealer is very likely to be the major beneficiary from the use of RPCs. The introduction of RPCs will bring additional costs into the trade, which are supposed to be offset by the expected higher revenue arising from quality improvements. For reasons of equity, it is important to ensure that the allocation of this additional cost burden mirrors, as far as is practicable, the distribution of benefits. Inequitable allocation of costs is bound to hinder acceptance of the RPC by stakeholders who may feel unfairly affected. This is particularly valid in the case of small-scale farmers.

C1.4.1 BACKHAUL DISTANCES

Since reusable packaging has to be returned for reuse, this backhaul operation imposes an extra cost on operations. As is to be expected, this cost is distance-dependent. Many successful systems involve company-owned or dedicated distribution vehicles, as is the case in the bottling company business in the country. Consequently, reusable packaging tends to do better when backhaul distances are low than when they are high. The distance involved in the case under consideration is about 900 km (for the north-south trade), and therefore that part of the case falls, by the above classification, at the extreme edge of the grey zone.

Widespread use of RPCs will inevitably have a significant negative impact on the raffia basket value chain, which accommodates a number of stakeholders (including raffia bamboo suppliers, makers, dealers and agents located largely in the south-south and south-east of Nigeria). This will worsen if the use of RPCs is later extended to other fruits and vegetables.

C1.4.2 ENVIRONMENTAL CONSIDERATIONS

In the developed world, the growth in the use of reusable packaging and reusable transport packaging has been driven principally by a growing concern for the environmental and regulatory intervention by the government. The inference to be drawn from this is that bottom line considerations sometimes have to yield to higher matters dealing with human life. There is no reason why this should not be so in Nigeria in general and in the case of the RPC in particular.

Raffia baskets are intended for one-off use in the north-south transport link and should not normally be reused. However, there is some local reuse in the Lagos area, but even with that, given the high volumes of tomatoes coming down south from the north, the trade generates a substantial amount of refuse for disposal. Mile 12 market, for example, was said to discharge an average of as many as sixty 12-tire trucks daily, which, at 360 baskets per truck, translates to 21,600 baskets daily or 648,000 baskets monthly during the tomato season.

One major advantage of the plastic crate is that it is more environmentally friendly, with a crate remaining in service for many years and, at the end of its useful life, being recycled into new crates. Life cycle analysis studies have shown conclusively that reusable packaging has a more benign ecological footprint than one-use packaging.

C1.5 THE WAY FORWARD

The issues that need to be reviewed and addressed in the process of designing an RPC rental system include the following:

- Current practice
- Scope
- Operational/management model
- Ownership of RPCs
- Cycle time
- Return rate
- Pool size
- Recovery incentives and rental policy
- Backhaul costs
- RPC maintenance
- Service life of RPCs
- Customer liability
- Sustainability
- Capacity building
- Regulatory intervention

C1.5.1 Suggested Operational Model

A fundamental design consideration is the choice between an open loop system and a closed loop one. The open loop system, in which customers collect RPCs from one depot and can return them to a different depot, tends to work well for items like pallets (e.g., the Europallet scheme) and in situations where the traffic is multi-directional and fairly balanced in those directions. Unfortunately, the agricultural commodities distribution system in Nigeria does not have the necessary configuration or attributes to support a multi-depot open loop system. The flow of production is largely unidirectional and as with all such systems, the backhaul of empties is unavoidable. Furthermore, the tomato trade is additionally constrained by food safety considerations which restrict the uses to which tomato crates can be put.

So, for long-distance trade, a single-depot CLSC appears to be the most suitable option available in the circumstances. Crates will be introduced into the system in the north, used to transfer tomatoes to the south, and thereafter are returned to the north for cleaning, sanitizing, storage and reuse. This requires an efficient organization for the speedy retrieval of crates from southern markets and their shipment back to the north without undue delay.

It is not considered efficacious to saddle the wholesalers in downstream with the responsibility for RPC retrieval and backhaul operations. The RPC owner has a vested interest in minimizing the cycle time to the largest extent possible, but dealers and wholesalers, who are preoccupied with their own business, may not share the same sense of urgency, particularly if the rental is not on a per diem basis. Having the RPC owner to handle the retrieval (rather than entrusting this to wholesalers) will improve visibility in the chain and reduce the impact of customer behavior on cycle times. This will require maintenance by the owner of some field staff and the provision of storage facilities in Lagos.

For the short distance trade (which has a much shorter cycle time and consequently fewer uncertainties than the long-distance trade), the loop will also be closed. The crate moves from the RPC owner to the farmer, thence to the local market and thereafter back to the owner (thus illustrating the integrated forward and reverse logistics).

This scenario assumes that the RPCs do not enter the retail segment of the chain, at least in the early stages of the project. While it may be possible for the service provider to effectively police retrievals from the wholesalers, the same cannot be expected to happen if the RPCs enter the retail segment of the chain, which is spread out all over metropolitan Lagos. Therefore, catering to the retail trade can be expected to drastically increase the number of actors in the chain, complicate and delay the retrieval of crates for reuse, increase the cycle time for crates (which will imply a bigger pool size), and probably raise the rate of structural and incidental losses. The combined effect of all these will be an increase in the number of crates needed to keep the system fully supplied and consequently higher capital and operational costs. Different provisions (involving a different set of recovery incentives) have to be made for the retail trade in the south.

At this point, it is pertinent to ask a fundamental question about the tomato industry in Nigeria: in what form does the final customer want to buy tomatoes? It is well known that Nigerian cuisine has a number of tomato-based dishes, of which the most popular are tomato stew, native soup and jollof rice. In these, the tomato is normally used in blended form (together with onions and other condiments), with the fruit being mostly used in salads and as garnishing. If it can be established that the bulk of the tomatoes sold in southern markets is intended for blending before use, it becomes relevant to question the necessity of transporting the fruit over 900 kilometers of bad roads (with all the attendant losses) instead of converting the tomato to paste up north. It is instructive to point out that the imported product usually comes in processed form and not as raw fruit, and it gets sold in the same market.

Also, the use of the RPC is likely to be extended to other products, e.g., pepper, tatashe, mango, etc. Widespread use of RPCs should generate a high volume of containers for the reverse trip, implying that the reverse trip will be as regular as the forward trips. This will have a positive impact on the level of stockholding of containers.

Case 2: Implementing Circular Economy in the Automotive Industry
A Case Study in Nigeria

C2.1 INTRODUCTION

Relying on the backdrop of Extended Producer Responsibility (EPR) implementation experiences in the different regions of the World, the Nigerian National Environmental Standards and Regulations Enforcement Agency (NESREA) adopted and released guidelines for the implementation of EPR policy in Nigeria. As far back as 2007, the social charter of the National Economic Empowerment and Development Strategy (NEEDS) had underlined the need for environmental sustainability and the inclusion of the private sector participation in Nigeria's waste management sector. Furthermore, it has been stated that the general priorities of the environment sector in Nigeria were conceptualized in the National Policy on Environment in 1989 and later reviewed in 1999 and also between 2010 and 2020. Although some awareness of cleanliness at the national level has been created by virtue of the setting up of the first Presidential Task Force (PTF) on clearance of abandoned/accident/scrap vehicles, vessels and aircraft from the road, inland waterways and airports, respectively in 2003, no mention of EPR was made in the old or any of the revised versions of the National Policy on Environment. Regarding the 33 National Environmental Regulations that NESREA released in 2014, companies operating in the identified sectors of the Nigerian economy are required to have in place an EPR program. Some of the national environmental regulations with EPR provisions for some sectors include National Environmental (Sanitation and Wastes Control) Regulations, 2009. S. I. No. 28; National Environmental (Food, Beverages and Tobacco Sector) Regulations, 2009. S. I. No. 33; National Environmental (Chemicals, Pharmaceuticals, Soap and Detergent Manufacturing Industries) Regulations, 2009. S. I. No. 36; National Environmental (Electrical/Electronic Sector) Regulations, 2010. S. I. No 23; National Environmental (Base Metals, Iron and Steel Manufacturing/Recycling Industries) Regulations, 2010. S. I. No. 14; National Environmental (Non-Metallic Minerals Manufacturing Industries Sector) Regulations, 2010. S. I. No. 21; National Environmental (Pulp and Paper, Wood and Wood Products) Regulations 2012, S. I. 34; National Environmental (Motor Vehicle and Miscellaneous Assembly Sector) Regulations, 2012, S. I. No. 35; and National Environmental (Domestic and Industrial Plastic, Rubber and Foam Sector) Regulations, 2010, S. I. No. 17 (Ajani & Kunlere, 2019). The EPR can be described as an integrated waste management policy that extends (rather than merely assigns) financial and physical responsibility for the management of post-consumption (end of life (EoL)) products to the producers (or importers and distributors) of such products, with the aim of reducing waste disposal, promoting resource conservation, increasing recycling, and encouraging more environmentally friendly product design.

According to the EPR program, there are six major stakeholders in the EPR process: Producers, Consumers, Producer Responsibility Organizations (PROs), Collectors, Recyclers and Government and its agents. Figure C2.1 shows the EPR implementation framework in the Nigerian context.

The Producer is the product manufacturer. Furthermore, *producers* could be regarded as converters in the product supply chain, franchisees, assemblers, fillers, brand owners, importers, distributors or retailers of a product. Within the framework of the EPR operational guidelines, producers are to ensure that wastes arising from the use of their products by the consumers are safely managed through effective monitoring of the entire lifecycle of the product.

Consumers are individuals or organizations who buy and use products produced by makers. Under the EPR Operational Guidelines, consumers are required to safely dispose of their wastes through legal and appropriate means such as at collection centers managed by accredited collectors. For those producers who are physically unable to effectively manage the EoL wastes of their products, they may assign a third party to help them oversee the process through a network of collectors, dismantlers and recyclers across the country. Also, producers in a related sector where the type of waste they produce are similar, for example, in the food and beverage sector, they may jointly delegate or transfer their responsibilities under the EPR policy to a single third party. Generally, such third parties are known as *Producer Responsibility Organizations (PROs)*.

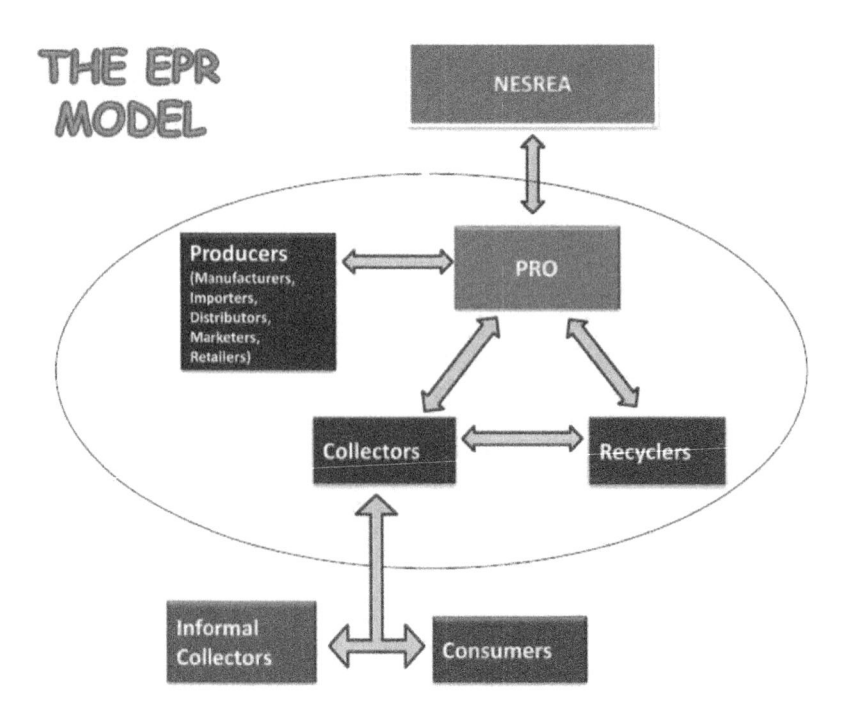

FIGURE C2.1 EPR implementation framework in Nigeria.

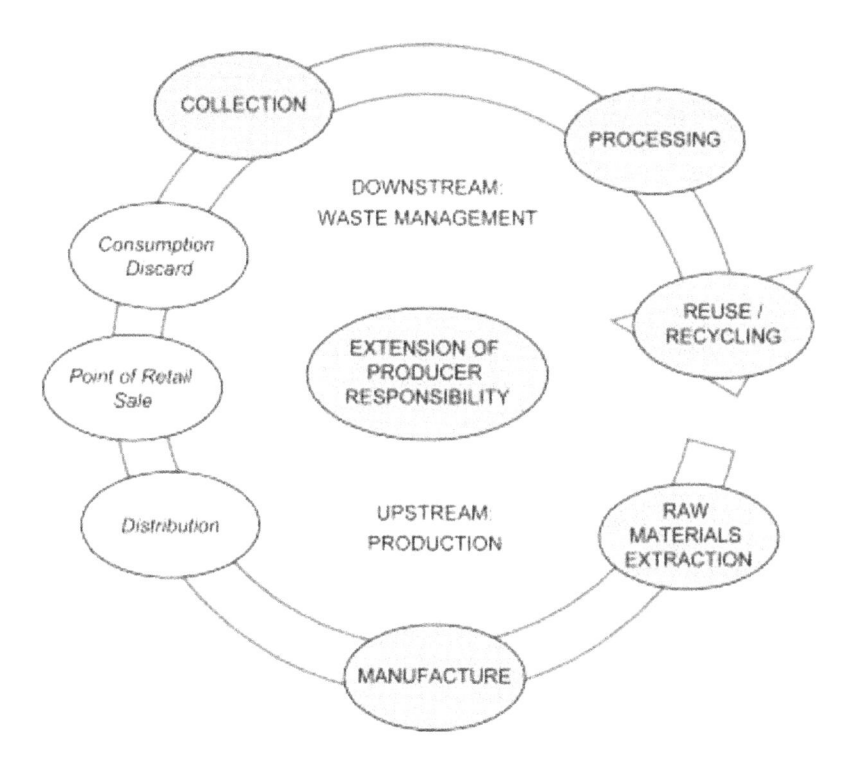

FIGURE C2.2 EPR implementation framework in Nigeria.

PROs are responsible for managing the entire process for creating awareness, collection and ensuring workable arrangements with recyclers. In Nigeria, some PROs have been registered. They include: Food and Beverage Recycling Alliance (FBRA) – a PRO that represents selected food, beverages and bottling companies, focuses on collection and recycling of plastic wastes; the Recycling and Economic Development Initiative of Nigeria (REDIN), which focuses on clean energy and; the Alliance for Responsible Battery Recyclers (ARBR) which focuses on recycling of hazardous battery wastes.

The Collector is described as a person or company that directly receives or retrieves post-consumption (EoL) products (otherwise known as wastes) from the consumers and may briefly store them before transmission to the recyclers. To enhance the process of collection, the collector may establish a collection center or a safe and effective means based on the operational exigencies. The collector may be informal – i.e., operates a simple, unregistered business. Informal collectors include scavengers and cart pushers. They are known to collect between 20% and 60% of wastes, making them a key part of the EPR process. The collector may also be formal, with registered businesses responsible for receiving or retrieving waste from informal collectors or directly from consumers.

The Recycler refers to person(s) or organizations that reprocess wastes into raw materials for producing new products of exactly the same kind or a somewhat different kind. Furthermore, the recyclers are also required to ensure that they adopt appropriate and global best technologies in their operations and provide to producers information that could help improve design, recovery, and recycling of their products and EoL products on a continuous basis.

The Government provides and implements the policy framework. It also regulates and ensures the effective implementation of the EPR process through monitoring and other means. While other government agencies may be involved in the EPR process, NESREA is the sole agency responsible for the implementation and coordination of the EPR policy in Nigeria.

C2.2 THE CASE STUDY OF THE PRESIDENTIAL TASK FORCE ON CLEARANCE OF ABANDONED/ACCIDENT/ SCRAP VEHICLES FROM POLICE STATIONS, HIGHWAYS AND PUBLIC PLACES IN NIGERIA

As of January 2022, Nigeria has practically 2 or 3 automotive semi-assembly plants. In the 1980s, it had the Peugeot and Volkswagen assembly plants which have all gone extinct as the economic restructuring of the country kicked in in1980s due to crude oil slump in the international market and the fact that the country is primarily dependent on oil sales for revenue. However, the Nigerian population continues to grow at about 3–5% annually. The repeated devaluation/adjustment of the local currency to the US Dollar (current official rate as of December 2021is $1 to N415) meant that practically used capital equipment, some consumables (e.g., apparels) than new ones are affordable. The list of affected items includes vehicles, industrial machineries and home appliances. This opened the flood gate for the importation of used vehicles of all sorts most of which were close to their EoL stage. Incidences of limiting the age of used imported trucks to eight years encountered resistance from the transport stakeholders. It was against this background that the PTF was introduced. The PTF on clearance of abandoned/accident/scrap vehicles from police stations, highways and public places in Nigeria was established in November 2003. The determination of the Government to address the problems of metal scraps and waste from accidents, etc. in the country was underscored as stated by the Secretary to the Federal Government: "metal scraps resulting from accidents or abandoned vehicles constitute not only avoidable hazards on our roads, they also, contribute significantly to environmental degradation".

A committee was set up with the following terms of reference (TOR) and a six-months duration:

- To make a full inventory of all scrap/abandoned/accident vehicles currently located at police stations, highways and public places across the country;
- To design an appropriate policy for removing the scrap/abandoned/accident vehicles from all police stations, highways and public places in order to clean up the country;
- To work out clear legal strategies for accelerated investigation and court hearing for those vehicles currently being held as evidence in ongoing court cases;
- To set out appropriate strategies for retaining a hauler that could move the vehicles from identified locations;
- To work out an effective commercial arrangement with Federated Steel Mills Limited, Otta and any other steel mill that government may appoint from time to time as the end user of the product;

Case 2: Implementing Circular Economy in the Automotive Industry 295

- To ensure that all monies raised in the sale of scraps are paid directly into the Federated account through the Ministry of Environment after deducting the cost of collection, haulage and delivery of the scrap metals;
- To articulate workable strategies and regulations, including sanctions that would guide the handling of accident and abandoned vehicles and other scrap metals in the future.

Specifically, the mandate provided a paradigm for coping with metal scraps generated in the country at the time and in future. The focus on "scraps" as the end activity out of the variables (scrap/accident/abandoned vehicles, etc.) stems from the fact that scraps evolve from metals through the life cycle or aging process; and/or through negligence, mismanagement and damages due to accidents and abandonment. In this context, Nigeria is a veritable ground for the accumulation of metal scraps, being a huge consumer of metal products generated locally and through imports.

The PTF mission implied the following specific objectives:

- generation and analysis of data for policy formulation;
- identification, enumeration, classification, valuation and disposal of metal scraps;
- negotiation with stakeholders in the metal scraps industry;
- providing framework for legislation and regulation of the industry; and
- working out financial outlay for all activities.

Other objectives also included:

- eliminating the environmental nuisance caused by scrap vehicles;
- providing inputs to foundries and allied steel mills and thereby obtaining salvage value for metal scraps that litter our environment.

There was an increasing concern among the members regarding the specific mention of police stations (numbering over 1000 locations across the nation) in TOR even though they fall within the generic public places, and the need for according that sector high priority since majority of the stations were littered with accident and abandoned vehicles throughout the Federation. Another major observation by the PTF members was that it would commence work from a zero-level budget, even when data were not available for realistic budgeting. The probability of internal funding was inferred from the TOR, but it was also acknowledged that expenditure would first be incurred in the process of collection, haulage and delivery of metal scraps.

In spite of the obvious limitations to forecasting, which is critical to budgeting, members considered and proposed an interim budget of 160 million naira. Other major decisions at the inaugural meeting were:

- appeal to the Nigerian Police Force to make available data on all vehicles at the various stations nationwide;
- appeal to members to individually embark on library and archival search for knowledge connected with scraps of metal.

C2.2.1 Work Design

A tentative plan of action, which was in the first instance to ensure clearance of the police stations in the states capitals, was, however, considered and approved.

The adopted work design hinged on:

- establishing contact with the organizations in whose premises the metal scraps were located;
- creating teams to carry out enumeration, classification and valuation in conjunction with the metal scraps keepers;
- select clearing agents who must effect disposal within ten days of signing the Memorandum of Understanding and on payment of the full value of scraps into a designated account.

C2.2.2 Funding of the PTF Activities

It became obvious that other sources of financing had to be explored and the search narrowed down to an offer by a local commercial bank to provide the "seed" money that would facilitate the gathering of data upon which a meaningful public/private sector initiative could be developed. This alternative funding proposal was rejected, and in its place, the Ministry of Finance and the Central Bank made the sum of 12 million naira available to the PTF for the assignment.

Out of the approved sum, 8 million naira was eventually released to the group to commence operations in March 2005, exactly 16 months after its inauguration.

Members took notice of the funding arrangement as contained in the TOR, which specified that "all monies raised in the sale of scraps are paid directly into the Federation Account through the Ministry of Environment after deducting the cost of collection, haulage and delivery of the metal scraps". To deduct the cost of collection, haulage and delivery of the metal scraps logically implies the existence of a holdback account to meet these expenses before direct payment into the Federation Account. A holdback account becomes even more imperative when the withdrawal procedure from the Federated account is considered, and such account was therefore opened with All States Trust Bank.

C2.3 METAL SCRAP INDUSTRY

C2.3.1 The Global Perspective

A visit to national capitals and other important cities in the developed economies would reveal that scrap business is big business as one would notice scrap metal processing – scrap facilities or yards, cranes lifting and sorting metals and trucks hauling scraps in and out of yards. Also noticeable is the avalanche of recycling plants that are dependent on designated scrap ponds, where scrap metals find usage in another form, even if, of lesser technological relevance. Recycling metal is important in conserving national resources, while the clearance of scrap metals from public places keeps the highways and cities free from debris and also preserves landfill space.

Not much has been achieved by Nigeria in adopting this general trend that keeps the environment safe for humanity and contributes to economic growth. Data on scraps generated in Nigeria is not readily available. What is known, however, is the number of scraps used by some of the industries that are located in different parts of the country.

C2.3.2 Types of Scrap Metals

Scrap metals are of two types – ferrous and non-ferrous. Ferrous scraps comprise basically iron and steel and include scraps from old automobiles, farm equipment, steel beams, railroad tracks and ships. Ferrous scraps account for the largest volume of metal scraps.

Internationally, ferrous scrap is classified into almost 80 grades. However, in Nigeria, only three major grades abound – heavy, medium and light. Non-ferrous scrap metal such as aluminum and copper is scrap metal other than iron and steel. While the volume of non-ferrous scrap is less than ferrous scraps, it is more valuable by weight.

Scrap metal, ferrous and non-ferrous, can be categorized as either "home" scrap or "purchased" scrap. Home scrap is generated at the steel mills and generally re-melted and used again at the same plant. Purchased scrap relates to scraps that are purchased from scrap collectors/dealers. The PTF assignment puts purchased scraps in its purview.

C2.3.3 Users of Scrap Metals/Utilization Capacity

Scrap metal is an essential raw material in the following industries:

- Iron and steel,
- foundries and
- Metal manufacturers and fabricators.

C2.3.4 State of Metal Scraps in Nigeria

In Nigeria, the Manufacturers Association of Nigeria (MAN) has no fewer than 14 companies that use scrap metal as basic raw materials. While the installed capacity of some of these industries is known, only the Federated Steel Mill, aside the Delta Steel Company (DSC), Aladja, can boast of up to 10 metric tonnes capacity furnace. The combined installed steelmaking capacity of DSC is 400 metric tonnes, of which 20% (i.e., 80 metric tonnes) is reserved for scrap usage while the rest is for sponge iron – made in-house in the pelletizing and direct reduction plants. The newly operational steel plant in Ikorodu, Lagos State, has only two induction furnaces of 5 metric tonnes capacity. At a maximum capacity utilization of about 80%, the scrap requirement for the other scrap metal users is far less than 1 million tonnes per annum.

At a projected growth rate of scrap metal requirement of 5% per annum, the users in Nigeria will require about 1.10 million metric tonnes in each of the subsequent years for the next five years.

C2.3.5 SOURCES OF SCRAP METALS

As articulated earlier, scrap metals abound in the country. While there were no immediate figures to indicate the volume of generated or purchased scraps, indications were that the supply of purchased scraps far exceeds the demand. Against this backdrop and coupled with the export ban on scraps, a significant glut of scrap metal (ferrous) is predominant in the country. This is illustrated by the then prevailing price of 10 to 12 naira per kilogram of the highest grade of ferrous scrap.

Compared with the international market price of $100 per tonne, the low price appears to act as some kind of disincentive to the development of scrap processing industry (adding value), since scrap processing involves heavy and costly equipment – cranes, crushers, etc. – and large space. Some degree of state intervention is, therefore, desirable.

Furthermore, the low price discourages the steel mills from investing in the growth of scrap processing industry, and so they pay only when the supplied scraps are delivered and accepted by them. Incidents of heaps of scrap metals purchased and dumped on the premises of the millers, without adequate management of them, were legion.

It was discovered that only Ikorodu Steel Mill had invested in scrap compressors which ensures that scrap metals supplied are compressed into "cubes" and stored properly, thereby freeing up a lot of space for other activities.

C2.4 THE TEST RUN PHASE

For the test run phase, police stations were the obvious choice and Lagos was considered a good starting point because of its concentration of police stations and other public places that will provide the basis for subsequent planning. Two things characterized the work during this phase, namely, vehicles, rather than scrap metals in general, were enumerated and evaluated; and secondly, police stations were the main target rather than highways and other public places as stipulated in the TOR. The work of the PTF was facilitated by the comprehensive returns, which the police had by then rendered.

Two teams, each comprising members of the PTF, supported by personnel from the secretariat, police escorts and other resource persons (i.e., professional valuers and other assistants) visited all police formations in Lagos; took inventory of relevant vehicles therein, evaluated them and reported back to the full house. The PTF stickers for IMMEDIATE DISPOSAL (Red) or PENDING (Yellow) were pasted on vehicles after a review of the case history of the items had been given by the "exhibit keeper" or the Investigating Police Officer (IPO). It was also agreed that vehicles thus labeled and recorded can still be released by the Divisional Police Officer (DPO) to their legitimate owners but only after proper documentation and clearance from the PTF. The task force ensured that in all places worked upon, the Chief Executive of that place nominates one of his officers to work with it and report to him on a daily basis.

A disposal committee was, thereafter, constituted to prepare and submit a schedule of scrap vehicles for allocation to accredited agents for immediate disposal. The

Case 2: Implementing Circular Economy in the Automotive Industry   299

PTF then met to ratify the proposal and appointed its members to coordinate the clearance by the agents.

C2.4.1   FINDINGS FROM THE TEST RUN

The moment the PTF commenced work, it was inundated by auctioneers who offered to help with the disposal on their usual terms. Indeed, some of them threatened that they were the only group statutorily mandated to effect sales of accident/abandoned/scrap vehicles in police stations throughout Nigeria. Such a claim was easily brushed aside because three of the members are practicing lawyers who readily punctured the claim. Their position was made worse during the fieldwork when it was discovered that items in police stations that were auctioned several years back merely had the valuable parts removed and the scraps left to continue littering the stations. It was at that point that it was decided that scrap agents would rather be employed to singly or in group, take away all allocated items within a stipulated time frame. The only concession to auctioneers was that they could serve as agents on terms agreeable to the PTF, which they readily acceded to.

In general, the original inventory of the target vehicles supplied to the PTF by the police did not exactly match the items found on the ground. In dealing with the discrepancy, team members had to include those items left out of the police inventory that had been in the stations for upwards of five years. By far the most contentious was the categorization of vehicles that the police claimed were either "under investigation" or were "evidence" in ongoing court cases. Most of the items the teams labeled "pending" fell under this category. In the spirit of decongesting the police stations as mandated by the Presidency, some vehicles, if they merited it, were ordered to be released to their bona fide owners either on bond or immediately.

Underestimation of the time needed to accomplish the tasks at hand proved a major insight and the lessons learned formed the basis of future exercises. Resource constraint, which delayed the take-off of the PTF, was somewhat overcome by the device of inviting monetary deposits from scrap dealers/agents who applied to work with the PTF. Five such agents worked with the PTF during the test run phase. They were subsequently allotted materials to the value of deposits they lodged into the PTF account. Complaints that some materials allotted to some agents did not match the values of the deposits they made were addressed.

Notable among the accomplishment during this phase were:

- an appreciable insight into the nature and the enormity of the tasks;
- an evolving (cordial) relationship between the police (scraps holders) and the PTF was established and
- an innovative resource generation for the activities of the PTF was devised.

C2.4.2   LIMITED EXPANSION STAGE

Encouraged by the appreciable success recorded during the test run stage, while remaining conscious of the financial limitation to the ambitious move, the PTF decided on limited expansion to its activities. Five states (Ogun, Ondo, Edo, Rivers and Bayelsa) were added to Lagos and grouped into three, viz: Lagos and Ogun; Edo and Ondo and Rivers and Bayelsa: with each group assigned to a team as constituted during the test run stage. The PTF secretariat was temporarily located in Lagos.

All the processes and procedures, the methodology and modality of work that were introduced during the test run stage were maintained and effectively deployed. The considerable distance of operation from the official base of the PTF in Lagos posed some problems in terms of a gap in immediate authoritative support in some emergency situations. The problem was particularly acute in the process of release of vehicles by the Divisional Officers to their rightful owners after the teams had left the various states. In some cases, agents who were formally allocated materials complained that they were denied the release of same on the excuse that the items were required in evidence at courts, whereas impostors were granted free access to the materials. The degree of cooperation between the police and the PTF varied from excellent in Lagos and Ogun; good in Ondo and Edo and bad in Rivers and Bayelsa.

Attempts to enumerate several oil tankers that were confiscated from illegal "bunkering" posed the greatest challenge to the activities of the PTF in Rivers State. The PTF then involved several state agencies including the military, the Special Operations Squad, the State Security Service (SSS) and many others. The cooperation of the Governor of the state, the SSS boss and other high government officials was sought to resolve contending issues. Many of the seized oil tankers by the police had substantial quantities of products of varying quality (refined, semi-refined and crude) in them.

C2.4.3   REVERSAL INTO LULL PERIOD

If the test run stage provided the PTF with direction in discharging its functions, the limited expansion stage could be ascribed with opening up the PTF to public scrutiny with its opportunities and challenges. Other stakeholders in the industry, at home and abroad, were making inquiries and opening discussions for collaboration in properly launching the nation into the metal scraps business. Investors were coming to enquire how they can come in to salvage the environment while still reaping the fruits of their investments. Agents were falling heads over heels to reap the benefits of a secured market for the scraps that they collaborated with the PTF to collect and dispose of and were only too willing to be officially appointed as agents. Members were learning to cope with these challenges as best as they could.

It was at that point in time that bureaucracy opened up its fangs. Coming as a surprise to the PTF was the information that the bankers would not honor withdrawals from the account on the instruction of the Accountant General of the Federation. The account was, in the first instance, opened as an operating holdback account with the funds from the Office of the SGF to meet with expenses for collection, disposal and haulage in accordance with the TOR and serve to receive deposits from agents for financing the PTF activities, which facts were well known to the supervising agencies. Resolving what was thought to be a minor issue moved from days to weeks and months and eventually led to the suspension of operations when the problem of funding again reared its head. This time, not because there was no money, but that bureaucracy wants it spent in a given way, which was not in cognizance with the TOR.

The attempt to employ a consultant at a fee on completion of task while a resolution to the impasse was being sought failed; and so, the activities of the PTF went on holiday after a not too successful operation in Delta, Anambra, and Rivers states.

C2.5   CRITICAL ELEMENT OF SUCCESS

The setting-up of the PTF was greeted with great enthusiasm and high expectation from a cross section of the people, and this was for justifiable reasons. Viewed from whatever perspective – environmental, security or economic – the PTF was expected to have a major impact on the society. The varied expectations of all stakeholders were, therefore, crucial to the successes and failures of the endeavor. Indeed, there were panic moves by some organizations within a week to provide remedies before the body took off, notably the Police and Federal Road Safety Corps, who saw the creation of the task force as an indictment on their statutory roles. In essence, the assignment was itself crisis laden with several conflicting interests and challenges to cope with.

The choice of the Task Force mode, which relies on shock effect to return situations to the right course or provide quick direction to a policy thrust, was particularly instructive. But then, the Task Force must be pre-planned, provided with the wherewithal to function and be freed from routine encumbrances that warranted its setting-up in the first instance. If these critical elements were missing as was the case in respect of the PTF, there were bound to be problems, some of them insurmountable, unless the convening authority is willing to support it at all times.

C2.5.1   ADMINISTRATIVE SET-UP

On inauguration, the PTF had fruitlessly requested for office space to establish its administration with ad hoc staff from ministries and other organizations. For a body that was to generate and analyze a large volume of data, it was thought inadequate for the appointed secretary to combine the administration of the PTF with his formal functions in the public service. Throughout the life of the PTF, the public service office of the secretary doubled as the secretariat of the organ: the Nigerian Press Council up to September 2006 and the Office for Veterans Affairs in the Presidency thereafter.

Since the secretary was not detached from routine duties and scheduled staff were not assigned to the PTF, priority of work was not assured, which perhaps explained why letters addressed to the Chairman or the PTF were long in delivering. Moreover, the PTF had no office equipment of its own; thus, most activities could not be shielded from those who should not know. Above all, effective coordination could not be achieved for an assignment that was to cover the 36 States of the Federation and the constituent 774 Local Government Areas.

C2.5.2   ROLES SPECIFICATIONS

The task assigned to the PTF was specific on police stations and highways and went on to mention the broader generic, public places in Nigeria, which was understood to mean that priority of work should go to the places with roles specified, without ignoring the other areas. It turned out that the definition of "public places" was desirable.

Even in the case of highways, it took the maturity of members to avert collisions on state roads in Lagos. This implies that the convening instructions could well have limited activities to Federal roads, which is, in any case, ridiculous for an assignment that was meant to cover the entire nation and borders on security and environment that have limited place for demarcation.

Surprisingly, an innocuous issue, such as when an equipment is deemed abandoned, came to the front burner of the PTF's activities. Heaps of scraps that had been under the Third Mainland Bridge in Lagos since the 1970s, road construction equipment abandoned at Ore after the construction of the Benin-Sagamu road in the 1980s and vehicles that were left in police stations for upwards of six years suddenly found owners when the PTF moved in to salvage the environment; only for the owners to disappear again, when other circumstances forced a halt to their disposal.

C2.5.3 BUREAUCRATIC INTERFERENCE

The delays in the authorization of requests, which were imposed for reasons that were not in consonance with the spirit of the assignment, were particularly frustrating. What does one make of the process to open an account that took five months for a Task Force that should complete its work in six months? What about the delay of three months to approve the budget proposal, the intervention of the President and another six months to finally direct the release of the money? Yet it was some of those on the line for these approvals that were always quick to refer to the time limit of the assignment. Indeed, the impression was ripe that certain interests did not like the idea in the first instance.

C2.5.4 EXTERNAL FORCES INFLUENCE

If there was one problem that was not hidden from the PTF, it was how to cope with the hindrances deliberately placed on its part by external forces. At the venue of inauguration were persons who claimed propriety of the ideas on which the Task Force was formed and bragged of their connections, which as far as members were concerned were hogwash since those connections could not be higher than the President who set the PTF up. The auctioneers also fell, heads over heels, to blackmail the PTF; and indeed, unsuccessfully sought court injunctions in Delta State to halt the assignment.

When the pronouncements and activities of these external forces were superimposed on the bureaucratic foot-dragging for routine approval, the formidable problem posed to the activities of the PTF would be appreciated better.

C2.5.5 HOSTILE ATTITUDE OF METAL SCRAPS KEEPERS

One amazing discovery of the PTF in the course of its work was the joy that metal scraps keepers derive from the junks in their control and their reluctance to part with them. They will gleefully relate the history of the scraps and optimistically posit that these would be easily made to function but would not bother at what cost that would be. Very often, the true state of the item is hidden from the teams that sometimes enjoy disagreement between the keepers and the engineering staff that are assigned by the management to the PTF.

These metal scraps keepers constitute the front line of those who deny genuine agents of the PTF from collecting items that are allocated to them.

C2.6 PROSPECTS

All the problems that were encountered by the PTF in the discharge of its functions are basically attitudinal, which implies that given the right attitude, the metal scraps industry would prosper in the country. One can only hazard a guess as to why there was that strong feeling in some circles that the PTF should not get the support so desirable for success because that was what their attitude translated to. It appeared there was a strong misperception that the PTF was sitting on a gold mine, of which many stakeholders equally aspired to take control. Such persons equate the assignment of the PTF to auctioning of vehicles at those specified places and would want to have a taste of the action.

C2.6.1 Environmental Sanity

The neglect of the past has resulted into indiscriminate dumping of metal scraps all over the place with mountains of it growing in the metal high consuming areas. The sight of these areas is sufficiently nauseating, but that is not a critical concern to humanity. Rather it is the health and security effects of indiscriminate dumping that calls for a quick solution. The chemical properties of metals and other items the disused metal products contain are directly hazardous to health and could be the cause of epidemic if there is direct link of the dump to public or private water source. Furthermore, accident/abandoned metal could be the cause of another accident and so, a threat to life.

Also observed in the past is the practice whereby miscreants turn these dumps into homes and resort for criminal activities along the highways, waterways and even in cities with unsuspecting persons becoming victims. These dumps are veritable sources of illegal arms whose manufacturers rely on uncontrolled scavenging for materials for their illegal business.

The establishment of metal scraps ponds to specification, which is the primary sector in metal scraps industry, would bring sanity to the environment and thereby enhancing the security and health status of the people. In addition, the ponds, which could be in public/private investment partnership, will provide employment for its management and persons engaged in metal scraps compression, cannibalization, categorization and packaging of parts.

C2.6.2 Growth of Recycling Plants

Also contributing to the generation of employment are the recycling plants that rely on inputs of the ponds as raw materials. With the growth of recycling plants either as adjoint to the metal scraps ponds or as separate establishments of their own, the life cycle of metal products in the country would be enhanced. These plants, with high profit yielding potentials, would preferably be on private sector initiative. Indeed, there were enquires and/or indications of interest from foreign and domestic investors in the course of the assignment.

C2.6.3 INPUTS TO EXISTING INDUSTRIES

Many companies of MAN use metal scraps as their basic raw material with prospect for expansion. A deliberate policy of compressing metal in situ would be of immense value to these end users, in addition to reducing the haulage cost that is presently prohibitive. Moving bulk scraps before compression occupies space and reduces the volume the trailers can lift at a time even where the weight becomes less.

C2.6.4 FUNDS GENERATION

The much-taunted economic value of metal scraps is correct at all times, in so far, that value is added to the scraps in situ before disposal. From our field experience, it was obvious that the sales of abandoned/accident/scraps vehicles would only be profitable for as long as some of these vehicles are within economic repairs. The agents only agree to bulk purchase for clearance which the PTF imposed, after considering the overall cost implications, and not necessarily, on the value of a particular item. When haulage cost of 10,000 naira per tonne is juxtaposed with scraps' current value of 10 to 12 naira per kilograms, it was obvious that the market would attract only a few desperate buyers. This was the major reason why the auctioneering system encouraged cannibalization on the spot leaving the environment worse off.

The large build-up of metal scraps over the years, the low demand and cost locally and the favorable price of scraps in the international market all point to one direction – freeing the market for exportation. The PTF was inundated by foreign enquiries, which go to show the importance of scrap metal business to the international community. Coordinated efforts at the identification, enumeration, classification and valuation of metal scraps that were accumulated over the years in Nigeria and those that are being generated on a daily basis would be high foreign exchange earner.

C2.6.5 COSTING THE PTF PERFORMANCES

In close to 5 years of its existence, no more than 15 weeks were dedicated to actual work of the PTF. Most of the time was devoted to solving problems that centered on poor administrative and logistic back-up; inadequate specification of roles, which certain forces explored; bureaucratic interference apparently for ego busting; external forces influence for selfish end; hostile attitude of metal scraps keepers and imposition of authorization procedure that stifled funding.

C2.6.6 GOING FORWARD

Government, in its wisdom, constituted the PTF for the clearance of abandoned/accident/scrap vehicles from the police stations, highways and public places; with the TOR and other directives making its overall objective the provision of a paradigm for metal scraps industry in Nigeria. The genuine intentions and the zeal of approaching the tasks appear not matched by the bureaucracy charged with empowering the Task Force to function properly and effectively.

There is no doubt that the metal scraps industry has a high prospect in Nigeria when one considers its high salvage value; the chances of restoring environmental sanity with impact on the citizens' health and security status; helping vehicle recycling plants to grow; and providing inputs to foundries, iron and steel mills and other metal fabricators. In the short run, the metal scrap industry in Nigeria has potential for foreign exchange earnings; only if the value is added to the scraps before exportation.

The PTF could not meet the target set for it and which members enthusiastically embraced and expanded upon due to extraneous/insurmountable factors placed on its way throughout the period.

SUGGESTED MATERIALS FOR FURTHER READING

Ajani, A., & Kunlere, I. O. (2019). Implementation of the extended producer responsibility (EPR) policy in Nigeria: Towards sustainable business practice, *Nigerian Journal of Environment and Health*, 2, 44–56.

Index

A

Artificial Intelligence, 129, 219

B

Badenhorst, 251
Behavior change tool, 233, 237, 243
Big data analytics, 48, 114, 129, 131, 133, 135, 152, 155–156, 158–159, 161, 222
Blockchain
  circular supply chains, 166
  technologies, 163–166
Blockchain-enabled circular supply chain, 170, 179
Boulding, Kenneth, 8
Business intelligence, 157–158, 161
Business management, *see* Sustainability
Business-to-business (B2B), 142

C

Capacity building, 220
Circular business models, 17, 31, 184–185, 198–199, 204
Circular economy
  action plan, 4, 79
  circular economy product-focused, 202
  circular economy rebound, 184, 203
  concepts, 8–9
  consumers, 221, 230, 238–245
  definition, 8–9
  principles, 193, 201, 213, 219, 225, 232, 263–264
  Promotion Law, 8
  risks, 227
  strategies, 204–206, 209
Circular economy business models
  environmental impact, 199
  experimentation, 198–199
  firm's dynamic capabilities, 200–203
Circular Economy Development Strategy and Recent Action Plan, 9
Circular flows, 23, 33
Circular public procurement, 79–83
Circular supply chain
  concepts, 13, 224
  definition, 4
  logistics, 18
  refurbish, 15
  refuse, 15
  procurement, 17
  product, 16
  production, 18
Circular supply chain management, 6–8
Circularity, 130, 135, 139, 142–143, 155, 159, 175, 179, 187, 190, 192–194, 196–198, 207–208, 222, 228, 234, 263–264
  strategies, 174
Closed-loop supply chain, 24, 64–66
Closed-loop systems, 27–28, 51, 62, 217
Closed Substance Cycle and Waste Management Act, 8
Cloud computing, 219
Coercive forces, *see* Institutional forces
Collaboration, 209, 216, 223, 228, 234, 255, 260–261
  horizontal collaboration, 27, 30, 46, 108–109
  pre-competitive collaboration, 143
  vertical collaboration, 27, 30, 46–47, 108, 124
Collaborative consumption, 143–144, 185
Communication, 69, 71, 82, 85, 129, 133, 177, 220–221, 225, 234, 243–244
  communication channels, 203, 235
  communication sustainability, 208
  communication technology, 130–131, 135, 152
Consumer
  business influences, 239
  perceptions, 239
  preferences, 239
Contemporary logistics, 263
Cradle to cradle, 25, 33, 183
Customer service, 6, 129, 165
Cycle time, 94, 281, 289

D

Danone, 110
Data information, 140, 152, 161, 174
Data-driven analytics, 216, 219
Data-driven insights, 157–160, 219
Design
  circularity, 25
  sustainability, 25
Design for disassembly, 12, 33
Design for sustainability (DFS), 25
Digital supply chain, 134, 223
  definition, 131–132
Digital technologies, 129, 157, 160
Disassembly, 93
  disassembly-to-order, 94–95
  disassembly lot-sizing, 94–95
  process, 64

307

E

E-waste, 11, 58, 66, 106, 106, 258, 260
Eco-efficiency, 32
Eco-label, 82, 232, 237–246, 242, 246
Ecological
    balance, 218
    protection, 218
Ellen MacArthur Foundation, 110, 183, 254
Enablers, 33, 112, 139, 155, 194, 213, 221
    environmental enablers, 223
    organizational enablers, 222–223
    technological enablers, 222
End of life (EOL), 7, 19, 58–59, 66, 250, 291
End of use, 3, 66, 254–255
Energy
    renewable, 218
    resource efficiency, 218
    waste to, 218
Environmental
    requirements, 96, 102, 175
    strategy, 203, 209
Ethics, 221
European Commission, 4, 79, 205
European Union (EU), 4, 58, 189
Extended producer responsibility (EPR), 61, 109, 264, 290
Externalities, 4

F

FedEx, 110
Finance, 6, 296
    finance-centric business performance model, 40
4R framework, 23–25, 31
Fuller, Buckminster, 25

G

Governance mechanisms, 71
Government policies, 219–220
Green design, 16–17, 21
Green employment, 31

H

H&M, 4
Horizontal collaboration, *see* Collaboration

I

IKEA, 4
Industrial Internet, 160
Industrial symbiosis, 37, 42, 46–47, 86, 105, 114, 139, 142–143, 193, 230, 257
Industry 4.0, 136–138, 161
Information flow, 130, 219
Information sharing, 7, 12–13, 28, 30, 47–48, 69–71, 173, 17
Intelligent systems, 219–220, 223, 228, 251, 295
Internet of Things (IoT), 127, 131, 152, 154–155, 160–161
Institutional forces
    coercive forces, 50
    mimetic forces, 50
    normative forces, 50
Intrapreneur, 234–236, 245
Inventory management, 19, 65, 96–97, 107, 259
IT-enabled supply chain, 130

K

Kalundborg Symbiosis, 143

L

Labeling scheme, 237–238, 240, 243
Leasing, 12, 14, 23, 114, 146, 174, 185, 198
Legislation, 21, 37, 65, 80, 219
Logistics
    Circular Economy in the Automotive Industry, 291–304
    contemporary logistics, 263–265
    returns' management process, 252, 264
    reusable plastic containers, 275, 277, 279, 281, 283, 285, 287
    reverse logistics process, 65, 73, 89, 169, 250–252, 264
    tomato logistics, 273, 283, 285, 287
Loop
    cultivating alternatives loop, 53
    double-loop learning, 53
    interpretation loop, 53
Lot-sizing problems with manufacturing options (LSR), 97–98

M

Maintenance, 133, 139, 146–147, 152–153, 200, 217, 219, 225, 243, 255, 279
Manufacturing, 1, 3–4, 6–8, 12–14, 291
Manufacturing companies, 3, 21, 54, 62, 64, 172, 175, 177
Mastos, 263
Mimetic forces, *see* Institutional forces
MUD Jeans, 194, 304

N

Natural resource base view, 51
Nestle, 110
New Plastics Economy Global Commitment, 110

Index

Nigerian National Environmental Standards and Regulations Enforcement Agency (NESREA), 291
9R concepts, 14
9R strategies, 19

O

Open-loop systems, 86, 99, 107, 280
Organizational changes, 28–29, 33
Organizational citizenship behavior, 233, 236–237
Organizational enablers, *see* Enablers
Organizational paradigm shift, 44
Organizational theories, 49–53
    institutional theory, 49–50, 108, 112
    organizational learning theory, 53, 54
    stakeholder theory, 50, 51
    potential theory, 52

P

Packaging, 109
Papanek, Viktor, 25
Partnerships, 43, 85, 193
Pay per use, 146
Pearce, Turner and Turner, 8, 256
Pearce and Turner, 8
Peer-to-peer (P2P), 143–144, 166, 173, 176–178
Philips, 4
Process management, 84, 187, 209
Procurement, 77, 79
    circular public procurement, 79–83, 99
    green public procurement, 79, 99
    sustainable public procurement, 79–80, 99
Product acquisition, 59, 147
Product flow, 86
Product labeling schemes, 238
Product recovery management, 60, 63
    product and material recovery, 66
    product recovery management model, 60
Product-as-a-Service (PaaS), 216–217, 249
Product-service systems (PSS), 12, 21, 147, 151–155, 186, 194
Product stewardship, 51, 203, 209
Production planning, 93–96
Products, serviceable, 96, 98
Purchasers, 233–237, 245

R

"R" frameworks, 23, 33
Reconditioning, 20, 58–59, 96, 250
Re-contextualizing, 20, 59
Recycling, 24, 93–99, 119
Refurbish, 10, 22, 24, 61, 67, 156, 169, 252
Regulatory initiatives, 214
Remanufacturing, 17, 20, 24–27, 32, 41–42, 57, 59–63, 66–67, 73, 86, 96–98, 103
RePack, 194
Repairs, 59, 66
Replacement, 14, 60–63, 156, 282
Required to acquire the initial stock (RTIs), 62, 284
Reselling, 148, 161
Resource-based view (RBV), 49, 51, 52
Repairs, 59, 66
Research and development, 48, 67, 171, 174, 187, 194–196, 209
Retail industry, 69, 261–265
Reverse logistics operations, 62
Reverse supply chain management
    definition, 57
    measuring, 66–67
    performance, 57, 66–67, 71
    supply chain leadership, 67–70, 72
    transformational supply chain leadership, 69, 72
Risks, 223–226

S

Sharing economy, 12, 142–147, 161, 186
Smart circular economy, 139–140, 161
Stock, 251
Strategic planning, *see* Sustainability
Strategies, 3, 28, 30, 112, 137, 153, 204–207
    win-win strategies, 214
Supply chain circularity, 7, 12
Supply chain configuration, 45, 49
Supply chain design, 17, 26, 28
Sustainability, 30, 288, 291
    business management, 187
    cost management, 189–190
    environmental management, 191–192
    objectives, 4, 222–223
    quality management, 191
    service management, 194
    strategic planning, 188–189
    strategies, 51, 175, 179
Sustainable business performance, 183
Sustainable development, 4, 9, 12, 18–19, 66, 132, 134, 137, 183,
Sustainable development goals (SDGs), 9, 37, 79, 104, 110, 137, 253
Sustainable packaging, 16, 104, 109, 110, 111–114, 140
Sustainable purchasing, 77, 84, 99, 233–234
Sustainable supply chain management, 38–45, 47–53
Sustainable supply chain operations
    consumers, 119–121, 124

    environmental, 108, 111–119, 124
    green supply chain management, 101
    investment decisions, 119
    pricing circular products, 115–118
Symbiotic ecosystems, 184, 187, 208

T

Take-make-dispose, 3, 59, 106, 113, 155, 171
Technological enablers, *see* Enablers
Technological fix, 25
Theories
    ecological modernization theory, 112, 114
    institutional theory, 112
    stakeholder theory, 113
    Technology-Organization-Environment (TOE) theory, 221
3R, 169, 216–217, 221
    principles, 16, 103, 123
Tomato, 273
    production, 273
    supply chain, 275

U

United Nations 79, 104, 110, 217
United Nations Environmental Programs (UNEP) 110
Unverpackt, 110
UPS 110
USPS 110

W

Waste electrical and electronic equipment (WEEE) 59, 64–65
Waste management, 58–60, 78, 102, 110, 112, 130, 134, 145, 192–193, 202, 218, 220, 227–229, 233, 256, 291
Willingness to pay (WTP) 118–119, 124
    definition, 115
Win-win strategies, *see* Strategies

Z

Zero-packaging, 110, 112